Encyclopedia
of Indians
of the Americas

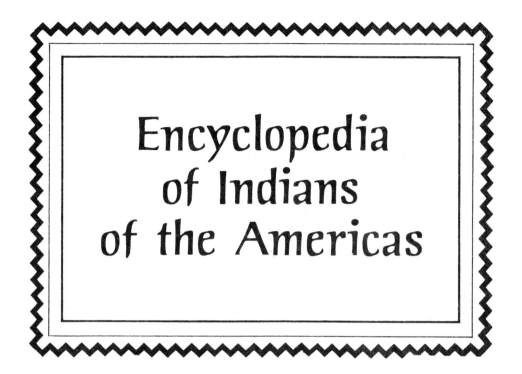

Encyclopedia of Indians of the Americas

VOLUME

6

Scholarly Press, Inc.

19722 E. NINE MILE RD., ST. CLAIR SHORES, MICHIGAN 48080

ENCYCLOPEDIA OF INDIANS OF THE AMERICAS

Copyright ©1974 by Scholarly Press, Inc.

Library of Congress Cataloging in Publication Data

Main entry under title:

Encyclopedia of Indians of the Americas.

    1. Indians. I. Harry Waldman, ed.
E54.5.E52   970'.004'97   74-5088
ISBN 0-403-01795-5 (v. 6)

Printed in the United States of America
First Printing - 1981

FLATHEAD RESERVATION, in Flathead County, Montana, an area of over 600,000 acres, is home to nearly 3,000 Salish Indians.

The reservation was established by the Hellgate Treaty of July 16, 1855, which ceded most of Montana to the United States for 1,234,969 acres for a general reservation for the Kootenai and Salish. A succession of Acts followed which dissipated tribal holdings through land allotment and non-Indian homesteading. About one-half the land within the reservation, including almost all of the better agricultural land located in the valley bottoms is non-Indian owned. The mountains, upland range, and valuable forest lands are Indian-owned.

History. The Salish and Kootenai people occupied western Montana, eastern Washington, southern British Columbia, and northern Idaho when the Europeans reached the continent. They moved in groups to other areas for visits and usually maintained friendly relations with the tribes to the north, south, and west. However, as the Plains tribes were confined by the wester expansion of the Europeans, conflicts with the neighboring Blackfoot increased.

Culture. The two tribes are from different linguistic families, but both are related to the other Pacific Northwest tribes. The Salish were originally fish eaters but in time acquired houses and many of the characteristics of the Plains Indians.

Government. The tribal government consists of a 10-man council elected from five districts. Five members are elected to 4-year terms in biennial elections. Following the election, a chairman and vice-chairman are chosen by the council and a secretary and treasurer are selected at large by the council.

FLEMING, DARRELL (Cherokee; June 22, 1911-), was a career official with the U.S. Bureau of Indian Affairs (BIA). Born in Bernice, Oklahoma, he began working for the BIA in 1933. He retired in 1970 after serving in many posts, including assistant area director of the Minneapolis Area Office (1966-70). In 1964 he received a Presidential Citation for outstanding contributions to improvement in government operations.

FLORES, WILLIAM VAN (Cherokee-Papago; Oct. 2, 1927   ), is a medical illustrator, who is best known as a cartoonist of Indian subjects. Flores, who is also known as Laughing Bull, was born at Appleton, Wisconsin. He worked as a printer from about 1942 to 1952 and then served with distinction in the U.S. Army in Korea (1952-54). Since 1958 Flores has worked as a medical illustrator for the Civil Aero-Medical Research Institute of the Federal Aviation Agency in Oklahoma City. He has been called a master of Indian humor because of his caricatures of Indian subjects.

FLORIDA. In the last decade of the nineteenth century an extensive investigation of the shell and sand

mounds of Florida was financed and directed by the archeologist, Clarence Bloomfield Moore. Prior to this time there had been little but amateur investigation of Florida's rich archeological remains. Relics had been carried off as souvenirs, shell mounds used to build road foundations, and bones and pottery scattered by plows and harrows. But thousands of mounds and earthworks in relatively inaccessible places have been preserved. Earthworks stand in swamps or on offshore islands in west Florida; along the southwest coast, burial mounds and heaps of shell, thrown up by the ancient Calusa to form dwelling platforms, are in mosquito- and snake-infested portions of the Ten Thousand Islands; sand and shell heaps remain unexcavated in the depths of the Everglades.

The work of Moore and the investigations (1895-96) of F.H. Cushing of the Bureau of Ethnology gave the first authoritative information on Florida's pre-Columbian tribes. Moore found that the existing mounds were built of sand or shell and were of four types: ceremonial, foundation, kitchen midden (refuse), and burial. Contents of refuse mounds reveal the varieties of food, methods of cooking, and a number of the implements and weapons used by the tribe. The size and number of mounds in some sections along the coast indicate that at certain seasons of the year the aborigines consumed extraordinary quantities of shellfish. The unusually heavy bone structure of the Florida aborigines was attributed by Ales Hrdlicka to the predominance of sea food in their diet.

Moore's initial investigations were in the sand mounds in the panhandle section. Some of the mounds

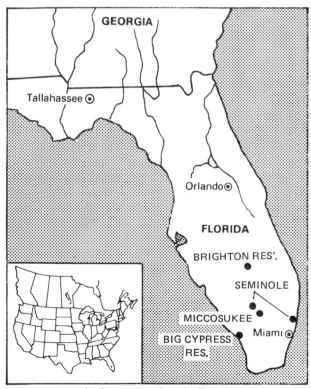

Indian reservations in Florida.

in west Florida, between the Perdido River and Tallahassee, were 80 feet across the base and 8 feet in height, and contained as many as 100 burials. Most of the skeletal material was fairly complete. Many bodies were orientated with the heads toward the center of the mound; some were flexed, lying on one side with the folded legs at right angles to the vertebrae; others were extended, and lay either on one side or face upwards. The absence of some bones in many of the skeletons tends to support the theory that these Indians removed the flesh from bodies before interment, leaving only the sinews to hold the bones together. This was done either by exposure to the weather or by cooking. This custom may have given rise to the early belief, now doubted by most authorities, that the Florida Indians were cannibals.

Implements found in west Florida were few and in many cases crude, but there were some ornaments and weapon points fashioned of bone, chert, or slate that were finely worked. These, together with the small pieces of copper found with them, may have been brought from northern sections where the Indians had gained greater proficiency.

The mounds of this section yielded ornamented clay vessels, similar to those described by Alvar Nuñuz Cabeza de Vaca, who in 1528 stated that the Indians of west Florida were very poor, but "before their houses were many clay pitchers of water." Some of those found were elaborate, having as many as five compartments, built up into the form of a human body or an animal, and fashioned so that the head protruded and served as a handle. The majority were ornamented on the outer wall with incised or printed lines, whorls, and dots to form a geometric design or formalized drawing of some bird or animal; and in many cases the lines were filled with an unidentified white substance in order to bring out the designs more sharply.

Receptacles here indicated a definite change in religious ideas over a period of time. An early custom was to break a hole in the bottom of a vase that was to be buried with the dead, and thus "kill" the vessel so that its soul might escape and join that of the deceased. Pots thus destroyed were found with many burials, sometimes placed over the skull, sometimes buried in caches. Later it became the thrifty custom to construct for funeral purposes an artistic reproduction of the utilitarian vessels, with ready-made holes as part of the design. Among these the best portrait vases are found.

Moore's investigations in the northeast portion of the State, particularly in the vicinity of the St. Johns River, were not as productive as those in the northwest. The sand mounds excavated here yielded artifacts, pottery, and skeletal material, but in small amounts and in poor condition. The results of the exploration seemed to show that the works were built before contact with the whites, but in some places articles of European manufacture were fond, indicating possibly that the historic Indians had used an early

mound to include later burials. Notable finds were a number of conch shells with holes bored at the base for the insertion of handles. The conclusion reached was that such a shell was used as a domestic tool rather than a weapon, for the hole would not admit a handle of sufficient size to permit the striking of a heavy blow without the handle's breaking.

The earth and shell mounds of the southwest and southeast coasts, investigated by Moore, Cushing, Hrdlicka, and later archeologists, were interesting more because of their form and manner of construction than for their content. Most heaps yielded few or no remains, and seem to have been built mainly for dwelling platforms above the high-water mark of a swampy country. Artifacts were crude, most of them constructed of shell, while pottery was simple and without elaborate decoration. Living on and by the sea, the natives built an elaborate system of canals and basins to transport their canoes between dwelling platforms and the open water. Breakwaters and causeways surrounded and connected village sites. An interesting custom noted here was the decoration of conch shells. These shell walls gave rise to early stories of aboriginal stone structures on the keys.

Some burials in this section were found embedded in a solidified matrix of sand and shell, and at first it was believed that the remains were of great age; now it is thought that the matrix was hardened quickly by the infiltration of water carrying minerals in solution, and that the deposits are of no greater age than those found in higher and drier burials.

Perhaps the greatest find in this section was the collection of carved wooden objects unearthed in 1895 in Key Largo. These, probably made of cypress, of good workmanship, are thought to hae been used for ceremonial purposes. In 1921 a wooden idol and two flat carved objects of wood called "altar slabs" were plowed up in the muck in reclaimed land north of Lake Okeechobee.

J.S. Fewkes in 1924 excavated a group of mounds at Weeden Island in Tampa Bay. The pottery here seemed to show a level of culture higher than that found in most parts of the section and resembled in design the claywork of northwest Florida. Fewkes reported that he found three levels of culture; the lowest, Antillean; the middle, Muskhogean; and the upper layer, modern. There was no evidence of European influence, although Spanish trading beads were uncovered.

In 1928 Henry B. Collins explored mounds south and west of Lake Okeechobee, doing the most extensive excavation in the shell and sand heaps on Captiva Island, south of Charlotte Harbor. A burial mound on this island, although destroyed in part by early treasurer seekers, yielded more than 70 skulls. Some of these, in the bottom of the mound, had been cemented together by a mixture of muck and water and were well preserved; others, lying in the loose sand at the surface of the mound, considered to be secondary burials, were in poor condition.

A large oval mound with three projecting arms 40, 100, and 300 feet long respectively, and somewhat resembling the effigy mounds of the Northern States, was also reported by Collins, east of Fort Myers near Citrus Center. It was partly inclosed by an embankment. Beginning less than a mile away and extending westward for more than a mile and a half was a canal of aboriginal construction that apparently had some connection with the mound. Excavation produced nothing more than a few potsherds.

Smithsonian archeological projects, investigated mounds in southeast and southwest Florida. Excavations in the vicinity of Belle Glade, on the shore of Lake Okeechobee, revealed the same culture at all levels. Shell and bone implements as well as muck pottery were abundant. Several carved bird heads of wood and parts of two wooden plaques were found deep in the sand. Some remarkable effigy carvings in fine-grained sandstone have been discovered in recent years.

The native population of Florida at the time of the Spanish conquest comprised approximately 10,000 Indians, divided into four major tribes who lived in the four quarters of this region. The Calusa in the southwest were mariners and fishermen who sailed their canoes as far as Cuba and Hispaniola and lived on the abundant oysters and fish along the coast It is possible that they were of Carib stock and had crossed from the islands to make a new home in Florida long before the coming of the white men. Attempts to land in their territories were fiercely resisted, and it was from a

wound inflicted by one of their arrows that Ponce de Leon died after returning to Cuba from the west coast of Florida. Because of their attacks, no Spanish colony or mission ever succeeded in long holding a foothold in this part of the State.

East of the Calusa and south of Cape Canaveral dwelt the Tegesta, a people as hostile to the white man as their neighbors, although not as warlike. Spanish missions were established among them, and many claimed to have been converted to the new faith, yet the Tegesta were long a source of trouble. They protested friendship for the Spanish settlers, but there were continual reports of shipwreck victims being murdered while attempting to make their way up the coast to St. Augustine. Letters from that city to Spain tell of cruelty and breach of faith, and beg that the Indians be enslaved and sent away, in order to insure safety in the future.

The Timucuan, who lived in central and northeast Florida, had reached a stage of civilization superior to that of the southern Indians. They cultivated extensive cornfields, constructed substantial houses, and traded with the tribes to the north. More is known of the Timucuan than of other early Florida tribes. Because their language was understood in all parts of the peninsula, it was used as a sort of *lingua franca* by the Spanish missionaries who needed a general dialect to carry on their work. Catechisms and texts were published in Timucuan to simplify the instruction of the different tribes, and the language became a medium of communication in most of Florida.

In 1564 the French artist LeMoyne accompanied the Huguenots who built Fort Caroline. He made pictures

A Florida Indian village. From a 1591 engraving by Theodore de Bry, after an on-the-scene drawing by Jacques le Moyne de Morgues.

Courtesy, Library of Congress.

of the native villages and customs, and his drawings, supplemented by the narrative written by leaders in the colony, are today a valuable source of information of this extinct tribe. Added to these Indians for many years, and left behind him books rated among the earliest and most valuable of Americana.

The Apalachee in northwest Florida were civilized as the Timucuan and more powerful because their chiefs were united in a strong league. "Keep on, robbers and traitors," the southern Indians warned the soldiers of De Soto, "in Apalachee you will receive the chastisement your cruelty deserves." The Apalachee area was reputed to be the richest country in Florida.

All the tribes were sun worshipers. On the dawn of a certain day every spring a stag's head, garlanded with flowers, was set upon a pole facing east. As the first rays of light touched the antlered head, the tribe bowed in prayer. If the crops were not plentiful, first-born children and captives were often sacrificed to appease the sun god.

Moon and sun worship were analogous. The moon was associated with moisture and the Indians' water worship included many rites. For example, when the people wished to overcome illness, they bathed three times in clear running water, and sometimes, as in the case of measles, this treatment resulted in appalling fatalities.

Descent among these tribes was through the mother, so that a chief was succeeded by his sister's son, rather than by his own. Likewise, when a man said he was going home he meant that he was going to his mother's house. There were also instances where women ruled the tribes, as in the case of Dona Maria, the chieftainess who ruled Nombre de Dios near St. Augustine in 1592.

What clothes these early Floridians wore were for ornament; men wore brilliant feathered mantles, metal breastplates, and leather breechclouts. The typical brave wore inflated fish bladders, dyed red, in his ears, and his long hair was piled high in a knot at the top of his head. Fingernails and toenails were worn long. Elaborate tattooing covered the warrior's body, and his neck, arms, and legs were strung with beads and rattles.

An Indian woman wore a moss skirt and mantle, and her hair was unbound. Upon the death of her husband her hair was cut short, and she was not permitted to remarry until it covered her shoulders again.

Many of these people became Christians through the heroic efforts of Spanish missionaries. During the seventeenth century, Indian villages in Florida presented a remarkable picture of civilized community life. Indian children learned to read and write, and adults went to church dressed in European fashion. No white people except the priests were allowed to live near these villages, and trade in firearms and liquor was unlawful.

The progress of Indian life was rudely interrupted in the beginning of the eighteenth century. The Creek of Georgia sided with the English against the Spanish,

and, beginning in 1702, made raids into Florida as far south as the Everglades, carrying thousands of cattle and Indian captives to Charleston. The Spanish Indians were sold as slaves in New England and the West Indies, where they were highly valued for their training. Those who escaped fled to the protection of the French at Mobile, or to the Spanish forts at St. Marks and St. Augustine. By 1706, the towns of the Spanish trail across north Florida were almost deserted.

Slave-raiding parties from the north were usually composed of a few hundred Creek led by a small band of their British friends. As the land was laid waste and the natives were carried off, the Creek invaders took over the fields and settled here. When Florida became a British territory, the English colonists who replaced the Spanish found their old Indian allies from Georgia firmly established in the State and banded together in a strong confederation. They had broken with their old nation in the north and were now known as the Seminole or "Runaways."

After the Revolution, when Georgia became a part of the United States and Florida again became a Spanish possession in 1783, the ranks of the Seminole were continually being swelled by fugitive Negro slaves who found refuge and freedom among the Indians, to whom they paid tribute in corn. Attempts by planters of Georgia to recapture the runawys resulted in friction between Florida and the United States, and Seminole animosity against the Americans was inspired by the British. These continuing disturbances culminated in the short Florida campaigns of Andrew Jackson in 1814 and 1818, the latter known as the First Seminole War. Four years later, when Florida became a part of the United States, the government realized that measures were necessary to check the hostilities between Seminole and white settlers, and a movement was started to send the Indians to reservations west of the Mississippi.

In 1832 a delegation of chiefs traveled to the western reservation to inspect the land. They were persuaded to sign a treaty that committed their tribe to immigration, but the Seminole disavowed the treaty. Attempts to move the Indians by force and the seizure of Osceola's wife as a fugitive slave were among the incidents that precipitated the Second Seminole War, a seven-year struggle (1835-42) involving great losses in life and property.

The principal figure in this war was Osceola. In 1808, when the second secession from the Creek occurred, Osceola, at that time about four years old, came to Florida with his mother and finally settled on Peace Creek. When he appeared at Fort King shortly before the Seminole War, he had reached manhood.

In his dealings with the whites he was proud. Osceola was not a chief and, according to Indian custom, had no voice in the councils of his tribe; but his natural talent for leadership soon asserted itself, for the nominal chief, Micanope, an irresolute and phlegmatic man, soon fell under the influence of this spirited, more determined warrior.

The unfair treatment accorded *Che-cho-ter* (Morning Dew), Osceola's wife, was one of the chief causes for his open hostility toward the whites. Although Che-cho-ter had been married long enough to bear Osceola four children, a trace of Negro blood gave white settlers an excuse to carry her off as a slave. Osceola never forgave what he considered a blood insult to his people and himself.

During the first half of the Second Seminole War, Osceola was the real, if not the nominal, leader of the Indians. The spirit of his leadership is well expressed in a message which he sent to General Clinch." You have guns, so have we. You have powder and lead, and so have we. Your men will fight, and so will ours till the last drop of Seminole blood has moistened the dust of his hunting ground."

In 1837, at a council with General Hernández, Osceola and his friends were surrounded and taken as prisoners to St. Augustine, but were later removed to Fort Moultrie, South Carolina. Here Osceola, although suffering from quinsy, to which he succumbed soon afterwards, posed for a portrait by Catlin. His last wish was that he should die as a Seminole brave in the war dress of his tribe.

Coacoochee (Wild Cat), one of the chiefs imprisoned with Osceola at Fort Marion, escaped and became the most influential leader of the latter half of the war. General William J. Worth finally won the friendship of this chief in 1841, and through him persuaded about 500 Seminole and their Negroes to emigrate.

The majority of the Seminole were transported west, where they formed one of the Five Civilized Tribes of Oklahoma, but about 150 fled to the unexplored wilderness of the Everglades.

The Seminole in Florida today are divided into two tribes: the Muscogee, who live north and east of Lake Okeechobee, and the Miccosukee, who occupy the region south of the lake and the Big Cypress swamp on the west. Customs and habits vary, but in general there is little except dialect to distinguish the tribes.

FLORIDA STATE INDIAN RESERVATION, more than 100,000 acres in size, is set aside for Miccosukee and Seminole Indians.

The State of Florida has set aside an approximate 104,000 acres, some 60 rented from Miami, for the use and benefit of the Seminole and Miccosukee Indians of Florida. These lands are administered jointly by the Seminole tribe of Florida (northern third of area) and the Miccosukee tribe (southern two-thirds of area). Although much of the land in the state reservation may not be developed, all Seminole enjoy hunting and fishing rights there. The land on the state reservation, outside of the conservation area of the Central and Southern Florida Flood Control District, will, in time, be developed and utilized by the Indians of Florida. There are no houses or commercial buildings on the state reservation now. One or two members of the Seminole tribe may have permits to run small numbers of cattle on limited acreage. However, much of this land is under water most of the year.

FLUTE and flageolet are among the few indigenous North American musical instruments capable of playing a melody. The flute probably developed from the whistle, having holes along the side to produce more notes. A slide might go over the main hole to vary the tone. When two or more whistles were joined side by side, they became a "Panpipe," found in Central America and California. Flutes were made of various materials, including bone, reed, clay, and metal. In post-European America, old gun barrels were sometimes transformed into flutes.

Flutes were most commonly used by young men in courtship to send secret messages and for love charms. The Sioux (Plains) called these instruments "elk whistles" because the sound resembled the bull elk's mating call.

In Mexico, Eastern, and Southwestern U.S., flutes were used in official and sacred ceremonies. De Soto was met by chiefs in Florida signalling their good will by playing cane flutes. The Hopi Pueblo held a Flute Dance every two years alternating with the Snake Dance; long flutes were played at ceremonies offering prayers at deep springs. Flutes were usually played solo, but the instrument was part of the official Aztec orchestra, and the Yaqui people of Arizona and Sonora had a clown dance where one person played drum and flute at the same time.

Bureau of American Ethnology.

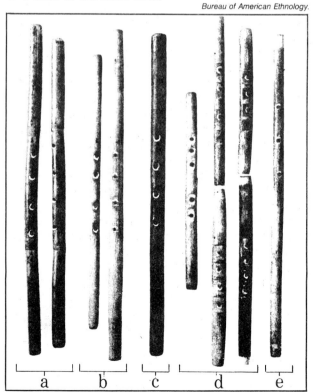

Flutes-a, Yuma; b, Yokuts; c, Miwok; d, Pomo; e, Karok

FOLKLORE Very few men have the gift of genuine creation. They can modify and improve on what is known already, but they cannot evolve an entirely new style of architecture, or a type of literature unlike any that has gone before. Similarly, when a people borrows folktales from surrounding peoples—and tales, or at least incidents in them, are transmitted more easily perhaps than anything else—it cannot assimilate them if they differ radically from its own folktales, but modifies them to conform to ideas and patterns that are already familiar, and imposes on them the individuality inherent in its own legends and traditions. A few tales, of course, often remain imperfectly assimilated and preserve their alien flavor. Nevertheless, taken in the aggregate, the folklore of each people has its own peculiar character, and often mirrors the lives and thoughts of its exponents.

The absence of writing among the Indians gave their folklore a higher and important role. It supplied the place of text-books in the education of the children, teaching them the traditional history, morality, and religion of their tribes both directly and through the ceremonies that in many cases dramatized the tales. Men used the folktales as public records, citing them to prove their claims to varius rights and privileges, such as that of painting certain emblems on their houses. On the Plains men validated their sacred medicine bundles by the legends attached to them, and in the East they established the claims of their bands to certain hunting and fishing territories by the recital of ancient traditions. There were many tales so closely interwoven with the social and religious life of the Indians that they were considered personal property, and although known to other individuals might be be recited only by their owners or at certain definite times and places. The world of the supernatural has always seemed very close to the Indians from the most ancient times. It figures even in personal narratives of the nineteenth century, vitiating many accounts of their early contacts with Europeans that in all other respects appear historical.

Every tribe separated its tales into two cycles, those that referred to the world of today with its familiar mountains, lakes, and rivers, and those that related to a supposedly earlier epoch before the earth and its inhabitants had assumed their present form. In that mythical "golden age," the Indians believed, man could freely communicate with the animals, which had the same thoughts, the same emotions as human beings and could even lay aside their animal dress at will. But mighty heroes transformed the world, and a chasm began to separate man and the animals, which culd no longer discard their animal forms except in their homes, far removed from human view or on special occasions when they visited the fasting Indian to confer on him their blessing.

The folklore of the first cycle inevitably abounds in nature tales, especially tales in which animals are the principal actors. There are anecdotes about beaver and mice, about a contest between owl and squirrel (and endless other stories of a similar character. One has yet to explain satisfactorily why such tales should have appealed to nearly every people both in the new world and the old.) They are exactly alike in all regions of the Americas. The Indians generally make of each animal a type. The coyote is a treacherous creature, the wolverine both treacherous and gluttonous, the deer timid, the raven greedy, the buffalo brave and honorable. Many of their tales, however, lack characterization, and a bird or animal has no other identity than that afforded by its name and outward description.

More interesting than these nature tales are the genealogical myths and the culture hero stories that are also attached to the first cycle. The Iroquoians and Algonquins have given us long cosmogonic myths in which the various episodes follow each other in more or less logical sequence. Another systematic account comes from Bella Coola, on the Pacific Coast, where the Indians had a fantastic but unusually well-ordered conception of the universe and its origin, built around the belief of the sky-god *Alkuntam*. Elsewhere these tales are short and utterly disjointed, even when the same characters figure as the principal actors. Nearly every tribe has in fact numerous tales that flatly contradict one another, for there was no organized priesthood to collate all the versions, reducing them to harmony, and individual families handed down their own traditions regardless of whether they conflicted or not with the traditions of their neighbors.

Although the Indians had myths explaining, for example, how daylight began, why winter and summer alternate, why the raven is black and the sea-gull white, and why the chipmunk, has stripes along its back, there were few creation stories, no myths attributing to the will of a creator the genesis of stars and planets, earth and water, day and night, the seasons, animals and plants. The great *Manitous* or high deities of the Indians were not "fathers of gods and men," and they could not be invoked as the ultimate causes of all things. Apparently the Indians felt no necessity for an ultimate cause, but assumed that the phenomena of nature had always existed somewhere, and in their myths merely described how they had been brought into their present relationship with man.

The principal character in many of these myths is a power "trickster" known to the different tribes under various names. The Algonquins call him *Glooscap, Nanibush,* or *Wisakedjak;* the Plains' Indians name him "the Old Man"; the Salish Indians identify him with the coyote; and the Pacific Coast tribes with the raven. Whatever his name, animal or other wise, he is always what the Carriers call him, "the trickster", who delights in playing pranks on everyone and everything. He invites the ducks to a new kind of feast so that he may twist their necks while they are dancing, and he frightens away his daughters with a rumor of enemies that he may surreptitiously eat all their food. They provided the folklore with a comic element that never failed to amuse the Indians, old and young alike.

Another group of tales widely spread relates how the "trickster", or else a separate culture hero, roams over the earth rearranging phenomena and destroying all the devouring monsters that prey upon mankind. There was no place for altruism in the character of the "trickster" himself, so that whenever there is a separate character, as among the Carriers, we have a hero (analogous to Perseus or St. Andrew) a genuine crusader who fights and sometimes dies for the cause of humanity. Many tales in this group afford glimpses of tribal life during pre-European days, and a few reveal romanticism. Thus in one story the hero begins life as a despised orphan, marries the daughter of a powerful chief through the help of his supernatural guardian, wins fame and honor by his skill and courage and becomes the champion of the countryside. After destroying various monsters that ravage the villages he receives a mortal wound in the death agonies of a supernatural lynx. His countrymen they carry home his body for honorable burial, but his widow, overwhelmed with grief because a faulty stitch in his moccasin had caused his death, commits suicide.

In the tales of the second cycle, those that refer to the world of today, human actors gain the foreground and animals drop back to a secondary place. The Indians believed that a stump could momentarily change to a man, that the caribou could push back the hood from its face and gaze out of a human countenance; that the snake or the owl could address the sleeping Indian in his own tongue. These things, however, happened rarely and not to all individuals, whereas there were many other tales of equal interest that they could narrate around their fires; adventures of the chase and of war, experiences of travellers among distant tribes, rivalries of chiefs and of medicinemen, medicine paraphernalia and their histories, and the everchanging incidents of village and camp life. Each tribe, of course, set its own stamp on these anecdotes, making them conform to certain patterns and reflect its own social life. The Eskimo had few tales of animals transforming themselves into men, but many stories of encounters with strange half-human beings, of shamans and their conflicts, of blood-feuds and quarrels over women; of orphans who grew up to avenge the murders of their parents; of famines, and long journeys by land and sea in search of food. The Indians on the West Coast told of the rivalry of chiefs, of potlatches and the struggles for wealth and position, and of journeys up and down the coast for trade and warfare. From the Plains there are anecdotes of the march and of the buffalo hunt, accounts of the bundles, and endless stories of raids for scalps and horses. Tales of war and of medicine-power were popular among the Iroquoians and Algonquins, but these tribes have absorbed so many European tales during the last three centuries that it is not easy to disentangle their original folklore.

In every area, particularly on the Plains, many tales are modelled on exactly the same plot. A story that

describes the origin of a certain medicine-bundle will be repeated with the change of a few names for several other bundles, as though this particular plot has carried a special appeal. Another stylistic feature is the repetition of the same incident over and over again for the purpose of holding the listener in suspense and retaining his interest. Thus in a Tsimshian tale a woman cries out for aid, and the animals come one after another to offer their services. Each asks the same question and receives the same answer, until the words become a refrain that lingers in the mind and serves as a text for the entire story. Many Plains' and west coast tales specialize in repeating the incident four times. Four brothers insuccession will start out on a journey and only the youngest be successful, or a man will undergo four tests and succeed only at the last. In this respect the folklore parallels some of the religious rituals, which were commonly repeated four times.

The most noteworthy feature about Indian folklore, however, is its purely anecdotal character. The emotions it portrays are few and simple—fear and anger, pity and love, jealousy and hatred—and even these are implied rather than expressed. Nowhere is there any attempt to analyse the characters, to depict their motives, or to introduce any psychological reflections. The stories relate events, and either end as soon as an incident is complete or pass on immediately to the next episode without comment.

Among a few tribes the moral sentence seems little more than a stylistic feature, a convenient literary device for bringing a tale to its conclusion. It is seldom the true *raison d'être* of the story or an integral part of it, for other tribes that relate exactly the same tales omit the moral.

Although they were not moral in form, a large proportion of the tales undoubtedly had a considerable ethical influence, especially when narrated at night in the firelight by some old man or woman who could add the comments suggested by a long experience of life. Public recitals of exploits, such as occurred among the Iroquoians before they set out on the warpath, stimulated the young to military valor. The great Sun Dance festival of the Blackfoot, at which the whole tribe extolled the purity of the Sun Dance woman and her predecessor, the warriors recited their earlier deeds, and the elder men related the tribal traditions, had something of the character of a prolonged spiritual revival; while the personal ownership of many tales, and their elaborate dramatization at public festivals under the mantle of religion, gave them inherent value and force.

The historical value of Indian traditions are not fixed even in a single tribe, but the versions given by one family contradict those of another. In Indian tribal traditions there is scarcely a semblance of agreement concerning movements and events in pre-European times. Even on the Pacific Coast, where the nobles were so deeply engrossed in matters of rank and inheritance that they kept count of potlatches and debts for three or four generations, traditions of events that happened more than a century and a half ago show little congruity. The Indians lacked interest in plain, historical facts, or at least found them difficult to understand without invoking such a wealth of supernatural causes and interferences. Many other peoples have preserved fairly reliable records of a great constitutional change such as the formation of the League of the Iroquois, which commenced only about the time of Columbus and was not perfected until a century later. Yet, although we know the names of its principal founders. Dekanawida and Hiawatha, there is little authentic information concerning their lives, which have become swallowed up in impossible legends.

Another reason for the unreliability of Indian traditions is the manner in which they were interpreted as they spread from tribe to tribe. There are stories that are well known to many tribes in the United States. One example is a tale about a girl and a dog, which is quoted by certain Eskimo tribes to explain the origin of sea mammals, by others to explain the origin and diffusion of the different races of mankind. The Tlingit Indians repeat the same story to account for the Milky Way, and the Blackfoot Indians to explain the origin of their "dog society." There are tribes that make it explanatory of nothing but narrate it as an anecdote. The story is fantastic, and nothing but an ancient folktale interpreted by the different tribes to suit their needs. Even if it were not imposible we should certainly err if we regarded it as the true explanation of the Blackfoot "dog society." Similarly we often find two tribes with the same migration tradition, although it can hardly be true of both. New myths and new traditions arose so easily that even when a tradition seems purely local and contains no improbable episodes one dare not accept its authenticity unless there is other evidence to support it.

One value the folktales possess for reconstruction the earlier history of the Indians comes from an analytical study of their diffusion. If two tribes now widely separated both relate the same complex story, we know that they have been in contact with each other at some period in their history, or else that one or both of them has derived it from an intermediate tribe. Tales like the girl and dog story are so ancient that one can hardly hope to discover their original sources or to trace the historical contacts suggested by their present diffusion. There are certain themes, such as stories about giants and dwarfs, that may even belong to the infancy of the human race, and have reached America with the first immigratns. Others, again, are so simple and natural that they could spring up in any country, and their distribution has no historical significance. Thus Indians have a tradition concerning a great flood, which we cannot reasonably connect with the biblical account or with each other.

A few tales stand out like flowers from a tangle of bushes and deserve the brush of a great artist. Such is the Tsimshian story given here which, in spite of its exoticism and impossibilities, appeals to us on account of its humanity:

"The son of a chief married a girl of his own village. They lived happily together for many months and the woman was about to bear a child. One morning she awoke very ill; by evening she was worse, and at midnight she died, the child being still unborn. The people mourned over her body for two days, and buried her on the morning of the third day.

The husband, stricken with grief, slept each night on his wife's grave. The people carried presents of food to him, but he declined to eat. At last his mother went and begged him to eat; and he entered her house and ate whatever she offered him. But at night he returned to his wife's grave and slept there.

The weather grew colder, and snow began to cover the ground. At first he cleared it away from the grave and slept on the bare ground; but when the snow grew deeper and the cold more rigorous he slept in his hut.

Spring came, and he went to visit his wife's grave again. As he drew near it he saw a little boy gathering fireweed, very quietly it entered the grave with a bunch of flowers, then came out again and began to pick more. The man concealed himself and watched. Sometimes the boy gathered flowers and took them inside the grave, sometimes he gathered other things. And all the time the man watched from his hiding place.

Now, as he pondered over this, he determined to try and catch the child. He returned to his house, speaking to no one, took down his tools, and made four tiny bows, which he covered with red paint. Next he cut some branches of the saskatoon tree and made four tiny arrows, which he feathered with great care. The villagers were glad to see him working again, although they did not know what he was doing, for they grieved that he should weep each day at his wife's grave.

Three days after he had first seen the boy the man returned to the grave, carrying his bows and arrows in a bag upon his back. Again he saw the boy, who was now a little bigger. When he entered the grave the man ran forward and planted a bow and arrow in the ground nearby. He planted the second bow and arrow a little farther down the trail toward the village, and the third and fourth a little farther still. Then he hid and waited.

Soon the boy came out of the grave again. He laughed softly when he saw the first bow and arrow, and ran to examine them. At first he seemed afraid to touch them with his hands; but presently he pulled out the arrow and looked at it. It was very beautiful, and a low laugh escaped him as he strung it on the bow and began to play with it. Looking around, he saw the second bow and arrow, and ran to get them likewise. Now he noticed the third, and, dropping the first two sets, which were rather heavy for him, he ran to gather them also. Both the third and fourth he gathered up and carried inside the grave, then returned a few moments for the first and second. The man waited for some time longer, but when the boy did not appear, he returned home pondering.

Now he made six more bows and arrows and set them out in the same way as before; and the boy came out of the grave and gathered them. Many more he made and also told his parents what he had seen. Twelve of the most noted medicine-men gathered in his father's house while he went out and planted them about six feet apart in a long line that led from the grave to the village. Then he rejoined the people in the house and they waited.

The boy was growing bigger now. He came out of the grave, gathered the bows and arrows three at a time, and returned for more. All day he worked, carrying his burdens into the grave; and nearer he approached the village, while the medicine-men watched him in silence through the part-open door. The last bow and arrow had been planted in the ground just behind the house. Thither the boy came, timidly, to draw it out; but just as he turned to go back the chief medicine-man ran swiftly and silently behind him, in a kind of trance, and caught him in his hands. The boy gave one frightened cry and shrivelled almost to nothing. The other medicine-men inside the house shook their rattles and sang their songs. They approached the child, one by one, and breathed on him, trying to restore him to life. Then they carried him inside the house, and sang over him for three days and three nights. On the fourth day the boy became truly alive. He was the man's own son, who had been buried in the grave with his mother but had been granted the semblance of life because of the father's constant weeping.

The boy was now alive, but he was not happy. He would not eat, but cried night and day. The villagers, unable to rest, called in a wise woman from another village and promised to pay her bountifully if she would cure the child. She came and listened to his weeping and to his constant cry "Dihl he Dihl he;" and she laughed as she heard the words. "I thought it was something big and great the child wanted," she said. "What he wants is only a little thing. He craves for the full free life of man, not the half life he enjoyed in the grave. He wants his cousin to accompany him half-way up yonder mountain where the giant spruce trees grow, and the people to set fire to the spruce trees so that the hot gum may fall on the bodies of them both as they stand underneath. Then the people must wash him and his cousin beneath a waterfall."

As the old woman instructed they did. The hot gum that fell on the children's bodies they washed off beneath a tumbling waterfall. Thus the boy gained the full free life for which he craved, and cried no more. The people named him "The Dead Woman's Son". And the heart of his father was glad as he watched him hunting and playing with his cousin, both growing up to manhood together."

Adapted from Bulletin 65, Anthropoligical Series No. 15, National Museum of Canada.

FOLSOM CULTURE, (9000-7000 BC). Following the last glacial period man lived in New Mexico and left

his chipped stone dart points embedded in fluvial deposits in conjunction with the bones of animals now extinct.

The Folsom culture derives its name from the site of discovery in northeastern New Mexico. A number of chipped stone dart points of unique shape were found associated with the skeletal remains of a post-glacial sub-species of bison. The artifacts are from one to three inches in length; they are thin and leaf-shaped, with a longitudinal fluting on each face, a concave base with earlike projections, and carefully retouched edges. The knapping technique developed by the Folsom hunters compares favorably with the percussion and retouching method employed by the inhabitants of the Scandinavian countries during the late Neolithic and Early Bronze periods, and the "ripple flaking" of craftsmen belonging to the pre- and early-Dynastic Egyptian horizons.

During the past years surface finds of Folsom points have been made throughout the Plains from Canada to Mexico; and camp sites of the eary "Bison Nomads" have been discovered. They encampment about fifteen miles south of Clovis, New Mexico, in one of the series of shallow basins known as Black Water Draw, yielded an assortment of stone artifact types and contained the remains of a charcoal-filled hearth. The Folsom people hunted such animals as the giant ground sloth, musk-ox, three-toed horse, camel, four-pronged antelope, mammoth, etc., which existed in the early post-glacial period. The early nomads probably frequented the country that is now New Mexico approximately 10,000 to 15,000 years ago.

FOLSOM, DAVID (Choctaw; Jan. 25, 1791-Sept. 24, 1847), the first chief of his people elected by ballot, was forced to cede Choctaw lands to the U.S. government and lead his people west. Folsom, who was a signer of several treaties between 1816 and 1825, was elected chief in 1826, replacing Mushalatubbee (q.v.). He was supported by a young, militant faction of the Choctaw who, like himself, opposed the cession of lands, and his election almost caused a civil war with the old chief. Although he was able to avert this threat through diplomacy, he eventually was forced to modify his position and agree to the cession.

Folsom led part of his tribe on the winter migration to the Red River in Indian Territory (November 1831-January 1832), and there he helped to establish missions and schools. He also set up a salt factory and became relatively wealthy. He died at Fort Towson, in present Oklahoma.

FOLSOM, FRANCES (Choctaw; 1864-1947), was the wife of Grover Cleveland, president of the U.S. (1885-89; 1893-97). They were married during Cleveland's first term on June 2, 1886, and she proved to be a popular first lady. She was the daughter of his former law partner, Oscar Folsom, and was descended from a prominent Choctaw family.

FOLSOM, ISRAEL (Choctaw; 1802-April 24, 1870), was a Presbyterian minister who was known among his people as a man of great spirituality. The younger brother of David Folsom (*q.v.*), *he moved west to Indian Territory (present Oklahoma) with his people in 1831. In 1861 he was in Washington, D.C., with Peter P. Pitchlyn (q.v.)* attending to business of the Choctaw Nation and, when they learned about the impending U.S. Civil War, they immediately returned home, where Folsom worked unsuccessfully to keep the Choctaw neutral.

FOLSOM, LORING (Choctaw; ?-after 1899), was one of the leaders of the Choctaw Nation in Indian Territory (present Oklahoma) and served as a circuit judge in his district for almost 20 years. The son of David Folsom (*q.v.*), he was noted for his wisdom. He retired from public life to a farm near Caddo, Oklahoma.

FOLSOM-DICKERSON, WILLIAM E. S. (Choctaw; Dec. 26, 1898-Dec. 5, 1974), was an educator and author. Born at Durant, Indian Territory (present Oklahoma, he was educated at the University of Texas. While a teacher in Texas public schools for more than 30 years, he visited the major Indian tribes in the U.S. researching his books. He is the author of *The Handbook of Texas* (1952, *The White Path* (1965), and *Cliff Dwellers* (1968).

FOND DU LAC RESERVATION, Minnesota, on an area of 21,000 acres, is home to nearly 800 Chippewa (Ojibwa) Indians.

The Fond du Lac Reservation lies immediately adjacent to Cloquet, population 10,000, which is a major trade center in Carlton County. Less than 20 miles from the reservation is Duluth, Minnesota, having a population of over 100,000.

The Chippewa, or Ojibwa, were one of the largest Indian nations north of Mexico and controlled lands extending along both shores of Lakes Huron and Superior and westward into North Dakota. Their migration to this area was instigated by Iroquois pressure from the northeast. Drifting through their native forests, never settling on prized farmlands, the Chippewa were little disturbed by the first onrush of white settlers. They maintained friendly relations with the French and were courageous warriors. In the early 18th century, the Chippewa drove the Fox out of northern Wisconsin and then drove the Sioux across the Mississippi and Minnesota rivers. By this time they were also able to push back the Iroquois, whose strength and organization had been undercut by settlers. The Chippewa of the United States have been officially at peace with the government since 1815 and have experienced less dislocation than many other tribes.

The Chippewa were nomadic timber people traveling in small bands, engaging primarily in hunting and fishing, sometimes settled to carry on a rude form of agriculture. These foods were supplemented by gathering fruits and wild rice. Their wigwams of saplings and birchbark were easily moved and erected. Birchbark canoes were used for journeys, but other travel was usually by foot. The tribe was patrilineal, divided into clans usually bearing animal names. Although their social organization was loose, the powerful Grand Medicine Society controlled the tribe's movements and was a formidable obstacle to Christianizing attempts of missionaries. A mysterious power, or manitou, was believed to live in all animate or inanimate objects. The Chippewa today are largely of mixed blood, mostly French and English.

The Fond du Lac Reservation is one of six Chippewa reservations in the state organized as the Minnesota Chippewa Tribe under the Indian Reorganization Act of 1934. The revised constitution of this organization, approved in 1964, provides for a local reservation business committee to be elected at each of the member reservations. The chairman and secretary-treasurer of each elected committee form the 12-member tribal council.

The only natural resources occurring on the reservation are sand, gravel, and peat. The forest timber has been overcut. The annual tribe income averages $1,900. Ninety percent of this comes from the forestry industry. Most of the remainder is earned in farming. The tribe has organized a Reservation Housing Authority and has an active Community Action Program. Many different types of commercial and industrial establishments are located in the reservation committees of Brookston, Sawyer, and Paupor, and in the bordering city of Cloquet.

The reservation lies in an area which averages 70 inches of snowfall each year. The annual precipitation measures 22 inches. The average summer high temperature is 66°; the average winter low is 9°.

FOOD AND DRINK. Many of the most widely used and important foods known in the Americas today are of Indian origin. They are sold, enjoyed every day, and often even prepared as the Indians did. Such classic dishes as barbecue, steamed lobster, succotash, spoon bread, cranberry sauce, and mincemeat pie, are inherited from Indians. Until the discovery of America, the rest of the world knew nothing of such foods as avocados, sweet or Irish potatoes, pineapples, tomatoes, peppers, pumpkins or squashes, maple sugar, and, of course, corn. Without corn, which most Indians regarded as a gift from the gods to be treasured and surrounded with ceremony, and which was cooked in numberless ways, the colonization of America might have faltered. The wild rice of the Great Lakes region, which is now considered a gourmet delicacy, was often used, and is still harvested by the Ojibua.

To a considerable extent, religious customs and beliefs determined both what foods were eaten and how they were prepared. For example, tribes of the Northwest, after eating salmon, would arrange every bone of the fish in a certain way to assure that the fish would return to life to be caught and eaten again. Many tribes had taboos against certain foods. Salt was tabooed by the Onondagas, for instance, and neither the Apaches nor the Navajos would eat fish or the flesh of bears or beavers.

Most Indians preferred cooked food to raw, and they had many methods of cooking and seasoning their food. Among the methods used were stoneboiling (putting hot stones into a basket or pot of water); drying; freezing; and smoking. The various cooking methods obviously affected pottery and basketry types. Flavoring was accomplished by the use of seeds, roots, flowers, and grasses. The north Pacific tribes used the tender inner bark of hemlock and spruce. In the southwest, mesquite beans, cactus and yucca fruits, and the agave were important.

Five distinct areas provided the Indian foods and recipes we use today. In the Southwest, the Pueblo tribes, the Papagos ("Bean People"), and Hopis grew peppers and beans which were made into savory chili, soups, guacamole and barbecue sauces. Along the Northwest Coast, seafood was the staple, and here women of the Tlingit, Kwakiutl, Salish, and other tribes steamed and broiled salmon and dozens of other fish and seafood from the Pacific and the western rivers. On the vast Plains, nomadic tribes such as the Sioux and Cheyenne roasted buffalo over campfires. In the South, Cherokees and other tribes had long enjoyed an impressive list of fragrant soups and rich stews, and they baked the same assortment of corn breads known today. Two particular American favorites, the clambake and Boston baked beans, were also staple favorites of the Narragansetts, Penobscots and Powhatans, who, like the Iroquois and other timber people of the East, steamed their dinners in earthen pits. Their method, still in use today, is now called "fireless cooking."

From all these regions, American Indians have bequeathed varied, imaginative and indispensable dishes. American Indian cuisine may rightly be considered continental cooking, indigenous and unique.

Securing and preparing

Among the Iroquois the women did the gardening; the men were the hunters. In the early days the Iroquois made much use of both fresh and dried fish and meat. The many lakes and streams of the Iroquois country yielded an abundant supply of fish during the spring fishing season. During the season of the fall hunt, long and toilsome expeditions to secure game were undertaken by the men. When times of scarcity occurred the Iroquois found it necessary to supplement the larger game by adding the meat of many of the smaller animals to the diet. In the old village site bones have been found of bison, deer, elk, black bear, porcupine, raccoon, martin, otter, woodchuck, muskrat, beaver, skunk, weasel and dog. Domestic pigs,

geese, ducks, and chickens became sources of food after their introduction into Quebec about 1620.

After the formation of the League, when the Iroquois became settled in more permanent villages, their food supply shifted more and more to an agricultural basis, and agricultural products came to form the major portion of their diet.

The entire process of planting, cultivating, harvesting, and preparing food for the family was in the hands of the women. A chief matron was elected to direct the communal fields, each woman caring for a designated portion. Certain fields were reserved to provide food for the councils and national feasts. Ceremonies were observed and special songs were sung at the time of planting and harvesting. Sacrifices of tobacco and wampum were made to the food spirits.

Through a mutual aid society, in later years known as a "bee," the women assisted one another in their individual fields when planting, hoeing, and harvesting. They laughed and sang while they worked. Each woman brought her own hoe, pail, and spoon. When the work was over a feast was provided by the owner of the field, and everyone went home with a supply of food, usually corn soup and hominy.

Corn (maize) has always been the principal food of the Iroquois. Corn pits have been found at old village sites. Even before the formation of the League, corn, beans and squash were cultivated. Because they were grown together they were sometimes called "the three sisters." The Iroquois spoke of them as "our life" or "our supporters." Considerable mythology and many ceremonies centered about them.

Ears of mature corn were neatly braided and hung to dry in long festoons within and without the Iroquois homes. Large quantities of corn were dried in a corn crib, built of unpainted planks in open slat construction, through which the air circulated freely. The corn crib is a characteristic feature of the small farm on the Iroquois reservations. Its use was adopted from the Indians by the early settlers.

The corn used by the Iroquois was of two common types, white dent and white flint, with occasional red ears. The white dent corn, called Tuscarora or squaw corn, was hulled or eaten on the cob, a custom adopted by the white settlers and still followed throughout the country. Flint corn was used in making hominy.

Both the green and the mature corn were used in the preparation of many popular dishes that continue in use today. Green corn was boiled on the cob, roasted on the cob in the husk, scraped and baked, scraped and fried in cakes, combined with green beans and stewed with fat meat as succotash, made in a soup when green or dried, or scraped when green and baked in a loaf.

Coarsely ground meal was made from mature corn either hulled or unhulled, pounded in a stone or wooden mortar. It was used as plain mush, combined with meat, dressed with oil, or baked as unleavened bread.

Hominy was made from the flint corn. It was prepared by soaking shelled corn in lye until the hulls could be removed. The plain hominy, hominy or hulled-corn soup in which the hulled-corn was combined with beans and pork or beef, and boiled corn bread in which the hulled corn was usually combined with beans, were popular dishes made of mature corn.

Charred corn was used the year around. Corn to be charred was selected when well along in the milky stage. The ears were set on end in a row before a long fire. Roasting proceeded until the moisture was dried from the kernels. Then the corn was shelled and further dried in the sun. The charred corn was so reduced in bulk and weight that it could be easily stored or transported. If to be kept for some time, it was cached in earthen pits. It could be preserved for several years and was used both uncooked and cooked or pounded fine and mixed with maple sugar. In the old days it was made up into cakes for the use of the hunter or warrior. In later years the charred corn has been used chiefly at ceremonial functions.

Many of the Iroquois food preparations, such as succotash and hominy, have grown popular on the American table and the names by which the Indians knew them have been added to the American vocabulary.

The cultivation and use of the several varieties of corn by the Iroquois gave rise to a need for special implements and utensils for handling the corn products. In every Iroquois home was to be found the mortar and pestle, the hulling basket, a hominy sieve basket, a netted scoop for removing ground corn from the mortar and for sifting out the coarser grains, a corn scraper, ladles, trays of bark and wood, and a long paddle for stirring corn soup and for removing the loaves from boiling water. The Mohawk used a soft hulling bag or basket in which the corn was twirled to remove the hulls after it had been boiled in lye.

Ten or more varieties of beans, varying in size, shape, and color, were cultivated by the Iroquois. Since the Iroquois did not use milk and cheese, beans were their only nitrogenous food when meat failed. The beans used were commonly known as bush beans, wampum, purple and white kidney beans, marrow-fat beans, string, cornstalk, cranberry, chestnut, lima, hummingbird, white (small), wild peas, bean vines, and pole beans.

Beans were used alone to some extent but seem to have been more often combined with corn or squash when prepared for eating.

Squashes and pumpkins, both fresh and when dried for winter use, have always been favorite foods of the Iroquois. Crook neck, hubbard, scalloped and winter squashes and hard pumpkins, artichokes and leeks, as well as corn and beans, have been cultivated by the Iroquois. Wild cucumber, turnips, and edible fungi were also used as food. Sunflower oil was used in the preparation of many dishes.

Blackberries, blueberries, checkerberries, choke cherries, wild red cherries, cranberries, currants, dewberries, elderberries, gooseberries, hackberries, hawthorns, huckleberries, June or service berries, red mulberries, small black plums, red and black raspberries, strawberries and thimble berries were all used by the Iroquois, though there is no evidence that they were cultivated. Acorns, beechnuts, butternuts, chestnuts, hazelnuts and hickory nuts were eaten. By 1779 apples, peaches, pears and cherries had been introduced from Europe. Muskmelons and watermelons were much used in later years. Fresh wild strawberries, dried blackberries, blueberries, and elderberries or huckleberries were combined with hominy and corn bread to give added color and flavor.

Maple sugar was an important article of the diet and was used almost as much as salt is today. Maple sap was used as a beverage, both fresh and fermented. Salt was little used. The sunflower was grown in quantities and its seed used for medicinal purposes.

Gourds and tobacco were cultivated by the Iroquois. The gourds were made to serve many useful purposes, as cups, dippers, spoons, and bowls in the home, and as rattles in the ceremonies and dances. Tobacco (Nicotiana rustica) was raised for both secular and sacred purposes. The Iroquois believed that tobacco was given them as a means of communication with the spiritual world. By burning it they could send up their petitions. Special tobaccos were used in ceremonies. Tobacco was cast on the waters, especially on falls and rapids, to propitate the spirits within and was put in small bags attached to masks to make them more effective. The men and some of the women smoked tobacco mixed with suma leaves and red willow bark.

Cooking

In the old days, fire for cooking was usually built in a sunken pit. Foods were grilled in the flames, boiled in pots of clay supported over the fire by stones or branches, or baked in hot ashes raked aside from the fire. Strips of inner bark, the ends which were folded together and tied around with a splint, formed a primitive emergency kettle. The bark kettle was suspended between two sticks over a fire and filled with water, into which the meat was dropped. By the time the bark had been burned through the meat was cooked.

The making of clay pots for use in cooking must have occupied much of the time of the primitive women. The characteristic extension rim on these early Iroquois pots provided a ridge where a bark cord could be tied around the neck without slipping, so that the pot could be hung from the crotches of branches set, tripod fashion, over the fire. The rounded base made it possible for the pot to maintain an upright position when set in the fire or soft earth. With the coming of the colonists, kettles of copper, brass, and iron replaced the baked clay pots. Cook stoves have been in use on the reservations for many generations.

Obtaining fire for cooking

Fire was made to serve many purposes in primitive life. The Iroquois used fire to hollow canoes and mortars out of logs, to fell large trees that were to be used for buildings, and to provide heat for cooking and for other domestic uses.

In pre-colonial days fire was started by friction, and the Indians had many devices by which a spark could be secured. The device characteristically used was a bow and shaft or pump drill. It consisted of a weighted upright stick or spindle of resinous wood about one inch thick and 1½ to 4 feet in length, to the top of which was secured a leather thong or string, the ends of which were attached to the ends of a bow that was 3 feet in length. A small wheel was set upon the lower part of the shaft to give it momentum. The base of the spindle was inserted in a notch in a piece of very dry wood, near which a piece of frayed rope (tow) or decayed wood (punk) was placed. When ready to use, the string was first coiled around the shaft by turning it with the hand. The bow was then pulled down quickly, uncoiling the string and imparting a spinning motion to the shaft, revolving it to the left. By the momentum thus given to the wheel the string was coiled up in a reverse manner and the bow was again drawn up. The bow was then pulled downward again and the revolution of the shaft reversed, uncoiling the string, and recoiling it in reverse as before. This alternate revolution of the shaft was continued until the rapid twirling of the spindle created a friction which, as it increased, ignited the powdered wood upon which it rested. The piece of tow that was placed near the point where the spindle rested on the board, took fire and quickly lighted kindling that had been placed nearby.

Preservation and storage of food

The Iroquois built shelters for their farm and garden equipment and well ventilated corn cribs of unpainted planks in which corn could be dried and kept, and they dug underground pits or caches (root cellars) for the storage of corn and other foods. The pit was dug in the dry season, and the bottom and sides lined with bark. A watertight bark roof was constructed over it, and the whole thing covered with earth.

Corn, beans, berries and other fruits were dried for winter use. Braided bunches of corn were hung beside long spirals of dried squash and pumpkin, outside the log cabin or from the rafters within the cabin. Charred and dried shelled corn was kept in bark barrels which were buried in pits. Pits of well preserved charred corn have been found near ancient village sites. The bark barrels were of all sizes, with a capacity ranging from one peck to three bushels. They were made of black ash bark with the grain running around the barrel, and were stitched up the side and provided with a well-fitting bottom and lid. In addition to storing corn, the barrels were also used to store beans, dried fruits, venison and other meats, and articles of clothing and personal adornment.

Surplus meat and fish were dried, smoked, or frozen for later use. For storing the dried meat bark barrels were lined with deer skin.

FOOD PRESERVATION was practiced throughout aboriginal America primarily by various methods of drying. Both animal and vegetable foods were often dried in the open air and sun, when and where weather permitted. Smoking or drying over fire were employed by most tribes, however, to speed the process and prevent insect infestation.

Meat or fish to be dried was most commonly hung on a simple rectangular frame with or without a fire underneath. In the western Subarctic and Northwest Coast, smoke houses were often used. Fish were primarily air dried in most of the Arctic, Plateau, Great Basin, and California. The smoking of fish was common mostly in the Subarctic, Northwest Coast, northern Prairies, and Eastern Woodlands. Dried meat, or "jerky," was used almost universally in North America. It was primarily air dried in parts of the Southwest, Great Basin, Plains, and California. Nearly everywhere else, smoking or drying over fire were usually used and were often necessary because of cold and damp climatic conditions.

Seeds, roots, herbs, and other wild and domesticated

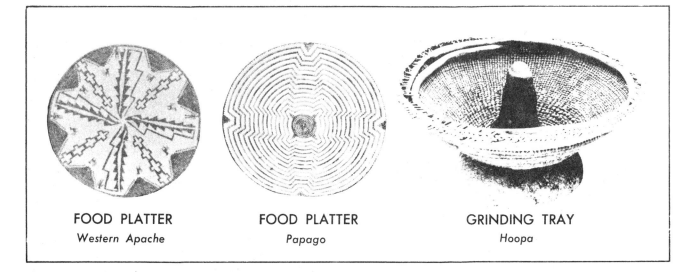

FOOD PLATTER
Western Apache

FOOD PLATTER
Papago

GRINDING TRAY
Hoopa

Smithsonian Institution.
Ojibwa woman drying fish over a slow fire, 1925.

Smithsonian Institution.
Dakota Indian boiling meat in the stomach of a cow, 1920.

plant foods were dried in a variety of ways. Among tribes who depended heavily on them, drying large quantities for the winter season was common. Plant foods were both air and fire dried and sometimes cooked or pulverized beforehand. Drying on frames or scaffolds as well as on trays or mats on the ground was common. Grain was often parched on a hot flat stone or in trays of hot ashes or sand.

In the Plains and parts of neighboring areas, dried meat was further processed to make pemmican. The meat was pulverized, mixed with melted fat, marrow, and fruit or berry paste, and packed in rawhide cases called parfleches. The mixture would last several years with proper care but was usually made in quantities adequate for a year or less. Dried fish was processed by somewhat similar methods in California, the Plateau, and parts of the Subarctic, Northwest Coast, and Eastern Woodlands.

Fish decayed under controlled conditions were used in parts of the Arctic, Northwest Coast, Plateau, and Eastern Woodlands. They were buried in pits or suspended off the ground and then allowed to partially decompose. Fish and meat were commonly allowed to freeze in the Arctic, Subarctic, and in some other areas with low enough temperatures. The salting of fish and meat is apparently post-Columbian, although salt was widely eaten in prehistoric times.

FORBES, JACK D. (Powhatan; Jan. 7, 1934-   ), is a noted educator and author in the field of ethnohistory. Born at Long Beach, California, he was educated at the University of Southern California, receiving his doctorate in 1959. After teaching at several institutions, including San Fernando Valley State College and the University of Nevada, in the mid-1970s he was on the faculty of the University of California at Davis. Among his publications are *Apache, Navaho and Spaniard* (1960), *Warriors of the Colorado* (1965), and *Native Americans of California and Nevada* (1969).

FOREMAN, STEPHEN (Cherokee; fl. 19th century), was a Presbyterian minister who preached in the Cherokee language and translated parts of the

Corrugated cooking pot, from Aztec ruins, New Mexico.

Bible into Cherokee. He attended a mission school at Candy's Creek, near Cleveland, Tennessee, and then studied under the Rev. S. A. Worcester at New Echota, Georgia, before attending one year at Union Theological Seminary in Virginia and another year at Princeton University. Foreman was licensed to preach by the Union Presbytery of Tennessee in 1833. In 1838 he was chosen as one of the leaders for the journey west to Indian Territory (present Oklahoma)— known as the Trail of Tears. He became the first superintendent of education in the Cherokee Nation in 1841.

FORREST, ERIN GEORGE (Modoc-Pit River; Jan. 12, 1920-   ), has served as tribal chairman of the XL Reservation, California, and is a prominent figure at both the state and national levels in Indian affairs.

Born in Alturas, California, Forrest enrolled in the all-white local public school system in 1929. Overcoming the difficulties of racial prejudice, he graduated from the Modoc Union High School in 1938 as student body president, an honor student, and an outstanding athlete in all sports. Following military service (1943-45), he became a rancher, raising beef and Appaloosa horses.

Forrest became politically active in gaining repeal of state and Federal Indian liquor laws in 1951. He was spurred to action when an Indian friend returning from combat duty in Korea, was denied purchase of a bottle of lemon extract, to be used by his mother in baking a homecoming cake, through enforcement of the Indian liquor law.

Among his many activities, Forrest has been a regional vice president of the National Congress of American Indians and a leading member of the National Tribal Chairmen's Association; California representative to the Governor's Inter-State Indian Council (1959-67); special consultant to Pres. Lyndon B. Johnson's task force on Indian affairs (1967-68); project director of the Modoc-Lassen Indian Health Project (1968-   ); and administrative assistant to a California state legislator (1969-   ).

Forrest was named the Outstanding Indian from the West by the American Indian Chicago Conference in 1961, and he was received numerous awards and commendations.

FORT ANCIENT was named for a prehistoric fort in Warren County Ohio. In this type there is rarely any sacred enclosure. The pottery is crude. Little copper work is found, and little mica; ornaments are confined to stone, bone, and shell. Awls of bone, and flat, long needles are usually found in the burials. (An important site of this culture is the great Madisonville works near Cincinnati, which had samples of pottery, implements, ornaments, and skeletal material. Other sites are the Baum Village and the Gartner mound village in Ross County, what was until recently Campbell Island in Butler County, and the Feurt mounds and villages in Scioto County).

A Fort Ancient village consisted of several hundred people who lived in skin or bark tepees and chinked, wattlework huts. They wore skins, feathers, and coarsely woven cloth, and adorned themselves with necklaces, bracelets, and beaded arm bands of shell, bone, or stone. While the craftsmen fashioned weapons and tools of stone, bone, or flint, and also pipes, pottery, and stone discs, the women toiled in the gardens with their hoes of mussel shell, raising corn, beans, squash, and pumpkins. Hunters returned with their spoils—deer and bear, and perhaps birds and mussels. The women cooked these in a big community pot from which all helped themselves. Refuse and waste matter were tossed aside and covered with earth—a custom that was to cause entire villages to rise several feet above their original ground level. Bones of animals in the refuse pits show that these people were not squeamish about their food. Besides the game animals known today, they ate Indian dog, otter, skunk, wildcat, toad, screech owl, crane, and swan.

The Middle Ohio Valley has known the presence of man from prehistoric times to the present day. Until the coming of the white settlers, the aboriginal inhabitants of the valley directed most of their time and energies toward obtaining food in sufficient quantities for the survival and perpetuation of their own social group. Some subsistence patterns, such as agriculture, involved a cultural elaboration of material items, whereas less diversity in the array of material traits generally was associated with earlier hunting and gathering populations. In other words, the earlier inhabitants of the Middle Ohio Valley concentrated on

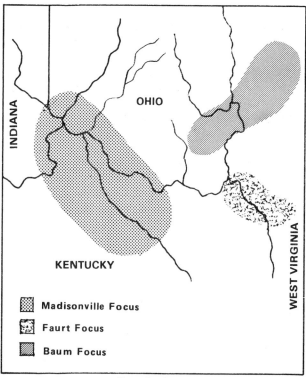

Fort Ancient

practicing their culture and left some of its products in passing.

Although the more recent immigrants to the region, the white settlers, were also interested in populating the area and gaining a living from it, they brought a new interest with them. They were inquisitive about the earlier occupants whose cultural items were frequently found on the surface of the ground or when the soil was cultivated. As a result, considerable attention was and continues to be devoted to the location, description, and identification of the cultures of the prehistoric inhabitants. This interest in extinct cultures has not been confined to the professionally trained investigator, as a perusal of early historic journals illustrates. More frequently, it is the amateur investigator who finds evidence of aboriginal occupations and who calls them to the attention of the trained specialist. Within the last one hundred years, many prehistoric sites have been found and subsequently given particular names in terms of location (name of landowner, town, etc.), of temporal placement (Archaic, Protohistoric, etc.), and of the population who made the material remains found on the site (Hopewell, Adena, Fort Ancient, etc.).

Physical remains of the population are often found in association with items of the material culture, and it then becomes possible to study not only the life ways of the people but the people themselves. For example, the skeletal remains found with the preceramic Southern Archaic shell mound manifestation at Indian Knoll display a combination of physical characteristics diagnostic of, and thus serving as, the type series of the Iswanid variety of North American Indians. A population which was responsible for a Middle Mississippi cultural assemblage tends to be representative of the Muskogid (formerly called Walcolid) varietal type. For the most part, the physical populations who produced the prehistoric cultures have not received the concentrated attention that has been directed toward their material products. Except for some reports such as H. Neumann's investigations of the relationship of the Walcolid (Muskogid) Spoon River Focus population of Central Illinois to the Muskogcan-speaking historic Choctaw-Chickasaw tribes and Funkhouser's (1938) proposal that some of the Norris Basin people greatly resembled certain Iroquoian groups to the north, few definitive attempts have been made to link the people of late prehistoric or protohistoric archaelolgical manifestations with historic tribes.

During the 1930s Dr. James B. Griffin made a comprehensive analysis of the Fort Ancient archaeological manifestation. The four foci—Baum, Feurt, Anderson and Madisonville—were established by Griffin on the grounds of artifactual similarities and differences and are accepted as archaeological subgroups. In his work, Griffin outlines the temporal and spacial distribution of the Fort Ancient culture. He presents ideas of cultural origins and traces cultural continuities as they relate to the aspect. He points out external influences upon the culture as witnessed by the diffusion of traits, and he demonstrates the cohesiveness of the groupings on the focus, aspect, and phase levels.

The ethnohistorical identification of the earliest tribes found in the region has been tested against the archaeological distribution in concordance with the temporal position of the Fort Ancient Aspect. While there is the possibility that the earliest historic tribes of the Middle Ohio Valley may have been derived from Siouan—, Muskogean—, or Algonquian—speaking stocks, it is more probable that the Fort Ancient people were Algonquian and therefore the ancestors of the historic Shawnee Tribe.

FORT APACHE. From its founding in 1870 until the capitulation of Geronimo in 1886, this fort was closely involved in the Apache wars (1861-86). Gen. George Crook, arriving in Arizona for his first tour of duty in 1871, organized there his first company of Apache scouts, one of his tactical innovations, before moving on to Camp Verde to conduct his Tonto Basin campaign.

Situated on the White Mountain (Fort Apache) Reservation, which adjoined the San Carlos Reservation, the fort guarded the Fort Apache Agency, while Fort Thomas watched over the San Carlos Agency. The two reservations were the focus of Apache unrest, especially after troops moved the Chiricahuas in 1876 from Fort Bowie to the White Mountain Reservation. In constant turmoil, the reservations were noted for their overcrowded conditions and dissatisfied inhabitants. Sparking the discontent were inefficient and corrupt agents, friction between civil and military authorities, attempts to make farmers of the nomadic Indians, and encroachment on the reservations by settlers and miners.

For a decade, until Geronimo laid down his arms, the resentful Apaches alternately fled into Mexico, returned to the reservations to enlist recruits, and raided along the Mexican boundary. Fort Apache troops spent much of their time in pursuit. In 1881, at the Battle of Cibecue Creek, a group of White Mountain Apaches defeated a force from the fort and then besieged it for a while before they surrendered. After 1886 Fort Apache ceased to be a significant frontier post, but it remained active until 1924.

Many fort buildings remain. The Fort Apache post office occupies the adobe adjutant's building. A log building, one of the oldest structures and reputedly the residence of General Crook, as well as the stone officers' quarters, are today the residences of teachers and other Bureau of Indian Affairs employees. The sutler's store and commissary building, cavalry barns, and guardhouse have not been significantly altered. One of the original four barracks, an adobe building in bad disrepair, houses the farm shop for the Indian school. The cemetery no longer contains dead soldiers, but does contain the bodies of Indian scouts.

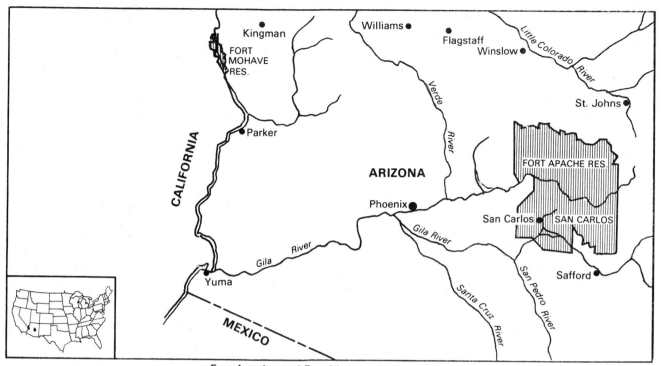

Fort Apache and Fort Mohave Reservations.

FORT APACHE RESERVATION, in Arizona comprises 1,664,872 acres, all tribally owned. It is home to about 6,000 White Mountain Apache Indians. This reservation was originally established in 1871 as a part of the White Mountain Reservation which was divided into the San Carlos Reservation and the Fort Apache Reservation in 1897.

The Apache were a nomadic people who were attracted to the Southwest by the abundance they saw there. They usually lived in mountainous areas and raided the pueblo villages for food, crops, and material goods. There were, however, peaceful periods when the two groups traded without hostility. The Spanish also became a target of Apache raids, and adopted the Zuni word "Apache" meaning enemy. Harsh treatment by whites increased animosity. Because they had not settled in any given area and lived by raiding other people, the Apache were difficult to subdue, and were the last tribe to be defeated by the United States Government. The Apache wars ended finally in the late 19th century. The White Mountain Apache donated the Nation's Christmas tree for 1965, a 70-foot blue spruce. It was the largest tree ever to stand on the ellipse.

The Apache were large, well-built people trained from childhood to be hunters and fighters. They were not horsemen and never fully adopted the use of the horse. Religious beliefs were centered upon the shaman, who was the religious leader. Mountain spirits, believed to possess great powers of both good and evil over people, are impersonated in the mountain spirit dances. The thatched wickiups in which the Apache lived were covered with hide in the winter. Clothing was made out of skins. The people were also skilled in basketry, sealing some with pitch to be watertight.

The tribe adopted a constitution in August 1938, according to the provisions of the Indian Reorganization Act of 1934, and amended the constitution in June 1958. The reservation is governed by an elected tribal council which holds office for a term of 2 years.

Eighty percent of the annual tribal income of $1 million represents forest industry profits. The remainder of the tribe's income is derived from farming and business profits. The tribe employs a total of 200 persons in various enterprises. The White Mountain Apache Enterprise and the White Mountain Recreation Enterprise are organizations to develop the recreational potential of the reservation.

The Fort Apache Timber Company works the reservation's impressive forest resources. Other tribal associations are the Whiteriver Construction Enterprise, and the Livestock Association, which manages a 2,000-head herd. Three private lumber companies are also located on the reservation: The Southwest Forest Industries, Western Wood Products, and Western Pine Sales. The tribe, through its membership in the Indian Development District of Arizona, has access to professional planning, technical skills, and funding assistance. Timber is the primary resource on the reservation and there are deposits of asbestos and cinders.

The climate of the reservation is strongly affected by the topography. Much of the reservation is mountainous with elevations ranging from 2,700 to 11,490 feet. The Mogollon Rim passes through the reservation. Rainfall averages from 12 to 30 inches yearly, varying with the elevation. The climate is mild, much cooler in the summer than the nearby desert area. Temperatures range from 90° to 15°.

Fort Belknap and Fort Hall Reservations.

FORT BELKNAP RESERVATION, in Blaine and Phillips Counties, Montana, is more than 600,000 acres in size. It is home to about 1,600 Gros Ventre and Assiniboine Indians.

The Treaty of Fort Laramie ceded a large block of land to the Assiniboine north of the Missouri in the western two-thirds of Montana. This was divided into the Fort Peck and Fort Belknap Military Reservations in 1873. The Fort Belknap Indian Reservation was established in 1888. It was reduced to its present acreage in 1895. Under the Allotment Act in 1921, almost half a million acres were allotted to individuals.

History. The Assiniboine originated in the Lake of the Woods and Lake Winnipeg areas of Canada where they early became allied with the Cree. Those that were within the United States when hostilities ended were placed on the Fort Belknap and Fort Peck Reservations during the 1800s, those within the United States were placed on the Fort Belknap Reservation.

Culture. The Assiniboine speak a Sioux dialect while the Gros Ventre speak a language of the Algonquian family. Despite this basic difference, earliest recorded history indicated that these tribes occupied adjacent hunting grounds and followed a nomadic plains culture centered on the buffalo. Both tribes also performed the Sun Dance.

Government. The Fort Belknap Community Council, which is the official governing body for the reservation is composed of 12 members from four districts. The Gros Ventre and Assiniboine tribes have equal representation.

FORT BERTHOLD RESERVATION, nearly 420,000 in acres in size, is home to over 2,500 Mandan, Hidatsa, and Arikara Indians in North Dakota.

History. Long before the Sioux migrated into the Dakotas from the east, three sedentary tribes had

settled along the Missouri River which bisects the two states. Of these, the Mandan are believed to have arrived first. They once occupied several villages of semisubterranean earth lodges in what is now South Dakota, but then moved farther north. Another agricultural tribe, the Arikara, were also settling along the river, occupying three villages of earth lodges between the Grand and Cannonball rivers. The Hidatsa established an agricultural life near Devil's Lake but were pushed west by the Sioux and settled at the junction of the Heart and Missouri rivers. All three groups were greatly reduced in number by the smallpox epidemic of 1837. Survivors were placed on the reservation established by Executive order in 1871.

Culture. The Three Affiliated Tribes have always been involved in agricultural activities. The remains of their original semisubterranean homes are objects of interest today. The Mandan and Hidatsa speak a Sioux language while the Arikara speak a Caddoan language. These tribes traded widely with other tribes as far away as Mexico.

FORT BIDWELL. Tucked into the extreme northeastern corner of California, Fort Bidwell (1865-93) was founded by Volunteer troops to protect settlers and emigrants from the Indians of northern California, southern Oregon, and western Nevada. In the 1890s the log post spread slightly to the south of its original location, and a town grew up around it. Its garrison fought with Gen. George Crook at the nearby Battle of Infernal Caverns in September 1867, during his 1866-68 Snake campaign, and in the wars against the Modocs (1872-73), Nez Perce (1877), and Bannocks (1878). The Indian Bureau succeeded the Army at the post and utilized it for a boarding school, which was operated until 1930. In that year the original two-story barracks, later a school dormitory, was razed.

All that remains, in varying states of preservation, are the stable; a school, now a private residence; a few other buildings; a graveyard; and the parade ground. The site, headquarters of the Fort Bidwell Indian Reservation is marked by a monument.

FORT BIDWELL RESERVATION, California, is 3,335 acres belonging to about 100 Pawte Indians.

A joint resolution of January 30, 1897, authorized the Secretary of the Interior to use former lands of the Fort Bidwell Military Reserve for an Indian training school. The reservation was enlarged in 1913 and in 1917.

The population varies with seasonal employment. The Indian language is spoken by the elderly. Indian religion is still practiced. Arts and crafts are produced in the individual homes.

The tribe is governed under an Indian Reorganization Act constitution and bylaws approved in 1936 and amended in 1940 and 1942. The nine members of the governing body are elected each November to staggered 2-year terms.

The reservation, located in northeastern California,

is rocky, hilly land covered with sage. The elevation varies from 4,550 to 7,000 feet. The tribe has an income of $3,400 per annum, half from forestry, and the other half from leases and farming. The tribal members have formed the Fort Bidwell Indian Cattleman's Association which is the only commercial enterprise on the reservation.

FORT COBB. In existence but a decade, from 1859 until 1869, this fort on the Washita River in Caddo County, Oklahoma nevertheless had an important history. It and the adjacent Wichita Indian Agency were established to receive Indians relocated from Texas reservations, to protect them and the local Wichitas from the Kiowas and Comanches, and to restrain the latter from raiding in Texas. When the post and the agency were only 2 years old, the Union abandoned them and the Confederates used the post spasmodically until the Indians drove them out and burned it. To clear the way for his 1868-69 offensive against the southern Plains tribes, General Sheridan ordered it reactivated in 1868 and the Fort Cobb Reservation (Kiowa-Comanche and Wichita Agencies) created as a refuge for all Indians in the area of the offensive who claimed to be peaceful, as well as for the Wichitas and the Texas tribes that had returned from their temporary haven in Kansas. In December 1868, the month after Custer's victory in the Battle of the Washita, General Sheridan moved his headquarters to Fort Cobb. To hasten the capitulation of the Kiowas, he seized and threatened to hang chiefs Satanta and Lone Wolf. The next March he activated Fort Sill to replace Fort Cobb and transferred the Kiowa-Comanche Agency to the new fort.

FORT DEARBORN located on the southern shore of Lake Michigan at the mouth of the Chicago River was built in 1803 and occupied intermittently until 1836. Its former site is in the heart of present-day Chicago.

In 1803 the U.S. Congress authorized the construction of a stockade and barracks at the mouth of the Onion (Chicago) River and the order was issued by Secretary of War Henry Dearborn. A six-square mile site had been ceded to the United States at the Treaty of Greenville in 1795. The fort's construction was occasioned by the recent Louisiana Purchase (1803) as the U.S. assumed control of a vast, unknown region far from the frontier.

Fort Dearborn was built and supplied by soldiers from Fort Detroit. When Detroit fell to combined British-Indian forces in 1812, Dearborn was ordered to evacuate to Fort Wayne. Nearby Indian tribes were sympathetic to the British cause and were probably angered by the disposal of the fort's supplies. Potawatomi Indians burned the fort and attacked the fleeing white families. Twenty five soldiers and 11 women and children survived what has been called the Fort Dearborn Massacre of 1812. The post was rebuilt in 1816 and finally abandoned in 1836.

FORT DEFIANCE. The name of this fort (1851-61) typifies the attitude of its garrison and that of the Navajos it sought to control. Only 3 miles west of the

Old Fort Dearborn.

Fort Dearborn, 1812.

Fort Defiance, 1850s.

Arizona-New Mexico boundary, it was the first Army post in Arizona and one of many established within the Mexican Cession (1848). After the failure of several treaties with the Navajos, who had disturbed residents of the Southwest since Spanish times, Fort Defiance was founded. In 1858, until which time only intermittent skirmishing had occurred, hostilities became intense. Two years later 1,000 Navajos besieged the fort but were unable to capture it.

In 1868 Fort Defiance became the Navajo Indian Agency, today at Window Rock. A Navajo tribal school and hospital, around which the town of Fort Defiance has grown up, now occupies the fort site. Modern construction has altered it considerably, but the fort outlines are visible.

FORT DODGE founded in 1865 on the Arkansas River and Santa Fe Trail about 60 miles southwest of Fort Larned and 25 miles east of the Cimarron Crossing of the trail was the most westerly in Kansas on the trail and one of its most important guardians and stopping points in the later years.

During the turbulent 1860s, the bloodiest period of Indian warfare on the southern Plains, Fort Dodge was active in military operations, especially Maj. Gen. Philip H. Sheridan's winter campaign of 1868-69. Contrary to their agreements in the Medicine Lodge Treaties of 1867, the thousands of Comanches, Kiowas, Cheyennes, and Arapahos who roamed in pursuit of the buffalo over his huge command area began a reign of terror the following spring and summer from Kansas as far south as the Texas Panhandle, raiding the Santa Fe Trail and even Fort Dodge itself. Sheridan, heading the Department of the Missouri, was stymied. His troops were unable to take effective offensive action against the swift-moving bands of warriors who lived off the land. Their initimate knowledge of the geography, especially the location of waterholes, allowed them to appear from nowhere and disappear just as suddenly. When troops pursued a war party, it dispersed in all directions and reunited at a prearranged point to continue raiding.

Sheridan, desperate by the end of the summer and barraged with demands from frontiersmen to exterminate the Indians and from eastern humanitarians to soothe them, finally decided to launch an aggressive winter campaign. He knew that the warriors preferred not to fight then, when they were immobilized and vulnerable, surrounded by women and children in their camps. Sheridan notified all friendly Indians to take refuge on the reservation set apart by the Medicine Lodge Treaties and report at Fort Cobb, Okla., which he ordered reactivated. He accumulated huge stores of supplies and winter equipment at Forts Dodge, Arbuckle (Okla.), Lyon (Colo.), and Bascom (N.Mex.); and formed wagon and pack trains to transport them. He also inaugurated a rigorous training program for the troops, and recruited white and Indian scouts.

The main column proceeded southward into Indian Territory from Fort Dodge and founded Camp Supply

Courtesy New York Public Library Picture Collection.
Navajo in Fort Defiance.

as an advance base. There Sheridan sent Lt. Col. George A. Custer and his regiment, the 7th Cavalry, on the expedition that ended in voctory at the Battle of Washita. Two other columns, which were supposed to drive the stragglers eastward toward the main column's line of advance, moved out from Fort Bascom, N. Mex., and Fort Lyon, Colo. The fort Bascom column won the Battle of Soldier Spring, Okla. Sheridan's campaign was very successful.

The 1868-69 campaign did not solve the Indian problem on the southern Plains. This occurred in the Red River War (1874-75), in which Fort Dodge was again a base. In 1872 the Santa Fe Railway had arrived in the vicinity and bought a change in economy from buffalo to cattle drives. Dodge City, the prototype of the wild and lawless cowtown, grew up in the shadow of the fort. By the end of the 1870s the frontier had moved westward from Fort Dodge with the railroad. In 1882 the Army evacuated the fort.

Numerous stone buildings, dating from 1867 and 1868, remodeled and used by the State soldiers' home that now occupies the site, stand among modern structures. They include two of the three original barracks, on the eastern side of the parade ground, which were connected in modern times; the commandant's house, in which Custer, Sheridan, and Miles may have resided, now the superintendent's residence; another unidentified structure, presently used as the administration building; the hospital, which now houses residents; a building currently used as a library that was probably the commissary; and three small cottages.

FORT DUQUESNE The growing French influence in the Ohio Valley region during the 1750s was incompatible with the westward thrust of England's seaboard colonies. George Washington visited the forks in November 1753, while en route to the French-held Fort Le Boeuf to warn the French away from the Ohio country. Washington strongly endorsed the forks as the most strategic position to command the rivers, and in February 1754 Englishmen began to construct the first outpost there. Two months later however, a combined force of French and Indians seized the weak stockade. The French proceeded to build a fort, which they named after Duquesne, the Governor-General of New France. This heightened the tensions that led to the 9-year conflict known in America as the French and Indian War and abroad as the Seven Years' War.

When Washington learned that the French had seized the post at the forks, he returned with a small force, which on May 28 surprised and defeated a French scouting party near Great Meadows, 11 miles east of the present city of Uniontown. Troops from Fort Duquesne besieged the hastily built Fort Necessity and forced Washington to surender on July 4. The French beat off a more threatening English effort the next year, when they shattered Gen. James Braddock's force several miles east to the forks. Thus, for 3 years longer, Fort Duquesne continued to serve as a French base for raids against the English frontier.

In 1758, 6,500 British and colonial troops under Gen. John Forbes, made a remarkable forced march through the rugged Pennsylvania wilderness and found Duquesne destroyed and abandoned by the French because of pressures elsewhere and the desertion of their Indian allies. Col. Hugh Mercer was left with 200 men to secure the position for England. In 1759, the English began to construct a major permanent fortification, named Fort Pitt in honor of the Prime Minister of England.

FORT GIBSON was one of the most important of the posts on the "Permanent Indian Frontier." The first fort established in Indian Territory, it was actively involved in the problems associated with the relocation there of the Five Civilized Tribes from the Southeast. A frontier hub of commerce and military activity, it was a key transportation point and a testing place for newly activated army organizations.

Established in 1824 by Col. Matthew Arbuckle on the east bank of the Grand River just above its confluence with the Verdigris and Arkansas Rivers, the fort was responsible for keeping peace between the Osages, who opposed any intrusion into their territory, and the Cherokees, who were already filtering into Indian Territory. The post replaced Fort Smith, which had been too far south to control the Osages effectively and was to remain inactive, except for several months, until

1839. During the period of Indian removal, in the 1830s and 1840s, the Fort Gibson garrison helped receive, care for, settle, and enforce peace among immigrant Cherokees, Creeks, Choctaws, Seminoles, and Chickasaws, as well as attempted to protect them from the Plains Indians. Troops provided escorts for surveyors marking the boundaries of Indian lands; established other posts in Indian Territory, such as Forts Coffee and Wayne and Camp Holmes; laid out a network of military roads; and tried to control the illegal liquor traffic.

In 1834 the fort was the base for the Dragoon Expedition, originally under the command of Col. Henry Leavenworth, who died of fever en route. His successor, Col. Henry Dodge, met with some of the southern Plains tribes at the north fork of the Red River and persuaded them to send delegates to Fort Gibson for negotiations. As a result, in 1835 the tribes made their first treaties with the U.S. government at Camp Holmes, Oklahoma.

Fort Gibson was also a center of trade and travel. Located at a point beyond which river navigation was virtually impossible, it was a supply depot for a large area. Keelboats and later river steamers came up the Arkansas to the fort a few months each year, and unloaded passengers, military stores, and Indian trade goods. Traders furnished return cargoes. The Texas Road, which ran from north to south and linked the growing American settlements in Texas with the Missouri River Valley, passed by the fort, which became a way station for emigrants, freighters, and traders. The troops also provided escorts for raod traffic. The fort continued to be a transportation and freighting center until the arrival in the region of the Missouri, Kansas, and Texas Railroad in 1872.

Originally a four-company post, the fort was expanded in 1831 to accommodate a regiment and it became the district headquarters, which overtaxed its limited capacity. Situated on low ground, it was also subject to flooding and threatened by malaria. In 1846 construction began of a new post on the hill overlooking the old site. But the project proceeded slowly and by 1857 only one stone building, the commissary storehouse, had been finished. That year, because the Cherokees had been requesting that the fort be evacuated and because the frontier had moved westward, the Army abandoned it and the tribe took possession.

At the outbreak of the Civil War the Confederates occupied the fort, but in 1863 Union forces made it a federal stronghold in Indian Territory and sought to strengthen the loyal element of the Cherokees. Regular troops replaced the Volunteers in 1866 and garrisoned the post until 1890. During this period the fort on the hill was completed; it consisted of seven large stone buildings and 10 frame ones.

Although the original fort has long since disappeared, the State of Oklahoma, under a Works Progress Administration (WPA) grant, completed in

1936 on a 55-acre tract a reconstruction of the original log stockade and a number of outlying log buildings almost on the original site. Except for the use of more durable materials, especially pine timber and lime chinking, the reconstruction is faithful to the original. On the ridge to the east overlooking the reconstructed stockade is the second fort site. Stone buildings, some now private homes, survive in various stages of repair.

FORT HALL RESERVATION, Idaho, one of the most famous in America, is 523,000 acres in size, and home to more than 3,000 Shoshone and Bannock Indians. It has played an important part in the history of the Basin-Plateau Indians.

History. In the late 1700s, 1000 Bannocks under their chief, Buffalo Horn, continued to wander over southern Idaho, fighting for their fields of camas. They had been ostensibly assigned to the Fort Hall Reservation. A series of murders and raids ended with the death of Buffalo Horn. The Bannocks, disorganized, were eventually assembled and returned to the Fort Hall Reservation.

Culture. The Shoshone and Bannock Indians were one of seminomadic Plateau Indian culture ranging over the dry uplands of Idaho, eastern Oregon and eastern Washington. All Plateau tribes were traditionally fishermen and hunters who wandered over the country in small, loosely-organized bands searching for game, wild seeds, berries, and roots of camas. With basketry techniques that ranked among the best in North America, they wove the grasses and scrubby brush of the plateau into almost everything they used, including portable summer shelter, clothing, and watertight cooking pots. Having no clans, Plateau Indians counted descent on both sides of the family. There was little formal organization. The few tribal ceremonies centered around the food supply. In the early 1700s, horses were introduced among the tribesmen, and they became highly skilled horsemen who counted their wealth in terms of the new animal.

Government. The tribe is organized under the Indian Reorganization Act of 1934, operating under a constitution approved on April 30, 1936, and a charter ratified on April 17, 1937. The Fort Hall Business Council is the tribal governing body. The business council consists of seven persons elected from the five districts on the reservation to 2-year terms. The council has authority over purchases, borrowing, engaging in business, performing contracts, and other normal business procedures.

Tribal econonmy. The tribe has an annual income of approximately $400,000. The tribe provides $13,500 annually for student scholarships based on need. The Land Purchase Enterprise is a tribal organization to increase the amount of tribally-owned land. Two industries are located on the reservation: The Food Machinery Chemical Corporation and the J. R. Simplot Company. Both are privately owned. Deposits of phosphate on the reservation are being extracted.

FORT INDEPENDENCE RESERVATION, in Inyo County, California, is 356 acres in size, and belongs to about 50 Paiute Indians.

The Fort Independence Reservation consists of 356 acres of open, level land. U.S. Highway No. 395 bisects the reservation. Currently a problem are the allotments fractionated by heirship. Most of the land is used for homesites, the remainder is leased. Camp Independence was established during the Indian Way on July 4, 1862, and later abandoned. The Fort Independence Reservation was established by Executive orders in 1915 and 1916.

The only remaining aspect of Indian culture is the Paiute language which is still spoken.

The Articles of Association were approved in May 1965. The tribe operates under a constitution and bylaws. Officers include the chairman and the secretary-treasurer.

The Sherwood Forest Animal Farm is leased from the tribe, providing the tribal income of $1,200 per year.

Because of its location in Owens Valley at the eastern base of the Sierra Nevada Range, the climate of the reservation is arid and irrigation is necessary to sustain agriculture. Rainfall measures only 5 inches per year. The temperature ranges from 100° to 5°.

FORT KEARNY. The tragic events associated with Fort Kearny, the Fetterman disaster, and the Wagon Box Fight form one of the most important chapters in the history of the Indian wars: the bloody 2 years of warfare in 1866-68 sparked by bitter Sioux opposition to the invasion of their hunting grounds by prospectors bound over the Bozeman Trail to the Montana goldfields. In one of the few instances during the Indian wars when the Army was forced to abandon a region it had occupied, the Sioux triumphed and the forts were evacuated. But the conflict forshadowed the final disastrous confrontation between frontiersman and Indian that ensued on the northern Plains as the westward movement accelerated after the Civil War in the United States.

Strikes in 1862 by Idaho prospectors in the mountains of western Montana triggered a rush to the diggings at Bannack and subsequently to Virginia City. The next spring John M. Bozeman and John M. Jacobs blazed the Bozeman Trail. Running north from the Oregon-California Trail along the eastern flank of the Bighorn Mountains and then westward, it linked Forts Sedgwick, Colo., and Laramie, Wyo., and the Oregon-California Trail with Virginia City. Spared the circuitous route through Salt Lake City, gold seekers soon poured over the trail, which crossed the heart of the hunting grounds the hostile Sioux had recently seized from the Crows. The Sioux, taking advantage of the absence of Regular troops in tlhe Civil War, quickly unleashed their fury.

In 1865, at Fort Sully, S. Dakota, the government concluded treaties with a few Sioux chiefs. In return for the promise of annuities, they agreed to withdraw from

An early view of Fort Kearny.

the vicinity of emigrant routes and not to attack them. The commissioners, however, had dealt with only unimportant leaders of the bands along the Missouri River—not the people who really mattered. Red Cloud, Man-Afraid-of-His-Horses, and other chiefs who roamed the Powder and Bighorn country to the west vowed to let no travelers pass unmolested.

In the late spring and summer of 1866 a U.S. commission met with these leaders at Fort Laramie, Wyo. In the midst of the council, Col. Henry B. Carrington and 700 men of the 18th Infantry marched into the fort. When Red Cloud and the other chiefs learned that their mission was the construction of forts along the Bozeman Trail, they stalked out of the conference and declared war on all invaders of their country. That summer and fall Carrington strengthened and garrisoned Fort Reno and erected Forts Kearny and Smith. Nevertheless, by winter Sioux, Arapaho, and Northern Cheyenne warriors had all but closed the trail. Between August 1 and December 31 they killed 154 persons in the vicinity of Fort Kearny, wounded 20 more, regularly attacked emigrants, and destroyed or captured more than 750 head of livestock. Even heavily guarded supply trains had to fight their way over the trail. The forts endured continual harassment, and wagon trains hauling wood for fuel and construction had to ward off assaults.

Sioux efforts focused on Carrington's headquarters, Fort Kearny, situated between the Big and Little Piney Forks of the Powder River on a plateau rising 50 to 60 feet above the valley floor. The largest of the three posts guarding the Bozeman Trail, it was one of the best fortified western forts of the time. It ultimately consisted of 42 log and frame buildings within a 600 by

800 foot stockade of heavy pine timber 11 feet high, and had blockhouses at diagonal corners. A company of the 2d Cavalry reinforced Carrington's infantry.

Strong defenses were necessary. The warnings of Red Cloud had not prevented the fort's establishment, but he soon put it under virtual siege. Carrington, saddled with 21 women and children dependents who had accompanied him from Fort Kearny, Nebr., maintained a defensive stance. A clique of his younger and more impetuous officers, who disliked him and resisted his attempts to impose discipline, were contemptuous. Prominent among them was Capt. William J. Fetterman, who boasted that he and 80 men could ride through the whole Sioux Nation.

On December 21, 1866, a small war party, in a feint, made a typical attack on a wood train returning eastward from Piney Island to the fort. To relieve the train, Carrington sent out Fetterman, two other officers, 48 infantrymen, 28 cavalrymen, and two civilians—81 men in all. Although warned not to cross Lodge Trail Ridge, where he would be out of sight of the fort, Fetterman let a small party of warriors decoy him northward well beyond the ridge and into a carefully rehearsed ambush prepared by Red Cloud. Within half an hour, at high noon, hundreds of Sioux, Cheyenne, and Arapaho warriors annihilated the small force to the last man. Relief columns from the fort, which scattered the Indians, were too late to rescue Fetterman and his men. They had suffered the worst defeat inflicted by the Plains Indians on the Army until that time and one that vied with subsequent defeats, such as the Battle of the Little Bighorn.

Following the Fetterman Disaster, Carrington hired civilians John "Portugee" Philips and Daniel Dizon to

Old Fort Kearny, 1847.

carry a message for Omaha headquarters concerning the disaster and a plea for reinforcements to the telegraph station at Horseshoe Bend, near Fort Laramie. Phillips continued on through a snowstorm to Fort Laramie. Carrington was replaced in January 1867.

By that summer the Indians had closed the Bozeman Trail to all but heavily guarded military convoys, but the troops won two victories. The Sioux and Cheyennes agreed to pool their resources and wipe out Forts Kearny and Smith. One faction, in the Hayfield Fight, attacked a haying party near Fort Smith on August 1, but suffered heavy casualties. The next day the other group, 1,500 to 2,500 Sioux and Cheyennes led by Red Cloud, set upon a detachment of 28 infantrymen guarding civilian woodcutters a few miles west of Fort Kearny. Most of the civilians succeeded in safely reaching the post, but four were trapped with the soldiers in an oval barricade that had been formed earlier as a defensive fortification from the overturned boxes of 14 woodhauling wagons that had been removed from the running gears. The troops were armed with newly issued breech-loading Springfield rifles—a costly surprise for the Sioux. Six times in 4 hours they charged the wagon boxes, but each time were thrown back with severe casualties. Reinforcements finally arrived from the fort with a mountain howitzer and quickly dispersed the opposition. The Army reported only about three dead and two wounded, but the Indians claimed the figures were at least 60 and 120, respectively.

The Hayfield and Wagon Box Fights exacted a modicum of revenge for the Fetterman disaster, but they did not deter hostilities. Forays increased steadily until the next year, when the Government was forced to come to terms with the Indians. In the Treaty of Fort Laramie (1868), in return for certain Indian concessions, it bowed to Red Cloud's demands and agreed to close the Bozeman Trail and abandon the three forts protecting it. As soon as this occurred, in July and August, the Sioux, unknowingly celebrating the zenith of their power on the northern Plains, jubilantly burned them to the ground.

Today, the basically unaltered natural scene of the sites of Fort Kearny, the Fetterman Disaster, and the Wagon Box Fight, despite surrounding ranch operations, are marred by but few modern intrusions.

FORT LARAMIE, TREATY OF was an 1851 agreement on a general peace amongst the Plains Indians and a cessation of hostility between the Indian and white emigrants.

Frontiersman Tom Fitzpatrick, appointed U.S. Indian Agent, called a peace council near Fort Laramie, a former fur trading post at the mouth of the Laramie River and the North Platte. The Indians assembled at Horse Creek, 37 miles east of the fort. They formed the greatest known assemblage of Plains Indians. They were 8,000-12,000 Assiniboins, Atsinas, Arikaras, Crows, Shoshonis, Sioux, Cheyennes, and Arapahoes. Many of these tribes had met previously only in battle. An increase in tensions and hostile incidents led to the council, for Indian lands were being crossed by a heavy flow of emigrants along the Oregon Trail as well as the California-bound "gold rushers".

The peace treaty guaranteed the Indian right to their lands. In return the westbound white emigrants were not to be disturbed. The U.S. government promised to protect Indian rights against white excesses. The Indians agreed to the building of roads and forts on their lands in return for an annual sum of money. The U.S. Senate cut the financial terms and the Indians later disputed this provision.

Three years later (1854), about 10 miles from the scene of the treaty, soldiers from Fort Laramie killed Conquering Bear, leader of the Brules (a subtribe of the Teton Dakota Sioux) over a minor dispute. The American people demanded retaliation when the soldiers, under 2nd Lieutenant John L. Grattan, were then killed by the Brules. These actions are often considered the beginning of the Plains Indian Wars.

FORT LEAVENWORTH on the west bank of the Missouri River, the oldest active Army post west of the Mississippi, is one of the most historic in the West and in the U.S. From the time of its founding in 1827 to the present, it has been a front-ranking installation. Centrally located on the main westward travel routes in the 19th century, it figured prominently in the Plains campaigns against the Indians and the Mexican and Civil Wars.

As early as 1824 Missouri citizens petitioned Congress to activate a military post at the Arkansas Crossing of the Santa Fe Trail to protect traders. Three years later, in a more defensible and logistically supportable location, just over the western boundary of Missouri and about 300 miles northeast of the crossing, Col. Henry Leavenworth founded the fort that came to bear his name. From 1827 until 1839 it was headquarters for the Upper Missouri Indian Agency, which had jurisdiction over all the tribes in the Upper Missouri and northern Plains region, and was the scene of many conferences and treaty councils. The garrison also inspected Missouri River steamboats to prevent the smuggling of alcohol to the Indians.

Replacing Fort Atkinson, Nebr., on the "Permanent Indian Frontier," the fort guarded the Santa Fe Trail and quelled Indian disturbances. The 1st Dragoons, mounted troops activated for use on the frontier to counter the mounted tactics of the Indians, came to the fort in 1834, the year after Congress established a regiment of 10 companies on an experimental basis. The regiment proved so effective that in 1836 Congress founded a second one. For three decades prior to the Civil War, particularly, the fort's location near the eastern termini of the Santa Fe and Oregon-California Trails made it a key frontier post and transportation mecca.

Exploring expeditions that used Fort Leavenworth as a base of operations between 1829 and 1845 included Maj. Bennett Riley's 1829 reconnaissance of the Santa Fe Trail to the Mexican border; Col. Henry Dodge's peacemaking mission in 1835 among the southern Plains tribes, during which three companies of

Fort Laramie in 1842 from *Fremont's Report.*

dragoons in 3½ months marched 1,600 miles to the Rockies via the Oregon-California Trail and returned via the Santa Fe Trail; and Col. Stephen W. Kearny's expedition to the southern Plains and the Rockies in 1845, which sought to impress the Indians with U.S. military powers, gathered information on the Plains country, and escorted caravans over the Oregon-California and Santa Fe Trails.

During the Mexican War (1846-48), the fort was the base for General Kearny's Army of the West, which occupied New Mexico and California.

After the Civil War, by which time the frontier had advanced well beyond the fort, it continued as a quartermaster depot and ordnance arsenal. In 1881 it became a school for infantry and cavalry officers, reorganized in 1901 as the General Service and Staff School. During the 20th century, it remained an officers' school, and in World Wars I and II served as an induction and training center. Today it is the headquarters of the Command and General Staff College.

FORT McDERMITT RESERVATION ,

in Nevada and Oregon, is 34,500 acres in size, and belongs to about 500 Pauite and Shoshone Indians.

This reservation was established as a military post in 1867 and abandoned some years later. The site was transferred to the Secretary of the Interior by Executive order in 1889 making the area public domain land. The Act of August 1, 1890, authorized disposition of this land under the Homestead Law. In 1892, allotments of this land were made to the Indians under the General Allotment Act of 1887.

With the exception of speaking the Paiute language, participation in a distinctly Indian culture is particlaly non-existent here.

The tribe is organized under the Indian Reorganization Act with a constitution and bylaws approved in 1936. The governing body is the tribal council whose eight members are elected to serve 4-year terms.

FORT McDOWELL RESERVATION, 24,600

acres in size, is in Maricopa County, Arizona. The population of more than 300 are Apache, Mohave, and Yavapai Indians. Approximately two-thirds of the land will be inundated by the Orme Dam, a diversion dam for the Central Arizona Project. Negotiations are being made to transfer an equivalent amount of acreage from adjoining Federal lands.

The people are descended from the Apache bands, Mojave, and Yavapai who were assigned to the Fort McDowell Military Reservation at the end of the Indian Wars. These tribes were known as strong, brave fighters.

Under the constitution and bylaws of the Fort McDowell Mohave-Apache Community and under the corporate charter of the community, the tribal council is the popularly elected organization which carries out the program of the tribe. They are assisted by a Planning Commission, Citizens Advisory Committee, Housing Authority, and various other committees.

Annual tribal income of $16,000 is derived largely from recreation fees and the City of Phoenix rental for a water facility. The remaining 10 percent comes from farming. There are four full-time tribal employees. The only commercial establishment on the reservation is a service station which is tribally owned.

Located near the Phoenix area the reservation has a climate dry and sunny. Rainfall averages 7 inches per year. Temperatures range from a high of 110° to a low of 30°.

FORT MICHILIMACKINAC

("place of the big wounded person", in Algonquian) was an important bastion of French and English power on the Straits of Mackinac and a vital furtrade center. French hegemony in the American heartland was closely related to its control of the highly strategic straits, the crossroads of the upper Great Lakes connecting lakes Michigan, Huron, and Superior. In the early interior exploration of North America, the Great Lakes and their related waterways were the main routes into the continent for the French, the first Europeans to penetrate them. The importance of the straits did not escape them.

The earliest French activity on the straits centered on Mackinac Island and at St. Ignace, on their north side. In 1670-71, Pere Claude Dablon founded a Jesuit mission on the island, which he named St. Ignace after the founder of his order, St. Ingatius. He was soon joined by Pere Jacques Marquette, who came with his Huron flock from the upper end of Lake Superior. In 1672, the mission was moved to the mainland on the north shore of the straits, at which time Marquette took charge, and a fort was added to the mission.

For a few years after 1698, the French officially abandoned the straits, but traders maintained contact with the Indians around the Mackinac area. Early in the 18th century, the French formally returned to the straits and during the years 1715-20 erected a new fort, Fort Michilimackinac, on the south shore of the straits at the site of Mackinaw City. The British took over this fort during the French and Indian War, but the garrison was surprised and most of its occupants massacred in 1763 during the Pontiac uprising.

The British reoccupied the fort in 1764, and it was the only British-garrisoned outpost on the Great Lakes above Detroit until near the close of the War for Independence. In 1781, when U.S. attack appeared imminent, the post was relocated at Mackinac Island. The British remained in control until 1796 and between 1812 and 1815. From 1796 to 1812 and after 1815 the fort belonged the the United States.

FORT MIMS, BATTLE OF

was an 1813 attack upon frontier settlers and militia by Creek Indians in

Old Fort Mackinac built in 1779 on Mackinac Island.

east-central Alabama that caused largescale U.S. retaliatory action in the Creek War.

The Creek people of Georgia and Alabama were visited by Tecumseh, the Shawnee Pan-Indian leader, late in 1811. At a meeting at Tukabatche he urged their support in a confederacy against the advancing white settler. The Creeks, divided in their support, erupted in civil war early in 1812. Those who supported Tecumseh's plan for resistance against the United States painted their war clubs red and were known as "Red Sticks". They were led by chiefs Red Eagle and Menewa.

Chief Red Eagle (William Weatherford), of mixed European and Creek ancestry, led a large war party against Fort Mims on August 30, 1813. Fort Mims, about 40 miles north of Mobile, was guarded by less than 100 militiamen and was occupied by refugee white settlers and their families and slaves. The invading Creeks killed almost 350 people in the massacre which followed.

William MacIntosh, the principal pro-American Creek leader, led a retaliatory force that killed 200 of the anti-American party. A U.S. force was dispatched to the area under Tennessee's General Andrew Jackson, later 7th president of the United States. After several engagements, Jackson's force won the decisive Battle of Horseshoe Bend in May, 1814.

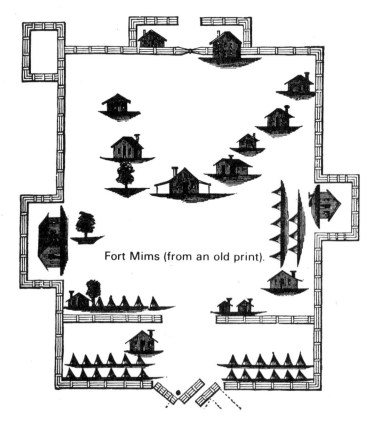

Fort Mims (from an old print).

FORT MOHAVE RESERVATION, in Nevada, California, and Arizona, is 38,384 acres in size. More than 500 Mojave Indians reside there.

In the early 16th century, the Mojave Indians were not part of the Mission way of life instituted by the Spaniards. The members were known as "wild" Indians. Originally they welcomed the Padres and soldiers, but forced Indian labor and Spanish raids soon changed their attitudes. The 1848 Treaty of Guadelupe Hinalgo, which ended the war with Mexico ceded California and other territories to the United States. Under that treaty, the U.S. government agreed to preserve recognition of the Indian people's right to the land they inhabited. The Mojaves have lived since prehistoric times engaged in small-scale farming, gathering wild foods, hunting, and fishing.

FORT PECK RESERVATION, 964,865 acres in Montana, had 6,000 Assiniboine and Dakota (Sioux) Indians residing on it. Under the 1908 Allotment Act, each member received 320 acres in addition to 40 acres of irrigable land. Heads of families also received 20

acres of timberland. Remaining lands were opened to homesteading in 1916. In addition to the land held in trust for the tribe, the tribe has control of 85,000 acres of submarginal land through a lease agreement with the Department of the Interior. Title to the Indian-owned land is complicated due to multiple inheritance. Indian lands are checker-boarded by non-Indian lands throughout the reservation.

History. The Assiniboines are a Siouan speaking people who originally lived in northern Minnesota. The Assiniboine and many Sioux tribes moved westward into Montana because of the pressure from the east exerted by the powerful Chippewa and the European settlers. Both tribes adapted to the Plains culture of their new enviroment. The Assininboine participated actively in fur trading with both French and British companies. In an 1851 treaty, the Assiniboines in the vicinity of Fort Peck were granted hunting and fishing privileges in common with the Blackfeet, Gros Ventre, and other tribes in the area. By 1871, large bands of Sioux had moved into the area. To accommodate these groups, the Fort Peck Reservation was established in an Executive order of 1873 as a home for both Assiniboine

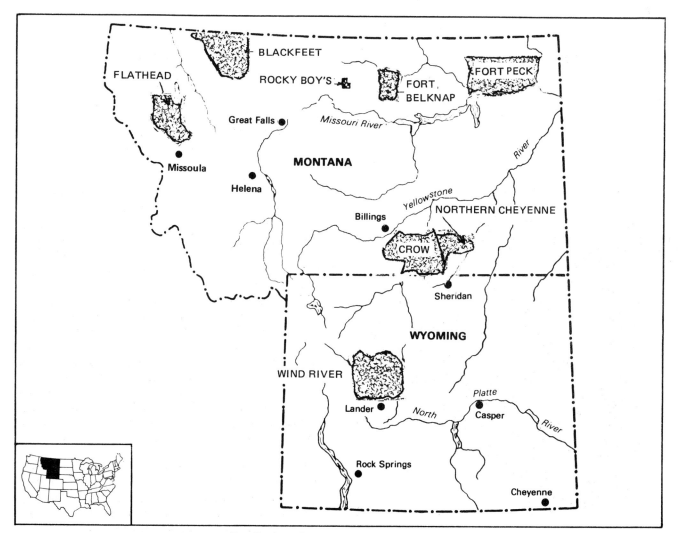

Fort Peck and neighboring reservations.

and Sioux Tribes. The reservation boundaries were set by Congress in 1888.

Culture. Approximately one-half the reservation population is Sioux, one-third Assiniboine, and the remainder mixed blood. They live in two distinct tribal groups, the Assiniboine occupying the southwestern and the Sioux occupying the southeastern portions of the reservation. The tribes, once nomadic hunters of the buffalo, still adhere strongly to their Indian customs, although subject to the white man's ways. Family ties are strong and tribal members still practice the Indian custom of sharing whatever they have with relatives and friends. During the summer months, Indian dances and celebrations are held in five different districts on the reservation.

Government. The Fort Peck tribes did not accept the 1934 Indian Reorganization Act. The tribe is governed by a 15-man council. Twelve members are elected at large from six geographic districts. The chairman, vice-chairman, and sergeant-at-arms are elected at large. Each elected executive board member serves a 2-year term. The board operates under a constitution and is empowered to act on all matters.

FORT PITT was involved in the Indian uprising led by Pontiac in 1763 and 1764.

In 1758, 6,500 British and colonial troops under Gen. John Forbes made a forced march through the rugged Pennsylvania wilderness and found Duquesne destroyed and abandoned by the French because of pressures elsewhere and the desertion of their Indian

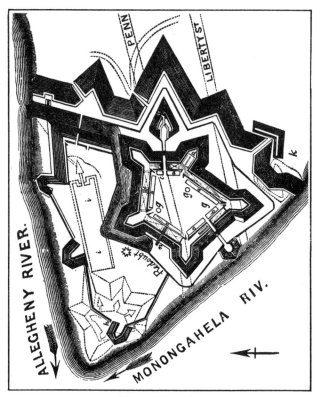

Plan of Fort Pitt.

allies Col. Hugh Mercer was left with 200 men to secure the position for England. In 1759, the English began to construct a major permanent fortification, named Fort Pitt in honor of the Prime Misister of England. The exterior walls of the pentagonal fort were earthen ramparts faced with brick. Frame and brick buildings were constructed inside, parallel to the interior walls. A town that subsequently became Pittsburgh began to take shape in the surrounding vicinity as settlers, mostly Virginians, followed Braddock's trail to take advantage of whatever opportunities might be available.

Fort Pitt was one of the few English forts to withstand attack during the Pontiac uprising of 1763-64. As the French and Indian threat receded, the fort deteriorated, while the settlement of Pittsburgh prospered as a base for traders, backwoodsmen, and westward-moving settlers. The United States built a fifth and last fort, LaFayette or Fayette, at the forks in the winter of 1791-92, when war with the Indians in the old Northwest flamed anew. Located a quarter of a mile above the site of Fort Pitt, which had fallen into ruin, the fort supplied troops during the Whisky Rebellion, in 1794, and served as a supply and training depot in the War of 1812.

FORT ROBINSON, Nevada, in the northern Plains, was founded in 1874 to protect the Red Cloud Agency, which had been moved the year before from its first location (1871-73), on the Oregon-California Trail and the North Platte River about 25 miles southeast of Fort Laramie, Wyo. The agency's mission was to control and issue food and annuities to the Sioux and Cheyennes. Among them was the Oglala Chief Red Cloud, who had refused to move onto the Great Sioux Reservation of western South Dakota, created by the Fort Laramie Treaty (1868), and insisted on residing in the unceded territory north of the North Platte.

Life at the agency was hectic. At times 13,000 Indians were camped nearby awaiting supplies. Aggravating the situation were their nonreservation kin and Arapahos, residents of the surrounding unceded hunting territory who wintered near the agency to procure food. De facto rulers of the agency, the Indians kept the inexperienced, and often dishonest, agents and their staff in a virtual state of siege. The braves in February 1874 killed the acting agent. The next month, to restore peace, the Army founded Fort Robinson adjacent to the agency and Camp Sheridan near the newly established Spotted Tail Agency, 40 miles to the northeast, which administered mainly the Upper Brules. Realizing the troops' daily presence generated friction, in May the commander relocated the fort about 1½ miles west of the agency.

But the Army could not prevent corruption in agency management, which infuriated the Indians. In 1875 a special government, infuriated commission conducting hearings at various locations throughout the Nation, including the Red Cloud and Spotted Tail Agencies, confirmed reports that agents, other government employees, contractors, and freighters were profiting from traffic in Indain food and annuities, many of them inferior. The nationwide publicity aroused the ire of eastern humanitarians.

A far stronger reason for Indian hostility was the violation of the Fort Laramie Treaty represented by the 1874-75 mining invasion of the Black Hills, for which the fort was a way station on the main route to the goldfields. In September 1875, first at the fort and than at a site 8 miles to the east, Government representatives tried to buy the hills from the reservation Sioux, but they refused. The fort supported campaigns in Wyoming and Montana the next year against the nonreservation and reservation Sioux and Cheyennes who united under Sitting Bull and other leaders and overwhelmed Custer in June at the Battle of the Little Bighorn.

Following this campaign and a victory over the Sioux in September in the Battle of Slim Buttes, S. Dak., Brig, Gen. George Crook returned via the Black Hills to Fort Laramie, Wyo. He then marched to the Red Cloud and Spotted Tail Agencies and put down a threatened uprising by disarming and dismounting Red Cloud's Oglalas and Red Leaf's Brules. Crook and the other generals triumphed in their retaliatory winter campaigns. Some 4,500 Sioux and Cheyennes, including the Cheyenne Dull Knife and the Oglala Sioux Crazy Horse, surrendered in the winter and spring at Fort Robinson and Camp Sheridan. As a result of a misunderstanding, in September 1877 the Fort Robinson commander attempted to arrest Crazy Horse. Resisting, in the guardhouse Crazy Horse pulled a knife, a soldier bayoneted him, and he died a short time later in the adjutant's office next door. An Indian rebellion was averted. The next month, however, the Red Cloud and Spotted Tail Agencies and their residents, in accordance with the Black Hills Treaty of 1876, moved to the Pine Ridge and Rosebud Reservations in South Dakota.

In September 1878 the Cheyenne Dull Knife and his band, who had been assigned from Fort Robinson to Darlington Agency, in Indian Territory, escaped and headed for their homeland. They were captured in the sandhills near Fort Robinson, where they were confined. They again tried to gain their freedom in January 1879, but troops killed some of them and captured the rest. In 1890, during the Ghost Dance rebellion, elements of the black 9th Cavalry and the white 8th Infantry from Fort Robinson were among the first troops on the scene at the Pine Ridge Agency.

During the late 1870s, ranchers had begun to move into the area around Fort Robinson and once the railroad arrived, in 1886, homesteaders followed. The presence of the post mitigated conflicts between the two groups. In 1890 the fort's importance increased as a result of the inactivation of Fort Laramie. Remaining active through World War II, in its final years Fort Robinson served as a cavalry base, remount depot, war-dog training center, and prisoner-of-war camp.

FORTS. Hundreds of forts once speckled the landscape west of the Mississippi River. Because the Plains Indians posed one of the greatest barriers to the westward movement in the 19th century, most of the forts are in the Plains region. Logically, they are also concentrated along historic routes of transportation and communication such as the Missouri, Yellowstone, Platte, Arkansas, Columbia, and Gila rivers, and the Rio Grande; the Oregon-California, Santa Fe, Southern Overland, Smoky Hill, and Bozeman Trails; and the Northern Pacific, Union Pacific, Kansas Pacific, Santa Fe, and Southern Pacific Railroads.

Only mounds of earth or foundations mark some fort sites today. In other cases the remains are extensive and well preserved. Between these extremes are scores of adobe, frame, and stone ruins in varying stages of disintegration, as well as numerous reconstructions. But even the best preserved fort is a far cry from the Hollywood and literary prototype—palisaded log fortresses with corner blockhouses and massive gates. The real forts were another matter. Few had stockades. Utilitarian, often simple or even crude in construction, and sometimes only tent sites or a motley collection of sod huts or dugouts, the posts were usually constructed of more durable materials. But, to facilitate Army mobility, they were often semipermanent.

As the 19th century opened, the Indians of the West unknowingly stood on the threshold of ethnic disaster. An alien tide rolled westward. Within a century it would engulf all tribes, appropriate all but a tiny fraction of their vast domain, and leave the survivors a way of life often grotesque in its mixture of the old and the new. The tribes east of the Mississippi were already suffering this experience. They were being pushed ever westward by the advancing frontier; or left in isolated pockets surrounded by hostile conquerors; or simply annihilated; or, in rate instances, absorbed by the newcomers. A few western tribes, notably in Spanish New Mexico and California, had experienced something of what was to come. Of the rest, only the occasional visit of a French or Spanish trader kept them from forgetting that white men even existed.

As the trickle of western migration swelled to a flood in the first half of the 19th century, the western Indians, as had their eastern brethren earlier, only dimly sensed the alternative responses open to them. They could unite in a desprate war to turn back the invaders. They could submit, borrowing from the invaders what seemed best and rejecting the rest. Or they could give up the old and adopt the new. The first choice usually proved impossible because of traditional intertribal animosities and the independence of thought and action that characterized Indian society. The last was rarely considered seriously. Sooner or later most of the tribes turned to the second, but few succeeded. For most groups, instead, the old culture simply disintegrated under the foreign onslaught—sometimes with, sometimes without, armed resistance—and left a void imperfectly and unhappily filled by parts of the conqueror's way of life.

In the wake of the official government explorers—Meriwether Lewis and William Clark, Zebulon Pike,

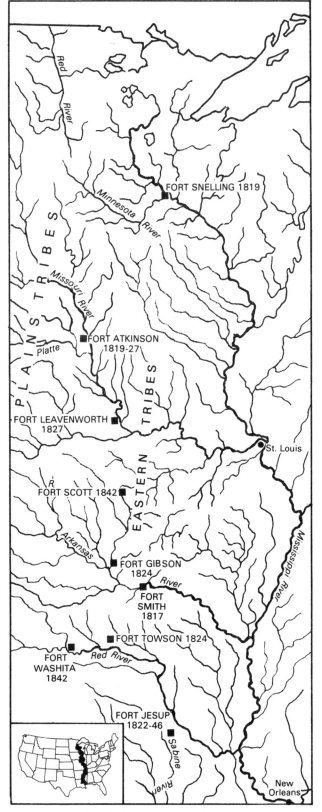

The Indian Frontier, 1817-48.

Stephen H. Long—came the roving fur trappers. Spreading through the wilderness, they afforded the Indian his first sustained view of the whites. Generally he liked what he saw, for many of the trappers in fact "went Indian," adopting many Indian tools, techniques, customs, and values. But the trappers also presented only blurred glimpse of the manners and customs of the white men. Free and company trappers roamed the West until the early 1840s, but the fur business came to be dominated by the fixed trading post, which relied on the Indian to do the actual fur gathering.

At Fort Union on the upper Missouri, at Bent's Fort on the Arkansas, at Fort Laramie on the North Platte, at Fort Vancouver on the Columbia, and at a host of lesser fur posts sprinkled over the West, Indian and white met on the latter's own ground. There the Indian acquired a fondness for alcohol that made it the chief tool of completion between rival companies, and there he contacted diseases such as smallpox and cholera that decimated tribe after tribe. There, too, the white man's trade goods—guns, kettles, pans, cloth, knives, hatchets, and a whole range of other useful items—fundamentally affected the Indian's material culture and thus bound him to the newcomers. Thereafter, even in time of war with the whites, he looked to them for a large variety of manufactures that had come to be regarded as essential.

Despite occasional armed clashes, the trapper-traders and the Indians usually dwelt compatibly side by side. Neither was bent on dispossessing or remaking the other. By the early 1840s, however, the Indian observed, coming from the East, other kinds of white men—miners, farmers, stockmen, adventurers of every breed—who did pose a threat to all he treasured.

The Oregon country, its ownership disputed between Great Britain and the United States, attracted some; Mexican California others. Then in the Mexican War (1846-48) the United States seized California and the Southwest from Mexico and extended its dominion to the Pacific. Texas, independent of Mexico since 1836, joined the Union in 1845. Settlement of the Oregon controversy in 1846 added the Pacific Northwest.

Territorial expansion stimulated emigration. The dramatic discovery of gold in California in 1848 opened the floodgates. Bound for the new possessions, few emigrants stopped to make their homes in the Indian country, but they pierced it from north to south with a tier of overland highways—the Oregon-California Trail, the Santa Fe Trail, the Gila Trail, the Smoky Hill Trail, and a multitude of alternate and feeder trails.

The overland trails destroyed a dream cherished by statesmen since the 1820s. They hoped to solve the Indian problem by erecting a "Permanent Indian Frontier," beyond which all tribes could enjoy security from invasion. To define the frontier, the Army laid out a chain of posts, running from Fort Snelling, Minn. (1819), on the north, to Fort Jesup, La. (1822), on the south. Roughly paralleling the eastern boundary of the second tier of States west of the Mississippi, it eventually extended through Forts Atkinson (1819), Leavenworth (1827), Scott (1842), Gibson (1824), Smith (1817), Towson (1824), and Washita (1842). Most of the eastern Indians were moved to new lands west of the frontier. Congress enacted a comprehensive body of legislation, the Indian Trade and Intercourse Act of 1834, to regulate relations with both immigrant and resident tribes. In 1838 Indian Territory—roughly modern Oklahoma—was established as a permanent home for the dispossessed easterners.

But in the 1840s the western trails breached the "permanent frontier" and bore streams of travelers across it. They demanded protection. By 1850 the "permanent frontier" had vanished and the federal government had moved west to confront the Indian. Along the trails and among the settlements at trail's end, the Army built forts. The Indians met new types of men—soldiers, agents, peace commissioners—who turned out to be not nearly so agreeable as the trappers and traders.

The agents and peace commissioners represented the Government Agency charged with Indian relations: the Indian Bureau, transferred in 1849 from the War Department to the newly created Department of the Interior. They negotiated treaties, disbursed annuity goods according to treaty obligations, mediated between Indians and whites, and tried to influence the tribes to accomodate themselves to government policies. Some of the officials, such as Tom Fitzpatrick and "Kit" Carson, were men of ability and dedication. Many, however, appointed as a reward for political services, were not only innocent of knowledge and understanding of Indians but frequently incompetent and dishonest as well.

Only dimly did the Indians perceive the implications of the first, seemingly harmless, requests of the government's emissaries. The latter asked the guarantee of safe passage to emigrants and withdrawal from the trails. In return, once a year the Great Father in Washington would send generous presents. Most tribes, still regarded under U.S. law as "domestic dependent nations," signed treaties committing the exchange of promises to paper, and they came at specified times to centrally located agencies to receive presents from an agent appointed for the purpose. The Treaty of Fort Laramie (1851), with the Sioux, Cheyenne, Arapaho, Crow, and other tribes of the northern Plains, and the Treaty of Fort Atkinson (1853), with the Kiowas and Comanches of the southern Plains, set the pattern for others that followed. The Upper Platte and Upper Arkansas Agencies represented the tentative and rather informal beginnings of management institutions that in four decades would bend the western tribes to the government's will.

The treaty system contained serious flaws that doomed it as an instrument for regulating relations between the two races. The signatory chiefs seldom represented all the groups whose interests were affected and could not enforce compliance by those they did represent. The white emissaries did represent the United States, but no less than the chiefs could they compel emigrants and settlers to respect the pacts. Moreover, because of cultural and language barriers, the two sides usually had sharply different understandings of what had been agreed upon. Sometimes, one or both sides lacked any serious intention to abide by a compact anyway.

And even the best of faith yielded to tensions. The

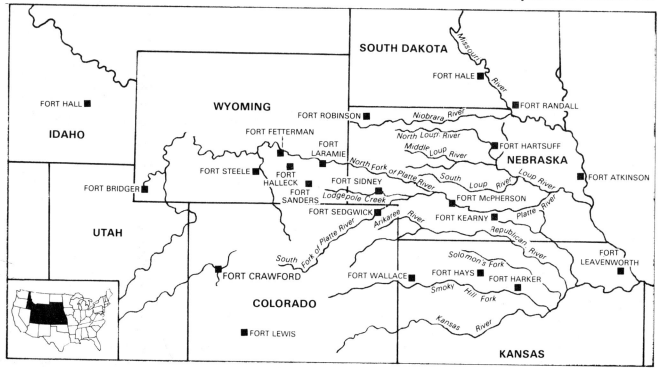

Western forts, 1874.

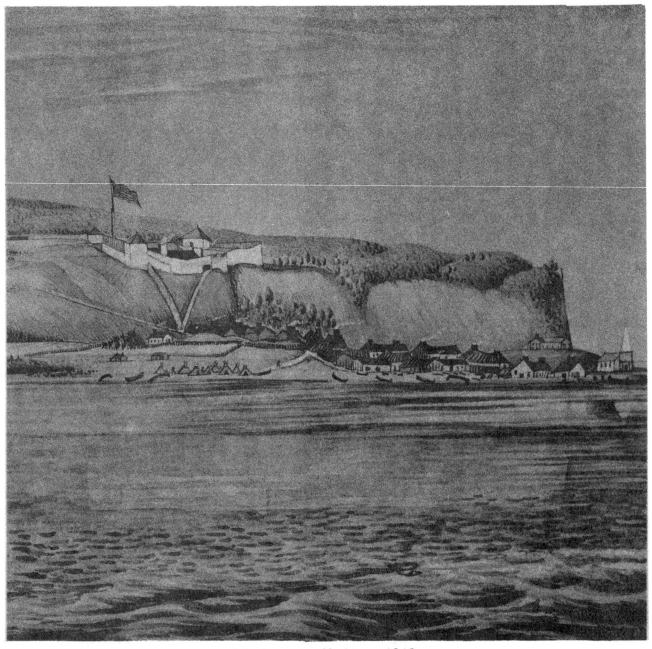

Fort Macinaw, Michigan, 1842.

Indian saw his buffalo and other game slaughtered, his timber cut, his patterns of seasonal migration disturbed, and in places ranges that had been held and cherished for generations appropriated—all by interlopers who also offered tempting targets to a people who set high value on distinction in warfare. The whites, on the other hand, saw the Indian as the possessor of an empire rich in natural resources that he had no means or ability of exploiting and that "natural law" commanded the "higher" civilization to exploit. Many whites saw him, too, as a savage who slaughtered their fellow citizens for mere plunder and the gratification of blood-lust.

Inevitably, friction occurred—among the Oregon, Santa Fe, and Southern Transcontinental Trails; on the expanding Texas frontier and the static New Mexico frontier; and in California and Oregon, where miners and settlers dispossessed the aboriginal occupants of lands coveted for mining or agriculture. For many of the tribes, the decade of the 1850s brought intermittent warfare with the soldiers, whose forts spread in increasing numbers.

Except for the tribes of California and the Pacific Northwest, the pressures of the 1850s did not fundamentally disturb the bulk of the western Indians. The forts represented a permanent encroachment on their domain. So did the handful of mining camps that appeared in the intermountain West toward the close of the decade. But soldiers and miners produced only local disruptions, causing but slight shifts in tribal ranges and alliances. Even the military campaigns again

Fort Benton, Montana, 1867.

This fort (Eaft) was strengthened and expanded by General Shirley in 1755. It was located near Lake Ontario at the channel entrance into the Onondaga River.

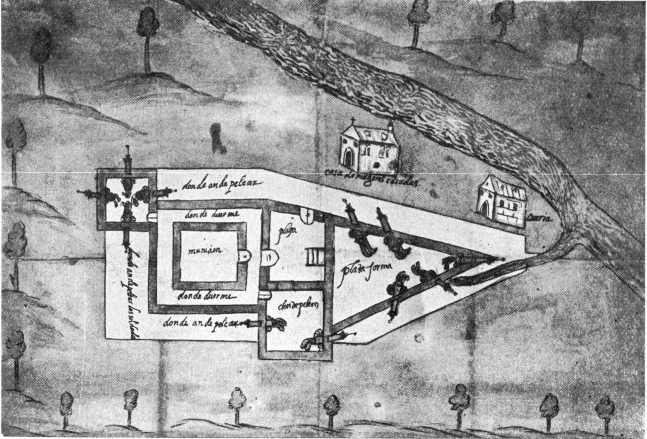

Spanish fort at Santa Elena, built 1566.

excepting those in the Northwest—proved mainly an annoyance. They demanded constant vigilance, occasional flight, and, rarely, a skirmish or battle that involved loss of life and property. This was nothing new to a people who had always regarded intertribal warfare as a condition of life. Growing numbers of trading posts represented an encroachment, too, but as an integral part of Indian life for almost half a century they were not regarded with antagonism. The close of the Civil War released American's energies to the westward movement. Thousands of emigrants and settlers pushed into the Indian domain with scant regard for the sanctity of hunting grounds or treaty agreements. Railroads supplanted the trails. The Union Pacific and Central Pacific, joined in 1869, were succeeded to the north and south by other transcontinental railroads, and a network of feeder lines reached into many remote corners of the West. Miners spread up and down the mountain chains of Colorado, Montana, Idaho, Nevada, and Arizona. Steamers, sailing up the Missouri River, carried passengers and freight to Fort Benton, Mont., for the land journey to the gold mines of western Montana. Stockmen moved onto the grasslands. Dirt farmers, attracted by the liberal provisions of the Homestead Act of 1862, followed. Towns and cities sprang up everywhere. The once huge herds of buffalo dwindled to the brink of extinction, a process hastened

by professional hunters interested only in the hides. Other game diminished similarly. Forts multiplied, and the soldiers came back in numbers unprecedented before the war. In a matter of two decades, 1865 to 1885, the Indian was progressively denied the two things essential to his traditional way of life—land and game. Often he fought back, and this period of history featured the last—and most intense—of the wars between the United States and its aboriginal peoples.

Nearly continuous hostilities swept the Great Plains for more than a decade after the Civil War as the flow of travelers, the advance of the railroads, and the spread of settlement ate into the traditional ranges of the Plains tribes. Red Cloud led the Sioux in opposing the Bozeman Trail, a new emigrant road that cut through their Powder River hunting domain to the Montana goldfields. The Army strengthened Fort Reno and erected Forts Phil Kearny and C. F. Smith along the trail but could not provide security. In December 1866 the Sioux wiped out an 80-man force from Fort Phil Kearny under Capt. William J. Fetterman. They tried to triumph again the following August but in the Wagon Box and Hayfield Fights were beaten back. When the Union Pacific Railroad reached far enough west to provide another route to Montana, in the Fort Laramie Treaty (1868) the government reluctantly yielded to the Sioux and withdrew from the Bozeman

Fort Snelling, Upper Mississippi.

Fort Pike.

View of Fort Snelling, Minneapolis *c.* **1850**. From an oil painting attributed to Seth Eastman.

Interior of Fort Snelling, 1853.

Old Bedlam (left to right) ruins of officers' quarters, additional officers' quarters and the sutler's store, erected in 1849, 1852 and 1884.

Trail. To the south, in Kansas, Gen. Winfield S. Hancock led an abortive expedition against the Cheyennes and Arapahos in 1867 and, instead of pacifying, aroused a people who had not yet forgotten Sand Creek. Kiowas and Comanches continued to terrorize the Texas frontier.

Despite the Medicine Lodge Treaties of 1867, which were designed to bring peace to the southern Plains, war broke out once more in August 1868. Gen. Philip H. Sheridan organized a winter campaign, in which columns converged on Indian Territory from three directions. One, under Lt. Col. George A. Custer, struck the Cheyenne camp of Black Kettle—the same chief who had suffered so grievously at Sand Creek 4 years earlier. At the Battle of the Washita, November 27, 1868, Custer decimated the band. Black Kettle fell in the first charge. On Christmas Day another of the commands, under Maj. Andrew W. Evans, attacked a Commanche camp at Soldier Spring, on the north fork of the Red River. Custer, Evans, and Maj. Eugene A. Carr, leader of the third column, demonstrated that the Army could operate during the winter months, when the Indian was most vulnerable. Most of the tribes yielded and gathered at newly established agencies in Indian Territory. The Battle of Summit Springs, Colo., the following July brought the last holdouts to terms.

FORT SILL, founded in conjunction with a new Kiowa-Comanche Indian Agency near the base of the Wichita Mountians in March 1869 by General Sheridan during his 1868-69 campaign, played a significant part in the pacification of the southern Plains tribes. Believing that the relocation of the fort and agency farther south on reservation lands and closer to the Texas frontier would facilitate Indian management, Sheridan founded the two installations to replace Fort Cobb and Fort Cobb Agency, Okla., about 30 miles to the north. Later in the year the Kiowa-Comanche Agency absorbed the Wichita Agency, which had been located at Fort Cobb.

Duress soon yielded to humanitarianism. That same summer, Fort Sill was the site of an experiment in Indian management, a part of President Grant's Peace Policy. Grant inaugurated the policy in reaction to the cries of eastern reformers over the brutality of the Battle of the Washita, Okla., and other examples of Indian mistreatment. Hoping to end corruption on the reservations and to provide the Indians with examples of morality, he decided to appoint church-nominated men as Indian agents. Quakers, representing the denomination that responded most enthusiastically, were soon on reservation duty. The southern Plains, where the gentle Friends fell heir to some of the fiercest tribes in the West, became a testing ground for the "Quaker Policy."

Illustrating the problems the Quakers faced was the experience of Quaker Agent Lawrie Tatum. Arriving in July 1869, to take over the Fort Sill Indian Agency, he attempted immediately to transform the Indians into farmers. They continued their forays into Texas. They had little fear of punishment, for the Peace Policy forbade military interference on reservations unless requested by the agent. And, because Tatum refused to believe they were guilty, the Fort Sill Reservation offered a refuge after each escapade. Their boldness growing in proportion to their success, they defied the Army to stop them. But in 1871 an unexpected turn of events dampened their ardor.

In May of that year a Kiowa war party from the Fort Sill Reservation, led by Santana, Big Tree, and Satank, wiped out a wagon trian near Jacksboro and Fort Richardson, Tex. Gen. William T. Sherman, inspecting Texas forts, narrowly missed a similar fate at the hands of the same party. Determined to put an end to Kiowa and Comanche hostilities, he moved on to Fort Sill. There he learned the Kiowa chiefs had bragged of their exploits on their return to the reservation. He had them arrested and sent to Fort Richardson, Texas, for incarceration pending an unprecedented civil trial. Satank, seeking to escape, was shot and killed en route. Satanta and Big Tree, serving only 2 years in prison, returned to Fort Sill late in 1873. The Kiowas then resumed their raids.

Their Comanche friends had not curtailed their activities. They continued to plague Texas until even Agent Tatum was forced to acknowledge their guilt. He reluctantly called on the Army to punish them, but in so doing incurred the displeasure of his more idealistic superiors. Discouraged, he resigned in March 1873. The Army welcomed an opportunity to chastise the Indians, but its small force could only show them that the Fort Sill Reservation was no longer a haven. The Indians were incensed over the loss of the lands they had ceded in treaties and the devastation wrought by the buffalo hunters, whisky peddlers, and horse thieves.

The failure of the Peace Policy to protect Texas settlers prompted the Army to revert to sterner measures. The Red River War (1874-75), against the Arapahos, Kiowa-Apaches, Comanches, Cheyennes, part of the Kiowas, and lesser tribes, was fought mainly in the Staked Plains of the Texas Panhandle and in Indian Territory (Oklahoma). Fort Sill was one of the major bases. The month after the Kiowas and Comanches attacked a group of buffalo hunters at Adobe Walls, Texas, General Sheridan ordered all professedly friendly Indians in the region to report to their agencies for registration. A severe drought delayed his operational plans until late summer, when 46 companies of infantry and cavalry took to the field. Columns from Fort Union, New Mexico, Fort Sill and Camp Supply, Oklahoma, and Forts Concho and

Griffin, Texas, gradually closed in on the Staked Plains, which became a haven for fugitive bands.

Although among the most comprehensive campaigns ever prosecuted against the Indians, the casualties on both sides were few. Involved was the sort of campaigning that General Sheridan viewed as the most effective and humane—relentless pursuit that kept the enemy always off balance, always on the move, always tormented by insecurity. Such tactics so damaged morale that surrender was but a question of time. The last fugitives gave up in the spring of 1875. The Army transported more than 70 Indian leaders from Fort Sill to Florida for imprisonment and placed their people back on the reservations. That same year Satanta was again sent to the Huntsville penitentiary in Texas, where he later committed suicide. Except for occasional raids by stray bands, the Red River War brought permanent peace to the southern Plains.

Fort Sill continued nevertheless as an active post. In 1894 Geronimo, his Chiricahua Apaches, and some of their Warm Springs kin, after their exile in Florida, were settled on the Fort Sill Military Reservation. Officially Geronimo was carried on the Army rolls as a scout, but he actually spent most of his time in retirement until his death in 1909. Four years later, 187 of the Chiricahuas were permitted to return to the Mescalero Reservation, New Mexico, and the rest stayed at Fort Sill. In 1905 the Army had extensively rebuilt the fort and expanded it into an artillery training and command center, which it has remained to the present.

FORT STANWIX, TREATIES OF were two 18th century treaties in which the Iroquois nation ceded their claim to large quantities of lands for white settlement, particularly land south and east of the Ohio River.

Although the Royal Proclamation of 1763 had closed trans-Appalachian land to white settlement, traders and settlers pushed hard for a new agreement with the Indians. In November, 1768 the Iroquois nation was persuaded with fancy gifts to give up lands in New York, West Virginia, Pennsylvania, and Kentucky. Represented by Sir William Johnson, the Iroquois signed a treaty at Fort Stanwix, located between the Mohawk River and Wood Creek, a waterway connecting to Lake Ontario. This agreement established the Ohio River as the frontier.

The southern portion of the cession was not Iroquois territory. It was inhabited by bands of weaker broken tribes, such as the Delawares, who had been forced to leave their lands east of the Appalachians. As settlers and speculators moved onto the land, they contested the treaty and a long and bitter era of frontier bloodshed began.

The British then turned to another powerful Indian nation, the Cherokee, and negotiated the southern portion of the Stanwix cession at the Treaty of Hard Labor in 1768 and the Treaty of Lochaber in 1770.

The second Treaty of Fort Stanwix, signed in

Views of Fort Stanwix, Rome, N.Y., built c. 1757.

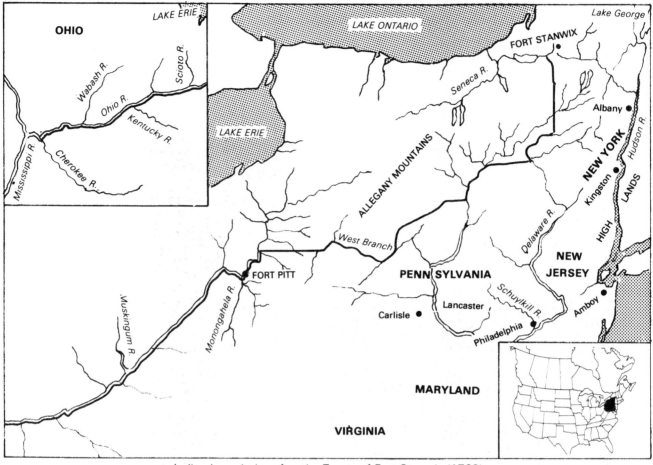

Indian boundaries after the Treaty of Fort Stanwix (1768).

October of 1784, was the first treaty between the United States and an Indian people. During the American Revolution, the Iroquois Confederacy, except for the Tuscarora and Oneida, had supported the British crown. The weakened league was forced to redraw their boundaries and pledge loyalty to the United States. In return, their right to live unbothered in their ancestral homelands was recognized.

In the treaty, signed by Cornplanter and other chiefs, they yielded part of western New York state and a large portion of land in Pennsylvania. Again, land near the Ohio, particularly west of the Ohio, was claimed by the Shawnee and other Indian nations who, in the Northwest Indian Wars, actively disputed the Iroquois right to cede such lands.

FORT TOTTEN RESERVATION, 50,000 acres in North Dakota, has about 2,000 Dakota (Sioux) Indians as residents. The reservation land is mostly allotted. Allotments account for 47,958.38 acres. The tribe owns 473.24 acres, non-Indians own 194,315 acres, and 1,800 acres are government owned. Fort Totten was built in 1867. The reservation was originally 360 square miles.

History. The Sioux were not native to the Great Plains area but migrated from their traditional homeland in the Great Lakes region near Lake

Superior. The Teton Sioux were the largest of the seven Council Fires Divisions, and the first to wander onto the Plains. They were first encountered by French explorers in the middle of the 17th century. As the 19th century began, they were the dominant tribe of the Northern Plains. Although habitually at war with other tribes, the Sioux did not actively resist white immigration until the whites began to intrude in great numbers and violated treaties. After the Minnesota Sioux uprising, General Sibley was sent to punish the Sioux and pursued them from Devils Lake southward. Battles followed at Whitestone Hill and Killdeer Mountain. The treaty signed in 1868 granted the Sioux freedom between the North Platte, Missouri, and Yellowstone Rivers. When discovery of gold in the Black Hills brought hordes of gold seekers into Sioux country in violation of that treaty, war was inevitable. Custer was defeated in 1876 at the Little Bighorn by the summer encampment of the Teton Sioux. The Wounded Knee massacre wiped out many of the Sioux people, mostly women and children, in the winter of 1890 and marked the end of Sioux resistance.

Culture. When the Sioux arrived on the Plains their culture changed from that of a forest and lake people to that of mounted horsemen whose primary source of livelihood was the buffalo. The Sioux Plains culture was one of the most highly developed both socially and

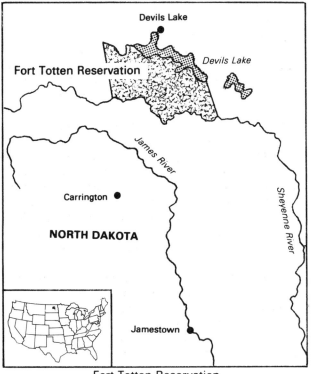

Fort Totten Reservation.

parts of that animal. The Sioux political organization and military strategy were both well developed, particularly as evidenced by the great summer encampments. Distinctive foods were corn balls, butter made from marrow, sausage, red bean, and tipsin roots. The tribe still dances the Omaha Grass Dances, the Rabbit, and the Hoop Dances.

Government. The Devils Lake Sioux are governed by a tribal council composed of a chairman, four councilmen, a vice-chairman and an acting secretary. The councilmen are elected from their districts for a term of 4 years.

FORT WAYNE, TREATY OF was a major land-ceding treaty of the Old Northwest in 1809 that increased hostility between Governor William Henry Harrison and Tecumseh, the Shawnee chief.

After the Indian defeat at Fallen Timbers and the subsequent cessions at the Treaty of Greenville in 1795, Chief Tecumseh rose to prominence among the Indians of the northwest. He traveled widely seeking an alliance among all Indian nations east of the Mississippi River to halt further white encroachment. He dreamed of an Indian buffer state between British Canada and the United States-populated by a confederacy of northern and southern tribes.

In 1800 the Northwest Territory was divided into two territories. The westernmost, called the Indiana Territory, had its capital at Vincennes and Harrison, later 9th President of the United States, was its first governor.

In September 1809, anxious to acquire further Indian lands, Harrison called a conference at Fort Wayne. In the treaty, the Delaware, Potawatomi, Miami, Kickapoo, Wea, and Eel River people ceded 3 million

politically of all the North American Indian tribes. Their sense of honor was strong, as was their sense of loyalty to the group. Greater praise was accorded a warrior who touched the enemy first without killing him than for enemy slain in battle. The ingenuity of the Sioux people with the products of the buffalo was unique and creative. All items of food, clothing, housing, utensils for water-carrying, tools for sewing and digging, and ceremonial dress, were fashioned from

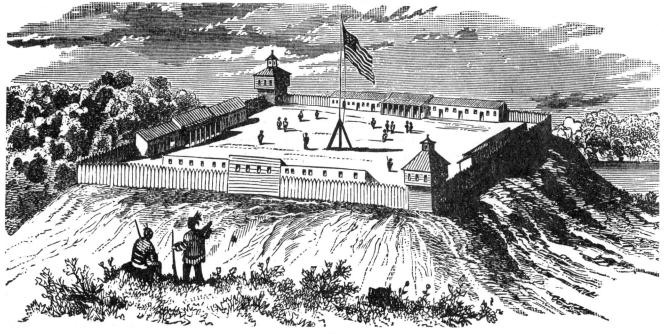

Fort Wayne.

acres of land. Unaware of the land's value, the Indians received approximately $2,000 in annuities and $8,000 in gifts. Part of the ceded land along the Wabash River belonged to the Shawnee, but not one Shawnee had signed the treaty. An infuriated Tecumseh fruitlessly argued at the Council of Vincennes in August 1810 that the Fort Wayne treaty was a fraud and that the lands must be returned to the Indians.

FORT WISE was established by Colorado Volunteers in 1860 on the north bank of the Arkansas River a mile upstream from Bent's New Fort. Two years after its founding the garrison marched into New Mexico and helped defeat a Confederate force from Texas in the Battle of Glorieta Pass. During the rest of the Civil War the post was the principal guardian of the Mountain Branch of the Santa Fe Trail. Cooperating with detachments from Fort Larned, Kans., and Fort Union, N. Mex., its troops escorted traffic along the upper reaches of the Arkansas to Raton Pass.

The fort was involved with the uprising of Southern Cheyennes and Arapahos in Colorado that reached a climax in 1864. Three years before, a few chiefs, pacified by Col. Edwin V. Sumner's 1857 campaign, had concluded the Treaty of Fort Wise. Guaranteeing peace along the Santa Fe Trail and in the region, they relinquished all the territory assigned to their tribes by the Fort Laramie Treaty (1851) and promised to settle on a reservation in the area of the upper Arkansas. But most of the other chiefs, refusing to be bound by the treaty, kept on hunting buffalo between the Platte and the Arkansas. Miners and settlers continued to flow into Colorado, whose Regular garrisons were serving in the Civil War. In the spring of 1864 the predictable collision occurred. Throughout the summer, warriors raided roads and settlements and practically halted traffic on the Santa Fe Trail. Coloradans obtained their revenge at Sand Creek, only 40 miles down the Arkansas from the fort, where a group of peaceful Indians who thought they were under the post's protection were slaughtered. Infuriated, the Plains Indians launched a full-scale war.

During the summer of 1867, because of floods, unhealthful conditions, and the decreasing supply of timber, the Army relocated the fort 20 miles upstream and renamed it. For a time, however, a Kansas City-Santa Fe line used the dirtroofed stone buildings at the first Fort Lyon as a stage station.

FORT YUMA RESERVATION, 9,281 acres lying in California and Arizona, has a Native population of 1,200 Yuma Indians. The reservation lies along both sides of the Colorado River. The land in Arizona, 480 acres, is entirely allotted.

The Yuman tribes had lived along the Colorado River for centuries before the arrival of the Spanish. The Fort Yuma Reservation was established in 1884, and included acreage in Arizona and California. Since that time, the tribe has lost most of the lands in Arizona and retains only a major portion of their California lands.

The Quechan, a subgroup of the Yuman Indians, lived in small farming communities along the Colorado River bottomlands. Principal crops included corn, beans, pumpkins, tobacco, and gourds. Both men and women tended fields. Their crops were supplemented through hunting, fishing, and gathering wild plants. Strong tribal unity with little formal government was characteristic of the Yuman tribes. Because of the hot climate, summer houses were principally roofs with open sides. Winter homes were more substantial earth-covered, rectangular buildings. These tribes were widely known as fierce, excellent warriors; they divided into two groups: archers and club men. Fighting well and bravely brought prestige. Dreams were considered important in the foretelling of events and the indicating of abilities.

In 1964, the tribe elected a paid president to devote full time to the socio-economic development of the reservation. The Quechan Tribe is organized according to the 1934 Indian Reorganization Act. The Quechan Tribal Council, as established by the tribe's constitution, administers all tribal affairs.

FOUR LAKES, BATTLE OF. The clash at this site in Washington on September 1, 1858, marked the beginning of a running engagement that culminated 4 days later in the Battle of Spokane Plain. In these battles, the army led by Col Wright revenged the victory of the Spokans, Palouses, and Coeur d'Alenes of eastern Washington over Major Steptoe in May about 25 miles to the southeast of the Four Lakes Battlefield. Wright's 600 cavalry men and infantry men, equipped with the new 1855 longrange rifle-muskets, whipped an equal-sized Indian force, emboldened by it triumph over Steptoe. The troops killed 60 Indians and wounded many others.

An arrow-shaped stone pyramid in the town of Four Lakes marks the site of the battle today.

In the wake of the Battle of Four Lakes, the Battle of Spokane Plain was the last in Colonel Wright's 1858 campaign in eastern Washington. Ranging over 25 miles and testing the endurance of the participants, it resulted in another Army victory. After the battle, shrugging off peace overtures, Wright marched through Indian country singling out the fomentors of the war and destroying the horseherds. The Yakima chieftain Kamiakin again made good his escape. But, before returning to Fort Walla Walla, Wright hanged 15 war leaders and placed others in chains. Like the Rogue River Indians of Oregon, the tribes he campaigned against in 1858 never again tried to stem the flow of settlers by force of arms.

FOX were a fierce warrior tribe that once lived in the Great Lake region.

Fox was an Algonquian language. Their actual name was *Meshkwakimy* meaning red earth people, the kind of earth their legends say they were created from. They got the name Fox when Frenchmen met a hunting party. The hunters told the French their band name was Fox but the French mistakenly applied it to all the nations. The Chippewa who drove them south from north Wisconsin called them *Dugamceg* which means people of the other shore. Originally the Fox came from Michigan's lower penninsula. For reasons still unclear, both the Sauks and the Fox who have many things in common emigrated west of Lake Michigan to Wisconsin. The Fox settled around Lake Winnebago.

The Fox generally were hostile, untrustworthy and avarious. Very primitive, but very brave, they were the only Indians who undertook a serious war against the French settlers. With the Sauks they drove the Illinois from part of their land. Also they constantly battled the Chippewa but were never successful against them. The Fox were colorful warriors wearing animal hair headdresses painted red and carrying shields covered with their coat of arms. Some braves who proved really outstanding were given the title of war chief. But actual leadership in war rested on that person who could raise an army.

Civil government was the responsibility of civil chiefs and a council comprised of the chiefs and all adult males. There were few regulations however.

An important social and religious unit was the gens, similar to the clan system of some Iroquois tribes.

Playing Fox, a chief of the Fox tribe, from the series of portraits of early Indian visitors to Washington.

Membership in these gens was hereditary. Members usually married and bequeathed property within the gen. On an individual religious basis any male wishing to lead a war party would fast for several days to communicate with the Great Spirit on the advisability of war.

Other social units with no religious importance were the male societies. There wre two branches, and each male belonged to one or the other. Membership was determined at birth, when the male infant's face was dabbed with either black or white paint. In the society, males learned games, hunting and war skills. Women held a lower social position and polygamy was common.

In village life birch bark was used extensively not

ONTARIO

Lake Superior

WISCONSIN

Lake Michigan

Lake Huron

MICHIGAN

ILLINOIS

INDIANA

OHIO

● Traditional locations

Fox

Sauk and Fox chief, Black Hawk and son from a painting by John Jarvis in 1833. The Black Hawk War was named in his honor.

only for canoes but for housing and containers. There was some agriculture and a specialty was collecting wild rice. Fox also hunted and fished.

Their first white contact was probably with French traders and explorers. At the beginning of the 18th century they became involved in the fur trade. As they continued in this trade they became more dependent on white traders. In 1806 Lewis and Clark remarked that the Fox trade was $10,000 a year. When Black Hawk lead the Sauks in war against whites, the Fox joined them and were nearly destroyed. They were then removed to reservations in Oklahoma, Iowa, and Kansas.

At their peak there were some 3,000. Today there are virtually no purebloods in Oklahoma. There are 436 Fox and Sauk in Iowa and Kansas. Those in Iowa rent land.

FOX, DAVID (Ottawa; 1934-), was head of the Great Lakes Indian Craftsmen, a Chicago-based company that markets Indian arts, in the mid-1970s. Born on a reserve at Wikwemikon on Manitoulin Island, Ontario, he later worked in sawmills and lumber camps, on road construction and structural steel.

FOX WARS, THE were fought in the upper Mississippi Valley between the French and their various Indian allies and the Fox nation in the first half of the 18th century. The French fought to preserve control of the midwestern fur trade.

The Fox were the only Indian people with whom the French directly waged war and their power was never completely broken. This incessant warfare in the west weakened France's Indian power base during the French and Indian War (1754-1763).

When first encountered by white men in 1670 the Fox, an Algonquian nation who called themselves Mesquakie ('red-earth' people), lived along Lake Winnebago and Fox River. They were bitter enemies of the Chippewa who, tradition says, had driven the Fox south from their northern Wisconsin homeland.

The French had supplied the Chippewa with firearms incurring the Fox' enduring enmity. The Fox received English supplies through the Iroquois at Albany rather than trade with the French at Montreal. In the wars which followed the French allied with various tribes including the Potawatomi,, Hurons, Kickapoos, and Menominees fought a Fox alliance of Dakota Sioux, Sauks, and French-hating Iroquois.

Early in 1712 the Fox, under Chief Pemoissa, planned an attack on the French fort at Detroit. When a large party of Potawatomis, Menominees, Illinois, and Osage came to French aid, the Fox were badly outnumbered and placed under seige. After 19 days without food or water some escaped to continue their nearly constant campaign against the Illinois Confederacy.

A French campaign of 1716 successfully surrounded their Fox River village (Little Butte des Morts) about 30 miles from Green Bay. The Fox agreed to peace demands. The French, now eager to expand their trade to the Sioux, built Fort Beauharnois near Lake Pepin on the Mississippi in 1727. Anxious to prevent a renewed Fox-Sioux alliance, the Fox village was burned, but most of the people and War Chief Oushala had fled the village in advance. The Fox now increased their campaigns in the countryside and against the Illinois to the south. Fort Beauharnois was abandoned in 1729.

In 1730 a large French-Indian army placed the Fox under seige near Le Rocher in Illinois country. Nicolas Coulon, the French commander, later was killed after making demands in a Sauk village. The Sauk, previously neutral, now joined with the Fox. They harassed French traders and their Indian allies, as well as the Illinois Confederacy. The Fox and Sauk together almost annihilated the Illinois despite repeated French expeditions. They occupied the Illinois country and controlled the Mississippi Valley from Wisconsin to the Des Moines and Missouri rivers. A major Fox settlement was Musquakinuk near the present site of Davenport, Iowa, while the Sauk occupied Illinois' Rock River region.

At St. Croix Falls in 1780, a combined Fox-Sioux force was badly defeated by the Chippewa. The remaining northern Fox moved south joining their people in the Illinois region. Early in the 19th century, they moved to Iowa and then Kansas in response to the pressure of white settlement.

FRANCISCANS are a religious order which played a role in the lives of the Indians in Spanish and Portuguese America.

At the time of the conquest of Mexico, the Franciscans were the first to enter the land of the Aztecs and preach conversion. They founded many missions and converted a great number of Indians as they acompanied the conquistadors. They founded such important early schools as Pedro de Gante, 1522, and Santa Cruz de Tlatelulo, 1536. From Mexico, the Franciscans spread their influence to California and Texas.

San Jose de Tumacacori Mission, Arizona. Built by Franciscan priests on the site of an earlier mission, San Jose served as the northern outpost of a Sonoran mission chain.

In California, the missions formed a chain of civilized outposts along the coast, spaced a day's journey apart. Each had its herd of cattle, its field and vegetable gardens, tended by the Indian neophytes. The Indians were taught by the padres to build irrigation systems and they became weavers, masons, carpenters, and blacksmiths. Thus the missions could be nearly self-sustaining, though they did receive clothing, furniture, implements, and tools from New Spain, in exchange for their surplus of meal, wine, oil, hemp, hides, and tallow.

The work of the padres, measured by the number of Indians reclaimed from their free life in the wilderness and put to tilling fields, was for a time successful. But even in 1786—at a time when the future of the missions was most promising—a discerning French scientist, Jean Francois Galaup de la Pérouse, visited California and wrote that he was not impressed with what the padres were accomplishing. He doubted whether the mission system would ever develop self-reliance in the aborigines.

In South America, the Franciscans established missions in Paraguay and Brazil, and replaced the Jesuits when they were expelled from all of South American in 1767. They, too, became powerful, like the Jesuits, and were granted privileges by the ruling monarchs and the Pope. At times, the Franciscans considered themselves independent of the state in their dealings with the Indians.

FRANCISCO (Yuma; *c.* 1820–1857) became chief after rescuing a white girl kidnapped by the Tonto Apache but later was killed by his tribesmen because of his friendship with the whites. In January 1856, probably out of fear of the troops stationed at Fort Yuma, Arizona Territory, Francisco volunteered information indicating that he knew the whereabouts of a white girl, Olive Oatman, who had been kidnapped nearly six years earlier (March 18, 1850). At that time, the Tonto Apache had killed most of the girl's family and carried off both Olive and her sister Mary into slavery. A brother, left for dead after the attack, survived and urged authorities in California to rescue his sisters, but no one could find a trace of them. Actually, the Tonto Apache did not keep the girls long, selling them in 1852 to the Mohave, in whose hands Mary died from starvation.

Francisco promised to rescue Olive if granted four blankets and some beads to pay her ransom. Given these articles, Francisco went to the Mohave village, but the natives denied knowledge of the girl. Then a young woman—whose skin had been stained with berries to disguise her white complexion—identified herself as the kidnap victim, whereupon Francisco won Olive's freedom and reunited the girl with her brother at Fort Yuma.

Francisco was chosen chief, possibly because his action saved the tribe from chastisement or because he received generous rewards and praises. He remained friendly with the whites, but his own people soon turned against him. Many believed that their chief's activities on behalf of the whites would bring an evil destiny upon them. For his part, Francisco only worsened the situation with his overbearing manner. Finally, in a raid against the Maricopa Indians in 1857, the Yuma warriors were all but eradicated. Out of the 75 or more Yuma warriors who had launched the attack at Maricopa Wells, only 3 survived. Convinced that Francisco had brought this catastrophe upon his tribe through his friendship with the whites, the surviving warriors turned on their chief and killed him.

FRANKLIN, MARVIN L. (Iowa; 20th century), served the U.S. Secretary of the Interior as Special Assistant for Indian Affairs, with full responsibility for all Indian programs, from 1973 until July 15, 1974, after demonstrations at the Bureau of Indian Affairs headquarters had caused the dismissal of Louis R. Bruce (*q.v.*) as commissioner. After leaving this post, Franklin rejoined Phillips Petroleum Co. (where he had worked in various capacities from 1947 until taking the government position) as director of legislative affairs. He is also a director of the American Indian National Bank (1974-). Born at Ponca City, Oklahoma, Franklin has been a leader in his tribal council and has worked to create job and business opportunities for Indians.

Franklin, Marvin L.

FRANTZ, ROSEBUD YELLOWROBE (Brulé Sioux; Feb. 26, 1907-   ), is a descendant of Sitting Bull, who since the early 1950s has been the director of the "Indian Village," an eduational exhibit on Long Island, New York. He is the author of *Album on the American Indian* (1969).

FREDERICKS, OSWALD WHITE BEAR (Hopi; Feb. 6, 1905-   ), is an artist, a wood carver, and an interpreter of the history, ceremonies, and crafts of his people. Born at Old Oraibi, Arizona Territory, he was educated at Haskell Institute and Bacone College. His drawings appear in *Book of the Hopi* (1963), which he authored with Frank Waters.

FREEMAN, ROBERT LEE (Yankton Sioux-Mission; Jan. 14, 1939-   ), is an artist who has won awards for work in several art media, including pen and ink, oil painting, and wood sculpture. He was born on the Rincón Indian Reservation, California. After serving in the U.S. Army in Korea (1958-60), he began working full-time as an artist.

FRENCH AND INDIAN WAR was fought from 1754 to 1763 and was the American phase of the European Seven Years' War. The American Indian was for the most part, allied to the French in the hard-fought conflict against the English over ultimate control of the New World.

Both France and England had laid claim to the Ohio Valley and lands further west. Each began to exercise its claim in the 1740s. Conflict was inevitable.

The Ohio region was populated by Indian refugees who had fled from either the British colonials or the powerful Iroquois Confederacy. The fraudulent Walking Purchase of 1737 had caused some Delawares, Shawnees, and other dispossessed Indian tribes to move from Pennsylvania to the upper Ohio area. There they were a hotbed of anti-English and anti-Iroquois sentiment. They encouraged French resistance to English encroachment and France built a series of forts from the Allegheny River to the site of present-day Erie, Pennsylvania.

In the 1740s the Iroquois gave control of the upper Ohio to the English. Developers, traders, and explorers arrived. The Ohio Company of Virginia dispatched explorers in 1750. Trading posts were set up along the Allegheny, Monongahela, and Ohio rivers. In 1748 an English settlement began across the first range of Virginia's Blue Ridge Mountains.

Artist's rendition of the Battle of Monogahela, in 1755, one of the bloodiest in the French and Indian War and a major French victory. A group of Frenchmen and their Indian allies are shown here ambushing Gen. Edward Braddock's troops. From a wood engraving by John Andrew after Billings, published in 1858.

In 1753 the French warned young George Washington, then 21 years old, that the English would have to fight the French for the Ohio country. Washington had been sent to a French woodland fort by Virginia's Governor Robert Dinwiddie to tell the French to get out. War began as the French destroyed Washington's newly-built fort and erected Fort Duquesne where the Allegheny and Monongahela unite to form the Ohio, the present site of Pittsburgh.

The French and their Indian allies resisted two early English attacks on Fort Dusquesne. In 1754 an English force was defeated and, the following year, General Edward Braddock and his troops were crushed by a force commanded by Pontiac, an Ottawa chief. Braddock's defeat caused most of the wavering Indian tribes from Canada to Kentucky and west to the Mississippi to join with the French. The exiled Pennsylvania Delawares were possibly the most fervent. At one point the English offered 200 pounds bounty for the scalp of Shinngass, the Delaware leader.

The French-Indian alliance defeated the English repeatedly in 1755. The western boundaries of Pennsylvania, Maryland, and Virginia felt the ceaseless pressure of Indian attacks. The western borders of these colonies shrank as much as 100 miles to the east.

Despite overwhelming French successes, the most crucial Indian ally, the Iroquois Confederacy, remained officially neutral. French territory and fortification covered a long defensive front line from Quebec to Louisiana. This line, however, was bisected by the Iroquois and their Great Lakes Territory.

The Iroquois neutrality was a deciding factor in the eventual British victory. Because of the efforts of William Johnson, an English fur trader, a limited number of Iroquois joined the British. At the Battle of Lake George in 1756, 200-300 Iroquois fought alongside 2,000-3,000 Englishmen. The very heavy casualties included the Mohawk Chief Hendrick, but the English were the victors in the crucial battle.

In 1756, war was officially declared. As though suddenly sensing the importance of the contest, France and England dispatched powerful new commanders. European forces became so large that the Indian factor became less strategic. Lord Jeffery Amherst took the French fort at Louisburg in 1758.

Peace with the Delawares was the assignment of Pennsylvania's Conrad Weiser. He won the friendship of Tedyuskung, leader of the eastern wing of the Indian nation. In 1758 they sent Christian Post, a Moravian missionary, to the western Delawares with a promise of renegotiating all the disputed land sales. Post was able to gather enough support to crack the French alliance and in November of 1758 Fort Duquesne fell to the English under General John Forbes.

In 1759, James Wolf defeated the Marquis de Montcalm on the Plains of Abraham, and Quebec was captured. The following year Montreal was taken by Amherst. The Treaty of Paris of 1763 officially ended the nine-year contest and the continent was partioned. Except for New Orleans, the entire eastern half of the continent came under British influence.

The Indian nations were very dispirited at the war's conclusion. The majority had fought with the lowing French and hated the British. The divided Iroquois soon felt their power erode as they were no longer a buffer between the French to the north and England to the south. Beginning in May 1763, many Indians continued their struggle for sovereignty under Pontiac. During Pontiac's war (1763-1765), the Indians recovered many abandoned French fortifications and used them as a base with which to control a wide region.

FRENCH GUIANA (Guyane) is the only French colony in South America, and the home to a small population of Coub and Arawak Indians.

The Guianas were sigted by Columbus in 1498. In 1499 Alonso de Ojeda anchored in the area while serving under Amerigo Vespucci and Spain subsequently claimed title to the area. In 1529 Charles V of Sapin permitted settlement on the Wild Coast (the Guianas). He granted control of Venezula and the Guiana Coast to one of his German banking creditors in 1531. All of this amounted to very limited and sporadic European presence. Phillip II claimed official possession for Spain in 1593. However, the gold and silver of Mexico and Peru received much more attention as did Cuba and Hispaniola (presently Haiti and the Dominican Republic), which served as safe havens for the formation of the annual treasure convoys which regularly carried the precious metals to Spain. Ready as ever to attempt to establish footholds in areas that the Spanish could not effectively control, the Dutch, British and French made many attempts to settle in the Guianas.

The area from the Orinoco River (presently in Venezuela) to northeastern Brazil was known as the Wild Coast. Aside from the Portuguese and Spanish, the Dutch were apparently the first Europenas interested in the area. The French soon developed an interest. Many colonization attempts were made from 1600 to 1650 and most failed for the usual reasons: conflict with the Indians, disputes with other Europeans, exposure to new diseases and problems of supply and contact. The first successful settlements were small earthen and wood trading posts. France bounded a colony in 1626.

These outposts, which were constructed often, had been established on rivers well into the interior. European goods such as knives, axes and cloth were traded for cacao, tobacco, red dye and other forest

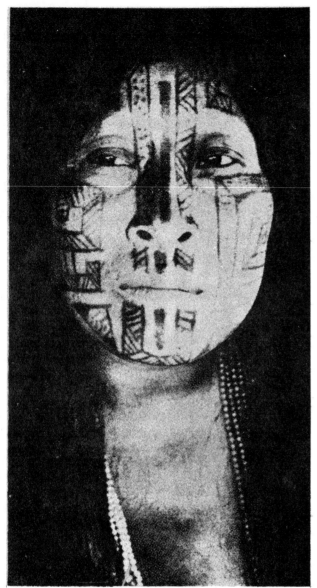

Tattooed Oyana women, French Guiana.

products. *Uitlopers* ('outrunners') was the term for the Europeans who first established trade with the Indians.

By 1674, France founded the colony of French Guiana. Off the colony's coast was located the unfamous Deuibs' Island (Iles du Salut-Isles of Safety) for unwanted Frenchmen.

Today, there are about 3,000 Indians—Caub and Arawak—among the colony's 30,000 population.

The knowledge of French Guiana's Pre-Columbian Indian inhabitants is sparce. The Guianas were peopled by Arawak (Locono) and Carib (Acuria, Carib, Kalina, Galibi, Caribice, Oyana, Oyaricoulet, Trio, Suppaye, Uparui) tribes.

In the fifteenth century, the Caribs, who probably originated further inland in Amazonia, waged a continuous campaign against the Arawaks. The Arawaks moved to the coast and then to the Caribbean Islands. These Insular Arawak developed a more

complex culture then their fellow continental cultural relatives.

The Warrau Indians migrated to the Guiana and Venezuela in the eighteenth century to escape Spanish and English control. Fishing is an important subsistence activity. Arrows, harpoons, lines and hooks and poison are used to catch fish. Bows and arrows are also employed in hunting. The Warrau seem to have learned agricultural techniques from the Arawaks. Among the crops raised are bitter manioc, chile peppers, and plantains. Men perform the heavy agricultural work and the women tend to planting, weeding and maintenance of the gardens. The Warrau live in large rectangular palm thatched structures and sleep in hammocks weaved of palm fiber and cotton. They build a bark canoe for up to three persons and a larger dugout canoe which can carry fifty. The larger canoes are famous for being well made and have been traded with the Arawaks. It is likely that these large vessels originated after European contact. Warrau society and political organization is not well known. They have a reputation for being the most polygynous of the Guiana Indians. Men may have two or more wives, often sisters (sororal polygyny). Although many Guiana tribes tend to be matrilineal, the Warrau reckon kinship bilaterally.

River Caribs are concentrated in several villages but smaller settlements do exist. There are dialectical differences in the Carib language spoken by different Carib Indians.

Villages can hold several hundred people living in large palm thatched structures and are usually located on the river banks. The kinship system is bilateral, with descent being traced through both the father's and mother's kin lines. Postmarital residence is usually matrilocal. There is a sexual division of labor like that of the Warrau: men hunt and fish and do the heavy agricultural work and weaving; women take care of the fields and extract the poisonous prussic acid from bitter Manioc (*cassava*) so as it is edible. Women also spin cotton and weave hammocks. Maroni River Carib society is sexually equalitarian. The sexual equality of women and their crucial economic role in subsitence is marked by the puberty rites of girls, which ritually denotes their transistion into adult womanhood. The ceromy takes palce after the onset of a girl's first menses. Her movements and diet are restricted. She must spin cotton and take part in other activities that symbolize an industrious wife and mother. Traditionally the girl had to place her hands in a bowl of biting ants and refrain from expressing pain. This still occurs, but seems to be growing less frequent. A feast is held for the villagers at this time and most of them are related to the girl. The initiate has little role here other than to be the manifest reason for the feasting. This initiation also has been associated with the matrilocal postmarital residence rule. Throughout their lifetime, daughters maintain continuous interaction with their mothers.

Funerals are also important and are the largest of the

village events. The death of an individual is announced by quiet cries. All of the villagers gather around the home of the deceased. The corpse is ritually washed and prepared for burial with its hammock. Burial takes palce within 24 hours after death. A second feast is held about one year later which is aimed at relieving the memory of the survivors. At this time either the wife, daughter, sister, mother or husband cuts their hair. Although the Carib are nominally Catholic, they still practice their tribal religion. One change that has occured is that illness, which was once attributed to supernatural causes, is now blamed upon deviant behavior. Magic is not often mentioned or even acknowledged—especially black magic.

The Amerindian tribes in French Guiana are a small segment of the population and those that remain are slowly accultruating to modern western society. This change will result in creative syncreticism of Indian and white cultural elements. Yet, the Guianas for many reasons, as well as one's interest in the Indians, is among the most exciting areas to conduct field research.

FRENCH POLICY. We are informed by some historians that "of all the white men, the Indians preferred the Frenchmen."

"In intercourse with them, the French neither treated them, as did the Spaniards, as minors or "wards" whose every action and opinion must be supervised, nor did they despise them as the English obviously did, even while recognizing their title to the soil and their right to bargain and make treaties. The attitude of the French was more like that of an older brother who might coax, scold, punish, deceive, or seek to impress his primitive kin, but who never attempted to enslave him or behave contemptuously toward him.

The French, it appeared, possessed a peculiar genius for securing the cooperation and retaining the good will of the Indians. In seeking the furs that were the most dependable source of revenue, it was the Indians of New France that led the *Coureurs de Bois* ever further into the interior, and that thereby aided the French in their westward exploration and discoveries. As they followed up on their contacts with the Indians, the French powers of endurance, skill in felling the forests, and ability to live under difficult conditions with a measure of cheerfulness and tranquility were "unrivalled by the people of any other European nation."

In keeping with their general approach to relations with the Indians, the French missionaries, in contrast to

Courtesy New York Public Library Picture Collection.

Oyana Indian women, French Guiana, 1953.

SAUVAGE matachez en Guerrier, ayant fait trois chevelure
cest a dire ayant tuez trois Hommes Natchez.
Bride les Bœufs Chef des Thonicas, il remply la place de
son predecesseur que les natchez Tuerrent au mois de juin
dernier. Femme chef Veufue du defiunt E. Iacob fils
du defiunt H cheuelures matachees et le baton pareillement
desinez d'apres nature Sur les lieux,
Redigez a la nlle orleans le 22. Iuin 1732.

Early French sketch of the chief of the Tunicas, with the widow and child of the former chief, who was killed by the Natchez. The living chief has his war paint on, and is carrying three Natchez scalps on his staff. *Peabody Museum, Harvard University.*

the Spanish and Portuguese, used only persuasive methods in their attempts to convince the native Americans they should become converts to Christianity. Although the end result of their efforts seem small, because the French eventually lost out in their efforts to permanently control an area in North America, In the French colonies, missionary efforts constituted perhaps the most admirable aspect of the whole colonial movement.

There was conflict between the missionaries and the frontiersmen in the French colonies as well as the Spanish. The fur trader wanted to use liquor as a trade item to facilitate the competition for the desired product. The French missionaries threw all their influence on the side of prohibition. In their efforts to secure the souls of the Indians, the missionaries often expressed the feeling that their job would be much easier if the government would keep the amiable and lusty fur trader away from the established Indian villages.

In 1609, while accompanying his allies, the Algonquin Indians on a journey to the lake that would later bear his name, Samuel de Champlain had a chance encounter with the Iroquois. To protect the Algonquins, Champlain ordered his men to fire on the Iroquois. As a result, the Iroquois later aligned themselves with the English against the French and the Algonquins, and thereby struck some telling blows against the success of the French in North America.

With the successful conclusion of the French and Indian War in 1763, the English inherited New France, which became Canada. By the Proclamation of 1763, the English established an Indian frontier. The area west of the line was temporarily reserved for the Indians. The success of the Indian policy of the French was evident even after their defeat, when in the conspiracy of Pontiac, the former French Indian allies lashed out at their English conquerors in an abortive attempt to cut them off from the outlying fortified trading posts established by the French to control the two great water systems of the Mississippi and the St. Lawrence.

The influence of the French fur traders continued to be felt among the Indians west of the Mississippi and along the upper Missouri River through the first quarter of the 19th century. It was a French trader Toussaint Charbonneau, with the Shoshone Indian girl Sacajawea as a companion, who served as guide and

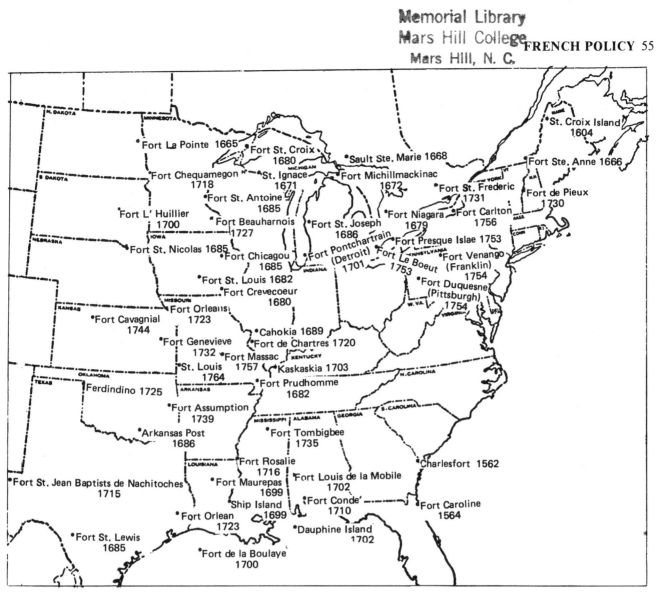

French posts and settlements, U.S.

interpreter for Lewis and Clark on their expedition west along the upper Missouri, across the Rocky Mountains, and to the Pacific Ocean.

The French policy in Canada was to make the Indians, to the extent this was possible, one with her own settlers. There was considerable intermarriage, and the Indians were not, as a practice, held at arms length or treated as an inferior or distinct people. Since the fur trade was of great importance throughout the French period in Canada, good relations with the Indians was a basic ingredient of policy.

Not long after the Spanish conquistadors began to move into the present southeastern United States, the French did so in the north. The French penetration—which ultimately extended from the Great Lakes to the Gulf of Mexico—was of an entirely different nature than that of the Spanish. Generally characterized by commercial exploitation of a fruitful but cold land, except in the warmer climes of Louisiana, rather than permanent settlement of a sunny and arid one, it was a veneer over the native life, not a lasting and deep-rooted influence. The tiny, scattered, and heterogeneous

French settlements also contrasted sharply with the well-ordered English, Dutch, and Swedish towns on the Atlantic Coast.

Adventuresome and individualistic *coureurs de bois* and voyageurs gradually penetrated the winding waterways and the deep forests. Ultimately exploring almost two-thirds of the continent, they founded small missions and temporary posts deep in the river-threaded heartland rather than great religious edifices and cities that could be easily supplied by sea. Lonely trappers and traders, living with Indian women, used their isolated huts as bases of operations. The amenities of civilization were rare in the far reaches of New France.

The soil of the Mississippi Valley was fertile, but the restless commercial activities of the French did not encourage stable agrarian development, and they did not recognize the immense agricultural potential of the rich soil that stretched away from the rivers of the heartland. Claiming a much larger territory than her major rivals—England and Spain— and beset with European wars, France never could enforce total sovereignty over the vast wilderness. For all these reasons, she was the first of the three major European powers to be driven out of the present United States—in 1763—and few physical remains of her occupation exist today except in Louisiana, where settlement was more intensive than elsewhere.

Like the other European powers, France was impelled by a desire to spread Christianity, to find wealth, and to counter the efforts of other nations; and her New World colonies were also closely tied to her under the mercantilistic system. She, too, hoped to find a new water route to the East through the North American Continent. Her exploring expeditions naturally probed the present northeast United States, whose shores were already known to her fishermen and were conveniently accessible from northern Europe.

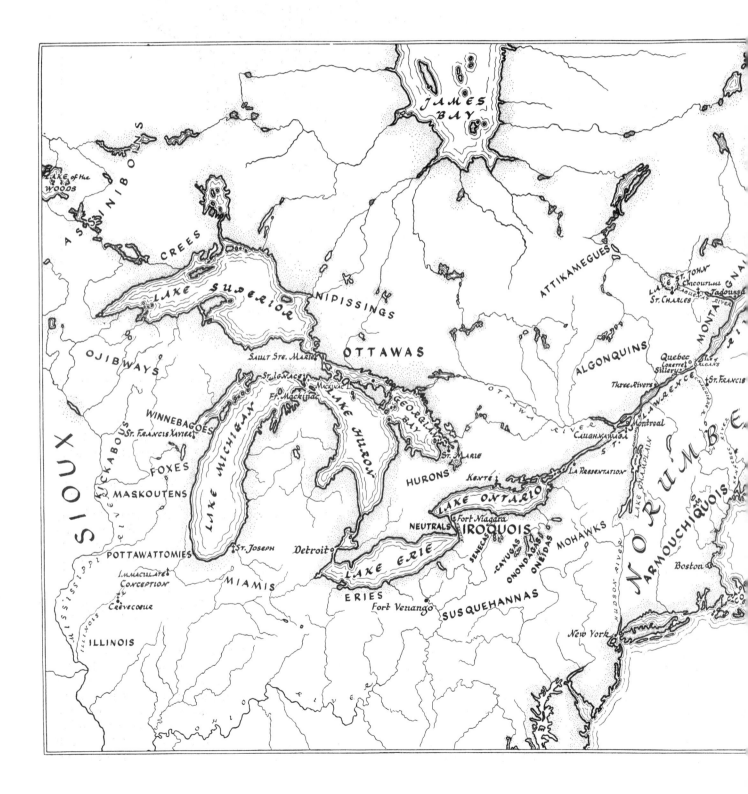

French explorers sailed down the St. Lawrence, across the waterways of Canada, through the Great Lakes, and finally to the Mississippi River and its vast drainage system. Instead of discovering a water passage through the continent, they found endless forests filled with fur-bearing animals and Indians eager to trade pelts for trinkets, muskets, and brandy.

The French empire in North America thus came to be based on the trade in furs, originally controlled from permanent settlements in Canada. Intrepid frontiersmen plunged into the wilderness to barter and bargain, while the mother country tried to control the lucrative business by granting monopolies, forming companies, and utilizing other administrative devices. During the 17th century, most of the furs were brought into Montreal to a great annual fair. But both licensed traders and freelancers operated with increasing freedom as the French empire spilled thinly into the heart of the continent. Frenchmen also did some mining for copper and lead in the upper Mississippi country, but transportation, manpower, and other problems hampered their efforts.

Side by side with the voyageurs, friars brought Christianity to the Indians. Most of them were strong-willed Jesuits, although Recollect Friars of the Franciscan Order accompanied Champlain and La Salle. French missionaries were far more mobile and had a less lasting influence on the native population than their Spanish counterparts. They founded no major missions, such as San Jose in Texas, San Xavier in Arizona, or San Luis Rey in California. Instead, scores of temporary mission stations, where priests read masses and performed the sacraments, dotted the forests of the northland. Nor did the French missionaries ordinarily attempt, as did the Spanish, to teach the "arts" of "civilization" to the Indians. The Spanish attitude toward the natives was paternalistic; the French, fraternalistic. The French adapted to the ways of the Indian; the Spanish "civilized" him.

With a few exceptions, mainly in Louisiana, the French settlements consisted of a few families of *hapitants,* who farmed the river lands in the vicinity of the forts, trading posts, missions, and Indian villages that were the centers of frontier life. Added to this small and more or less stable population were scores of restless traders, soldiers, and missionaries, continually on the move into the wilderness.

In 1608, Champlain planted a permanent settlement, called Quebec, adjacent to the Indian village of Stadacona, as a base for his explorations. The colonists survived the rigors of the winter only because of his grim determination. During the period 1609-15, Champlain struck boldly into the wilderness; he penetrated as far to the south as the southern tip of the lake that bears his name, up the Ottawa River into Canada, along the shores of Georgian Bay to Lake Huron, and back to the eastern end of Lake Ontario. Sometimes with him, and always with his encouragement and support, Jesuit fathers and some Franciscans carried the cross up the rivers and into the forests. Some successes, many disappointments, and a few failures attended their efforts.

To insure Indian acquiescence in his designs for colonization and development of the fur trade, Champlain early cultivated an alliance with the tribes that formed an unwilling buffer between French Canada and the powerful Iroquois. In 1609, he had been

Map of New France

persuaded by his Huron Indian friends to join them in an attack on the Iroquois near Lake Champlain—and again, in 1615, on the Oneida village south of Oneida Lake. Thus the French incurred the undying hatred of the five-nation Iroquois Confederacy, of which the Oneida were members, and this had repercussions for nearly a century. When the Iroquois finally overcame the Hurons, bands of the Confederacy—armed by Dutch traders in the Hudson Valley—spread out across southern Canada threatening to leave no Frenchman alive. In the Iroquois War (1642-53), the Indians twice nearly captured the newly founded Montreal and killed hundreds of Frenchmen, including several priests.

The year before Champlain's death, his lieutenant, Jean Nicolet, had traversed Lake Huron and the northern tip of Lake Michigan, and initiated trading compacts with the Indians in the Wisconsin area. In 1654 and 1655, the Sieur de Grosseilliers and his brother-in-law Pierre Radisson traced his route and established a lucrative trading post on the Wisconsin shore of Lake Michigan. Subsequently they explored Lake Superior, and in 1661 founded a post called Fort Radisson on its western shore.

Quashing the Indian threat

The demise of the Associates and the arrival in New France of such powerful leaders as Jean Talon, Count Frontenac, and Rene Robert Cavelier, Sieur de la Salle, stimulated expansion. Under Talon, a French army of more than 1,000 troops arrived in Canada; in 1666, it defeated the aggressive Iroquois and their allies and achieved relative peace for two decades. The same year, to prevent future Indian depredations, as well as to check the incursions of English trappers, the French built Fort La Motte at the upper end of Lake Champlain; one year earlier, Fort Chambly had been constructed on the Richelieu River, north of the lake. Their position strengthened, Frenchmen plunged again into the forests and soon pushed the frontiers of New France all the way to the Gulf of Mexico.

Extension of French influence

In the mid-17th century, the French possessions lay on a chain of waterways extending from the great river system of the St. Lawrence, through the Great Lakes, and down the Mississippi Valley to the Gulf of Mexico. French claims to this vast region were announced by explorations such as La Salle's; and they were affirmed by the establishment of forts and small settlements, the extension of the fur trade and missionary efforts, and the spread of influence over the Indians. After 1670, conditions were especially favorable for the development of the frontier. The French had quelled the Iroquois in 1666. To check further Indian depredations

and the incursions of English trappers, they then founded a series of forts.

Jesuits and trappers spread out into the western country. In 1668, at a well known and strategic location on the straits between Lake Superior and Lake Huron, Pere Marquette had established a mission to the Chippewas. There, in 1671, the French held a grand council with the Indians of the region, and over the years a village called Sault Ste. Marie arose. An equally strategic point was the Mackinac Staits, a few miles to

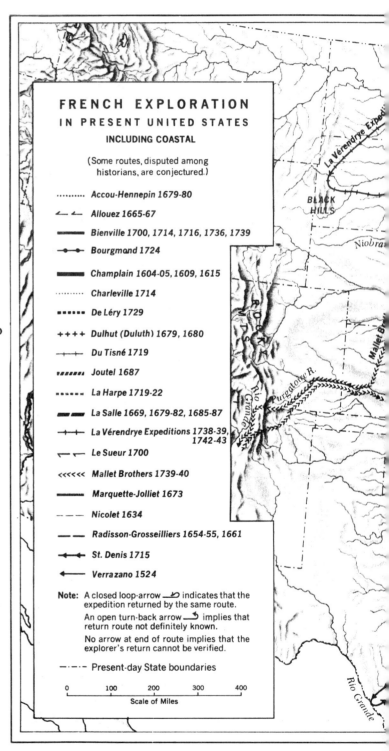

FRENCH EXPLORATION
IN PRESENT UNITED STATES
INCLUDING COASTAL

(Some routes, disputed among historians, are conjectured.)

.... Accou-Hennepin 1679-80

←-←- Allouez 1665-67

———— Bienville 1700, 1714, 1716, 1736, 1739

-•-•- Bourgmond 1724

▬▬▬ Champlain 1604-05, 1609, 1615

········· Charleville 1714

▪▪▪▪ De Léry 1729

++++ Dulhut (Duluth) 1679, 1680

-+-+ Du Tisné 1719

✧✧✧✧ Joutel 1687

▪▪▪▪ La Harpe 1719-22

▬ ▬ La Salle 1669, 1679-82, 1685-87

+-+- La Vérendrye Expeditions 1738-39, 1742-43

⌐-⌐ Le Sueur 1700

<<<<< Mallet Brothers 1739-40

———— Marquette-Jolliet 1673

– – – Nicolet 1634

▬ ▬ Radisson-Grosseilliers 1654-55, 1661

←-←- St. Denis 1715

←——— Verrazano 1524

Note: A closed loop-arrow ⟲ indicates that the expedition returned by the same route.

An open turn-back arrow ⟳ implies that return route not definitely known.

No arrow at end of route implies that the explorer's return cannot be verified.

–·–·– Present-day State boundaries

0   100   200   300   400
Scale of Miles

the south of Sault Ste. Marie, between Lakes Michigan and Huron. In 1670-71, missionaries founded St. Ignace Mission on Mackinac Island, and 2 years later relocated it at the tip of the peninsula on the north side of the straits, where soldiers built a small fort to protect the missionaries. Later, during the period 1715-20, the French erected Fort Michilimackinac on the southern shores of the straits. The straits area and Sault Ste. Marie were centers of missionary, as well as fur-trading, activity. From these and other bases, French missionaries penetrated the hinterland and carried the word of God to the Sioux, Chippewas, Illinois, Fox, and other tribes. The missionaries established small outlying stations for visitations.

Meanwhile, the fur trade expanded into the western country. Along the upper Mississippi, traders founded a number of posts, some of them temporary. Among the prominent were Fort St. Croix (1680), near the portage to western Lake Superior; La Baye (1684), at the southern tip of Green Bay; Fort St. Antoine (1685), on

Map by Harry Scott

the Mississippi between the St. Croix and Wisconsin rivers; and Fort St. Nicolas (ca. 1685), at the mouth of the Wisconsin river, around which arose the settlement of Prairie du Chien. Troops occasionally occupied these posts, but they were primarily used as bases by the *coureurs de bois*—dare-devil Frenchmen who took to the forest to trade with the Indians.

The passage between Lakes Huron and Erie was the last of the connecting links in the chain of the Great Lakes that the French fortified. In 1686, they erected a small post, Fort St. Joseph, north of Lake St. Clair near the entrance to Lake Huron. Then, in 1701, Antoine de la Mothe Cadillac built Fort Ponchartrain at the southern entrance to Lake St. Clair. This fort proved to be the most important and durable of those along the Great Lakes, and around it grew up the village of Detroit. The two forts protected the water route through lakes Ontario and Erie.

Western fur trade

St. Denis' post at Natchitoches was one of the first centers of the western fur trade. From there, in 1719, Bernard de la Harpe explored the Red River and crossed the prairies to the Arkansas River just above its junction with the Canadian River. Three years later he returned to the same region and made commercial alliances with the Plains Indians that resulted in a thriving trade in buffalo robes. Thereafter, French traders followed both the Red and the Arkansas into the Plains country with increasing frequency.

Meantime, the traders Etienne Veniard de Bourgmond, during the period 1712-17, and Claude Charles du Tisne, in 1719, explored the Missouri country and traded with the Pawnee, Osage, and Arapaho tribes. In 1723, Bourgmond erected and garrisoned Fort Orleans, on the Missouri River, in present Carroll County, Mo., to exploit the trade of the region and serve as a French outpost. He maintained the fort until 1728, when he abandoned it. In 1724, illness forced him to turn back from an attempt to reach Santa Fe. Bourgmond and Du Tisne probably probed westward individually as far as the North Platte River.

(It was from one of the posts in the Illinois country that a remarkable French exploration departed. In 1739, Pierre and Paul Mallet led a small trading expedition across the prairies and plains into Spanish New Mexico. They probably followed the general route of the Santa Fe Trail of a century later, and entered Taos by way of Raton pass. Their arrival at Santa Fe caused consternation among the Spanish officials. Already rumors of French activities had reached the Spanish through the Apache Indians; now there could be no question. Because the two nations were not at war, however, in 1740 the officials allowed the Mallets to return peaceably to New Orleans).

Twilight of empire

French energies in North America were soon diverted from exploration and settlement to defense against the expanding English over their Indian allies. As early as

1613, England had reacted to the French threat in North America by sending an expediton from Virginia under Capt. Samuel Argall to wipe out the feeble French colony at Port Royal, which had been reestablished in 1610 following the failure and abandonment of the first colony there 2 years earlier. In 1629, the English occupied Quebec itself for a short time.

When the French quelled the Iroquois in 1666, they may have had a moment of opportunity to dominate the English by moving into the Hudson Valley and New England. But they vacillated too long. England seized the initiative by capturing the Dutch settlements on the Hudson River and taking over the Iroquois fur trade, which the Dutch had found so profitable.

Three European wars between England and France were reflected in minor struggles between their colonies and their respective Indian friends: King William's War (1689-97); Queen Anne's War (1702-13); and King George's War (1745-48). Because in all of these wars French colonists suffered losses to their British counterparts, in the period of peace after 1748 France determined to so strengthen her hold on the Mississippi Valley that England could not shake it. In 1749, she dispatched Celoron de Blainville from Montreal into the Ohio Valley, occupied by Indian and English traders, to affirm French claims to the region. The principal result of his trip was increased hostility on the part of the pro-English Indians.

In the period 1750 to 1755, the French augmented the fortificaitons at old Fort Niagara as well as those at Fort St. Frederic, which in 1731 had been built on Lake Champlain; also in 1753, they rebuilt Fort de Chartres. New posts included Fort St. John (1748), on the Richelieu River north of Lake Champlain; Fort de la Presentation (1749), northeast of Lake Ontario; Fort Rouille (1749, on the western shore of Lake Ontario; Fort Presque Isle (1753), east of Lake Erie in present western Pennsylvania; Fort Le Boeuf (1753), also in western Pennsylvania; and, of primary importance, Fort Duquesne (1754), at the Forks of the Ohio.

Thus by the mid-18th century the final conflict, long deferred by the unwillingness of either side to make an all-out effort, was at hand. Englishmen were spilling over the Appalachians into the Ohio Valley, erecting trading posts and blazing trails into the heartland claimed by France.

It was the construction of Forts Le Boeuf and Duquesne that provoked the French and Indian War and brought disaster to the French in North America. Shortly after they built Le Boeuf, a small contingent of troops from its garrison seized and occupied Venango, an English trading post. Maj. George Washington, only 21 years of age, was dispatched from Virginia in the winter of 1753-54 to protest the action. His remonstrations were in vain, both at Venango and Le Boeuf, although he was courteously treated despite his youth.

To counter the rebuff, English officials in Virginia decided to drive the French out. In March 1754,

Washington and 300 Virginia militia set out across the mountains to construct a defensive post at the strategically located Forks of the Ohio. (A month earlier Capt. William Trent and about 30 men had proceeded to the site. Unknown to Washington, they had been captured by an overwhelming force of French and Indian allies, who constructed Fort Duquesne as their own defensive outpost against the English.) While Washington advanced steadily but slowly through the mountains, French scouts carefully watched his progress. On May 28, the first skirmish occurred.

Learning from prisoners of the strong force ensconced at Fort Duquesne, Washington attempted to provide a defense for his troops from the certain French attack. At Great Meadows he and his men hastily threw up a log palisade they called "Fort Necessity." On July 3, 1754, more than 600 French and Indians, skilled at forest combat and attacking from natural forest cover, invested the little fort. After 9 hours of heavy fighting, Washington surrendered, but he was allowed to march from the post with the "honors of war," on a date that was to prove portentous—July 4.

The martial conflagration thus ignited soon spread to most of the nations of Europe and about 100 colonial posts around the globe. The next year, the French troops successfully defended Fort Niagara and routed the proud British force under Gen. Edward Braddock that attempted to conquer Fort Duquesne. In 1756, the war, so far confined to the New World, broadened to Europe. The following year, when the British were still off balance, the French brought in fresh European troops and captured post after post along the English frontier. But in 1758 the tide of fortune turned. When Quebec fell to the British in September 1759, the war in America was over to all intents and purposes—even though hostilities continued for another year. In the spring of 1760, the French besieged Quebec; and, late in the summer, the British surrounded Montreal. Finally, in September, the Governor of Canada surrendered the whole of Canada to England.

As the defeat of France elsewhere in the world became assured, in 1762 she hastily consigned western Louisiana to her ally Spain by the secret Treaty of Fountainebleau. Then, in the Treaty of Paris the following year, she surrendered the rest of her North American possessions to Great Britain. Spain had to relinquish Florida in return for the restoration of her key posts of Havana and Manila, which had fallen to the British Navy. The French Empire in the New World was no more—although for a few weeks in 1803 France repossessed Louisiana from Spain, but almost immediately transferred it to the United States.

FRUITS, botanically, refer to the ripened ovary or ovaries of a flower, and thus both grains and pumpkins are fruits. The tomato, the husk-tomato, and the avacado are among the important fruits utilized as vegetables by the Indians of the Americas. Whether the origin of the cultivated tomato (*Lycopersicon*

esculentum) was in Mexico, or in western South America where its wild relatives occur, is still uncertain, but it seems clear that the fruit was more important in Mexico than in South America in pre-contact times. A husk tomato (*Physalis philadelphica*) was an important vegetable in Mexico, and may have been domesticated earlier than the tomato. The tree tomato (*Cyphomandra crassifolia*), another member of the nightshade family, was cultivated for its fruits in western South America. The avacado, a food rich in oils, was fairly widely grown. It apparently was domesticated independently in Middle America, the West Indies, and Peru.

Fruits that appealed to man because of their sweetness were rather numerous, and both Middle America and South America contributed many kinds. A large number of species of *Anona*—ilama, cherimoya, guanabanana, sweetsop, soursop, and anona—were domesticated. Other important cultivated fruits were pineapple (*Ananas comosus*), a cherry (*Prunus serotina*), the papaya (*Carica papaya*), sapodilla (*Achres zapota*), the guava (*Psidium guajava*), the hog plum (*Spondias mombin*), sapote (*Calocarpum viride* and other genera), cactus or prickly pear (*Opuntia*) and many more. The cashew (*Anacardium occidentale*) was valued more as a fruit than as a nut.

The coconut (*Cocos nucifera*), another fruit that eventually became an important food source in the Americas, apparently had an exceedingly limited distribution in Middle America at the time of the conquest. The coconut was at one time considered to be a native to the Americas, but it is now known to be indigenous to southeastern Asia. Whether its arrival in America was by floating or through the agency of man is still somewhat controversial.

FULLER, WILLIAM (Miwok; *c.* 1873–1958), was a hereditary chief who was the last of his tribe to speak the native language. With Fuller's assistance, the now-extinct language was recorded by Columbia University before the chief died. He was born at Bald Rock, where the town of Twain Harte, California now stands.

FUNDACHO NACIONAL DOS INDIOS Indians are the second largest group not yet fully integrated into Brazilian culture. An Indian has been defined as "any individual recognized as a member of a community of pre-Columbian origin, who identifies himself as ethnically different from nationals and is considered indigenous by the Brazilian population with whom he comes in contact." Estimates of their numbers range from 100,000 to 190,000, although these are highly tentative figures. There are many wandering tribes that are known to Brazilian authorities in name only. Tribes are continually disappearing through assimilation or disease. For the most part these Indians live in small family groups much as they did 400 years ago and continue to be dependent on hunting, fishing, gathering, and some incipient horticulture. The isolation and diversity of the tribes is marked. There are approximately 150 tribes, speaking an estimated ninety languages and 300 dialects. Most Indians reside in one of three kinds of communities: traditional villages, either isolated or on the outskirts of a modern settlement; national reservations, such as the Xingu National Park in Mato Grosso; or religious missions.

Those Indians who remain in their traditional villages are under the protection of the (National Indian Foundation) Fundacao Nacional dos Indios—FUNAI successor to the Indian Protection Service, which had been founded in 1910. The aims of the Indian Protection Service fluctuated over the years until it was disbanded in 1968, its policy and directives reflecting changing conditions and sentiments. Some saw the agency's role as protection of the Indians and preservation of their culture, others felt it was their obligation to educate the Indians in the ways of modern society, and a few practiced a laissez-faire policy. Both agencies have been consistent, however, in their approach to pacification of the Indians, basing their policy on nonviolence, even to the point to forbidding the use of force for self-protection in the face of death. In this manner agents have managed to establish contact with and gain the confidence of the Indians who, despite any other reluctance they may show, are assured of their physical safety. In 1979 FUNAI looked after an estimated 80,000 Indians.

Many Indians residing in traditional villages are being intergrated either into the larger society through close trading association with Brazilian communities or into one of the national reservations. The latter option is becoming increasingly necessary if the Indians wish to maintain a semblance of preconquest life. Their life-style and often their lives are threatened by roadbuilders, ranchers, woodsmen, miners, and other settlers who flock to the Amazon area, Bringing with them civilization and disease. As a consequence, entire tribes have been made aware of the threat to their existence and have migrated to protected areas. This move is usually accompanied by another set of problems, as newly arrived tribes still find themselves subject to diseases through contact with other Indians. Moreover, they may find they have moved within easy reach of traditional enemies. Nevertheless, the common will to survive has caused many warring tribes—both inside the reservations and outside—to sign peace pacts.

To the Indian the national society has presented different faces, alternately threatening or concerned, depending upon whether its representatives were Indian agents or pioneer settlers. Although the Indians have learned not to fear the agents, pioneer groups have not inspired such confidence, forcing the Indians out of their land and subjecting them to other kinds of exploitation. Raiding parties and skirmishes have often resulted over a disputed piece of land. In the early 1970s the government passed a law designed to defend the Indians against encroachment by white settlers. It guaranteed the preservation of the Indians' habitat and respect for their culture and tradition. It gave them permanent property rights to lands they occupy as well as the exclusive benefit of the natural resources.

Although the overall aim of the government in the late 1960s and early 1970s was the gradual integration of the Indian, many stopgap measures were being pursued because of other priorities. It was considered vital to economic expansion into the Amazon Basin that the Indian at best be integrated and at least not be allowed to interfere. The government's policy as stated by the president of FUNAI in mid-1971 was that "assistance for the Indian must be as complete as possible, but it cannot obstruct national development and the work to settle the Amazon."

In mid-July of 1971 President Emilio Garrastazu Medici ordered the formation of three new Indian reservations. The president's action was interpreted as a reaffirmation of Brazil's intention to move the Indians out of the way of the national development program affecting the area. He also altered the northern boundaries of the Xingu National Park to conform with the Transamazon Highway, which was nearing completion. In the winter of 1973 FUNAI announced plans for a program of land distribution that would set up a system of agricultural settlements for Indians in Roraima Territory. Because these Indians were in an advanced stage of acculturation, agricultural settlements were deemed preferable to a reservation.

FURNITURE, HOUSEHOLD. In a discussion of furniture, it is often difficult to distinguish the items included under this topic from the rest of the material culture of an Indian tribe. In this review, the items considered as furniture are those which belong essentially to the house and its use, rather than to other activities of the culture.

Under the topic of habitations, some special house features were described in terms of the major areas of South America. These overlap, to a certain extent, the category of house furniture. For example, the use of house lofts for storage, special storage platforms, wall niches, shelves, projecting pegs, and bins or compartments within the house—might all be called either "furnishings" or "house features." Furthermore, many Indian villages have small houses or sheds associated with the principal dwelling. These smaller constructions are used for storage, cooking, and the like, and consequently fulfill some of the functions served by furniture in other cultures.

The following discussion starts with a brief summary of household equipment and furniture by major areas, and continues with a more detailed description of the principal items of furniture and their distribution.

Area Summaries

The Southern Hunters of the Archipelago, the island of Tierra del Fuego, the Patagonia and the Pampas regions, have little that can properly be called house furniture. A fire bed is an important part of every shelter, but there are no prepared fireplaces or stoves. Floors are commonly covered with branches. For sleeping, mats of brush, skin, or plaited material, are spread on the ground. Around the habitations one finds such miscellaneous equipment as hunting weapons, simple split-stick fire tongs, grease stones, whetstones, scrapers, awls, and a variety of skin bags, some for storage, some for water containers. In the *Yahgan* camp other items are found, including seal bladders for oil containers, bark buckets, baskets, special bark-peeling wedges, and shell scrapers. The tribes of the Pampas and Patagonia add pottery, stone mortars for grinding seeds, wooden objects, and, in post-European times, a great variety of horse trappings.

In east Brazil, a raised platform bed is common. The houses may also contain stone baking slabs, wooden clubs, sword clubs, other weapons, baskets, calabashes, gourds, bamboo containers, bark bags, and various types of ceremonial equipment. The Chaco houses usually have pottery, skin bags, weapons of various kinds, fire tongs, skin and plaited sleeping mats, and a variety of wooden bowls and spoons. Also prominent in the Chaco are such Amazonian features as manioc equipment, wooden mortars and pestles, and fire fans.

Some of the typical items of furniture in the Amazon region are platform beds, hammocks, carved wooden stools, storage baskets, fire fans, manioc equipment, wooden mortars and pestles. The standard household also has pottery vessels, many wooden objects, baskets of various shapes and sizes, looms, woven pieces of cloth, gourds, and calabashes. Ceremonial equipment may also be kept around the house, such as feather costumes, bark cloth, and various musical instruments. The houses usually have fish, meat, and vegetable foods stored or hung around the interior of the houses.

Solid platform beds, clay cooking stoves, and grindstones are standard furnishings in the Andean region. Most houses also contain quite a variety of manufactured objects: ceramics, cloth, calabashes, woodwork, and metal work. Both blankets and skins are used as sleeping mats. Ceremonial equipment may be found in the house, but it is usually stored in a separate building. The *Araucanians* of Chile differ from other Andean groups in the variety of wooden objects found around their houses.

Even in so brief a summary, it is obvious that none of the South American Indian habitations contains much furniture. In recent years some European furniture has been introduced, such as tables, chairs, and frame beds, but in general, even these have not been widely accepted by the Indian groups. The archeological evidence shows that the Indian houses of today have little more furniture than they did in the past. In the following pages some of the outstanding articles of furniture are described in more detail. However, most of the common articles found around the households are described elsewhere, under the topics which cover the various crafts.

ARTICLES OF FURNITURE

Sleeping mats and blankets. The simplest beds found in South America consist of branches or brush mats laid directly on the ground. These are found among the *Caingang, Gorotire,* and *Botocudo* of east Brazil; among the *Nambicuara;* and among all of the southern hunting groups. The use of untanned skins for sleeping mats and for blankets is also found among most of the hunting groups, including the *Bororo, Caingang,* and *Botocudo* of Brazil; most tribes of the Chaco; all of the hunters of the Parana Delta, the Pampas and the Patagonia regions, the island of Tierra del Fuego and the Archipelago; and among the *Araucanians.* The *Inca* as well as the modern *Aymara* and *Quechua* use tanned skins in the same manner. Likewise, tanned deerskin bedding is used by some of the Montana tribes, such as the *Jivaro.*

Plaited sleeping mats are utilized in many parts of the Amazon, in east Brazil and, more rarely, in the Andes. The mats are made of thick totora reed in the Andes, of buriti palm in the east Brazil, and elsewhere of other types of palm leaves. Cloth is woven in most parts of Amazonia, but the use of woven blankets of cotton or wool is generally restricted to the Andean region. However, in post-European times, woven blankets were also used by the Pampas and Patagonia tribes.

Platform beds. Platform beds are found in east Brazil, in the Montana region, and in certain parts of the Andes. Many authors think that this form of bed is an early type, which was replaced in many regions by the hammock.

In east Brazil, the *Timbira,* the *Bororo,* the *Southern Cayapo,* and the *Caingang* use a platform bed which consists of four posts, two cross bars, and cross strands of buriti bast. Such beds are about 20 inches high, and from 20 inches to 10 frrt in width. The beds for the young girls are raised to a height of 6½ feet, and partitioned off with mats. Platform beds are not found in the Chaco proper, but such typical tribes as the *Mbaya, Kaskiha,* and *Guana* adopted them after they moved into the Mato Grosso region. Some of the *Guarani* groups have adopted platform beds in recent years, and this type has a questionable antiquity among the *Chiquito* and *Churapa* of the Mojos-Chiquitos region.

In the Montana area, platform beds are found among the *Omagua* and *Cocama,* and appear to be ancient among such tribes as the *Quijo, Canelo, Candoshi, Andoa, Cahuapanans, Yuracare,* and *Chane.* Later they spread to the *Panoan* groups and to the *Yameo, Leco, Mosetene,* and *Chimane.* Today the standard type of bed for the *Jivaro* is composed of four upright forked posts and two cross bars, with split banboo laid between. They are usually covered with deerskin mats. These beds measure 1½ m. long, 30 to 40 cm. high at the back, and 25 cm. at the front. A horizontal bar near the foot of the bed serves as a foot rest. Platform beds, screened with cotton cloth, were used by the *Chibcha* of Colombia, and are also mentioned for the *Cueva* and *Choco*. There are descriptions of *Inca* platform beds, but their antiquity in this region is doubtful. The modern *Araucanians* make a four-posted bed, with two cross-poles, and skins hung between.

Sleeping benches. In the houses of the modern *Aymara* and *Quechua,* and also in some of the *Inca* houses, a solid sleeping bench of clay or pirca is built across one or both ends of a room. This is then covered with skins and blankets, and serves as a bed for the entire family.

Hammocks. Hammocks are common in most parts of the Tropical Forest. They have many advantages for this type of environment, since they offer protection against damp ground, snakes, ticks, and the like. Fires are sometimes built under the hammocks so that the smoke furnishes further protection from insect pests. Hammocks are not found in east Brazil, with the exception of the *Cre'pumkateye,* who are known to have borrowed them. They are likewise rare in the Chaco, although used as baby cradles by some groups. The *Guana,* who arrived in the Chaco area recently, and the missionized *Zamuco* are exceptions. Hammocks are not used by some of the simpler Amazonian tribes, such as the *Nambicuara, Paumari, Macu,* and the *Bororo.* Furthermore, hammocks and platform beds have a mutually exclusive distribution. However, hammocks have a wide distribution in Amazonia, the Guianas, Venezuela, and the West Indies, and are also found among the *Goajiro* of Venezuela, the *Cuna* and *Choco* of tropical Colombia, and the *Cueva* of Colombia.

There are several types of hammocks. The simplest is that used by the *Ipurina* while traveling: three long bark strips tied at both ends. The *Timbira* and *Sherenta* of east Brazil likewise improvise a hammock by interlacing buriti leaves. The *Witoto* hammock consists of a series of cross-strings tied between two heavy side cords. Some hammocks, like those used by the *Tucuna,* are made in a netting technique. Others are made with long warp threads joined together at set intervals, as illustrated by the *Chiriguano.* Finally, the commonest type of *Carib* and *Arawak* hammock is woven on a loom.

Hammocks are made of many materials, of which palm fibers are the commonest. Chambira, tucum, and caraguta are other fibers utilized. Cotton is likewise common and some use is now made of wool. Combinations were also used, such as fiber warps and cotton wefts. Hammocks are used for other purposes than sleeping. For example, they are used as capes by the *Caraja,* and as cradles in the Pilcomayo-Bermejo region. Among the *Choco,* hammocks are only used by children. The *Chiriguano* and others use their hammocks only in the daytime.

Miscellaneous sleeping equipment. True mosquito nets were manufactured by some of the Amazonian groups. The *Guato* make a tent-shaped net of tucum fibers, intertwined with cotton cloth, which they stretched between two trees or posts. Similar woven cloth nets are reported for the *Omagua,* and the *Choco* tribes. The *Choco* used wooden blocks for pillows which are unknown elsewhere. In post-European times, the *Tehuelche* of Patagonia made a bolster of cloth stuffed with horsehair.

Wooden stools. Wooden stools, carved from a single block, are a common article of furniture in most of the Tropical Forest region, although rare elsewhere. They are not found in east Brazil, in the Chaco, or in the southern hunting region, and they are rare in the Andean area. In many groups such stools were reserved for honored guests or individuals of high prestige.

One type of stool, for example, that of the *Witoto,* is nothing more than a tub-shaped wooden block. Commoner types are low benches supported by two projecting side feet, or by four legs. The seats are oval and slightly hallowed. The four-legged seats, often carved in animal shapes, are found among the *Guato, Omagua, Tucuna, Guarani, Cocama,* in the Guianas, and along the upper Xingu. Somewhat similar four-legged carved stools are mentioned for the *Inca* of Peru, where they were reserved for people of high rank. The two-sided stools, also carved or painted, are used by the *Jivaro, Yurina, Shipaya, Asurini, Tupi,* and *Curuaya.* Turtle shells shaped into stools are mentioned for the Guianas tribes. In Colombia, low stools made of one piece of wood, both with and without backs, are reported for the *Chibcha.* In the archeological sites of Manabi in western Ecuador, stone stools are found which have U-shaped seats supported by carved animal figures.

Finally, the *Araucanians* used crude wooden stools.

Log benches. Short logs are used for benches by many Amazonian tribes. Some of these, such as those used by the *Guato,* are crude; others, in the Guianas, have the top side of the log smoothed; and still others, common in the Montana region, are split logs which serve as stools. Among the upper Xingu tribes, logs are placed along each side of the guest house to be used as seats. In this latter region, the *Naravute* make bark benches.

Tables and chairs. Tables and chairs, such as the rawhide ones made by the *Goajiro,* are generally considered to be European intorductions. However, there are reports of the use of tables in southwest Brazil, and this implies that it is an ancient practice.

Storage articles. Storage baskets are common house articles in the Amazon and in east Brazil. Large jars are used for storage by the *Chiriguano,* the *Inca,* and some of the modern *Aymara* and *Quechua.* In modern times, the *Araucanians* have made wooden trunks for storage purposes, and also use hide sacks for storing clothing in the house.

Fireplaces. In general, constructed fireplaces are not common anywhere in South America. However, firepalces amde of three logs are reported for the *Cuna,* and those built of stones are mentioned for the Guiana tribes and the *Southern Cayapo.*

Stove. Underground or earth ovens are used in east Brazil and many other places, but true clay stoves are found only in the Andean region, among the *Aymara, Quechua, Uru-Chipaya,* and the *Inca.* These are a type of pottery brazier with three top holes for burners, and a side opening for inserting the grass fuel.

Fire fans. Fire fans with handles are found throughout all the Tropical Forest region and in adjacent Chaco area. In western and southern Amazonas, the fans are made of feathers, but in northern and eastern Amazonas, they are of plaited fibers.

Lamps. In general, the only light at night was that of the fire, although torches may have been used. The *Omagua* and *Cocama* lighted their houses with copal resin wrapped in leaves. The modern *Aymara* use pottery-bowl lamps with rag wicks and fat tor fuel.

Manioc equipment. In the Chaco, east Brazil, and throughout the Tropical Forest area where bitter manioc is a principal crop, the standard equipment for preparing manioc and extracting the prussic-acid poison is practically part of the household furniture. Such equipment consists of grating boards, a press to squeeze the pulp of the grated manioc, a sifter for separating out the flour, and various containers and platters for cooking the final product. The graters vary regionally. In east Brazil, the grater is any piece of rough bark, and in eastern Bolivia, the prickly root of a palm is used. In the southern Amazon, upper Amazon, and the Atlantic coast region of Brazil, the grater is a curved board with inserted wooden points. In the north, in the Guianas, and in Venezuela, the curved board is fitted with stone points. In the Chaco, the board is flat, fitted with wooden points, and has a handle at each end. A cylindrical, basketry press with a loop at each end is used as a squeezer everywhere except East Brazil. There the grated manioc is wrapped in buriti bast strips which are then twisted in order to squeeze out the poison. The sifter is also of basketry, either square or oval in shape. Large, flat, clay platters are usually used for baking the cassava bread. In east Brazil, flat stones are substituted, or the batter may be made into a pie and cooked in an underground oven.

Mortars and Pestles. In all of the Tropical Forest region, and in the Chaco, wooden mortars and pestles from part ot the household equipment. The commonest mortar is made from a cylindrical log, with a hole, about 5 inches in diameter and 15 inches deep, hallowed out of one end. Some mortars, used in the Guianas, have an hourglass shape and are painted in geometric designs. In east Bolivia, the mortar is a hallowed-out log in the form of a trough. The pestle is a wooden pole as much as 10 feet in length.

Metates. Throughout the Andean region, from Colombia to Chile, stone metates, without legs, have been in use from early archeological periods up to the present. Grinding manos are equally common, but in Bolivia, and perhaps elsewhere, a curved stone was used as a rocking grinder, called a batan. The *Tehuelche* used a stone grinder for preparing seeds, and the *Tupinamba* made a wooden grinder fitted with two handles.

Ladders. In spite of the size of many of the houses in the Amazon, ladders or stairways are rare. Notched logs were used as ladders by the *Cuna* of Panama and by the *Timbira* of East Brazil.

Cradles. Cradleboards, in which children were securely tied, are mentioned for the *Ona, Tehuelche,* and *Araucanians,* and are represented in pottery designs in the early archeological periods of Peru. The *Araucanians* use basketry cradles, suspended from the roofs of the houses. The *Bororo* make a cradle by attaching the four corners of a mat to the roof beams. A skin swung between two posts served as a cradle for the *Mocovi* of the Chaco. As previously mentioned, hammocks are used as cradles by the tribes of the Pilcomayo-Bermejo region, and also by the *Omagua* and *Cocama.*

Fly swatters. In spite of the troublesome insect pests, fly swatters are a rarity. However, fine fiber cloth attached to a handle was used for this purpose by the *Guato, Chamacoco,* and *Morotoco.*

Drums. Large signal drums, made from hollowed-out logs, are a standard part of the household equipment among the tribes of the northwest Amazon, such as the *Jivaro,* and the *Witoto.* These are used both as war and as signal drums. To give better resonance, logs are suspended from the house rafters, with one end raised higher than the other.

It is quite evident that house furniture was not elaborate anywhere among the South American Indians. In fact, everywhere the house served principally as a shelter rather than a center of constant activity. Even in the Andean region, where houses were made in more pemanent fashion, most of the daylight hours were spent in activities outside the house, which in turn was used principally as sleeping quarters. The absence of windows, proper heating, and general uncleanliness, made houses a place to spend as little time in as possible. As a consequence, little attention and effort went into the manufacture of furniture.

FURS were used by the North American Indians primarily for warmth in clothing and were the most effective natural material available for protection in cold environments. They were also used to some extent for clothing ornamentation and as items of luxury or wealth. Fur was most commonly worn in the Arctic, Subarctic, northeasten United States, Prairies, and Plains where tribes lived primarily by hunting and had an abundant supply of hides. They were used to a lesser extent in all other major areas north of Mexico.

The fur robe, taken from large game such as buffalo, elk, or bear, was commonly used in the Eastern Woodlands, Northwest Coast, Plateau, and California, and used to some extent through much of the Subarctic, northern Plains, and Southeast. Fur robes of smaller skins also were widely used, especially where larger game was scarce. These were made by two methods: sewing small furs together to form a patchwork robe, or cutting the furs, especially of rabbits, into long strips and weaving these in various ways into blankets.

The Eskimos utilized fur to the greatest degree, incorporating it in their tailored clothing to the extent demanded by climate. Elsewhere in North America fur was incorporated in a variety of ways in stockings, leggings, moccasins, shires, dresses, and skirts. Detachable fur sleeves, fur mittens, fur hats, and muffs with the fur turned inside were used in many areas where climate encouraged them. In parts of the Arctic and Subarctic, fur sandals were sometimes worn over boots to afford quietness in stalking or traction on smooth ice.

Before the arrival of Europeans, the Indians hunted primarily for the food, hide, and fur necessary for survival. European settlement brought the steel trap, the gun, and a tremendous new demand for furs. The fur trade and the efficiency of steel hunting devices encouraged wide scale hunting primarily for fur and hide for trade by many tribes and Anglo-Americans. Serious depletion of furbearing populations including the beaver in the Northeast and Subarctic, the sea otter on the Northwest Coast, and many others followed. The loss of furbearing game and their ranges, the introduction of modern textile clothing, and other factors largely eliminated the use of fur in Indian culture.

FUR TRADE in North America was an attraction for all traders and has been a social, economic, and political influence from the beginnings of settlement. The trade involved not only the acquisition of furs from the Indians, but the giving in exchange for the furs the products of European manufactured cloth, beads and metal ornaments, copper and iron kettles, awls, spoons, knives, hatchets and axes, hoes, firearms, powder, and lead for shot.

To the English colonies in North America the Indian trade was important. To the Dutch, Swedes, Russians, and French it was indeed the very life-blood of their North American colonies. (Of the dominantly fur-trading groups, the Russians appear very late and very far away from the Atlantic coastal area where North American history was shaped.)

The French were as early on the scene as the English in Virginia, and they remained on the scene until late in the eighteenth century.

The fur traders policy appears to have undergone early developments which later continued to determine its direction independent of influence by or upon the contemporary development of English policy.

The French Crown and the trading companies, alike in their activities on the St. Lawrence River and in the trans-Allegheny regions, were concerned almost exclusively with the development of the Indian trade.

The success of this trade depended upon having the Indians spend as much time as possible in hunting fur-bearing animals, notably the beaver. The beaver furnished the raw material of the important French hat industry. In exchange for the furs of the Indians industrial products such as firearms and ammunition, cloth, copper kettles, iron hoes and knives, and such were paid. French industries and the trading companies were also concerned in the maintenance of the Indian trade.

The missionaries wanted to see the Indian settled the year round in villages well-equipped with ploughs and hoes, axes, cattle, and orchards. They wanted the Indians to be allowed firearms only for defense of the mission villages. They wanted prohibition of the sale of liquor. But the trading interests urged the Indian out into the wilderness, gave him firearms to hunt with, which the Indian used as much to fight with; and in order better to cheat the Indian, or merely to please him and increase his dependence on them, they sold liquor. The missionaries were often, through the favour of the Crown, a real political power in the French colonies; but so long as the Indian trade was the dominant motive for French colonial development, the laws which they obtained to favour the mission policy were rather futile in the face of contrary practice on the part of the traders.

The trading interests sought to prevent the development of an agricultural colony in French North America, excepting the case of Louisiana,—which, however, was not under way until the early eighteenth century and was not of great importance. They not only objected to seeing the Indians reduced to a more settled life, but they objected to introducing French farmers. The only immigrants they wanted were men to serve as agents for the trade. Expansion of agricultural settlements would drive away or kill off the fur-bearing animals, and settlement of the Indians would take away the cheapest and best supply of born hunters of these animals. The Crown (and men like Champlain) frequently urged immigration and agricultural development. The New France Company during the period of its government, about thirty-five years, up to 1663, had established a population of only about two thousand French in North America and these were mostly concerned with trade. The West India Company was chartered partly on the condition that it introduce more and more immigrants, and in one year after receiving its charter in 1664 it had shipped over two thousand more French.

Fond du Lac spans the full story of the fur trade: established by the French, the post fell to the British after the Battle of Quebec, despite the revolution, they held it until after the war of 1812, when the U.S. took over.

Pierre Radisson and Sieur de Grosseilliers, fur traders and explorers, with Indian Guides. They were among the first white men to explore and trade in the Lake Superior region. From a painting by Frederic Remington, published in 1906.

A fur train from the far north.

Trading posts were established further and further to the westward by agreements between the colonial administration and the various Indian tribes. The Indian tribes were treated as independent nations, but the tribes invariably entered into alliance with the French and permitted the building of fortifications at the trading posts. Of course this method of treating the tribes as sovereign states was merely viewed as a temporary, necessary expedient. It was anticipated that gradually, under the influence of the spread of Christianity among the Indians, they would in time be brought to submission to the sovereignty and administration of the Crown and its agents. It was a policy of peaceful penetration dictated by the peculiar nature of French interests in America. And, especially through the activity of the mission establishments, beginning on the coast at the mouth of the St. Lawrence, tribe after tribe was gradually brought to surrender its sovereignty and submit to French administration, retaining, of course, its tribal government as a village or local government.

There was never any buying of land from the Indians of French North America. The trading interest and the government were gladly given land for posts and forts by the Indians who appreciated the advantage of a trade through which they obtained metal kettles, iron hoes, firearms, and so on; and who realized that the French were not planning to cut down the forests and plant the soil. And when an Indian tribe, in the regions of older settlement where French farmers were moving in, accepted French tuition and supervision usually in the person of the missionaries, it appreciated the fact that with a knowledge and use of European agricultural economy it had no need of its hunting lands. The Spanish method was then followed. Indians submitted to the Crown and received title only to their cultivated lands. The hunting grounds became Crown or company property and was sold to French Immigrants.

GABOURIE, FRED WILLIAM (Seneca; Oct. 5, 1922–   ), is an attorney whose practice has been concerned primarily with legal problems of minority peoples, especially Native Americans. Born in Los Angeles, California, and raised on the Six Nations Reserve, Ontario, he became a movie stunt man for Walt Disney productions in 1948. He was admitted to the California bar in 1965. Among his many activities, he is an advisor to the American Indian Law Center at the University of New Mexico and is a member of the steering committee of the Native American Rights Fund, Inc. Gabourie has produced two Indian radio programs in the Los Angeles area and is the author of *Justice and the Urban American Indian* (1971).

GABRIELINO were a complex, powerful, wealthy ethnic nationality whose influence spread throughout southern California. The name *Gabrielino* derives from the San Gabriel Mission. They spoke a Cupan language of the Takish family, were divided into small triblets, each with its own territory, based on a unilineal descent. They occupied the watersheds of the Los Angeles, San Gabriel and Santa Ana rivers, all of the Los Angeles basin from Aliso Creek in the south to Topanga Creek in the north, including the islands of San Clemente, San Nicholas and Santa Catalina. They lived in large villages occupied continuously in multiple lineage groupings. Predominant food resources were acorns, sage, yucca, cacti, deer, and small game, e.g., rabbits, wood rats and other rodents, quail and various waterfowl. Shellfish, sharks and fish were also important. The off-shore kelp beds were exploited as fishing areas for tuna and swordfish. On the islands, sea mammals, sea fowl, and several species of fish were important, e.g., sea lions, harbor seals, sea otters, scallops, mussels, limpets and sea urchins. Little clo-

Location in the 1500s

Tribes of California, 1500.

thing was used by the Gabrielino, body painting and tatooing were common. Women's skirts, breechclouts, rabbit blankets, deerhide capes, sandals, were used. Ritual costumes were made with the colorful plumage of different birds, decorated with shells and beads. Basket making was highly developed and stone steatite carvings decorated with incising, painting and insertion of clamshell beads and the like were used for practical everyday use as well as ceremonial and aesthetic use. Mortars and pestles, metates and monos, wooden stirrers, paddles, shell spoons, bark platters, wooden bowls, saws made of deer scalpula, bone or shell needles, fish hooks, scrapers, flakers, wedges, knives and flint drills were part of the ordinary tool inventory. Weapons included wooden war clubs, sinew backed bows, cane arrows, throwing clubs and slings. Houses were dome shaped, circular structures thatched with tule, holding up to 50 people, three or four famiies characteristically living in each. Sweat houses, menstrual huts and ceremonial enclosures were also built.

A moiety system existed and they were organized in a heirarchically ordered social class system with an elite class including chiefs and their immediate families, a well to do middle class, and a third class comprised of those engaged in ordinary socio-economic pursuits. Many individuals owned real estate and property boundaries were often marked by painting a copy of the owner's personalized tattoo on trees, posts or rocks. Villages were usually autonomous, but some were confederated. The authority of leaders was legitimized by possession of the sacred bundles and esoteric knowledge which was privileged. Chiefs were wealthy, usually polygamous and sometimes were heads of multi-village confederations. They administered to community solidarity and welfare. A bureaucracy of others, chief's assistants, messengers, shamans and ritualists assisted in the political and religious functions of the group. Rituals were held for birth, puberty, marriage, and death. A constant state of enmity existed between some groups within the Gabrielino and their neighbors. Feuds were commonly passed from father to son, for generations. Ritualized song fights served as ways of expressing hostility of a feud. Interpersonal disputes were adjudicated by village chiefs. Intermarriage with neighboring tribes was common, e.g., Luiseno, Chumash, Cahuilla. They traded materials as far as the Colorado River and the central valley of California. They obtained acorn seeds, obsidian, and deer skin in exchange for shell beads, dry fish, sea otter pelts, shells, and seatite. The presence of southwestern pottery in some Gabrielino sites suggests a very long and ancient trade relationship over long trade corridors. Not much is known about Gabrielino religious systems. Several creation stories exist. The world was created out of a state of chaos and it was fixed upon the shoulders of seven giants. Their prime sacred characters are heaven and earth, brother and sister; six different creations made the world and gave birth to a god-like being Wiyot, who ruled the people for a long time but was eventually killed by his sons. Later a god-like person called Chingishnish established a religion practiced at the time of European contact. Other important cosmological figures were sun, moon, crow, raven, owl and eagle. Prime values of Gabrielino religious life include respect for the aged, maleness and secrecy.

There were possibly from 50 to 100 mainland villages occupied simultaneously by Gabrielinos. Populations were decimated quickly after contact with Europeans. European explorers observed Santa Catalina in 1520 and Santa Catalina in 1602. The Spanish settled in 1769, Mission San Gabriel was established in 1771. Conversions came rapidly and the social organization of the Gabrielino changed significantly. By 1785, Indian protests and revolt were frequent. By the early 1800s, many Indians were integrated into the mission system. Others continued to resist the European presence. In 1833 the missions were secularized and many of the Gabrielinos were shifted to other areas. Many remained in the immediate vicinity of the area. Gabrielino presence in the area was significant until the 1860s; after this the Gabrielino disappeared as a visible ethnic entity, but in 1979 Gabrielinos still maintain their ethnicity and identify very closely with their cultural heritage.

LOWELL JOHN BEAN

GALL (Hunkpapa Sioux; 1840– Dec. 5, 1894) was a war chief, famed for his military genius, especially for his conduct in the Battle of the Little Big Horn.

Born along the Moreau River in Dakota Territory, Gall (Indian name Pizi), who was a half-orphan, learned early the skills of hunting and fighting from tribal elders, one of whom, Sitting Bull, adopted him as a younger brother. From Sitting Bull, too, he learned to distrust and detest the white man, although he later turned against his mentor and became a friend to his former enemies.

Gall was with Sitting Bull on June 25, 1876, when Col. George A. Custer attacked the combined Indian village on the Little Big Horn. Maj. Marcus Reno's command was the first to approach the village— with such speed that the Indians were on the verge of retreat. Gall's two wives and three children were among the first to die. "It made my heart bad," Gall said later. So it was with vengeance that he led the Indian counterattack that drove Reno back into the woods. He then forced him into making a full-fledged, hasty retreat that turned into a rout. With Reno held impotent, Gall was able to divert many of the warriors for a frontal attack on the hapless Custer.

With Sitting Bull, Gall fled to Canada after the Custer battle, but in 1880 he separated his followers from the old chief's and, on January 1, 1881, surrendered to Maj. Guido Ilges at Poplar River, Montana.

Gall spent the remainder of his life on the Standing Rock Reservation. The rift between Sitting Bull

Gall

and Gall was permanent. The old chief never changed his mind about the perfidity of white men, while Gall became a highly respected friend of the whites. He was influential in seeking government education of Indian children and in bringing about the ratification of the treaty of March 2, 1889, by which the Sioux agreed to the division of their large reservation into separate reservations, with some portions ceded to the U.S. From 1889 he served as a judge of the court of Indian offenses at Standing Rock Reservation in North and South Dakota.

GALLINAZO. The Mochica culture reached its climax and declined without apparent outside interruption. The type site of the Gallinazo Period which follows is in Viru Valley, and the style is also found elsewhere in the Mochica area. Gallinazo is quite distinct from Mochica, although certain influence is seen in the vessel shapes such as modeled figure jars, stirrup-spouts, and dippers. On the other hand, Gallinazo ceramics are characterized by negativepainted rather than positive designs, and by some new shapes which include spout and bridge forms, bird vessels of a simple style, and double jars. The period shows little if any Coast Tiahuanaco influence, and its closest affiliations are with the Recuay culture of the North Highlands. The Gallinazo style is associated with rectangular house foundations on the platforms of pyramids. Burial mounds contain both extended and flexed skeletons. Spindle whorls, textile fragments, figurines, and copper, gilded copper, and siver are all found.

Neither the Gallinazo nor the Coast Tiahuanaco Periods completely eliminate the Mochica tradition, which is revived in modified form in the later Chimu Period. One hypothesis is that with the intrusion of outside cultures, such as Gallinazo and Coast Tiahuanaco, Mochica moved northward to the valleys of Lambayeque and Piura, where it was able to carry along in modified form.

Gallinazo ceramics.

GAMES. Indians were fond of games of chance and had a great variety of them. For each there were special pieces of equipment and special rules. Dice games were played with wild plum or peach stones and cherry pits, beans, deer and elk horn or bone buttons, and carved wooden tally sticks or counters.

Peach Stone Game. (Also known as Dish Game). Peach stones were filed or cut down to an oval shape so that they looked like smoothed-off hickory nuts. One side was slightly burned to blacken it. The game was played by placing six of the peach stones, all with the same color up, in a flat bottom earthen or wooden dish carved out of a knot or burl of a tree, sometimes decorated with carving. The bowl was then shaken violently and brought down on a pile of skins with a whack. The count was based upon the number of pieces of each color exposed. If all of one color were up the count was ten, all but one of the colors up counted five, and two of a color up counted two. The counters were red beans. An equal number of beans were given each side and the game was played until one side had won all the beans. Sometimes it took as long as four days or more to play a game.

The peach stone game was played three times a year in the longhouse — at the Indian New Year, the Maple Sugar Thanksgiving Festival, and the Green Corn Festival in September.

Deer Button Game. The deer button game was played by two or more with eight buttons, an inch in diameter, carved out of deer bone and blackened on one side. They were cupped in the hands and thrown down, usually on a blanket. The relative number of black and white faces turned up determined the count. If they all turned up white, the count was twenty; if seven of the eight turned up white it counted four; if six turned up it counted two. The game continued until one player had won a bank of fifty beans. Sometimes the buttons were decorated with dots and with circular and radiating designs.

Ring, or Cup, and Pin Game. The ring, or cup, and pin game enjoyed by many Indian tribes was played with seven conical bones loosely strung on a leather

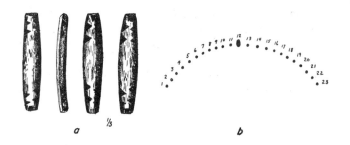

Tsuka game, Choroti. A, dice; B, arrangement of holes for game.

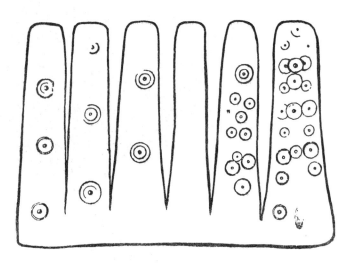

Huayru die, Quechua of Equador. Schematic drawing of the six sides with circles indicating count.

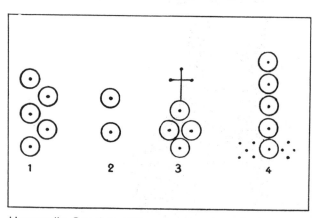

Huayru die, Quechua of Ecuador. Counts on the four faces of the pyramidal die.

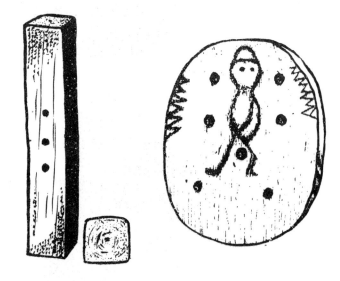

Canelo gaming die and disk. Left; prism die. Right: disk board for maize-grain game.

thong, about eight inches in length. The bones were usually smaller at one end and could be slipped into each other. At one end of the thong was a small piece of fur and at the other a hickory stick three and one-half inches long. The game was played by holding the stick in the hand, swinging the bones upward, and trying to insert the pointed end of the stick into one or more of the bones as they were descending. Each bone had a value of its own, the highest value being on the lowest bone, and the one who could total up the highest score was the winner.

HOOP GAMES

Hoop games were played with shooting sticks, poles, spears and javelins. Hoops of different sizes were made of a bent, unpeeled sapling, usually of hickory or maple, tied around the overlapping ends with bark. Some of the hoops were filled with an elaborate hexagonal weaving. Spears varied in size from small darts to poles fifteen feet long.

Hoop and Javelin Game. The javelin was five or six feet in length and three-fourths of an inch in diameter and was usually made of hickory or maple. It was sharpened at one end, finished with care and striped spirally. The hoop was eight inches in diameter and left open or filled with a netting. Sometimes the javelin was thrown horizontally by placing a fore finger at its end and supporting it with thumb and second finger; in other cases it was held in the center and thrown with the hand raised above the shoulder.

Fifteen to thirty players with three to six javelins apiece were arranged on each of two sides, according to tribal divisions. The javelins were the forfeit, and the game was gained by the party which won them. A line was mapped out on which the hoop was to be rolled and the two bands of players were stationed on opposite sides at designated distances from it. The hoop was rolled on the line by one party in front of the other and the javelins were thrown. The players who failed, handed their javelins over to the other side.

The side which threw the greatest number of javelins through the hoop as it rolled, won the game.

Hoop and Dart Game. The hoop and dart game was played with a hoop, made of a sapling, and darts four or five feet in length, of which each player usually had two.

The players lined up on two sides about ten feet apart. A member of one party threw the hoop so that it went spinning along the ground at a rapid rate and the others launched their darts at it. The object was to stop the hoop as it rolled by, impaling it. If a player missed, his dart was forfeited, but if it went under the hoop, he retained it.

Hoop and Pole Game. The hoop and pole game was played with a hoop made of an unpeeled bent sapling tied with bark, sixteen inches in diameter, and six poles, seven feet in length. Five or six persons played. The hoop was rolled and all threw their poles. The one whose pole stopped the ring owned it. The others then

shot in turn, and the owner of the hoop took all of the poles that missed it, and shot them at the hoop, winning those that he put through it. If two men stopped the hoop, they divided the poles.

Snow Snake. Snow snake, which may be called the national game of the Iroquois, is still a popular winter sport. Snow snakes were smooth, polished, flexible rods made from various kinds of hard wood (maple, walnut, or hickory). They were from five to nine feet in length and one inch in diameter at the head, tapering to about half an inch at the tail. A slight notch was made near the small end, or the upper surface was left slightly concave near the end to allow for a better finger hold. The head was rounded and turned up slightly on the under side like the fore part of a skate runner. Today the head is pointed with lead to help its balance. The snow snake was made with precision and given a fine finish.

When there had been an abundant snow, a smooth, shallow course was laid out on a level stretch, sometimes slightly down grade, by pulling a smooth barked log from ten to eighteen inches in diameter in a straight line through the track for from 90 to 120 rods. This packed the snow, making a trough 10 to 18 inches deep. Any protruding objects were removed. The course was then sprinkled with water to form an ice crust.

When the game was to be played those taking part gathered at one end of the track and in turn threw the "snakes" with force, skill, and accuracy so as to make them travel the longest distance possible in the shortest time. Before it was thrown the snake was rubbed with a skin saturated with some secret "medicine" (oil or wax). The player grasped the snake firmly in the right hand placing the forefinger in the notch that had been cut in the snake toil and, balancing it with the left hand, stopped toward the ground with the snake held horizontally over the rut in the snow. There with a few quick, short steps he threw the snake with considerable force along the rut. The snake travelled with a speed of 60 or 80 rods. A goal-maker indicated where each snake stopped. Victory was declared when the player or team had sent four or more sticks over the greatest distance in specified number of trials.

Target Shooting. Target shooting was carried on with a bow from three and one half to four feet long. It had a difficult spring which could scarcely be bent by an inexperienced person and the arrow was shot out with great force. The arrows were three feet long, feathered at the small end with a twist to make them revolve in flight. Every man had his arrows marked so that he could identify them. Originally the arrows were pointed with a piece of flint, horn bone, or chert (rockflint) which made them exceedingly dangerous missiles, penetrating deeply any object which they hit.

Throwing the Arrow. Throwing the arrow was a game requiring swiftness and muscles. The person who threw the greater number of single arrows into the air before the first one thrown fell to the ground won.

SOUTH AMERICA

GAMES. Some of the more striking general features of the game and amusement complex of South American Indian culture are: the relative poverty of the game pattern in the Fuegian and early Patagonian and Pampean areas, and strangely enough in the Andean, as compared with that of the areas north and east of these; the particularly rich pattern of the Chacoan area, at least in the modern period; a seeming predominance of quiet games, mostly dice games, in the Andean area, contrasting with the prominence of active, often strenuous or violent, sports in the *Araucanian* area to the south and in most of the remaining areas of the continent east of the Andean Cordillers; the absence of team games toward the southern end of the continent, in the Fuegian area and earlier it seems in the Patagonian; the marked western distribution of gambling, in earlier times confined almost entirely to the *Araucanian* and middle Andean areas, and even in more recent days found almost exclusively in areas (Patagonian, Pampean, Chacoan, Northern Andean) adjacent to and influenced by these. The *Araucanian* area links typologically and probably historically with both the Andean through its characteristic dice games and gambling and with the Chacoan through its equally characteristic hockey game.

A comparison of the South American games and amusements in which implements are employed with those of North America reveals some interesting resemblances and contrasts.

Such North American games and amusements as *(a)* Games of chance: dice games, guessing games (stick, hand, four-stick, moccasin); *(b)* games of dexterity: archery, snowsnake, hoop and pole, ring and pin, ball (racket, hockey, double ball, ball race, football, ball juggling, and four additional highly localized and specialized ball games); *(c)* minor amusements: shuttlecock (with and without battledore), tipcat, quoits, stone throwing, shuffleboard (resembling ninepins), jackstraws, swing, tilts, tips (hand-, cord-and whip-spun, simple and humming), bull-roarer, buzzer, popgun, beanshooter, and cat's cradles.

Of these all are found in South America except guessing games of chance, double ball, ball race, the four specialized and localized ball games, tipcat (European?) and jackstraws (European?). The chief North American games lacking in South America are the first three of the foregoing: guessing games of chance, double ball, and ball race.

Of the implement games found in South America but lacking in North America the most striking are the log race of the *Ge* of the Eastern Brazilian area and the pillma ball game of the *Mapuche-Huilliche* of the *Araucanian*.

The data are not available for an adequate corresponding comparison of South American with North American games and amusements in which implements are not used.

Chocktaw ball players with lacrosse sticks, from a lithograph by George Catlin, 1836.

GANADA MUCHO (Navajo; fl. 1860s and 1870s) was a headman at the time of the Navajo roundup at Bosque Redondo, New Mexico Territory, in the early 1860s. He was one of the tribal leaders who signed the treaty of June 1, 1868, and returned with his people to the new Navajo Reservation. In 1871, together with Manuelito, he succeeded Barboncito as co-chief of the Navajo.

GARCIA, MARCELINO (San Juan Pueblo; June 2, 1932–   ), is a tribal official and a founder of the Oke-Oweenge Arts Cooperative in San Juan Pueblo, New Mexico. Garcia has worked for the Bureau of Indian Affairs as a counselor at the Santa Fe Indian School (1955–62) and as an adult educator at the San Juan Pueblo (1962–).

GARRY, JOSEPH R. (Coeur d'Alene; March 8, 1910–   ), is chairman of his tribal council, the first Indian elected to the Idaho State Legislature (first as a representative and then as a senator), five times the president of the National Congress of American Indians, and long-time president of the Affiliated Tribes of Northwest Indians. Born in a tipi on the Coeur d'Alene Reservation, Idaho, he did not speak English until he was ten years old. One of the most prominent spokesmen for Indian rights, he was a leading opponent of the U.S. government's policy of terminating federal services for Native Americans.

GATEWOOD, HENRY, III (Navajo; March 17, 1929–   ), was the first Arizona Indian to become a superintendent in the Arizona public school system. Born at Fort Defiance, Arizona, he was raised on the Navajo Reservation. He directed the Navajo Community Center in 1961, helped bring a sawmill to the reservation as a board member of Navajo Forest Products, and became superintendent of the Chinle Public School District in 1969.

GAVIÕES are those Indians which belong to two Timbira tribes, currently divided in: The Gaviões of the West and the Gaviões of the East. This division occurred approximately in 1850. This article focuses on the Gaviões of the West.

The name *Gavião* was given by the Brazilian people. The Timbira call themselves *Pukopüe* or *Pukobye*, originating from the names *pukóp* or *pukób* (*Dioscorea*, sp.). This denomination is still given to Gaviões of the East. The Gaviões of the West refers to the division *Parkateyê* and *Kuikateyê*.

Social and Cultural Boundaries and Subdivisions. The Timbira, as well as other Gé Indians, were classified as "marginal people"—hunting and food gathering nomads. However, during their early period they worked in agriculture due to a possible influence by neighboring groups in the tropical forest. The Gaviões, as well as the other Timbira tribes

are placed in the Eastern nucleus of the cultural area Tocantins - Xingú. There is a basic cultural pattern among the tribes, whose groups are distincted by the accessory elements.

Territory. The Timbira live in an area between the 3rd-9th south Lat., 42°-49° of Long. west (states of Maranhão, Pará and Goiás). The predominant part of this area consist of steppes of *campos cerrados*, with galeria forests along the brooks and rivers. Absolutely pure steppe occured only in the upper Pindaré Country, where the Pukopüe and Krikati live. The Gaviões of the West, after the division of tribes in 1850, had moved to the tropical forest, between the Tocantins and Capim rivers.

Language. The Gaviões speak a dialect of the Gé linguistics family, that is closely related with the dialect of Krikati, neighboring of Pukopüe.

Summary of tribal culture

Subsistence and economy. Gathering of fruits, hunting, fishing and agriculture. Crops: sweet potato, yams, manioc, maize, peanut, cotton, papaw, bottle, annato, *banana* and *kupá* (*Cissus* sp.), the most important of the traditional Timbira crop. They have not cultivated tobacco and other plants used as stimulants and narcotics.

Technology and arts. Basketry-Weaving baskets, firefans and mats, palm leaves and *aruma* (a Maranthaceae). Feather headresses only worn by males. Cotton stripes and cords applied in female dresses.

Musical Instruments: a horn with a resounding bottle, bamboo flute and a bone whistle.

Labor division: man— hunting, fishing, basket wearing, weapons, housing, agriculture; women—cotton eaving and planting crops; both sexes—planting and moving the crops. The Gaviões do not make pottery and canoes.

Life cycle: *Couvade* when a son or daughter is born. The father does not work for several days and eats vegetables only.

Puberty. During the first menstrual period the girls are isolated in tents, where their mothers or other women can visit them only during their meals.

Burials. The corpses are buried in rounded caves (today, they are also rectangular), with their head placed toward the sunrise. They are buried with their personal items.

Mourning. The relatives of the dead have a short haircut. The one who fills has a short round haircut in the form of a crown, scrapes his body and remains inside his tent for several days.

Social Organization: monogamic marriages. Marriages between close relatives are not allowed. However, this kind of marriage may happen when there is not enough women. The local groups were composed by extensive families, with matrilocal residence; now they are composed by nuclear families. The kinship terminology is Crow, including the names denomination from the mother's side—from the mother's brother to the sister's son.

Leadership. In the beginning there were two leaders in each group and the other outside. Now, there is only one leader. The transmission is not by heredity.

Traditions and folklore. The festivities are after the planting, and in the corn crops. In the beginning there were also festivities after war victories. During the festivities there is singing, dancing and a log race (the most traditional Timbira sport). The participants are divided into two ceremonial groups—*Pano* (macaw) and *Hok* (hawk).

Folk medicine and other systematic knowledge. The medicine man (*xamã*) is one who sucks with his mouth and massages the ill and makes him drink teas of roots, fruit peels and tree leaves. The xamã is also a soothsayer and it is believed that he can modify the course of things.

Religion and philosophy. The Gaviões have as divinities the *Piti (Sun) and Ingagê* (Moon), both considered males. When these divinities lived on earth, so they believed, trees were grown and the sky moved away from the earth. The distinction between days and nights started as well as the birth and death of humans and other beings. The fire was gotten from the jaguar. According to a modern myth the white-men (*kupen*) originated from the children of those who moved away from the group. Kupen's "new God" had taught them how to make "fire weapons" in order to kill their ancestors.

Summary of tribal history. In the beginning of the 19th century, the Gaviões were already considered as the best warriors among Timbira. In 1814, they attacked the Chapada Fort (today Grajaú) and burnt alive 30 people, and set fire to houses and boats. In 1815 they dispersed an expedition formed by those who lived at Pastos Bons and São Pedro Alcântara, with the participation of the Macamẹkran Indians. The Gaviões of the west, after settling at a new environment (Tocantins and Capin Rivers), had serious conflicts with the other Indian groups.

After 1920, the Brazil nuts collectors and the Gaviões started having serios conflicts in an area of about 180 kms (3°-5° south Lat.) The Gaviões were accused of serious acts of savagery, especially around the city of Marabá, whose population constantly asked for the total extermination of the tribe.

In 1937, the Indian Protection Service (IPS) established an agency called *Ipixuna*, in order to pacify the Gaviões, but they did not obtain any positive results. After one year the agency was visited on twelve occasions by friendly Gaviões. However, later during other visits they killed two of the agents because they could not supply them with tools and manioc flour. After this incident they never returned. Due to this situation, in 1943, the IPS obtained from the State of Pará, the place Mãe Maria for future location of Gaviões, while also changing the location of Ipixuna for another one called *Ambaua*.

The final pacification of the Gaviões of the West started in 1956. It started after a conflict between the two remaining Parkateyé groups. The losers searched shelter among the inhabitants of Itupiranga municipality (Tocantins). However, in 1957, as a small group due to illness, the Gaviões moved to the region along the Praia-Alta River (Coval) about 42 kms from Tocantins. There, they worked in the regional economic system as producers of nuts, animal hides and meats of wild animals until 1966. At this time the IPS moved them to Mãe Maria.

In 1958, the other group attacked the Brazil nuts plantation named *Chiqueirão*, and killed 2 people. After reacting to an enemy attack which used shotguns, they killed 2 and wounded other attackers. In 1959 twelve members of the group attacked the agency. They destroyed the hedges and killed the animals. In 1960, afraid of being attacked again by their enemies, they left their old village (Moju River) to live in Ambaua. Soon, they started to trade with inhabitants of Tucurui, under the supervision of the IPS. In 1972, FUNAI (former IPS) moved the remaining group to Mãe Maria. The Indian Payaré did not move with the group. He married a civilized woman and decided to incorporate into the Brazilian society.

The Kuikateé, after the massacre of 1955, isolated themselves in the "Igarapé dos Frades" between Pará and Maranhão. However, after 1964, their condition became more and more critical. At the beginning, the region where they lived was invaded by hunters who killed seven members of this group. Later, came agricultural settlers. In 1968, FUNAI, after contacts with the group, obtained from the federal government the isolation of the place to be used by Kuikateyé only, but the settlers did not leave the place. Then, they were attacked by the Indians who killed three of them and caused the evacuation of 600 familes. In 1969 after an agreement with the government of the State of Pará, FUNAI moved the Kuikateyé to Mãe Maria.

Parkateyé and Kuikateyé under the jurisdiction of FUNAI remained at Mãe Maria divided in two distinct Indian villages, along the PA-70 highway, which crosses the Indian reservations.

Contemporary tribal situation. The integration of the Gaviões of the West in the Brazilian society in short, is as follows: A decrease in subsistence activity due to their interest in obtaining commercial products especially Brazil nuts; disappearance of the large families and a change in the monetary economic system; the decline and alternation of the traditional practices as a consequence of the population decrease and external influences; and a negligence in the use of the tribal languages especially in the communication between adults and children. Today there are about 125 Gaviões of the West.

ARNAUD EXPEDITO

GEIOGAMAH, HANAY (Kiowa-Delaware; 20th century), is a playwright and the company director of the Native American Theatre Ensemble. His play *Foghorn* was first performed at Theater im Reichskabarett in West Berlin, Germany, on October 18, 1973.

GELELEMEND (Delaware; *c.* 1737–1811) was a chief at the outbreak of the American Revolution when the Delaware tribe, having been pressed west from their ancestral lands in the Delaware River Valley, was settled along the Muskingum River in Ohio. Although the precise date and place of his birth are not on record, Gelelemend ("Leader") was probably born in eastern Pennsylvania about 1737.

His father, a well-educated war captain called John Killbuck, was the son of the principal Delaware chief Netawatwees (*q.v.*). Following the death of Netawatwees, on October 31, 1776, Gelelemend—then known as Capt. John Killbuck, Jr.—became one of the three ranking chiefs of the Delaware. At that time each of the three subgroups, which were named after animals (Turtle, Turkey, and Wolf), had its own chief. U.S. Congressional records of 1779 describe Gelelemend as the "first chief," an honor reserved to the Turtle group.

During the Revolution, a majority of the Delaware fought with the English against the Americans. Gelelemend joined the Americans, fighting under the command of Col. Daniel Brodhead who commissioned him, and he became known as Col. William Henry. He was a signer of a peace treaty at Fort Pitt on September 17, 1778. In 1882 Gelelemend narrowly escaped death when he was with a band of pro-American Indians who were attacked by a group of American whites returning from the massacre of nearly 100 Christian Delaware at the village of Gnadenhütten, Ohio.

At the close of the war Gelelemend remained disassociated from his tribe and declined several invitations to resume the chieftaincy. He was baptized by the Moravian pastor David Zeisberger on April 12, 1789, under the name William Henry, and his three sons were also baptized and given the names John Henry, Charles Henry, and Christian Gottlieb. In 1792 he, his wife Rachel, and his sons migrated to Ontario, Canada, with other Christian, or Moravian, Indians settling at Fairfield on the Thames River. He lived there until August 15, 1798, when he and his family joined a party of Christian Indians who returned to the Muskingum and established a mission town called Goshen. Gelelemend died at Goshen in 1811 and is buried there. His descendants, who intermarried with whites, continued to use the surname Killbuck.

GEMMILL, MICKEY (Pit River; 1944–   ), is a former tribal chairman of the Pit River Indians of northern California and in the early 1970s was a leader in the demands for the recovery to his people of most of the land between Mt. Lassen and Mt. Shasta. The land was taken by the U.S. without payment in the 1850s when the U.S. Senate did not ratify the treaties made with the Indians. Gemmill and his followers were arrested several times in 1970 in attempts to occupy parts of these lands.

GENERAL ALLOTMENT ACT. *See* DAWES GENERAL ALLOTMENT ACT.

GENS. *See* CLAN AND GENS.

GEORGE II (Mosquito; fl. 18th century), the most independent and effective Mosquito Indian king of British-controlled Nicaragua, took his throne in 1776, a year after he visited his "cousin," King George III of England. An associate of such notable Mosquito chiefs as Colville Breton and Alparis Delce, George II profited from the conflict between Spain and England. The regent Stephen I succeeded him in 1800.

GEORGE III (Mosquito; fl. 19th century), was the Mosquito Indian king who succeeded the regent Stephen I in 1816. Son of the relatively independent George II, George III was firmly controlled by the British masters of Nicaragua's Mosquito Coast. After his premature death, his brother Robert took the puppet throne in 1825.

GEORGE IV (Mosquito; fl. 19th century), the Mosquito Indian king who ruled from 1841 to 1846, was 10th in a line of puppet kings controlled by England. Under his reign, the British forced Nicaragua to recognize an independent Mosquito territory. George IV was succeeded on his death by George V.

GEORGE V (Mosquito; fl. 19th century), was the Mosquito Indian king who ruled from 1846 to 1865. During his reign the British granted Nicaragua uncontested independence in the 1860 Treaty of Managua, foreshadowing the eventual end of the Mosquito puppet rulers. George V was succeeded on his death by William I.

GEORGE VI (Mosquito; fl. 19th century), was the Mosquito Indian king who ruled from 1879 to 1888. Under him, Mosquito rule became totally nominal. George VI was succeeded on his death by his nephew Jonathan I.

GEORGE, "CHIEF" DAN (Squamish; 1899–   ), is an actor who won acclaim and several awards, including the New York Film Critics Award for best supporting actor in 1970, for his portrayal of Old Lodge Skins in the film *Little Big Man.* Born near Vancouver, British Columbia, he worked as a logger and then for more than 25 years as a longshoreman. He began playing small parts for television and movies about 1960. Dedicated to improving the acceptance of Indians, he acted in "Cariboo County" (Canadian Broadcasting Company), *Cold Journey* (Canadian National Film

George, Chief Dan

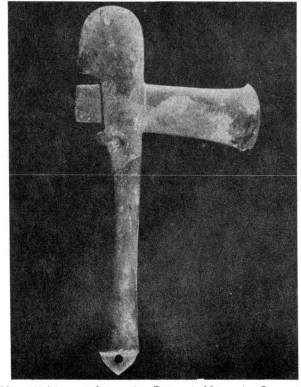

Monolithic axe from the Etowah Mounds, Georgia.

Board), and *The Ecstasy of Rita Joe*, a contemporary drama about Indians.

GEORGE, Lucy Squirrel (Cherokee; Nov. 17, 1897–   ), is a craftsman who taught herself basketweaving during the Great Depression, using honeysuckle instead of the usual river cane or white oak to gain a sales advantage. The results were strikingly original designs that have been exhibited worldwide. Born at Cherokee, North Carolina, she teaches her craft to the young on the Cherokee Reservation.

GEORGIA. In colonial times most of what is now Georgia was dominated by the Creek confederacy, except for the northern highlands that belonged to the Cherokee. These tribes formed a buffer between the Spanish of Fiorida, the English of Carolina, and the French of Louisiana, whose claims all overlapped. The Creeks allied themselves with the English, and grew rich in trade goods and dreaded in war power.

In 1733 James Oglethorpe founded the colony of Georgia at Savannah with the Creek's consent. Intended as an idealistic social experiment, the colony originally forbid slavery and rum, and was scrupulous in observing all treaties with the Creeks. Oglethorpe brought Tomochichi and other important chiefs to England where they were presented to George II, entertained, and shown off. But the Georgian utopia failed, and in 1752 became a normal colonial business venture.

English traders flourished through marriage alliances with prestigious Indian families. In time this game rise to a prosperous, elite Anglo-Indian class who lived in mansions and often held slaves. These families tended to be "progressive," *i.e.*, adapted to white culture, while the full-bloods remained "conservative." Some Anglo-Indians were self-serving adventurers, but others became great leaders of their people.

During the Revolution the Creeks supported the British, and consequently, in 1790, were forced to cede land to the Americans. Their treaty, however, guaranteed their right to most of Georgia. This angered the Georgia settlers who had not fought against England to secure their state for the Creeks. The Georgians were further angered when, in 1802, they ceded their western frontier (present Alabama and Mississippi) to the U.S. in exchange for a promise of Indian removal that the government took no steps to implement.

In the war of 1812, the Creeks again supported the British. Defeated by Andrew Jackson at Horseshoe Bend, they were forced to cede Alabama and southern Georgia, but still held central Georgia, a situation that the Georgians found intolerable. The U.S. sought further treaty consessions, but after 1824 the Creeks refused to cede any more land and made it a capital offense for any Creek to do so. When chief William McIntosh later ceded land he was summarily executed.

Oglethorpe, the founder of Georgia, presenting Chief Tomochichi of the Creeks and other Indians to the Lord Trustees of the Colony of Georgia in 1734 in London.

LOCATIONS OF
CREEK (MUSKHOGI) INDIANS

(And Original Range)

LEGEND

Location
(Broken-line area — former Indian Reservation)

Original Range

None of these consessions appeased the Georgians. Only when the Georgians threatened the U.S. with war in 1827 did the government negotiate the Creek's removal to the west. This left the Georgians free to turn their attention to the Cherokee, who had meanwhile developed into a nation of propserous agriculturists, with their own constitution, alphabet, and schools, and a firm determination to remain in Georgia.

Ignoring the Cherokee's independent status, Georgia extended its laws over them. When Samuel Worcester, a minister to the Cherokees, was arrested for an infringement of Georgia law, he took his case to the Supreme Court. The decision that Georgia had no jurisdiction over the Cherokee, handed down by John Marshall in the case *Worcester v.s. Georgia,* is today the basis of Indian legal status.

In defiance of this decision, Georgia allotted Cherokee lands to whites who seized them by force, making life intolerable for the Indians. A faction of Cherokees ceded their lands in self-defense, but the great Cherokee chief John Ross refused. The forced removal of the Cherokee, known as the Trail of Tears *(q.v.),* occurred in 1838. Their subsequent history, except for a small group who escaped to North Carolina, belongs to Oklahoma.

JEANETTE LERNER

Embossed copper, Georgia.
Incised and painted pottery

Pottery Pipe, Georgia.

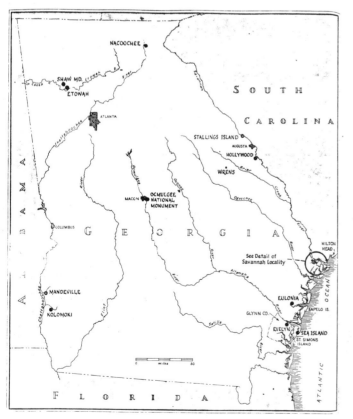

Map of Georgia showing archaelogical site and localities.

Petroglyphs in Georgia.

GERARD, FORREST J. (Blackfoot; Jan. 15, 1925–), is a U.S. government official in the field of Indian health. Born at Browning, Montana, he worked for several years as a tribal relations officer and then chief of the Division of Indian Health, U.S. Public Health Service. He also served as legislative liaison officer for the U.S. Commissioner of Indian Affairs. Gerard became director for the Office of Indian Affairs, U.S. Department of Health, Education, and Welfare in 1967; is executive secretary of the Surgeon General's Advisory Committee on Indian Health; and has been a consultant on Indian programs to the U.S. Senate since 1971.

GERONIMO (Chiricahua Apache; June 1829–Feb. 17, 1909) was the last and most feared of the Apache leaders; he outwitted, outmaneuvered, and outfought thousands of U.S. troops for a decade ending in 1886. Although his name is linked with Cochise, Victorio, and Mangas Coloradas, he continued to spread terror in frontier settlements long after those bold chiefs had passed from the scene. Born a Bedonkohe Apache at No-Doyohn Canyon (near present Clifton, Arizona, he married a Chiricahua woman in whose tribe he gained his reputation as a warrior. Although known to whites as Geronimo (or Heronimo), his Indian name was, according to vari-ous spellings, Goyathlay, Goyakla, or Golthlay, meaning "One Who Yawns."

Admitted to the Warriors' Council when he was only 17, he soon managed to steal enough horses from a rancheria to give 20 of them to Ne-po-se in exchange for his daughter Alope. She, their three children, and his mother were killed by Mexicans in 1858. It was then that Geronimo entered upon a life of bitter revenge. Never a chief, he nevertheless achieved fame equal to that of the hereditary chiefs.

In the early 1870s Gen. George F. Crook, commander of the Department of Arizona, was able to establish some semblance of peace in the territory. He made great use of Indian scouts to track renegade Apache to their retreats. Among the last to succumb were the Chiricahua under Cochise, who died in 1874. In 1876, because of Indian raids on whites, it was decided by the U.S. government to move the Chiricahua from their reservation in southeastern Arizona to the San Carlos Agency on White Mountain Reservation where they would farm parched bottomland. Geronimo was among those who fled across the border into Mexico. From an isolated stronghold in the Sierra Madre they raided Mexican settlements, stealing, burning, and killing. Geronimo had soon accumulated a large herd of cattle and horses, which he sold to white ranchers in New Mexico. He then settled in a hideout near the Warm Springs (Ojo Caliente) Reservation in New Mexico.

In 1877 Geronimo was caught by surprise near Warm Springs and was taken to San Carlos in irons. The following year he managed to slip away to the Sierrra Madre. He surrendered again in December 1879, but then bolted the reservation in October 1881 with Juh, Nahche (a son of Cochise and the hereditary chief), and about 70 Chiricahua. They returned to their Mexican stronghold in the Sierra Madre and to their life of raiding and plundering in Mexico and Arizona.

In April 1882 Geronimo led a bold maneuver of his renegades onto the reservation, where they persuaded or forced most of the remaining Chiricahua, and many other Apache as well, to go with them to Mexico. Many of the escaping Apache were caught between the pursuing cavalry forces under Col. George M. Forsyth and a Mexican infantry regiment. Geronimo was among those who escaped.

General Crook returned to assume command of the Department of Arizona in September 1882. He took advantage of some minor raiding incidents to cross into Mexico after Geronimo. In May 1883 Crook located the Chiricahua camp in the Sierra Madre and convinced Geronimo to surrender. The Apache agreed but he asked for time to gather his people and bring them with him. He failed to show, and Crook was severely criticized for trusting the wily Geronimo. Crook, however, maintained that Geronimo would eventually keep his word—which

Geronimo

he did the following March. The reason for his delayed arrival was evident: he had with him a large herd of cattle and a pack train loaded with gifts, all stolen, for his friends and relatives at San Carlos.

Infighting among government agencies over conduct of Indian affairs, particularly the matter of Indians making and drinking *tizwin* (a native beer made from corn), brought such chaos that Geronimo abandoned his farm home near Fort Apache on May 18, 1885, taking with him 42 warriors and 92 women and children. Indian scouts again tracked the renegades to their hideout in a remote canyon. Geronimo agreed to a peace conference in "two moons," but would talk only with General Crook, unaccompanied by soldiers, at the Cañon de los Embudos, just below the border. At the rendezvous, late in March, Crook was blunt: he would accept only unconditional surrender. He had orders to send the renegades as prisoners of war to Florida, and they could accept the terms or fight until they were all killed. The leaders agreed to surrender, providing they could return to the Apache reservation in two years.

Enroute to Fort Bowie, the plan was sabotaged by an unscrupulous trader who provided the Indians with free whiskey and told them they were all to be killed as soon as they crossed the border into Arizona Territory. Geronimo and 21 other warriors and their families vanished.

Criticism from his superiors forced Crook to ask for relief, granted in the person of Brig. Gen. Nelson A. Miles, who arrived in April 1886. Under his command, Capt. Charles B. Gatewood and his Indian scouts found Geronimo and his band in the Torres Mountains of Mexico. In all sincerity, Gatewood assured the Indians that they would be reunited with their relatives at Fort Apache. Unlike Crook, however, Miles did not consider keeping his word a matter of honor, and Geronimo never returned to Arizona Territory. A military band played "Auld Lang Syne" on the parade ground of Fort Bowie as Geronimo and the last of the Apache hostiles were loaded on wagons to be taken to the railroad and deported from their Arizona homeland. They, along with many of the most loyal Indian scouts, were sent as prisoners of war first to Florida and then to Mount Vernon Barracks in Alabama.

Bowing to the inevitable after he was moved to Fort Sill, Oklahoma, in 1894, Geronimo tried to "take the white man's road." He joined the Dutch Reformed Church, farmed, sold his handiwork and photographs of himself at exhibitions, rode in the inaugural parade with Pres. Theodore Roosevelt in 1905. To Steven Melvil Barrett he dictated his autobiography, *Geronimo's Own Story.*

GHOST DANCE MOVEMENT was a mystic movement among the Plains Indians which began as the Plains Wars were coming to a close in the late 1800s. Realizing there was no hope for containing the white man and preserving their traditional way of living, the vanquished Indians pinned their future to the hope of a messiah, as had other beleaguered cultures in history.

There was an earlier messianic movement when Tecumseh's half-brother, Tenskwatawa, was regarded as the Prophet to lead the Creeks and others back to their ancestral lands. This movement died with the Battle of Tippecanoe in 1811.

As the realities of an ever-shrinking reservation system became intolerable, the Plains Indians turned in emotional desperation to the promise of a redeemer. Wovoka, a Nevada Paiute, declared himself a messiah as his father or uncle had been before him. He said that the spirits of ancestors would come to rescue them in this, the Indian's hour of greatest duress. The Great Spirit would aid them and the dead would live again. The buffalo would return, the white man would leave, and the Indians would again be free, he promised. Ritualized dances were held to make the Indians invulnerable to the white man's bullets. White men named this the Ghost Dance Movement because of the reliance on the ancestral spirits.

This mystical religion gained more and more converts as conditions on reservations deteriorated. The Sioux at Pine Ridge reservation were cold and hungry. By December their August rations had not yet arrived. Kicking Bear began the first Ghost Dance at Pine Ridge. A Sioux from the Cheyenne River agency, he

Arapaho Ghost Dance shirt.

had been to see Wovoka and promised that if the Indians wore Ghost Shirts painted with magic symbols they would be safe from harm. Soon the Sioux adopted it with such zeal that Indian schools, stores, and farms were empty.

As the movement became more fervent, authorities began to fear revolt and unrest. They authorized the arrest of some leaders as a precautionary move. Sitting Bull, invited to a Ghost Dance at Pine Ridge, was killed on December 15, 1890 as he was being taken into custody.

The end of the mystical movement, as well as the Plains Wars, began with the death of Sitting Bull. Angered and terrified at the news, a large number of warriors under Crow Dog fled the reservation to the Bad Lands. Big Foot, a Sioux chief, waited at Wounded Knee Creek, South Dakota, to join others. The 7th Cavalry, equipped with four Hotchkiss guns, was dispatched to the area. On December 29, 1890, about 200 Sioux men, women, and children were massacred at Wounded Knee.

GHOSTS. Everywhere in the Americas funeral rites expressed the desire of the living to placate the dead, to prevent their return, or to facilitate their journey to the other world. These practices developed into a cult of the dead in the restricted sense of the word, that is to say, into a worship of the souls of the dead because they directly affected the welfare of their descendents.

Worship of the dead was an important component of the religions of ancient Peru. There the ancestral mummies were attended by priests and were offered sacrifices; during certain feasts they were taken on processions. A feast celebrated in the month of October in honor of the dead of the group was later assimilated to All Saints' Day and is still observed by the Highland Indians of Peru and Bolivia. On this day the dead returned to receive offerings of food and drink.

The care with which the Guiana and Amazonian Indians *(Carib, Mundurucu, Apiaca, Yuruna, Ipurina, More)* preserved the bones of the dead in their huts suggests a cult of the dead. The *Island Carib* and the ancient *Guarani*, however, believed that the souls could return to the bones and advise their living relatives.

Cubeo religion to a large extent was based on a cult of the Ancestors, who were invoked during tribal meetings, when they were represented by gigantic trumpets. The *Bororo* also believed that the ancestral souls continued to maintain a close relationship with the living and often came to their villages to eat, drink, and dance. The link between the dead and their living relatives was provided for by a special category of shamans, the *aroettaware* who served as mediums for the souls of the dead. The great feasts celebrated by the *Guaicuru* in their cemeteries probably were the expression of a cult of the dead.

The *Cagaba* regarded the Ancestors, whom they

called aluna (souls), as superior to demons. They attributed the origin of all human institutions to the Ancestors, whose actions were always beneficial to mankind; demons, on the contrary, were harmful unless they were controlled by the Ancestors. The aluna long ago ceased to take any interest in human affairs, but men continued to exist, thanks to their teaching and to the celebration of ceremonies introduced by them.

Likewise, ancestor worship was a salient feature of the religion of the ancient *Taino,* for the great Zemi of the caciques were believed to contain the souls of the chiefs' ancestors, and certain cotton and wooden zemis contained the skulls and bones of deceased relatives.

The most important religious celebration of the *Shipaya* was the dance of the ghosts, which took place at the special request of the headman of the dead. In order to dance and drink, the ghosts had to borrow the body of a shaman whose soul supposedly remained idle in a hut while his body, covered by a long cape, danced on the plaza. The feast continued for several nights until each ghost and some animal spirits had in turn executed a dance and sung a song.

GILA RIVER RESERVATION, in Maricopa and Pinal Counties, Arizona is 371,933 acres in size, and home to more than 7,500 Pima and Maricopa Indians.

The Pima, or River People, have occupied the same locality for centuries, continuing the Hohokam tradition of irrigated farming, industriousness, peacefulness, and artistic excellence. The original reservation of 64,000 acres was designated by an Act of Congress in 1859. Subsequent executive orders have increased it to its present size. As a result of their extensive use of irrigation as a community project, and the necessity of uniting for their mutual protection against the Apaches, their government structure was well organized.

The Spaniards, first encountering the Pimas in the late 16th century, found them to be advanced in agriculture. The Spaniards introduced new farm crops such as wheat, and a religion new to the Indians, Christianity. The Pima were always peace-loving, and developed a highly organized culture. They were wealthy compared to the neighboring tribes.

The 17-member, popularly-elected tribal council represents the seven districts of the reservation. The sources of power for the governing body are granted in the constitution adopted and approved in accord with the Indian Reorganization Act of 1934.

GILLESPIE, ROBERT C. (Dakota-Cheyenne; July 1918–   ), is an official with the Indian Health Service of the U.S. Department of Health, Education, and Welfare. Born in Oglala, South Dakota, his long experience in the health field has included positions as executive director of a rehabilitation center, associate director of a children's hospital, assistant administrator of a 600-bed hospital, and community organizer for Chicago's Hull House. He is the author of several books on Indian arts and crafts.

GLADSTONE, JAMES (Blood; 1887–1971), was the first treaty Indian appointed to the Canadian Senate, and he gave part of his acceptance speech in his native tongue. Also known as Akay-na-muka, or Many Guns, he was raised on the Blood Reserve in Alberta. At the reserve Gladstone acted as a scout and interpreter for the Royal Northwest Mounted Police in 1911 after a brief period of typesetting at the *Calgary Herald*.

During World War I, Gladstone was charged with promoting bigger production from farms on the reserves. Following the war, he became stockman for the Blood Reserve, while farming and ranching his own 800 acres. He was the first reservation Indian to buy a farm tractor or have electricity.

Gladstone was one of those who pressed for the initial meeting at which the Indian Association of Alberta was formed in 1939. He was president of the organization from 1948 to 1954 and again in 1956.

Before his Senate appointment in February 1958, Gladstone was frequently called to Ottawa to represent Indians in negotiations with the Canadian government. A year after joining the Senate, he was named cochairman of a joint committee of the Senate and House of Commons to study Canada's Indians. In 1960, while he was on the committee, treaty Indians were given the right to vote in federal elections.

Gladstone's efforts on behalf of his people were recognized in 1960 when he was named "American Indian of the Year." In 1969 he was a member of the Canadian delegation to the Moral Rearmament Asian Assembly held in Japan. His philosophy was that Indians should cling to their Indian heritage with one hand and reach forward with the other.

GLASS, which was unknown to the Indians, was brought to the New World by the conquistadors. Coarse beads of glass were offered to the Indians in ex-

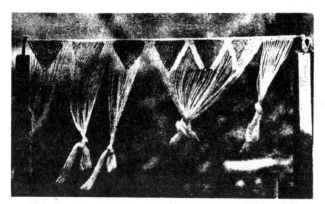

Mohave frame for weaving glass bead cape.

Indian glass works, Mexico.

change for valuable pieces of gold, and the Spaniards were often displeased when this gold was "low gold," that is, copper mineral with some percentage of gold and silver.

In 1542, the first glass-shop was established in the city of Puebla, Mexico, on the street which was later called "Glass Furnace." During the following centuries, this factory seems to have prospered, although its production was evidently limited to the making of household glassware, for there are no examples of artistic glassware during this era.

During the middle part of the 19th century, the Quinar family, of French origin, acquired the only workshop which existed in Puebla, although it is not known whether it was the original shop on Glass Furnace street. From this shop emerged the first Mexican glass-maker, Camilo Avalos Razo, who in 1862, having emigrated to Guatemala, founded his first glass-shop in that city. Upon his return to Mexico, he founded, or helped found, the shops in Texcoco, Mex., Sta. Ana Chiauhtempan, Tlax., Apizaco, Tlax., Guadalajara, Toluca, and the well-known Carretones factory in Mexico City. About this time, pressed glass began to be made and has remained extremely popular among the modest "catrinas" and "tornillos," the former with a feminine face pressed on them, and the latter of a spiral shape; water glasses, small goblets for refino or mezcal, and the famous little hens which served as salt-cellars.

Don Camilo Avalos' sons took charge of the shops in Guadalajara and Mexico, Odilon, in Guadalajara, and the twins, Francisco and Camilo, in Mexico City. Both shops were dedicated exclusively to the making of blown glass. The variety of objects, forms, quality and colors which these shops put out is astounding. The Carretones factory is a veritable glass museum. There, besides those products which are for sale, the Avalos exhibit their own marvellous collection of glass sculpture: exotic gardens, acuariums with multicolored fishes and marine plants, bulls, horses, caricatures of famous people, and dozens of other objects.

The Avalos' factories still preserve their original character, technique and implements, and their products maintain the same elegance and good taste.

The glass-shop in Texcoco also makes objects of excellent quality, although it has never acquired the importance or prestige of those of the Avalos brothers.

GLIKHIKAN (Delaware; ?– March 8, 1782), was a warrior and orator who was converted to Christianity in a famous debate to which he challenged the Moravian missionaries on the Allegheny River in 1769. He had earlier confounded some Jesuit missionaries in a similar debate and won the plaudits of his tribesmen; the result of the second debate was his baptism in 1770.

Glikhikan went to live with the missionaries at the Moravian settlement of Lichtenau, Ohio, and in 1777 he protected them from massacre at the hands of Half King and his Huron warriors. Out of respect, the Huron chief spared him from death in another encounter on September 4, 1781, at Gnadenhütten, Ohio. When the Pennsylvania militia under Col. David Williamson massacred the peaceful Christian Indians at Gnadenhütten on March 8, 1782, Glikhikan was among the slain Indians.

GOAJIRO Indians live on the *La Guajira* Peninsula in Colombia, a narrow strip of which is still controlled by Venezuela. These South American Indians are unique in the New World because of their adoption of nomadic herding of goats and cattle from the Spanish in the mid-sixteenth century—an innovation which in this case did not destroy, but strengthened, the indigenous culture. Indeed, selective Indian borrowing from the Europeans contributed to their cultural continuity and is a rare example of positive results in Indian-European contact. The pre-Columbian hunting and gathering subsistence economy and social organization of the Goajiro underwent dramatic changes with the onset of herding. Livestock, particularly cattle, became objects of great value. The Goajiro also acquired pigs, sheep and chickens in their trade with the Spanish, in exchange for pearls which came from beds lying the coastal Goajiro fishing waters.

Goajiro Indians.

Prior to the arrival of the Spanish the Goajiro ate shellfish and other marine foods and women collected wild vegetables, fruits and roots. Men hunted deer and small game such as peccary, rabbit and birds with traps and bow and arrow. Although rifles are present today, the cost of ammunition is prohibitive, minimizing their use. Fishing is done off the coast and in lagoons using hooks, lines and nets. Today, hunting and fishing are secondary to pastoralism. Cultivation is small-scale and found only in the foothills of the Upper Goajira. This is a rough upland region in the northern part of the peninsula. Lower Goajira is a plain to the south. Cultigens include manioc, millet, beans, melons, plantains, sugar cane, tobacco and gourds. Whereas hunting, fishing and pastoralism is predominantly the work of the men, agriculture is carried out by the women, together with the brewing of the harvest corn beer, *chicha*. The fermentation is started by the chewing of kernels and placing the resulting combination of saliva and mashed corn in containers to brew.

By the mid-sixteenth century cattle and cattle products had become the mainstay of Goajiro subsistence, although they have continued to maintain a mixed subsistence economy. Meat and milk products are important in their daily activities and cattle raising became the most important unit of measure in social life. Beef, hides and other by-products are now sold for cash, which is used in turn to buy other foods and merchandise. The increasing dependence upon European and modern South American goods today comprises an important material tie between the Indians and the larger world economy.

The Goajiro are organized matrilineally and clans play an important role in social life. Descent within an individual's defined bloodline is traced via the women and only women can pass on membership to their children. The lineage is comprised of people who can genealogically depict their consaguineal or blood relations. Each clan comprises various lineages, the members of which trace their descent to a common ancestor, real or mythical. The matrilineal or uterine kin are considered to be relatives of the flesh, the *casta*. *Casta* is a term which refers to the extended family, the lineage and/or the matriclan, depending upon one's useage. The clan and lineage include both living and deceased members, and both the living and dead (spirits) within the *eiruku* (clan) participate in the cycle of the flesh: a belief in regeneration wherein each newborn child is believed to be the returning of a matrilineal kinsmen, a spirit from the afterwork, to the land of the living. As of 1972 the Goajiro had approximately 40 *castas*.

The origin myth of the Goajiro has several variations. In most the beginning tells of a woman who lived alone. During one of her menstrual cycles a tremendous thunderstorm occurred and engendered her pregnancy. The child, a boy called Maleiwa (the creator), is seen as the child of a virgin birth. Maleiwa created the world and flora and fauna. In waves breaking on the coast he created female animals, who later are changed to women. They are brought to the land and meet man. Copulation occurs and so in this way each *casta* has its origin. The *castas* of today are viewed as reincarnations of the original ancestors, and the myth clearly demonstrates the matrilineal principle of Goajiro society.

Within a matrilineage the most important person is the mother's brother or maternal uncle. Usually it is the eldest brother who acts as the head of the matrilineage and, more importantly, is the person who is ultimately responsible for the care of the lineage herd. Upon marriage a man usually lives near his wife's family, who in turn frequently resides avunculocally (near the maternal uncle). Great respect is accorded the senior maternal uncle since he is head of the *casta* and has jural authority within it. As in most unilineally organized societies, the lineage as a whole is responsible for the actions of its members and vice-versa. The maternal uncle symbolizes and embodies this principle of mutual rights and obligations within the *casta*. It is essential to note that in a matrilineal society the mother's brother is the person in authority and it is through him that livestock is inherited. Inheritance of responsibility for the *casta* and parts of its herd goes from elder to younger brother then to sister's son. A man's chief responsibility, therefore, is to his sister's children and not to his own. However, sons and daughters are treated with affection. As is the obligation of all of the matrilineage members, but even more for the senior maternal uncle as lineage head, the continuity of the lineage must be encouraged and preserved; especially in view of it being the most important institution in Goajiro social, political and religious life. Indeed, the adoption of cattle pastoralism probably was a crucial contributing factor to the continuation and preservation of Goajiro cultural/social organization, unlike those Indians who had become culturally more hispanicized.

In life as well as death it is the *casta* which protects the individual and he depends upon it. The role of cattle is significant here as cattle and women both are identified with the perpetuation of the *casta*, as well as with each other. A matrilineage is only as strong as its herd is large and productive and its women marry and reproduce new lineage members. The symbolic equating of women with cattle and the flesh canot be overemphasized. Transgressions against both are treated very seriously and depending upon the offense, require substantial punitive fines to be paid in cattle and other livestock from the offender's lineage to the victim's *casta*. Just as sick humans are treated by shamans, so are cattle who become ill.

Upon marriage brideswealth is given to the bride's lineage. Many of the groom's matrilineage members contribute to the gathering of this herd, which in turn is distributed to different members of the bride's *casta*. This brideswealth serves several functions: it socially recognizes the marriage; legitimizes the children; and marks the establishment of an affinal relationship between *castas*. A further singular feature of Goajiro life is that just as cattle are identified with women and the *casta*, horses are identified with boys and men. A boy usually receives his first horse from his maternal uncle, who assumes the responsibility for teaching him the ways of manhood. Prior to adolescence, however, the father is the child's teacher. Horsemanship is highly regarded and important in caring for the herds.

The Goajiro are quarrelsome and feuds between lineages are fairly common. Active fighting sometimes occurs. The eventual settlement always involves the payment of *cobro* or compensation. Mothers will restrain their children from playing with those of other lineages to prevent incidents which might require *cobro* payments. During fiestas men will liberally consume large quantities of rum and beer and women busily keep the men away from crowds; again, to prevent instances which may precipitate feuds. Once started, feuds can last for years. If *cobro* compensation, arrived at through negotiations among senior lineage males, is not paid the offended lineage may organize a raid and take that which they claim. When raids occur women will use charms or *contras* to safeguard their lineage men. In such situations a husband may find himself in the unwelcome position of being a member of the lineage which has transgressed against his wife's *casta*.

When a Goajiro is born he is believed to share the flesh of his mother's matrilineage and the blood of his father's. As he grows older and dies, most of the blood is gone and after death the individual can join the spirit world of the *eiruku* and the cycle of the flesh. Eventually the spirit re-enters the womb of a lineage descendant and will be reborn to the living *casta*. When a woman discovers her pregnancy, she will go out alone to discover which of her ancestors has entered her womb to be reborn. Upon death, all the matrikin gather for the funeral. As it is women who give birth, it is the kinswomen who also care for, wash and prepare the corpse. The body is placed in its hammock for three days. Kinswomen wail, cover their faces with black cloth, and bend over the corpse. Kinsmen enter the home of the deceased through the back of the house with their faces covered. They also bend over the body. Large quantities of food and drink are provided for the grieving kin. Animals from the dead man's herd are slaughtered for the guests, but matrikin cannot eat these animals. This would be seen as the equivalent of incest. A record is kept of the sacrificed animals which together form the deceased's spirit herd. The deceased's status in the afterworld will depend upon the number of cattle and other livestock sacrificed at his funeral by his kinsmen. This ritual slaughter is therefore of great importance. Again, these acts are not so much for the particular dead man as for the rest of the *casta*, both living and spirit. The body is buried in the matrilineage burial ground, wrapped in a bull's hide. After a year or more the corpse is re-interred in a secondary burial. A second funeral feast is held at this time. The corpse is

now with its spirit herd and travels to a cave believed to be an island off the *La Guajira* Peninsula, Jepira. The dead must pass through several tests before full incorporation into the spirit world.

The dead cannot communicate with humans who visit them nor be addressed by their personal name. This is a variation of a common South American Tropical Forest Indian taboo against speaking the name of the dead. After several months the spirit leaves the cave and begins its journey t the afterworld. Ultimately the person will be reborn to a matrikins woman and the reincarnation cycle of the flesh will be completed, only to begin once again.

JOHN H. PHALEN

GODFROY, FRANCIS (Miami; 1788–1840), was the last war chief of his tribe. His father, Jacques Godfroy, was a Frenchman from Detroit. Francis grew up in the vicinity of Fort Wayne, Indiana. During the War of 1812, he led the Indians who attacked Col. John Campbell's force along the Mississinewa River, Indiana, and drove the Americans back to Greenville, Ohio.

Following the war, Godfroy opened a trading post at a place on the Wabash River called Mount Pleasant and became wealthy for his day. He carried on an extensive correspondence with leading citizens of the day, including U.S. Vice Pres. Richard M. Johnson. Between 1818 and 1840 he signed treaties which ultimately disposed of all Miami lands, in return for which he received grants of land and cash. He died near Peru, Indiana, where a monument has been erected in his memory.

GODS AND GODDESSES. Just as mysterious forces varied in their powers to the Indians gods and goddesses varied. Above a multitude of *genii locorum,* obscure and usually nameless, rose higher beings like the Plains' thunder-god who perpetually warred against the water-spirit, the Eskimo sea-goddess Sedna who presided over the supply of seals, and the sun or sky-god, recognized under different names by many different tribes, who looked down deities, generally more of less coordinate; the Bella Coola Indians of British Columbia arranged them into a regular hierarchy culminating in a great sky-god, the All-Father Alkuntam. The sky-god always occupied the highest position, but many tribes regarded him as too remote, too detached from human affairs, to require much attention or worship. The Haida Indians, while acknowledging the supremacy and occasionally offering a few prayers to the "Power of the Shining Heavens," reserved nearly all their sacrifices for the ocean spirits, especially the Killer Whales; and the Montagnais, who believed Atachocam created the world, "spoke of him as one speaks of a thing so far distant that nothing sure can be known about it." Yet in two regions at least the sky-god reigned supreme. The Huron and other Iroquoian tribes offered vows and sacrifices not only "to the Earth, to Rivers, to Lakes, to dangerous Rocks, but above all, to the Sky. They have recourse to the sky in almost all their necessities, and respect the great bodies in it above all creatures, and remark in it in particular, something divine." Of the Plains' tribes: "All these Indians believe in the existence of a Great Spirit, the Creator of all things . . . They think this great medicine pervades all air, earth and sky: that it is omnipresent, omnipotent, but subject to be changed and enlisted on their side in any undertaking if the proper ceremonies and sacrifices are made. It is the author of both good and evil according to its pleasure, or in accordance with their attention to their mode of worship . . . Power is its attribute, and its residence is supposed by some to be in the sun."

Although the great body of the Indians lingered in a polytheistic stage, particularly on the Plains, the more speculative had arrived at a true monotheism. Their All-Father was not the omniscient and benevolent Being of the Christian religion who created and governs this universe to fulfil some unknown purpose. Rather it was the personification of the mysterious powers or forces operating in man's environment, forces that were conceived as emanations from some higher force. The Algonquins called both this higher force and its individual mainfestations *manito,* the Iroquoians *orenda,* and some Siouan tribes *wakanda.*

The supernatural spirits of the Indians, like the mysterious forces which they personified, might be either helpful or harmful, but they were not ethical forces in any sense. (Indian thinkers hardly attacked the problem of evil in the world). The tribes on the Plains considered that their All-Father was the ultimate source of both good and evil, and attempted by rituals and prayer to gain only the blessings. The western Carriers of British Columbia made *Sa* a sky-god of righteousness who punished violations of the moral code, but this was perhaps the result of Christian teaching. The Iroquoians alone vaguely perceived the great depth of the problem. They predicted a dualism in nature and in various elaborate myths described how two rival spirits, one good and one evil, fought for the mastery of the universe, and how the good spirit finally overcame his adversary without being able to undo all his mischievous creations. After all, the main problem for every tribe of Indians, as it is for all mankind, was not the explanation of evil, but its avoidance. Since many of the forces or supernatural beings in nature were hostile or at least productive of evil, it behooved the native either to render these powers innocuous, or to ward off their influences by other means.

Mesoamerica

In most Indian areas God and Christ now reside at the top of the aggregate of supernatural beings, but are considered too remote to be approached directly. Catholic saints and Maya nature gods populate the descending hierarchy and are classified as lesser deities acting as intermediaries between God and man. The lesser gods usually are visualized as anthropomorphic beings, but are also considered to have supernatural power.

The separation between the Catholic and Maya deities is often vague, for in many areas a Catholic saint has assumed the powers and duties of a Maya god. In the Department of Chiquimula, for example, the gods of rain are collectively referred to as *chicchans,* but individually bear the names of Catholic saints. In some places the two sets of deities are so closely interwoven that they perform integrated tasks. In one township St. Michael Archangel is in command of the four Maya rain gods and gives orders for them to ride across the sky, pouring water from their gourds. They are often accompanied by the Virgin Mary who, for some, has become the guardian of the maize.

There have been many confusions about the concept of the Virgin Mary. Because Spanish painting always show her standing on a crescent moon, she has become associated with the moon goddess; however, she is also variously represented as Mother Earth, guardian of the corn, and the wife of Christ. Every Indian is expected to have a wife, so it is logical that they expect the same of their gods. Most village churches contain at least one of her images, but each individual image is considered a separate person with distinctive characteristics.

Furnerary urn. Zapotec.

CARVED STONE
PANEL, MAYA

In most townships the Christian deities are worshipped principally in the villages; and Maya gods, in the fields. This separation, however, is never rigidly maintained as evidenced by the interchange of powers and personalities between the two sets of deities. In a prayer to the wind gods in preparation for burning a *milpa,* an Indian always addresses both sets of gods.

On the whole, however, the local church is considered the center of the Catholic faith, and all the images of Christian saints and of the holy family are kept here in places of honor. The images are brought out of the church into the village for religious festivals and, if the *cofradia* system is strong, the statues of certain saints may be moved to the homes of leaders of the brotherhoods for special rituals. The images seldom leave the boundaries of the village.

Most Indians consider the images themselves divine and not mere representations of a spiritual being. The statues of the saints are dressed in Indian clothing and, like the images of the holy family are considered local personages. Two townships may have saints of the same name, but they are not considered the same person. The two are more like relatives.

The saints are perceived as very influential and powerful beings, yet they are also believed to have human weaknesses and desires. In the township of San Miguel, St. Ann is thought to be the wife of Santiago (St. James), the patron saint. Some time ago, she was supposedly unfaithful to him and, consequently, he beat her and threw her into jail. A very similar story, involving the sun and the moon, can be traced to pre-Columbian origins.

Each township has its own patron saint, who is considered the personal god of each member of the village. He cares for his people and watches over their crops and their health. The religious brotherhood devoted to him is the most important, and his name is invoked in almost every ritual. Most of the villagers pray directly to him because it is believed that heeek readily intercedes with God on their behalf. The patron saint is so vital to the community that often the township is named for him, as in San Gregorio or Santo Tomas. It is illustrative of the syncretic and localized character of their religion that often an Indian name is added, as in Santo Tomas Chichicastenango.

Townships in the Northwest value their patron cross as much or more than the saint. The cross is an intermediary deity whose roots lie in both Maya beliefs and Christianity. In pre-Columbian times the cross symbolized the four sacred directions. When the

Spaniards arrived more emphasis was placed on this symbol, and it gained great significance in the new syncretic religions. Today crosses are personalized and, according to many Indians, can see, hear, and speak to certain shamans. They are often dressed in Indian clothing and are found at the four entrances of a village, on mountain tops, in caves, and outside of churches. The cross, as such, is seldom seen within a church.

Another supernatural being that has been taken from Christian theology is the devil. The early friars saw the Indian religion as communication with Satan, and they attempted to convince the Indians of this. The Indians did not completely accept this belief, but they did assimilate the concept of the devil. Maya religion had many malevolent spirits, but the Christian devil, being in charge of the underworld, became the dominant one. It is generally believed that his powers are extensive and that anyone who wishes to become a witch or sorcerer must first make a pact with him. He is usually depicted as the early Spaniards visualized him — with horns, a tail, and cloven feet. In many of the dramatic presentations performed by the Indians, the devil plays a role and is inevitably converted by the Virgin Mary.

Many of the supernatural beings found in present-day Indian religion can be traced directly to the ancient Maya religion or to Spanish folk beliefs. These spirits and deities are usually invoked in the *milpa* or by shamans at ancient shrines, but many comprise the superstitious beliefs, which indirectly affect daily activities, and are not worshiped. They form the legends and folk beliefs that belong to no organized religion.

The Maya nature gods are still influential and are propitiated throughout the cultivation cycle. The rituals vary with the township, but in many towns a turkey is taken to the field at the beginning of planting and sacrificed, his blood poured upon the ground to feed the earth. Incense is burned, and prayers are said to the various gods. These rituals are continued throughout the cycle with seasonal variations. In choosing the proper day on which to commence cultivating or harvesting, a farmer generally goes to the shaman, who consults the sacred Maya calendar or, at least, surviving portions of it. The calendar is also used in divination and in setting the dates of agricultural feasts. Most Indians know of the existence of the calendar, but only the shaman understands how to use it.

In addition to the nature gods, there are many supernatural beings who are mixtures of Spanish and Indian spirits. Their appearance, powers, and names vary from one township to another, but the pattern of beliefs is similar. Many of the malevolent spirits such as Juan Noq, Don Avelin Cabellero Sombreron, and the Duende are depicted as *ladinos*. The first two are in charge of witchcraft and those who practice it. The last-mentioned is a dwarf who, in some townships, seduces women, causing them sadness and sometimes death. In other towns he distributes favors and riches to those who worship him, but people must be willing to risk death in order to receive his good will.

The majority of spirits, however, retain the appearance and power that they had in the Maya legends. The Sigvanaba and Llorona are phantom women who lure men to their destruction. The first of these appears to a man as a beautiful woman, but turns into a skeleton or a figure with a horselike face if he follows her. The Dueno de los Cerros (Lord of the Hills) is particularly influential in the northwestern highlands and, supposedly, guards all the resources of nature within his domain. Some townships consider him a protector of the village as long as he is appeased with offerings. To others, however, he is a malevolent being causing disease and destruction.

The most widely known supernatural concept is that of the *nagual*. The term is the subject of much debate and confusion for it is used differently throughout Central America. Basically, however, it concerns two phenomena. The first is derived from an ancient Maya belief that every person is born with an animal counterpart that serves as his protector. The fate of both is interwoven, and when one dies, so does the other. This animal can be discovered from the sacred calendar or by scattering ash around the home in order to clearly record the animal's prints.

A second definition of the *nagual* phenomenon is a sorcerer who by the power given him by the devil, can transform himself into an animal. An evil individual who wishes to make this pact with the devil sleeps in the cemetery for nine nights, and on the tenth the devil appears. The two fight, and if the man wins, the devil teaches him how to change himself into an animal. If the man loses, he dies. The purpose of this transformation is to perform evil deeds, usually against virtuous people. It is believed that his most common act is nocturnal thievery.

STONE, AZTEC

South America

Inca religion with its array of gods, its numerous priesthood, and complex ritualism differs from the diffuse and often amorphous animism of the tropical tribes as well as from the simple theism of Tierra del Fuego. On the one hand, only strong animistic beliefs can explain the cults of the countless huacas or minor deities and fetishes of ancient Peru; on the other hand, some of the nature gods of the *Inca* pantheon crop up here and there among the tribes of the forests.

Throughout South America natural objects and phenomena are personified or are believed to be the abodes or manifestations of supernatural beings. There is, nevertheless, considerable variation in the degree of individualization of these spirits, in their functions, and in the nature of their relationship with people.

In Peru the heavenly bodies, the natural phenomena, and the elements as well as the earth and the sea were conspicuous deities that were worshiped in temples and served by priests. In most of the primitive tribes the same natural objects were either mythological figures without religious significance or were animated by spirits with little individuality. The personification of nature sometimes brings about situations which are difficult to define. For example, among the *Mataco,* Sun was a mythological figure but not a functioning deity, for no prayers were addressed to him and no ceremonies were performed in his honor; yet shamans "visited" him to take advantage of his great knowledge in solving their problems.

Outside of Peru, where Sun was the ancestor and the principal god of the *Inca* dynasty, Sun and Moon were potent deities only in three small *Ge* tribes of Eastern Brazil: the *Apinaye,* the *Sherente,* and the *Canella.* There were also traces of a solar cult among the ancient *Guarani* and their modern descendants, the *Apapocuva,* but its importance probably was slight.

Although from Tierra del Fuego to the Guianas, stars and constellations were visualized as Culture Heroes or mythical animals that had migrated to the sky, the phenomena were deified only in Peru and among the *Sherente,* to whom they appeared in visions as deputies of Sun and Moon.

The sky never has been personified in South America, but human will and feelings were attributed

PUMA GOD

MULTIPLE-HEADED GOD

CENTIPEDE GOD

to it in Chaco mythology when, for instance, the sky changed place with the earth so as not to be soiled by it.

The Thunder God ranked very high in the *Inca* pantheon and survived to modern times under the name of Santiago. In the Chaco and in the Tropical Forest, thunder was attributed either to birds or to spirits. The Thunder Spirit of the ancient *Tupi-Guarani* of the Brazilian coast underwent a strange metamorphosis after the Discovery. The missionaries, in their search for the notion of a Supreme Being, heard the Indians refer to this sky demon, and raised him to the dignity of a High God. Today Tupan is the name of the Christian God among all the people of Brazil and Paraguay who speak a *Guarani* dialect; tupan also has taken on the meaning of "sacred."

The Earth-mother is a typical Andean deity whose cult was perhaps more important in the popular religion than that of the Sun or other *Inca* major gods, for it remained almost intact from Ecuador to the Argentine long after most of the gods of the *Inca* pantheon had been forgotten. The cult of the Earth Goddess has been reported among the *Jivaro,* but there she was probably a simple vegetation demon, for only female plants were under her protection.

BIRD GOD

FISH GOD

BIRD DEMON

PERUVIAN DESIGN UNITS

GOGGLES were used by all Eskimos and some neighboring Indians to protect the eyes from sunlight reflected from snow and water. Various types of visors also were worn commonly in northern regions, but goggles afforded the greatest protection and were a necessity during the Arctic spring. They were usually made of wood and less often of ivory, were contoured to fit the face, and were provided with small elliptical holes or one or two horizontal slits to see through. Goggles were worn throughout the Arctic to prevent snowblindness and were worn when using the kayak in Greenland, Alaska, and the Hudson Straits region.

GOING SNAKE (Cherokee; *c.* 1758– ?) was a prominent chief at the time of the removal to Indian Territory (present Oklahoma). He fought with a contingent of Cherokee on the side of the U.S. at the Battle of Horse Shoe Bend, Alabama, in May 1814, when the Creek warriors were defeated by forces under Gen. Andrew Jackson. He was a member of the Cherokee National Council in 1822, and in October 1830 he was elected Speaker of the council. He was still Speaker in 1838 when, together with several other tribal leaders, he petitioned Gen. Winfield Scott to defer the Cherokee removal from the summer to the autumn because of the unusual heat of that year.

GOLD AND GOLDSMITHING were almost unknown by the Indians of North America. A few gold objects resembling Mexican work found in mounds of the Ohio valley probably indicate that these mound builders had contact with Mexicans. The most interesting gold ornaments made by Indians were a few found in mounds in Florida. They include flat pendants and discs of thin sheet gold. Most gold seen in Florida by early Spanish explorers was probably recovered by Indians from Spanish vessels wrecked on their way home from gold producing areas of Mexico and Central America.

In the Southwest today gold is set with turquoise in jewelry made by a few of the best Hopi and Navajo silversmiths.

In pre-Conquest days the Indians practiced placer mining, and were in possession of large quantities of gold. The Spanish were fascinated by the prospect of reaping huge riches from the gathering of gold in the Western Hemisphere, and mining began soon after the Conquest. It started first on the island of Hispaniola (Santo Domingo (1492-1515), and was continued in Cuba and Puerto Rico (1515-1530).

Peru

In Peru, the center of the Inca empire, Inca gold was used almost entirely for luxury articles and ceremonial objects. Bangles and sequins to be sewn onto clothing, tupu (Topo) pins for fastening women's garments, plates to be hung around the neck, and figurines representing men, women, llamas, and alpacas were

found at the *Inca* shrine of Titicaca on the island of that name. Cups shaped like the wooden ones (Qiro), earplugs, larger statues, and a variety of ornaments for litters and costume are mentioned by the chroniclers. Certain walls of the Temple of the Sun in Cuzco had gold bands across them. Lists of gold objects taken by the Spaniards at the time of the Conquest give an excellent idea of the variety of objects made and the ingenuity of the *Inca* craftsmen.

Colombia

The main producer of gold during the colonial

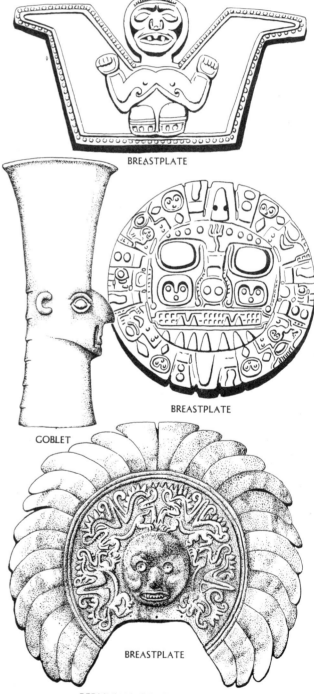

BREASTPLATE

BREASTPLATE

GOBLET

BREASTPLATE

PERUVIAN GOLD AND SILVER

Gold work, Central America.

Gold breastplates from Azuay.

period was Colombia, where the gold produced until the end of the 16th century has been estimated to have reached approximately 4,000,000 ounces.

The first scientific studies of indigenous goldwork were made only a century ago by the Colombian philologist Ezequiel Uricoechea. His *Memorias sobre las Antiguedades Neogranadinas* (Reminiscences of New Grenadine Antiquities), published in Berlin, contained the first descriptions, as well as drawings and chemical analysis of Chibcha objects.

Nearly 30 years later a number of pieces were found in the Department of Antioquia. One, in the form of a raft bearing a chief and seven retainers, appeared to depict the investiture ceremony that gave rise to the legend of El Dorado. Liborio Zerda wrote a series of

articles describing and illustrating the objects that were published in book form in 1883.

In 1892 the government commissioned Vicente Restrepo and his son, Ernesto Restrepo Tirado, to prepare archaeological contributions for the Madrid and Chicago international expositions. They assembled, classified, and photographed hundreds of gold objects from all over the country for the Madrid Exposition catalog. Each also published basic works on Colombian archaeology. It was about this time that individuals began building collections by buying from the *buaqueros,* diggers who made a business of robbing prehistoric tombs.

In 1936 the government restricted the export of archaeological material and organized official ar-

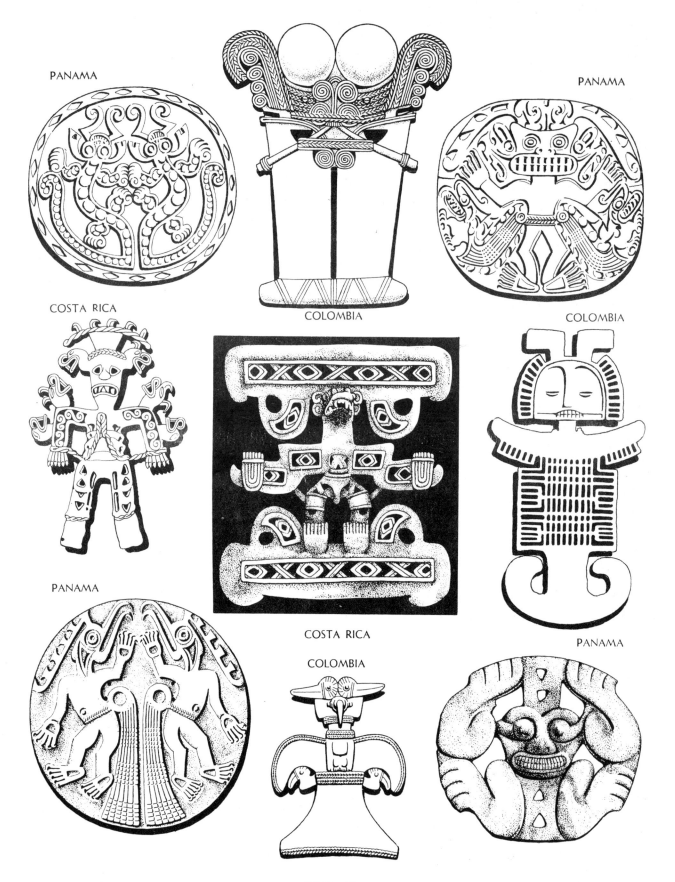

PANAMA

PANAMA

COLOMBIA

COSTA RICA

COLOMBIA

PANAMA

COSTA RICA

COLOMBIA

PANAMA

GOLDWORK

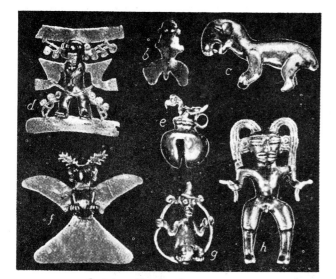

Gold artifacts, Costa Rica.

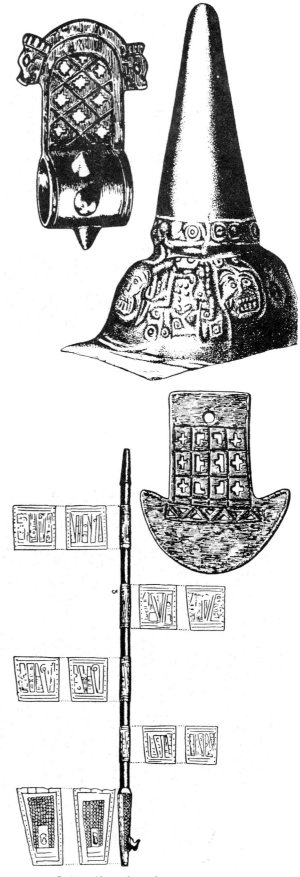

Gold artifacts from Azuay.

chaeological services under the Ministry of Education. Three years later the Bank of the Republic decided to buy up indigenous goldwork, not as a form of capital investment, but to establish the Gold Museum for the enlightenment and enjoyment of the people.

During the next 15 years the bank acquired 6,276 pieces — over four times the total number of goldwork in collections throughout the world. In 1969 the Gold Museum was housed in modern quarters in the bank in Bogota. The bank's cultural center also includes a library of books printed before and during the colonial period and contemporary works on philosophy, history, science, and technical subjects.

The largest and most significant part of the bank's gold collection, from the standpoint of art and archaeology, came from burial grounds uncovered since 1939 in the upper valley of the Calima River in the Department of Valle del Cauca. These pieces of the so-called Calima style include complete sets of body adornments from a single burial and are related stylistically to the famous stone statues of San Augustin on the upper Magdalena River. They are considered older than either the Chibcha or Quimbaya pieces.

The Calima pieces also reveal stylistic similarities to the coastal cultures of Peru and Central America. Since the Calima goldwork is highly developed as a craft and is apparently contemporary with the beginnings of the Chavin Period in Peru about AD 300, archaeologists believe that the earlier, primitive stages of prehistoric goldwork antedated the Christian era by several centuries. No Colombian objects have yet been found, however, that use the primitive method of simple hammering alone; all reveal more advanced techniques.

The Indians melted gold in stone or baked-clay crucibles, using wooden or clay blowpipes to fan the flames. The gold was poured into single open molds or closed two-piece molds. The more complex cire-

Gold artifacts from Coclé, Panama.

Gold breast plate.

Gold disk represinting the crocidile god.

Quimbaya gold objects.

perdue, or lost wax, method was also used. The lost wax method consisted of modeling a core of clay and powdered charcoal with a bone or wood instrument, coating the core with wax, then adding an outer shell of the clay and charcoal mixture pierced by entrance and outlet openings. After drying, the entire piece was heated, causing the melted wax to run out. Molten metal was then poured in to replace the wax. When the mold cooled, the outer shell was broken and the cast polished.

Sometimes metal, wood, stone, or shell objects were sheathed with gold foil. Metallic plating was achieved by dipping pieces in molten gold, by sheathing them with a veneer of fine gold leaf, or by surface oxidation of the copper present in gold alloy. Soldering was very common, so that sometimes a single object could be made up of three different types of gold alloys. The decoration includes both engravings pressed into the surface and designs standing above the surface in relief. Decorative bangles and precious stone inlay work are also found.

In Brazil the first gold mine was opened at the end of the 17th century in Minas Gerais, and Brazilian economy, then lagging, was stimulated as the rate of the population increase of the country was greatly stepped up. Soon after the discovery in Minas Gerais there were big strikes in Matto Grosso, 1721, and Goiaz, 1726. The economic development of Goiaz was helped greatly by the mining.

GONZALES, LOUIS (San Ildefonso; Sept. 10, 1907–), is a noted mural painter whose painting career was cut short by a hunting accident in which he lost his right hand. Gonzales, also known as Wo Peen ("Wolf Mountain"), was a pioneer Pueblo muralist and painted actively in the early 1920s, until his accident. Since then, besides painting occasionally, he has traveled extensively, lecturing, giving pottery demonstrations, exhibiting his paintings, and presenting native songs and dances. In 1944–45 he was governor of the San Ildefonso Pueblo, New Mexico.

GOODWILL, JEAN CUTHAND (Cree; 20th century), is a Canadian government official who, since 1971, has been coordinator of Native Youth and Native Women's Programmes, Citizenship Branch, Department of the Secretary of State. Born and raised on Little Pine Reserve (near Paynton, Saskatchewan), she was licensed as a registered nurse. After working for the Indian and Northern Health Services at an Indian hospital and outpost nursing station in Saskatchewan, she became executive director of the Indian and Metis Friendship Center in Winnipeg, Manitoba (1963–65). She married Ken Goodwill, a Dakota, in 1965.

Jean Goodwill was co-editor of *Indian News* (1967–68) and then editor of *Tawow* (1969–71), the first Canadian Indian cultural magazine. She served as provisional chairperson of the steering committee for the National Native Women's Association and was involved in the study of the Royal Commission on the Status of Women, with particular reference to recommendations concerning Indian and Inuit women.

Goodwill, Ken

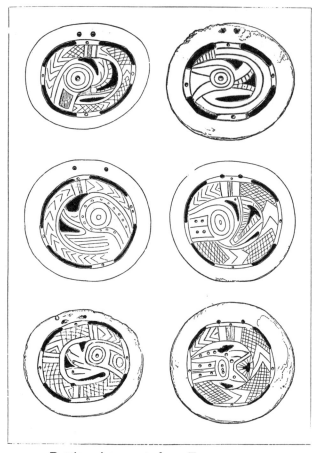

Rattlesnake gorgets from Tennessee.

GOODWILL, KEN (Dakota; 20th century), is a Canadian government official who, since 1972, has worked as a personnel officer in the Native Employment Program of the Public Service Commission. He was born on Standing Buffalo Reserve at Fort Qu'Appelle, Saskatchewan. Goodwill has worked as director of the Brandon Indian Friendship Center in Manitoba (1965– 66); head of the Indian Participation Programme of the Canadian Centennial Commission (1966– 68); chief of the Indian Participation Division, Citizenship Branch, Department of the Secretary of State (1968– 71); and director of the Indian Cultural College at the University of Saskatchewan (1971– 72).

Goodwill served as an executive board member of the National Indian Council and as chairman of the National Indian Cultural Committee. He is performance manager of the Canadian Prairie Inter-Tribal Dance Troupe, which toured Holland and France in 1969 and has performed at various special functions in Canada, and he is president of Nikamona Recording Company, which produces Indian dance and song records and cultural films.

GORGET is a breastplate, worn as a pendant or collar or attached to clothing. Sometimes gorgets were in-signia (perhaps of military rank) and other times may have been amulets. They also may have served as armor. Many gorgets have been found in the southern U.S. mounds of the Mississippian Culture(c. 700-1500 AD). As in other areas, these were made of various materials, including copper and stone. But most were of shell, such as irridescent abalone or carved conch. Sea shells were traded far inland, and their water origin probably gave them sacred meaning. Carved designs often seemed symbolic — serpents, spiders, costumed dancers. Sometimes these Mississippian carvings were reminiscent of Mexican styles, motif, and ceremony, suggesting prehistoric cultural exchange between the two areas.

Another ornament that might be called a gorget was the Plains Indians' breastplate of long bone beads (hair-pipe beads). These were strung horizontally with buckskin, two or three across and 30 to 40 down, making a rectangular bib covering a man's chest. The value of such a breastplate increased by the quality, size, and number of beads.

GORMAN, CARL NELSON (Navajo; Oct. 5, 1907–), is an artist who was reared in a traditional atmosphere on the Navajo Reservation in Arizona, but who has achieved outstanding recognition in nontraditional Indian art forms, including oil and watercolor paintings, ceramics, mosaics, jewelry, textile design, silk screening and industrial design. He is in demand as a lecturer on Navajo healing sciences and is active in their preservation, development, and promotion.

Gorman, whose Indian name is Kinyeonny Beyeh ("Son of the Towering House People"), was born at Chinle, Arizona, where his parents founded the Presbyterian Mission in 1921. His early schooling was in Arizona and New Mexico at U.S. government and Indian mission schools, with high school graduation from the Albuquerque Indian School in 1928. During World War II, he served in the U.S. Marine Corps and participated in such major campaigns as Guadalcanal and Tarawa as one of the "code talkers" whose use of the Navajo language baffled the Japanese. After the war he used the benefits of the G.I. Bill to acquire a formal art education at the Otis Art Institute in Los Angeles, from which he graduated in 1951.

Gorman has participated in art exhibitions throughout the Southwest and West Coast; has received numerous awards; and is represented in public and private collections. With deep concern for his tribal associates, he undertook the management of the Navajo Arts and Crafts Guild at the tribal seat of government in Window Rock, Arizona, from 1964 to 1966. He served as director of the Navajo Culture Center at Fort Defiance and taught art and Navajo language at Tuller College in Arizona. In 1970 he became a lecturer on Indian art and Navajo history and culture at the University of California in Davis. He accepted directorship of the Office of Native Healing Sciences with the Navajo Health Authority in 1973. Gorman's dedication to Navajo culture was honored in that same year with the dedication of the Carl Gorman Museum at Tecumseh Center, University of California in Davis.

GORMAN, RUDOLPH CARL (Navajo; July 26, 1932–), is an artist who, like his father, Carl Nelson Gorman (q.v.), is at home in both the traditional art and culture of his people and the art and culture of the 20th-century white society. Although he often paints native subjects and speaks of the reservation as his source of inspiration, his style and technique are nontraditional. He paints in a variety of media, often in the fully abstract, and makes great use of washes, bleeding colors, and fade-outs. Gorman—who is known as "R.C."—was born and raised on the Navajo Reservation at Chinle, Arizona. He served in the U.S. Navy (1952–56) and attended Mexico City College and Arizona State College, where he majored in literature. He operates his own gallery in Taos, New Mexico.

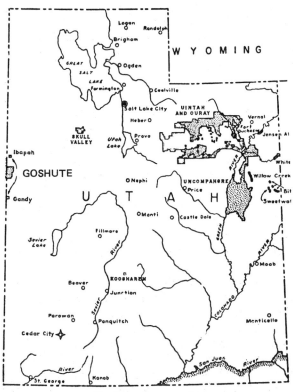

Goshute Reservation.

GOSHUTE RESERVATION, in White Pine County, Nevada, and Juab County, Utah, is more than 108,000 acres in size. The population, Western Shoshonean, numbers around 100. The land for the reservation was acquired by two purchases by the Bureau of Indian Affairs for the tribe.

The population is largely Shoshonean; however, there are also some Paiute and Bannock living on the reservation. These Indians eked a living from the hostile Great Basin climate by gathering roots and berries and hunting small game. The people traveled in small bands which were usually the extended kin groups as this was all a given area could support. Because of the struggle to survive, the Indians developed only very simple organization and culture.

The tribal government is organized according to the Indian Reorganization Act of 1934. The constitution and bylaws were approved in November of 1940 which provide for the Gosiute Business Council to be the governing body. The council's membership is made up by five tribal members who are elected to serve 3-year terms.

GOSIUTE. See SHOSHONE, WESTERN.

GOUGE is a chisel-like instrument with a curved or hollowed blade, used in many parts of aboriginal North America primarily for working wood and stone. Indians in some areas where maple sap was collected reportedly used gouge-like instruments for tapping the trees. Most gouges were of stone or bone, but some were of shell, antler, or copper. Many are hard to distinguish from adze and scraper blades unless they were supplied with a handle which is still intact. A gouge used by the Eskimos and Indians of the Eastern Woodlands consisted of a wooden handle with a beaver tooth set in one or both ends.

GOURDS are fruits that were widely employed for vessels as well as in a number of other ways by the Indians of the Americas. Before the invention of pottery these plants must have been particularly valuable to man, and their use continued after the arrival of pottery, as it does today in many parts of the Americas. The fruits of both plants have been called both gourds and calabashes and sometimes the distinction between them is not made. However, the plants producing them are very different. One, usually called the *bottle gourd,* comes from a cucurbit *(Lagenaria siceraria)* whereas the other, the tree gourd, comes from a bignoniaceous plant *(Crescentia cujete)*. The latter is a small tree, widespread in the American tropics, whereas the former is a large vine, also widespread in the tropics but whose cultivation extended into the temperate zone as well. It is generally agreed that the bottle gourd is native to Africa, but it is found in Mexico at 7000 BC and nearly as early in Peru. Thus it appears to be one of the oldest domesticated plants in the Americas, and how it arrived here has been the subject of much discussion. Some have held that it must have been carried by man, whereas others believe that the fruits must have floated across the Atlantic. Since the fruit has been shown to float for long periods in salt water without losing seed viability, the latter view is quite plausible.

GOVERNMENT. The Indian tribes began their existence as sovereign nations, with full power to deal with other politically independent communities on the one hand (external sovereignty) and to regulate their internal affairs on the other (internal sovereignty). Their external powers were limited by European governments which "discovered" and extended their jurisdiction over areas of the New World, and the external sovereign powers of Indian tribes in the United States were extinguished with the adoption of the American Constitution in 1789.

The American Constitution gave Congress the power to regulate commerce with Indian tribes and provided the basis upon which the federal government took jurisdiction over Indian affairs to the exclusion of the states. After 1789, the federal government rapidly expanded its regulatory role in its relationship with Indians.

With national expansion in the 19th century, Indian tribes were obliged to move westward or they were placed on reservations — during the latter part of the century many of the reservations were broken up into allotments. The resulting turmoil and disruption of tribal life led to a breakdown in tribal government on most reservations. There were some exceptions — for example, the Pueblos of New Mexico retained their traditional governmental organizations; and after two centuries of contact with European culture before their removal westward the Five Civilized Tribes were able to maintain their tribal governments, organized on the basis of tribal constitutions patterned on American forms. They adopted law codes, built jails, maintained tribal police, operated schools and otherwise acted in the interest of their survival as tribes.

For the majority of the tribes, federal agencies had to step into the vacuum left when native governmental

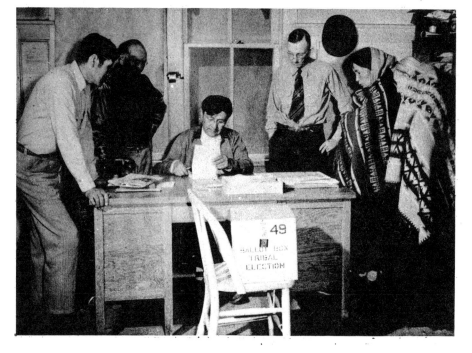

Modern tribal self-government voting in the Navaho general election. A special system of ballots on which the pictures of candidates are printed is used, since most Navahos cannot read.

organizations ceased to operate. Some tribes had never functioned as tribal political entities — they had been organized traditionally on a band or local group basis, with varying degrees of autonomy.

Initially the tribes had administered justice on the basis of tribal law and custom, punishing not only their own members but non-members and non-Indians, as well, for crimes committed on the lands under their jurisdiction. However, even before the adoption of the American Constitution the trend was to provide that Indians committing crimes against citizens of the United States be turned over to the United States for punishment. Treaties with the Wyandotte and the Cherokees so provided, as early as 1785. The punishment of crimes committed by Indians against Indians remained in the hands of the tribes as long as the tribal governments were capable of administering justice.

The Federal Courts have limited jurisdiction and state jurisdiction was excluded until very recent times (Act of August 15, 1953; Act of April 11, 1958). The gap had to be filled by tribal jurisdiction or by makeshift arrangements.

The Act of March 3, 1885, gave to the Federal Court jurisdiction over certain major offenses committed by Indians against Indians, including murder, manslaughter, rape, assault with intent to kill, arson, burglary and larceny. Later, robbery, incest, assault with a deadly weapon, embezzlement and certain other offenses were added. The action of Congress in conferring jurisdiction over these offenses on the Federal courts filled the gap that had formed on most reservations as a result of the breakdown of native governmental organizations, while at the same time it was a further invasion of the internal sovereignty of the tribes.

In 1883, the Secretary of the Interior authorized the establishment of Courts of Indian Offenses which dispensed justice on the basis of a code of laws developed by the Department of the Interior. Courts of Indian Offenses were established only where tribal organizations had broken down. They reached their peak in about 1900 at which time two thirds of all reservation agencies had them.

The Courts of Indian Offenses were not very successful. They received very little financial support — in fact, the Indian judges in the Courts of Indian Offenses received no salary at all until 1888, and thereafter they were paid only $3-$8 per month. The judges were recruited from the "progressive" element within the tribal population and they reflected non-Indian attitudes and prejudices against such native institutions as religion, ceremonialism, medicine men, polygamy and other cultural features. The judges were not trained and their "decisions" were often dictated by the Agent or by the police.

After passage of the Allotment Act of 1887 — also known as the Dawes Act — Indians receiving allotments went under state civil and criminal jurisdic-

tion. Under the terms of the Act they became citizens and Commissioner T.J. Morgan held, in 1892, that "there can be no system of Indian Courts where Indians have become citizens, and no system of Indian police."

The Curtis Act of 1898 dealt a death blow to the tribal courts and police of the Five Civilized Tribes, applying the allotment principles of the Dawes Act, and providing for the dissolution of their tribal governments by 1906.

The Competency Act of 1907 opened the doors wider to further shrinkage of tribal lands and internal tribal sovereignty. Conditions on the reservations grew steadily worse until the initiation of a reform movement after World War I which culminated in the Indian Reorganization Act of 1934. In its original form, it contemplated special court of Indian affairs but the section embodying this court was eliminated. However, Section 16 of the Act authorized tribes to reorganize under tribal constitutions, and the modern tribal courts came into being with the reorganized tribal governments. They administer justice pursuant to a tribal code of laws, usually subject to approval by the Secretary of the Interior — or, in the absence of such a code, they use that contained in the Code of Federal Regulations, Title 25.

On the basis of Chief Justice Marshall's decision the principle was established that Indian tribes retained all of their internal sovereign powers to the extent that they were not waived or limited by treaty or by positive enactments of Congress. Those powers of self-government that were not thus limited or extinguished were still retained and could be exercised by the tribes. Furthermore, it was held that residual tribal sovereignty was not lost or impaired by failure of a tribe to exercise it. Consequently, tribes that reorganized under the Indian Reorganization Act or otherwise could exercise all of their residual sovereign powers even though they might not have exercised them previously on a tribal basis — or even though there might have been a period during which they ceased to exercise them.

In the administration of justice on Indian reservations the trend has been in the direction of adoption of European-American concepts of law and punishment rather than continuation of traditional tribal concepts and usages. To some extent there has been a blending of the two systems and philosophies, and in a few tribal situations traditional concepts and practices are still important. Title II of the 1968 Civil Rights Act (The Act of April 11, 1969) further limits internal tribal sovereignty to the Indian people under their jurisdiction, most of the same restructions and guarantees as the American Constitution applies to the Congress under the Bill of Rights.

Title II of the Act of April 11, 1968, (Public Law 90-284, Civil Rights Act of 1968) also provides that any Indian person who believes himself to be wrongfully held in jail by order of an Indian Tribal

Court can petition a Federal Court for a writ of habeas corpus, i.e. a court order that has the effect of testing the legality of the order issued by the Tribal Court.

In addition, the 1968 Civil Rights Act limits the punishment that can be meted out by the tribal courts to a maximum of six months in prison or a fine of $500, or both, for conviction of any one offense.

Under existing law Indian tribes can elect to abandon their judicial and law enforcement functions entirely and permit the states to assume criminal and civil jurisdiction over the reservations.

Traditionally the tribes varied somewhat in their customs and usages in the area of social control. However, in most instances ridicule and social pressures were relied upon to obtain conformity with tribal law. Punishment, when necessary, might take the form of personal embarrassment, corporal punishment, payment to the victim or his family, vendettas, retribution, banishment or execution. Crimes against property were insignificant in most traditional Indian societies. Sharing and cooperation were stressed as cultural values, and the scarcity of personal possessions made stolen objects conspicuous in a closely knit community.

Among the Plains Indians homicide, adultery and violations of hunting rules were paramount crimes. The tip of the nose or the entire nose of adulterous wives was cut off, and among the Cheyenne murderers were banished.

Cherokee law required 100 lashes for horse theft, while rapists were punished with 50 lashes and the left ear was cropped close to the head for the first offense. A second offense brought 100 lashes and the right ear was cut off; a third offense led to death.

Among the Pueblos of the Southwest, offenses fell into two broad categories: (1) those against the community, including witchcraft and crimes against the religious-ceremonial system; and (2) those against individuals, including theft, murder, rape, adultery and slander.

Witchcraft was greatly feared and accused witches were dealt with harshly. Such a person might be hung from a horizontal bar set up in the plaza, suspended by his feet, thumbs or by his arms tied behind his back. He would be "encouraged" to confess, sometimes by periodic clubbings, on the premise that powers confessed were powers lost. Accused witches were sometimes wiped out as nests of sorcerers—or villages split with part of the population leaving. After confession, accused witches might be required to undergo purification before being released.

Among the Zuni, the only crimes punishable by death were witchcraft and cowardice in battle.

Violation of ceremonial procedures and re-

Crow delegation to Washington, 1880. Indians left to right, Old Crow, Medicine Crow, Two Belly (standing), Long Elk, Plenty Coups and Pretty Eagle.

The coronation of the Emperor, Inca Mancho.

quirements among the Pueblos was sometimes punished by whipping. The divulging of religious secrets was a serious offense against the entire community, especially in the face of Spanish religious persecution, because the religious-ceremonial system was thus jeopardized, and it was considered to be an institution of first importance in the life of the Pueblos.

Ridicule was a means of restraint and punishment. An offender might be obliged to dress in clothing proper to the opposite sex; sit alone in the middle of the plaza exposed to the mockery of all who passed by; or be the butt of public jeering at the hands of the clowns during ceremonies.

At Zuni, thieves were obliged to repay stolen items — ten for one, in the case of sheep. Trials were conducted by civil leaders, (the Governor and his staff) or by the entire council.

Murder was considered a crime against the individual and his family. The murderer could be required to make retribution in the form of goods; he might be obliged to substitute his labor for that of his victim; or he might be punished privately by the kinfolk of the victim.

Rape was viewed as an offense, not because of the sexual relationship involved, but because of the lack of consent of the victim, and the offender could be required to make payment to the victim.

Among the Navajo, as among the Pueblo peoples, harmony between man and nature, and between men was a primary value. Chaos and disharmony were to be avoided at all cost, and crime was a prime source of disorder. Ridicule, restitution and private punishment administered by one's kinfolk were among the media used to secure conformity with social requirements. As among the Plains Indians, the nose tip or the entire nose of adulterous women might be cut off among the Navajo and Apache.

It was difficult, historically, for Europeans to understand Indian concepts of crime and punishment. At Fort Defiance, in 1858, the soldiers shot a number of Navajo owned horses. The owners could not force the military to pay compensation for the lost horses, so they killed a slave belonging to the commanding officer by way of retribution. This angered the military and, to mollify them, the Navajos killed a Mexican and dragged the body into Fort Defiance in lieu of surrendering the killer of the slave. The behavior of the Navajos was incomprehensible to the military; and the behavior of the military was beyond the understanding of the Navajos.

The military, the Agents in charge of reservations, and the Courts of Indian Offenses administered justice in conformity with European-American concepts of law and justice, whereas the tribes continued many of their traditional practices well into modern times; traditional practices continue to the present day, and traditional concepts of justice influence the decisions of tribal judges despite the fact that the tribal law codes are generally patterned on non-Indian concepts of justice.

The Cherokee Nation maintained a tribal police force in pre-Civil War times, and during the period 1860-1878 Indian Agents on a number of reservations informally organized a force of Indian police to assist in keeping order. The Navajo, Pawnee, Klamath, Modoc, Apache, Blackfeet, Chippewa, and Sioux had such force during the period in reference and, in 1878, the Commissioner of Indian Affairs directed all Agents to organize Indian police on their reservations. However, the Indian police were poorly financed until recent years and, until the tribes reorganized their tribal governments the Indian police functioned primarily as arms of the federal government rather than the tribe.

Following reorganization of tribal government after 1934, many tribes not only established tribal courts for the administration of justice, but tribal police forces as well, for the enforcement of tribal laws. The modern tribal police are an arm of the tribal government today. Their organization and procedure differ little from those of municipalities elsewhere in the nation.

All in all, Indian tribal government has been re-established as one of the several institutions of democratic representative government on the American scene — national, state, county and municipal Tribal governments function generally within the limiting framework of federal laws, and most of them are organized along Anglo-American lines. The major distinguishing feature between tribal government and the other forms of American government lie in the derivation of their right to exist — tribal governments derive this right, along with their basic powers, from residual tribal sovereignty, in contradiction to the national government which derives its powers from the American people through the federal Constitution; and the state, county and municipal governments which operate within the framework recognized by state and federal constitutions, state laws and charters.

Tribal government is federal because the federal government took exclusive jurisdiction over Indian Affairs.

Reservation Indians are citizens of the United States as well as members of their several tribes. As such they may participate fully in national and state political life including not only the right to vote, but the right to be elected to office in state and national, as well as tribal, government. Within the boundaries of their reservation they are generally subject to tribal and Federal laws and regulations exclusively; outside their reservations they are subject to the same Federal, state and municipal laws and regulations which affect all other citizens. Tribal government has much in common with municipal government except that it is limited by Federal, rather than State law.

GRAND MEDICINE SOCIETY. *See* MIDEWININ SOCIETY.

GRAND PORTAGE RESERVATION, in Cook County, Minnesota, is more than 44,000 acres in size and is owned by more than 200 Ojibwa (Chippewa) Indians. This reservation was established in 1854 by treaty with the United States government.

The Chippewa, or Ojibwa, were one of the largest Indian nations north of Mexico, and controlled lands extending along both shores of Lakes Huron and Superior and westward into North Dakota. Their migration to this area was instigated by Iroquois pressure from the northeast. Drifting through their native forests, never settling on prized farmlands, the Chippewa were little disturbed by the first onrush of white settlers. They maintained friendly relations with the French and were courageous warriors. In the early 18th century the Chippewa drove the Fox out of northern Wisconsin, and then drove the Sioux across the Mississippi and Minnesota Rivers. By this time they were also able to push back the Iroquois whose strength and organization had been undercut by settlers. The Chippewa of the United States have been officially at peace with the government since 1815 and have experienced less dislocation than many other tribes.

The Chippewa were nomadic timber people traveling in small bands engaging primarily in hunting and fishing, sometimes settling to carry on a rude form of agriculture. These foods were supplemented by gathering fruits and wild rice. Their wigwams of saplings and birchbark were easily moved and erected. Birchbark canoes were used for journeys but other travel was usually by foot. The tribe was patrilineal, divided into clans usually bearing animal names. Although their social organization was loose, the powerful Grand Medicine Society controlled the tribe's movements and was a formidable obstacle to Christianizing attempts of missionaries. A mysterious power, or manitou, was believed to live in all animate or inanimate objects. The Chippewa today are largely of mixed blood, mostly French and English.

The governing body is the Reservation Business Committee. The committee has five members elected to 4-year terms. Elections are held every 2 years on a staggered basis. The Grand Portage Band is a member of the Minnesota Chippewa Tribe which is organized under the 1934 Indian Reorganization Act. The tribe's constitution and bylaws were approved in 1936 and revised in 1964. The governing body of the tribe is the Tribal Council.

GRAND SOLEIL (Natchez; fl. first half of 18th century) was the traditional title for the head chief of the Natchez Indians, but it is associated particularly with a chief in the early 18th century who resisted white claims upon tribal land and later butchered a great many of the French during a bloody uprising. The French called him Grand Soliel ("Great Sun"), but his Indian name remains a mystery. He and his Natchez followers lived in the village of White Apple, near the present city of Natchez, Mississippi. Although Grand Soleil had always behaved well toward the French settlers in the region, the French commandant—named Chopart—ordered the chief to move the Natchez off their ancient tribal lands. Chopart would not even permit the Indians to harvest their crops prior to their removal unless they bribed him for the privilege.

Apparently, the French commandant never suspected that the formerly submissive Natchez would resist his orders, despite a good deal of evidence to the contrary. For example, Grand Soleil sent out bundles of sticks to the various Natchez villages; Chopart merely assumed that the sticks were to instruct the villagers how much tribute to pay. In reality, however, the sticks told the Indians how many days remained before the uprising. Even when a Natchez woman warned some French officers of the impending attack, Chopart refused to take adequate precautions.

The uprising began on November 30, 1729; in short order the Indians killed all 700 white persons in the nearby French settlement. From Natchez the Indian attack spread southward, destroying French plantations in Louisiana and killing the white inhabitants. Finally, the governor of the French colony—named Perier—launched a counterattack and recaptured the Natchez outpost. Grand Soleil, after making a pretense of agreeing to peace, snuck off with his people during the middle of the night.

The chief built a fort on a secluded portion of the Red River, and it was not until a year later that the French forces found him there. A brief battle ensued, after which Grand Soleil surrendered. Many of the captured Natchez women and children died in an epidemic following their surrender, and those who survived were shipped to Haiti where they were sold as slaves to French planters. The Natchez men—Grand Soleil and his warriors—were taken to New Orleans and probably executed for their crimes.

GRANGANIMEO (Secotan?; ?–*c.* 1585) was a leading figure among the Indians in the vicinity of Roanoke Island (North Carolina) who befriended the first English settlers on the island. He aided Captains Philip Amadas and Arthur Barlowe during their exploration of the island in 1584 and then offered friendship and provisions to the settlers who arrived the following year. Together with his father Ensenore (*q.v.*), he protected the English from his brother Wingina. Unfortunately for the colonists, he died soon after they arrived.

GRANGULA (Onondaga; fl. late 17th century) was an Iroquois chief who refused to heel to French demands that the Five Nations not trade with the English. Grangula's name was a corruption of the French *grande gueule* ("big mouth"); his proper name was Haaskouan ("His Mouth Is Large") or sometimes Otreouati. In 1684 the French governor of Canada, De la Barre, crossed Lake Ontario with an expedition to crush the Five Nations because they were interfering with French trade. But the French force was weakened by sickness and, when De la Barre finally confronted Grangula, the Onondaga chief hosted him courteously but refused to be intimidated. He said that the Five Nations would trade with the English or French as they chose and would continue to treat as enemies French traders who supplied guns and ammunition to their Indian enemies.

GRANT'S PEACE POLICY. When Ulysses S. Grant became President in 1869, he attempted to achieve some of the Indian reforms recommended during the previous decades:

> He promptly adopted a new policy as regards the appointing of Indian agents by delegating their nomination to the several religious organizations interested in mission work among the Indians. This was a rather curious acknowledgement of the power of the politicians

in controlling the appointments of the President. As the law required Indian agents to be confirmed by the Senate, the President evidently felt that he could not secure the confirmation of men selected for other than political reasons unless there was some well-defined organization that Senators would fear to offend. In the early days of the administration of the Society of Friends selected the agents in Nebraska, Kansas and Indian Territory.

What the religious and humanitarian groups had succeeded in securing from President Grant was the opportunity to conduct an experiment. Although the Society of Friends and other churches were invited to submit lists of persons who would be suitable for selection as agents, actually Grant at first filled most of the posts with military officers. On July 15, 1870, however, the Congress passed a bill forbidding military personnel to hold civil office. In reaction to this, although under great pressure to make political appointments, with the support of the Board of Indian Commissioners President Grant decided to further extend appointments to individuals recommended by religious bodies.

GRASS, JOHN (Blackfoot Sioux; fl. late 19th century), was a leading chief at the Standing Rock Agency from about 1883 who, despite the opposition of Sitting Bull, signed the agreement in 1889 ceding land to the U.S. and breaking up the Great Sioux Reservation into smaller reservations. For more

Chief John Grass

Smithsonian Institution, Bureau of American Ethnology.

Lithograph of a Wichita village seen in 1852.

than 30 years, he served as a judge of the Court of Indian Offenses at Standing Rock Reservation in North and South Dakota.

GRASSWORK was used for ornamental, utilitarian, and ceremonial purposes among various tribes.

Indians of the South, the Hopi and Pima of the Southwest, the Tlingit of the Northwest Coast, and Eskimos sometimes wove grass into their baskets. Some tribes used polished white and yellow grass stems as basket decoration. The Hupa of Northwest California used stems as fringe on clothing. Flat grass stems, sometimes dyed, were sewn onto dressed skins as decoration in a manner similar to that used with porcupine quills.

In the Midwest the Wichita and Caddo Indians made loose grass into domed, thatched houses in which several families lived. Grass was used for bedding, fiber for cord, perfume, and tinder. The Cheyenne burned grass to make paint of the ashes mixed with blood and tallow. Pueblo Indians tied stiff stems into bundles for use as hairbrushes.

Grass was used in ceremonies by several tribes. Some Plains Indians burned grass for lighting the pipe in rituals. Some placed balls of grass into the eye sockets and nose of sacred buffalo skin in the belief grass would make it live. The Pawnee used sod in a ritual as a symbol of life and growth.

GRATTAN INCIDENT was an encounter between the Sioux and the U.S. military from Fort Laramie that is often considered the beginning of the Plains Indians Wars.

In 1854, three years after the Fort Laramie peace council, a Minneconjou Sioux killed an emigrant's sick and probably abandoned cow for its hide. The Sioux offered $10 retribution but the owner demanded $25. The commanding officer at Fort Laramie planned to negotiate a settlement; however, 2nd Lieutenant John L. Grattan was allowed to handle the matter.

Grattan had arrived at the fort that year with little respect for the Indians as warriors. He insisted that he could whip the entire Cheyenne nation with 10 men; with 20 he felt he could empty the Great Plains.

Grattan went to the nearby Sioux camp with 32 men and 2 howitzers. The camp held three Sioux groups: the Brules, Oglala, and Minneconjous. After an emotional verbal exchange, a solider fired a shot and one of the howitzer crew fired a round. Conquering Bear, the Brule chief, was mortally wounded. The Sioux then retaliated, killing Grattan and all his men.

Several Sioux had been killed during a misunderstanding the previous summer; but this incident was the scene of the first white blood shed since the Treaty of Fort Laramie. Although the commander at the fort quickly sent a detailed report, newspapers called it "Grattan's Massacre" and the War Department sent an expedition. In the summer of 1855, Colonel William L. Harney left Fort Leavenworth with 1,300 men. At Ash Hollow on the North Platte River, he attacked the Brule camp of Little Thunder; of the 86 Indians who died, a significant number were women and children. Five of Harney's men died.

GRAVE. *See* BURIAL CUSTOMS.

GREAT BASIN CULTURE AREA. The Great Basin of Utah and Nevada was like a huge bowl, rimmed by mountains. The streams feeding the lakes, swamps, and forests began and ended in the "bowl." When glacial waters ceased to feed them, the lakes began to dry up. The mountains prevented most of the coastal precipitation from replenishing the rapidly diminishing water supply, and as lake levels dropped, salinity increased. When the change was complete, there remained the stretches of desert, salt flats incapable of supporting life, Utah's Great Salt Lake, and the petrified residue of the great forests that we know today. For the hunter, only antelope, migratory or indigenous birds, small adaptable mammals, rabbits, and other rodents remained.

Colorado was more fortunate. Ancestors of today's Utes inhabited forested mountain slopes filled with game, deep canyons with productive streams, fed by the Continental watershed. Their land remains much the same today as it was in prehistoric times. With the exception of the Uintahs, a Ute Tribe that roamed Central Utah, they lived in relative affluence compared to Utah and Nevada neighbors who eked out a living at minimal survival level after the change. The fact that the ancestors of the Paiutes, Shoshones, Goshutes, and Washoes survived the cataclysmic transition at all is a testimonial to their intelligence, stamina, and extreme adaptability.

Early residents of the Great Basin learned to utilize every asset in their environment in their progress toward recorded history. Hunters became harvesters of seeds, roots, herbs, sagebrush, lichens, cacti, reeds, and grasses, from which they derived all subsistence items and even a few luxuries. No seed, however minute, no plant, animal, insect, or even larva was overlooked in the all-encompassing quest for survival. These resourceful people became interested in the art of healing and had developed almost 100 vegetable medicinal compounds, a contribution which is believed to rank as the largest body of pharmacoepia known to primitive man.

A shelter of brush, reeds, and grasses lashed to poles bent in a conical shape was the typical housing. Fibers from milkweed and sagebrush bark, reeds, and grasses were woven into clothings and utensils. Wealthy was the man who possessed a woven rabbit skin blanket. To a migratory people, skins were more valuable for shoes than for clothing.

The grim realities of survival limited the bands to a single or extended family seldom exceeding 15 persons. Personal possessions were limited to the loads the woman could carry suspended in large burden baskets from their heads as they followed the harvest.

Each band member, of necessity, was an active contributor to the common welfare. Cooperative sharing was the essence of survival. It was mandatory, in the common interest, that competitive or rebellious members, and those incapable of, or indisposed to, sharing the workload be abandoned to fend for themselves. At night, the member who was a liability was abandoned, as the others stole away in the darkness to reconvene at a predetermined point. Subdued rebels and converted sloths could rejoin a band if they mended their ways. A crime against one was a crime against the whole, and often serious offenders were stoned to death. For lesser offenders, and in training children, ridicule and shame were potent chastisement. Children and their happiness were of primary concern — first as the realization of the racial

survival instinct, and only secondly as contributors to a society where life was a daily struggle and death a constant threat. Orphans were adopted and no child ever lacked love.

Arrow and spearhead makers were honored individuals and enjoyed many privileges. Weapons were basic, limited to nets, snares, and the *atlatl* (throwing spear) which was largely superseded by the bow and arrow, introduced around AD 500. Skill in the hunt consisted more of stalking and surprise than accuracy with weapons.

Annually, in the fall, communal game drives were organized at times considered propitious by the *shaman,* or medicine man. If he misread his signs, and game was scarce, he could be ostracized or stoned. For these hunts, several bands, seldom more than 50 persons, joined to pool manpower and equipment. Nets, knotted from milkweed fiber twine, sometimes more than 100 feet long, were held taut while "beaters" drove game into them.

Only two bands practiced farming to any degree. The Washoes were located where more fertile land enabled some of them to plant corn, squash, melons, and beans, but their majority shared the migratory life of their neighbors. The Kaibab, a small Paiute band, were the only true agriculturalists, even developing a rudimentary irrigation system.

Tribes of the Great Basin.

In defiance of their harsh realities, members of several of these tribes had great personal pride, expressed in self adornment. Body painting in ritual designs for beauty and for success in both hunting and warding off misfortune was the custom. Special importance was attributed to the hair, worn long and plaited. For its care they evolved six types of vegetable shampoos, raccoon tail brushes, combs, and even a perfumed pomade. Shampooing by the bridal couple of each others' hair was part of the marriage ritual, and grief was expressed by shorn locks.

The annual pine nut harvest, and the communal game drives afforded these Indians rare social occasions from which they extracted the last drop of pleasure. Dances were held, accompanied by rhythmic music provided by the elders, using drums, rattles, simple flutes, and thrummed bowstrings. Simple evening fireside exchanges, a full stomach and a shared pipe were the limit of their daily pleasures. This, then, was the life pattern well into recorded times.

In the 16th century the horse, acquired from Spanish explorers, freed the Utes of Colorado and the Shoshones from the land. Horse stealing became a fine art, especially among the Utes. The Spaniards, who sought to lure them into conversion to Christianity with the first horses as a bribe, soon saw their mistake, as mounted Utes with tough-minded practicality raided, rather than traded, for horses and livestock. The Plains Indians, too, became acquainted with the Utes, who swooped down the eastern slopes of the Rockies in lightning raids on horse and buffalo herds. The

horse brought war to the Utes as Plains Indians tried retaliatory invasions. The Utes have been compared to the Swiss in their almost invincible defense of mountain strongholds. They were said to be the first tribe north of Mexico to use stone forts in defensive war, and even early Anglo-American military expeditions were to come to grief against them.

Proud and fierce as mountain eagles, the Mouache and Capote bands who roamed the eastern face of the Rockies were the forebearers of today's Southern Utes. On the western side, the Weeminuche, Yampa and Uncompahgre (Tabequache) bands are known today as the Ute Mountain tribe. These five bands, and the Uintah in Utah, with the acquisition of the horse, became the powerful Ute empire which early settlers encountered.

The Shoshones of Nevada and Utah had also become skilled mounted hunters who swiftly extended their territorial boundaries into Wyoming, Montana, and Idaho. For a time they conducted a brisk trade with the Spaniards and Mexicans in slaves, acquired in mounted raids on the unfortunate Paiutes and Washoes.

The second great transition these peoples were to undergo was now imminent — the first had been environmental; the second was to be cultural — the acquisition of the West by the United States.

GREAT LAKES. When 17th century European explorers pushed into the area of the Great Lakes, they found it the homeland of many tribes. There were Hurons; Ottawas; Chippewas or Ojibwas;

An Interfaithful metting.

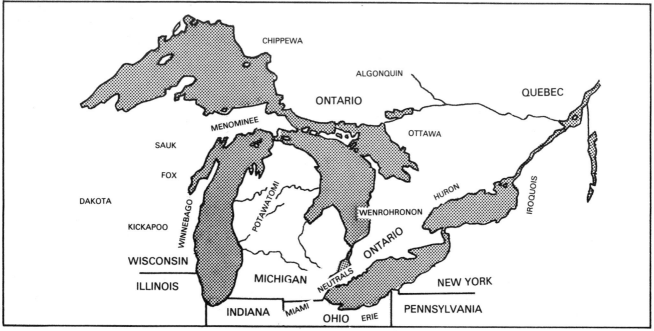

Tribes of the Great Lakes Region.

Potawatomis; Winnebagos; Menominees; Sacs; Foxes; and Miamis. Most numerous probably were the Hurons and Chippewas. The Foxes and Menominees were fewest in numbers.

The Indians living on the shores of Lakes Superior, Michigan and Huron were hunters and farmers in varying degrees. Where agriculture was practiced, population clusters were found. Where the hunting of forest game was the chief means of livelihood, there were fewer Indians. Relatively less land area will support a farmer than a hunter.

Each tribe had its own language, belonging to one of three main language families. The Hurons spoke an Iroquoian language; the Winnebago speech has been classified as Siouan and the other tribes belonged to the large Algonquian family of languages.

Although the white man raised the curtain on Great Lakes Indian culture, the area had known a long history of development by aboriginal peoples. Archaeological findings indicate that men began to enter these lands as early as 7,000 years before the birth of Christ, as the continental glaciers retreated. By 500 BC the lakes had assumed the approximate forms they have today.

A succession of cultures developed, culminating in the Late Woodland-from AD 800 to 1600. From primitive hunters who pursued the mastodon and giant beaver, through the mysterious period of the copper workers and the highly developed Hopewell culture that flourished and died long before Europeans came, there was bustling life around the Great Lakes. The cultures developed by groups long resident in the region became mingled with those of peoples wandering in from the river valleys of the south, forming patterns that are now fascinating problems for archaeologists and historians.

PREHISTORIC INDIANS IN THE GREAT LAKES AREA

Early Archaic	8000 BC to 2500 BC
Paleo Indians	7000 BC to 5000 BC
Aqua Plano	7000 BC to 4500 BC
Borea Archaic	5000 BC to 500 BC
Old Copper	5000 BC to 500 BC
Red Ocher	1000 BC to 500 BC
Early Woodland	1000 BC to 100 BC
Hopewell	100 BC to AD 700
Upper Mississippi	AD 800 to AD 1600
Late Woodland	AD 800 to AD 1600
Middle Mississippi	AD 100 to AD 1300

GREEN CORN CEREMONY. *See* BUSH CEREMONY.

GREENLAND. The first Icelanders to settle in Greenland under the leadership of Eirikr found traces of human dwellings in various places, but they saw no natives. The first record of what were probably Eskimo is given in an account of a shipwrecked party high up on the east coast.

The repopulation of west Greenland took place after the establishment of the Icelandic colony there. The whole west coast is now inhabited from Igdluligssuaq, south of Holm Island, southward.

The southeastern coast is little inhabited. Capt. W. A. Graah estimated that there were about 600 natives here in 1829-30, but even then they had begun to leave for the mission posts on the west coast. In 1884 Gustav Holm found only 135 here, and they were still leaving for the west coast. After the establishment of a trading post in 1894 at Angmagssalik, where there was already a considerable Eskimo population (now about 800), some of the natives went there. The last 38 left Tingmiarmiut in

1899 and in the summer of 1900 arrived on the west coast. One family of eight members remained, but later left for Angmagssalik.

After the depopulation of the southeastern coast, probably largely induced by the reduction in the numbers of the seals through wholesale slaughter by European sealers, the Angmagssalik District was the only inhabited region on the east coast until the estalishment of the new settlement in Scoresby Sound by the transfer of 70 Eskimo from Angmagssalik in 1925.

On the north coast between Polaris Bay and Bronlund Fjord a meat cache has been found at Frankfield Bay, slightly to the west of St. George Fjord, which shows that hunters have penetrated to this region. Dr. Birket-Smith says it is remarkable that no other traces of Eskimo have been found, for it is certain that if the Eskimo migrated to the east coast by way of the north they must have wintered here. He suggests that they may have lived exclusively in snow huts, like the central Eskimo tribes of Canada.

As described by Dr. Birket-Smith, the Polar Eskimo, the most northerly people of the world and the only ones living under extreme Arctic conditions, have a high Arctic culture which centers entirely around ice hunting. This Arctic culture is found in the Thule District where the occurrence of fjord seal and walrus, and to a certain extent, bearded seal and bear, determine the location of the dwelling places. Where the ice lies smooth and unbroken without being pressed into ridges and hummocky fields, the seals have their breathing holes, and in spring they creep up on the ice in order to bask in the sun. The walrus is to be found under young ice which it can break with its hard and solid skull, and in Melville Bay the bear wanders regularly between the open water and the glacier. A smooth floe which offers the best conditions for sledging is essential for the site of a dwelling place. A necessary condition for the existence of a high Arctic culture is that ice floes remain practically throughout the year, so that the kayak is not necessary; but at the same time there must be an alternative to resort to when the hunt for sea mammals fails. Dr. Birket-Smith says that this is the case in the Thule District. Along the north coast of Greenland the sea is never entirely free of ice, but is covered with the so-called paleocrystic or permanent ice, or in the fjords with permanent sikûssaq ice,which is very unfavorable for mammals. It is possible that an Eskimo population in these regions would have to depend on musk ox hunting to a very large extent. It is doubtful whether even the Eskimo could exist along the north coast of Peary Land where steep mountains covered with ice and destitute of hunting grounds drop down to the permanently frozen ocean.

Arctic culture requires, in winter, lasting and smooth floe ice on which the hunter can look for the breathing holes of seals. This culture type is not sharply differentiated from the preceding. The fjord seal is still the chief game, and the requisites for dwelling places are in several respects the same. The occurrence of other animals, as walrus and bearded seal at Nugssuaq, and bear in the direction of Melville Bay, only exceptionally influence the location of the dwelling places. Open water in winter here begins to be a factor to be taken into account. This occurs partly in icefjords where the motion of the glacier produces open leads in the ice, and partly at tidal rapids where the tide keeps large holes open. Around such open waters the seals gather.

A transition stage between the Arctic and Subarctic types is seen in the habitations in the Egedesminde and Holsteinborg Districts. Here the fjord seal still plays a part, though a far less important part than farther north, and the saddleback now, perhaps, ranks first as the chief objective of the hunt. For this reason the inhabitants shun the long and narrow fjords and keep to the island belt where the saddlebacks pass. Now that the fjord seals have greatly decreased in number, the natives in the fjords of Holsteinborg are in winter mostly restricted to fishing for Norway haddock and fjord cod.

The Subarctic culture is characterized especially by kayak hunting, accompanied by the disappearance of the dog sledge, which is not found farther south than Holsteinborg, and by cod fishing. The Subarctic culture area proper corresponds very nearly to the west coast from the Arctic Circle south to Cape Farewell, the culture reaching its climax on the southern west coast. When, in addition to favorable conditions for kayak hunting, there is a special abundance of seals the cultural possibilities are developed to the maximum, as was originally the case at Julianehaab Bay, to which great quantities of bladdernose were carried by the pack ice around Cape Farewell from the east coast.

But there is no sharp dividing line between these cultures. North of the Arctic Circle the area as far as Disko Bay forms a transition to the Arctic phase, and on the east coast there is a similar transitional region on the King Frederick VI coast and in the area about Angmagssalik. Some of the most expert kayakers live on the small group of islands at the entrance to Disko Bay, and also at Angmagssalik, and in both regions there is also dog sledging.

By far the greater number of Eskimo live on the west coast south of Disko Bay, and along the greater part of this coast the kayak can be used, with short interruptions, throughout the year. Here also seals are especially abundant.

Linguistically the dialects of the language of the Greenland Eskimo are phonetically related, and are distinguished from other Eskimo dialects by certain common characteristics. In their culture the Greenland Eskimo, especially beyond the Thule District, also show a very few endemic characteristics.

The present native peoples of Greenland are properly referred to as Greenlanders, not as Eskimo, for they have advanced far beyond the stage usually associated with the term "Eskimo." They number at present about 18,000. They have increased steadily during the past years. In 1901 there were 11,600; in 1911, 13,000; in 1921, 14,000; and in 1931, 16,800. They are more or less extensively mixed with European blood, chiefly Danish. The greatest mixture is about Disko Bay, where it would now be difficult to find a native of strictly pure blood. Mixed-bloods are decidedly in the majority all along the easily accessible west coast. In the isolated Julianehaab region, in the southern part of the Egedesminde District, and in the Upernivik District mixed-bloods are at a minimum.

History

The early history of Greenland from the year 900 to the year 1492 is the history of an Icelandic colony that perished and was all but forgotten. This colony is memorable because it was from Icelandic Greenland that the North American mainland or "Vinland" was discovered in the year 1000, and its settlement attempted.

The history of this colony has no connection with the rediscovery of Greenland which led to its permanent settlement, but is properly speaking an integral and interesting part of the history of Iceland.

The rediscovery of Greenland leading to its colonization by the Danes was one of the results of the attempt to find a route to China by sea through the northwest passage. Strongly encouraged by King Alfonso of Portugal, King Christian I of Denmark in 1472 or 1473 sent out an expedition under two adventurers, Diedrick Pining and Hans Pothorst, who were joined by the Norwegian Johannes Scolvus and a Portuguese nobleman, Joao Vaz Cortereal. This expedition reached Greenland in the vicinity of Angmagssalik, where it was attacked by Eskimo. According to Dr. Louis Bobe, it is likely that Columbus learned of this expedition when he visited Iceland in 1476.

In 1537 and 1539 sailors from Hamburg had been blown out of their course to or from Iceland and driven toward Greenland, but they had been prevented from landing by bad weather. This les to an expedition from Hamburg under Gert Mestermaker which found the country, but did not see any of the inhabitants. At this time there was much talk about Greenland, but nothing was done.

The Englishman, Martin Frobisher, in 1576 sighted the east coast of Greenland in latitude 61° N. and circumnavigated Cape Farewell, but was prevented from landing by the ice, in which one of his ships was lost. He undertook another voyage in 1577, but again was unable to reach the coast because of the ice. On his third voyage in 1578 he landed somewhere on the southwest coast, without appreciating the fact that it was Greenland, and took possession of the territory in the name of Queen Elizabeth of England. He found that the Eskimo were in possession of some metal instruments from which he concluded that they had had intercourse with strangers.

In 1579 a Danish expedition under the command of an Englishman, Jacob Allday, was on the east coast of Greenland, but it did not reach land, and in 1581

Faroese Magnus Heinesen tried to reach the east coast.

The Englishman John Davis in 1585 (the year of the first attempt to establish a colony in Virginia) discovered Gilbert's Sound on the west coast of Greenland in latitude 64° 15' N, the site of the present settlement to Godthaab) where he met Eskimo, but found no trace of the Icelanders. He made a second voyage in 1586, and a third in 1587 (the year in which Virginia Dare, the first child of English parentage, was born in Virginia). On his last voyage he sailed far up the strait named for him and reached a lofty granite island in latitude 72° 41' N. which he named Sanderson's Hope (now called Qaersorssuaq) in honor of a merchant, William Sanderson, one of his backers. Davis called the country "The Land of Desolation."

GREENVILLE, TREATY OF was a 1795 agreement between the Indians of the Old Northwest and the U.S. government which officially moved the western frontier north and west of the Ohio River. This treaty was the first of many land cessions wrested from the Indians of the region over the next 25 years.

For nearly two decades the Indians of the Northwest Territory had resisted white encroachment. In 1790 and 1791 two U.S. military expeditions had been defeated; however, in August of 1794 General Anthony Wayne, in command of a large and well trained military force, had routed the Indians at the Battle of Fallen Timbers.

Peace negotiations were called for the following June at Fort Greenville, Ohio, on the southwest branch of the Maumee River. Approximately 1,100 Indian chiefs and warriors were present, representing the Wyandot, Shawnee, Ottawa, Potawatomi, Kickapoo, and other Indian nations. Miami Chief Little Turtle, negotiating for the Indian confederacy, was forced to cede 25,000 square miles, nearly all of Ohio and parts of Indiana, Illinois, and Michigan.

The treaty gave the United States enclaves for fortification in Chicago and elsewhere throughout the Northwest Territory. These enclaves and the right of access to them led directly to further Indian-white hostilities throughout the years.

General Wayne used the recently concluded Jay Treaty (November 1794) between the United States and England as a weapon to push the Indians into the cessions. The Jay Treaty and the Treaty of Greenville combined to drive British influence further out of the area and to ease fears of a possible British-Indian alliance against the United States.

GRIFFIS, JOSEPH K. (Osage; fl. late 19th and early 20th centuries), was an author who had a varied background as warrior, medicine man, outlaw, scout, Salvation Army captain, clergyman, and scholar. Known as Chief Tahan and born in the middle of the 19th century, his books were *Tahan: Out of Savagery into Civilization* (1915) and *Indian Circle Stories* (1928).

GRINDING STONE is any of a wide variety of hard abrasive stones used universally from earliest times in North America for grinding stone, bone, ivory, wood, shell, and metal in the shaping, sharpening, and polishing of a side range of tools, weapons, and other objects. Any hard, gritty rock was used such as diorite, quartzite, or granite. Grinding stones varied in size from those easily held in one hand to large exposed surfaces of rock. They are often distinguishable from ordinary rocks only by signs of wear such as narrow grooves left from sharpening projectile and other points or broad channels made in shaping larger implements.

Grinding, as well as being an important means of shaping softer materials, was one of the principle methods of working stone, for which it was usually employed after a rough shape was first attained by percussion fracturing and pecking. The tools formed were numerous, including adzes, axes, hatchets, celts, clubs, picks, chisels, hammers, and pipes. Grinding stones with specialized shapes were themselves formed by grinding, examples being a hand-held nephrite whetstone used by Eskimos and the widely used arrowshaft rubber. The latter was a grooved piece of stone, usually sandstone, used for smoothing and polishing arrow shafts.

GRINDSTONE CREEK RANCHERIA, in Glenn County, California, is only 80 acres in size and is owned by fewer than 100 Wailaki Indians. The rancheria was purchased under Acts of 1906 and 1908 by the Secretary of the Interior on January 7, 1909. The rancheria is located 7 miles from Elk Creek City.

Culture still exists on the rancheria, such as Indian burials, songs, language, games, foods, arts and crafts, and medicine.

The general council is the governing body of the rancheria consisting of a chairman, vice-chairman, and a secretary-treasurer. Tribal officials are elected to serve 1 year.

GRITTS, FRANKLIN (Cherokee-Potawatomi; Aug. 8, 1914–), is an artist who has also served as an art instructor at Haskell Institute in Lawrence, Kansas. Gritts—also known as Oau Nah Jusah ("They Have Returned") and Oon Nah Susah ("They Have Gone Back")—attended several Indian schools before entering the University of Oklahoma, where he received a bachelor of fine arts degree about 1939. He studied mural technique under Olaf Nordmark and painting under Acee Blue Eagle (q.v.). Gritts served in the U.S. Navy during World War II as an aerial photographer, receiving a medical discharge after two years of hospitalization resulting from combat injuries.

GROS VENTRE. The Gros Ventre or Big Belly Indians who roamed over North America were an offshoot of the Arapaho, one of the many tribes that hunted the buffalo on the prairies of the United States. They were organized on much the same lines as the Blackfoot, having graded military societies and other institutions that differed only in secondary details from the corresponding institutions of their neighbours. After harassing some of the fur-trading posts towards the close of the eighteenth century, they retreated to the south under pressure from the Assiniboine and Cree, and ceased to exert any further influence on the development of the prairies.

GUACANAGARI (Arawak; fl. 15th century), ruled a rich region of Cap-Haïtien, modern Haiti, when Columbus arrived there in 1492.

Gros Ventre on upper Missouri, 1843. Copy form engraving in Maximilians Travels, 1843.

Guacanagari became one of Columbus' first Indian allies.

Guacanagari was probably born about 1450. When the Spanish flagship "Santa María" ran aground off Haiti, Guacanagari assisted in salvaging the ship's contents. The Indians then helped build Fort Navidad. But when Columbus returned to Spain, the fort and all its Spanish inhabitants were destroyed. On Columbus' rearrival, Guacanagari tried to reestablish peace, but the Spanish sailors kidnapped several Indians. Guacanagari lost an ensuing battle and his people's respect. He fled to the mountains, where he died in 1499.

GUACHI*(Guachie, Guachicas, Guajie, Guacharapos, Guarapayo, Guasarapo, Guajarapo, Guajnie, Guaichaje, Bascherepo, Guaxarapo).* This tribe of traders and fishermen is mentioned several times in the chronicles and documents concerning the discovery of the upper Paraguay River. In the 18th century, they lived on the northern side of the Mondego (Miranda) River and in the "canadas" formed by the heights of the Serrania de Amambay, and, like the *Guana* were vassals of the *Mbaya.* They were divided into a few "capitanias" (probably bands) and, though canoe Indians, had permanent villages and fields where they grew maize, sweet potatoes, gourds, and tobacco. They wove beautiful striped blankets which were much in demand among the *Mbaya.* About 1800 their able-bodied warriors numbered only 60. In the middle of the past century they were almost extinct. Their name appears for the last time in 1860 in an official document which refers to their presence near Miranda.

Guamontey and *Guamo* designated whole groups of tribes. Some sources called the *Guamo,* both in the east and the west, *Guaikeri (Guayquiri, Gaiqueri, Guaycari),* but both names refer to the same people.

The territories occupied by the *Guamontey* and the *Guamo* stretched from the eastern to the western extreme of Venezuela in two wide, parallel bands. The *Guamontey* were found along the lower Orinoco and the Apure River to its junction with the Zarare, and on the Guanare River. The *Maiba (Amayba, Amayva, Amaygua, Amaiba)* and the *Guaypura* were found camping with the *Guamontey* and may have been related to them. The *Guamo* lived more to the north of the latter, principally on the Portuguesa, Pao, Cojedes, Guanare, Guanaparo, and Acarigua rivers. The *Dazaro,* on the Guanare River, seem to have been closely related to the *Guamo.* The *Taparita,* on the Arauca, stand culturally somewhat apart from both the *Guamontey* and the *Guamo,* although linguistically they were closely related to the latter (but also to the horticultural *Otomac!).* The *Guarico* lived between the Guarico, Portuguesa, and Apure rivers. They were enemies of the *Atature, Masparro,* and *Colorado,* on the Portuguesa, Sarare, Colorado, Bocono, and Masparro rivers. These last four tribes are nearly unknown culturally, but seem to belong to this culture area. The *Zavire,* on the Capanaparo River, are known only by name, but are included in this area on the basis of their geographical location.

The physical appearance of the *Guamontey* and the *Guamo* is surprising. Our sources stress that they were taller and better built than other tribes (the comparison is probably with their sedentary neighbors) and describe them as markedly dark-skinned.

The two groups of the *Guamo,* that near the junction of the Apure and the Orinoco Rivers and that north of the junction of the Apure and Sarare rivers, maintained close relations with neighboring horticultural tribes, the *Otomac* and the *Caquetio,* respectively. The first was not only linked to the *Otomac* through constant intermarriage, but had learned from them a certain measure of cultivation. The westernmost *Guamo* had retained their fishing culture, but their settlements were intermingled with those of the *Caquetio,* who seem to have been their overlords, and these tribes carried on an active exchange of their respective products.

The few demographic data our sources provide give the impression that these tribes, or at least some of them, were as numerous as the *Guahibo* and *Chiricoa.* The *Guamontey* were estimated to have numbered 30,000.

Hunting.—Although fish or shellfish was undoubtedly the most important food to these tribes, and occasionally a tribe was said to have lived "only on fish," all them probably did some hunting. Animals living in the rivers and lagoons, especially manatee, may have been more important, especially to the *Guamo,* than land animals, among which tapirs, peccaries, and deer are mentioned. Most tribes are said to have eaten all nonpoisonous animals. The bow and arrow, which apparently was never poisoned, is the only hunting weapon mentioned by most sources. The *Guamo* caught caimans by the same method used by the *Otomac.*

Fishing and shellfish-gathering.—The *Guamontey* and the *Guamo* seem to have been true fishermen, the latter specializing in the catching of large fish, whereas the *Atature, Masparro,* and *Colorado* are accredited with the gathering of shellfish. The *Guamontey* used bows and arrows and "fisgas," the latter either three-pronged spears or harpoons. The *Guamo* used ropes to haul big fish and aquatic mammals from the rivers.

Gathering of vegetable food.—All these tribes probably dug roots, including caracaras and guapos, the latter an item in *Guahibo* and *Chiricoa* diet. They also gathered fruits, especially palm fruits. Collecting wild honey was of special importance in the west, between the Barinas and the Apure rivers, a region which is described as "one great bee-hive."

Cultivation and domestic animals.—Except for the *Guamo* who had come under *Otomac* influence, these tribes knew nothing of cultivation. When the Spanish conquerors showed grains of maize to the *Guamo* and *Guamontey* of the lower Orinoco, the Indians "sniffed at them as something strange." The food-gatherers, whom Losada and Reynoso met between the "province of Catapararo" and the great causeway near Buena Vista, cultivated a root called "lerene," but he insists that these people did not cultivate maize.

No source mentions dogs among any of these tribes.

Food preparation.—Dried fish and roots were ground, the latter in deerskins, in holes that were dug for that purpose and trampled smooth. Fish and root meal were also mixed together and made into tamales or mush. When the land was flooded, meal was stored in calabashes or baskets. Jerked meat, preserved in lye made of a salitrous plant, called coa, was stored in the same way.

GUADALUPE, VIRGIN OF.

Generally, religious practices and beliefs are strongly imbued with paganism in the remote Indian villages and in other isolated areas in Mexico. A fusion of Roman Catholic and pagan elements prevails in most rural mestizo communities and in lower middle-class densely populated areas; and traditional Roman Catholic practices, devoid of indigenous influence, are observed by Mexico's urban upper classes. Certain symbols and observances are meaningful in all three of the environments—isolated, rural, and urban—including the image of the Virgin of Guadalupe, patron saints *(santos)*, fiestas, churches, domestic shrines, and crosses.

The Virgin of Guadalupe is the most widely recognized and universally worshiped of all Mexican saints. During the early days of the conquest she appeared in a vision to a poor Indian named Juan Diego. The dark-skinned virgin asked him to build a church in her honor so that she could be near his (the Indian) people to protect and love them. The apparition appeared directly over a destroyed Indian shrine to Tonantzin, the Aztec earth goddess. The new virgin enabled the Aztecs to indianize the white man's religion and make it their own. This miracle was officially endorsed by the Roman Catholic Church, and the Virgin of Guadalupe became the patron saint of all Mexico. The shrine is the holiest in Mexico, and large crowds congregate daily in the plaza near the basilica. Upon entering they kneel and crawl forward to a spot where they can gaze at the image and pray.

GUADALUPE HIDALGO, TREATY OF

ended the Mexican war on February 2, 1848 and brought dozens of Indian nations under United States jurisdiction.

The Mexican War began in 1846, a year after the annexation of Texas, as a dispute arose over Texas' southern border on the Rio Grande. The Treaty of Guadalupe Hidalgo brought the United States the present areas of California, Arizona, New Mexico, western Colorado, Utah, and Nevada. The territory was primarily occupied by Indian nations, although there were Spanish settlements in California and along the Rio Grande. The Indian inhabitants included the Pueblo, Hopi, and Zuni people (New Mexico and Arizona), the Mission Indians (California), Apache groups, and the Navajo, Ute, and Shoshoni tribes.

The United States paid Mexico $15 million for the cession. Except for the Gadsden Purchase (1853) and the purchase of Alaska (1867), U.S. continental expansion concluded with the "Mexican Cession."

GUAHIBO

are the largest surviving indigenous population of the llanos (plains) of eastern Colombia and western Venezuela. This diverse, dispersed people has maintained a viable culture despite centuries of Western disruption.

Ethmology of the term Guahibo is unknown; it has many variants: Guajibo, Guajivo, Guayba, Guagiva, Guaiva, Guahivo, Gaivo, Goagibo, Guagibo, Guaibo, Guagiva matafora, Guagivo, Guayva, Catomae, etc.; Chiricoa, Chiricoy, Chiricau, Chicoa, etc.; and Cuiva, Cuiba, Cuyba, etc. Guahibo understand, but do not employ, these terms. Guahibo is usually applied to cultivating segments of the population, Cuiva to noncultivating segments. Chiricoa is a Yaruro name for Guahibo speakers. Guahibo call themselves *hiwi*, people; or in contrast to their indigenous neighbors, *wayapopihiwi*, people of the savanna.

Sociocultural subdivisions are related to subsistence patterns and degree of contact with Western society. Hunters and gatherers and seasonal cultivators, as more isolated groups, are called *sikuani* or *matasinipi-*

Location of Guahibo Indians.

hiwi by cultivators along major streams to emphasize their lesser sophistication. These categories are cross-cut by membership in mythologically sanctioned, regional-dialect units.

Once Guahibo spread over all the llanos of Colombia and the west-central llanos of Venezuela. Their center, as today, was the Comisaria of Vichada, Colombia. Some still live in Meta, Casanare, and Arauca, Colombia, and Apure, Venezuela. Missions took them to the east bank of the Orinoco, in Territorio Amazonas, Venezuela. In recent decades they have expanded there and into Guárico and Bolivar, Venezuela.

A Guahibo-Pamigua language family is usually placed within the Quatorial Stock of the Andean-Equatorial Phylum. The status of Guahiban languages is yet undetermined, but usually Guahibo, Cuiva, Guayabero, Yamu, Churoyan, and Amorua are listed. Missionaries have translated some biblical texts into Guahibo and have taught reading and writing. Members of the Summer Institute of Linguistics helped a small Guahibo newspaper to begin in 1978 in the Comisaria of Vichada.

A few nomadic Guahibo live by hunting, fishing, and collecting. Bands of fluctuating size stay only a few weeks at a site, living in temporary shelters. Travel is usually by canoe. A varied and abundant diet includes fish, wild plants, palm fruits, insects, turtle eggs, birds, and such game as picure, paca, iguana, armadillo, and capybara.

Most Guahibo live in villages and depend, to varying degrees, on slash-and-burn cultivation. Seasonal cultivators garden only during the rainy season, dispersing in the dry season to live as nomadic hunters and gatherers. Others are tied to the Western market economy and spend most of the year in villages, growing cash crops, producing craft items, and staying near wage labor sources. All grow bitter and sweet yuca (manioc); permanent village dwellers give more time to maize, sweet potatoes, plantains, and rice than the others.

The division of labor is based on sex and age. Men clear and burn fields, and cooperate with their wives to cultivate them. Men hunt, fish, make basketry, and work wood. Women gather wild foods, manage households, and make some pottery. Metal utensils and tools, cloth, and Western food items are obtained by barter and by income from sales or wage labor.

Social organiation is bilateral. Local groups based on kinship form around a central sibling core, with families attaching themselves to this core through consanguineal and affinal ties. Group composition is changeable; individuals and families move from one to another as economic and social conditions change. Marriage ties (preferentially cross-cousin) extend kinship links for individuals. Divorce is frequent, polygyny desired but limited, and genealogical memory shallow. Initial bride service is followed by matrilocal or neolocal residence. The nuclear family is the primary socioeconomic unit.

Endogamous, named, regional bands were formerly important. Members shared association with a territory, distinctive speech habits and behavior, and belief in descent from, or connection with, an animal, plant, or mythological being. Beyond this there is no unity or occasion for members to congregate. Fifty-three have been identified, but many have disappeared or lost their importance.

There is no Guahibo tribal organization. Each local community listens only to a headman with nominal authority based only upon personality and proven success. Headmen lead by example, counselling rather than commanding, and relying on kinsmen for support. He represents the community to the outside world, and organizes communal fishing, hunting, drinking, and work parties. He is expected to be knowledgeable and generous, and his sons may be exempted from bride service. The position is personal and lasts only so long as his influence. Shamans are often headmen because of their supernatural knowledge. Relationships within and beyond communities are based on kinship. Social control is maintained through gossip, ridicule, individual action, and socialization. Formerly, local groups united for warfare under influential leaders, but today no such cooperative efforts exist.

Despite centuries of Christian proselytizing, most Guahibo retain their traditional belief system. *Kuwai* leads the list of creator, culture-hero, beings who

Guahibo Indian.

people the spirit world. The universe is full of anthropomorphic and zoomorphic beings, dangerous and harmless, and ghosts, and souls. Humans and animals have two souls. Religion is individualistic, with no true communal ceremonies and no coherent body of myth or dogma.

Misfortune, illness, and death are due to breaking a taboo, supernatural interference, šorcery, or, rarely, natural causes. The shaman diagnoses and cures illness and practices sorcery. He has special power to contact and influence "other beings", and knowledge of magical formulas. His special power is earned and enhanced through training and long use of hallucinogens (*Anadenanthera peregrina*).

Since 1538, the Guahibo have been most often described as nomadic foragers, raiders, and traders, but some changes began in the seventeenth century. Cultivators who had controlled the major rivers disappeared because of disease, slave raids, and flight. Some Guahibo moved in to take their lands for seasonal cultivation. Guahibo also entered the expanding slave trade. During the eighteenth and nineteenth centuries Guahibo gained control over most of the Colombian llanos and much of Apure, Venezuela. They resisted missions, enhanced their reputation as raiders, and expanded their cultivating activities. Distinctions begin in the nineteenth century between peaceful cultivators (Guahibo) and aggressive nomads (Cuiva).

Twentieth century guahibo are increasingly subject to prejudice, persecution, and exploitation. The civil war (*Violencia*) in Colombia, from about 1948 to 1953, took many Guahibo lives. Massacres and torture of Guahibo since then have made international news, such as the massacre of unarmed Cuiva men, women, and children in Arauca, Colombia, in 1967, and the killings and tortures in the Planas region of Vichada in 1970-71. They follow a long tradition of Guahibo hunts (*Guahibiados, Cuiviados*) in the area. Guahibo are now threatened by increased colonization, restriction of mobility, and loss of land. Reserves in a few regions seem to have lessened the threat of genocide, but not of cultural destruction. Western society is now causing cultural disorganization by reducing Guahibo subsistence options and creating greater dependence on the market economy.

No early population figures exist. We know only that colonial missionaries compared the Guahibo to the most numerous of their cultivating neighbors, indicating a population in the several thousands. Unlike their neighbors, the Guahibo expanded in colonial times. Only the twentieth century has seen curtailment of their territory and, perhaps, of population size. Today there are probably between 15,000 and 20,000 Guahibo in Colombia and Venezuela.

Guahibo adaptability made them successful survivors of the European invasion, but today they face new and more difficult problems that their ingenuity may not be able to surmount.

ROBERT V. MOREY
AND NANCY C. MOREY

GUAICAIPURO. In the 1560s, the Teque Indian chief Guaicaipuro organized the Indians of the Caracas region of Venezuela into a strong but short-lived alliance against the Spanish invaders. His valor in defense of the territory, and the tragic end of his bold plans, have inspired poets to enshrine him as a national hero.

The Spanish first became aware of Guaicaipuro in 1560, when through terror he and a small band of Teques drove the Europeans from two lucrative gold mines discovered by Pedro Miranda. After defeating and killing his most feared rival, the sailor Juan Rodriguez Suarez, Guaicaipuro decided to make a concerted effort to expel the Spanish altogether. He enlisted the help of such major tribes in the area as the Caracas and Taramainas. His efforts gained momentum when his strongest opponent, a half-breed named Francisco Fajardo, was unable to organize a counter-insurgency among the natives, éven with the help of the Spanish governor Pablo Collado. With an army of about 10,000, Guaicaipuro gained virtually total control of the area.

The Spanish colonial government continued to vacillate until finally the military leader Diego de Losada assigned to Francisco Infante the specific goal of killing Guaicaipuro. In 1568 a force of 80 men under Infante trapped Guaicaipuro in a small house. When Indian villagers came to Guaicaipuro's assistance, the Spaniards resorted to fire. Forced into the open, Guaicaipuro and his men made easy prey.

The confederation likewise went up in flames, but two men's fame endured. Guaicaipuro was immortalized in literature and history, and Diego de Lasada assured his reputation as the founder of Venezuela's modern capital, Caracas.

GUAJA are called *Wazaizara* (wazai, an ornament of small tufts of feathers stuck with wax in the hair, plus zara, "owner") by the *Guajajara* and *Tembe,* and *Aiaye* by the *Amanaye. Guaja* is a form of gwaza in Portuguese.

The tribe is rarely mentioned in literature. In 1774, Riberio de Sampaio mentions the *Uaya* among the tribes of the lower Tocantins. A list of the tribes exixting in 1861 in the region along the road from Imperatriz to Belem mentions the *Ayaya* as "wild; very few of them are tame, but are timorous and therefore are pursued and killed by the others". The *Uaiara (Guajara)* at times appeared on the upper Gurupi River but did not have a fixed residence.

The *Guaja* wandered without fixed living places through the jungles between the Capim and Upper Gurupi rivers and between the latter and the Pindare River, northward to about lat. 3° 40' S. In 1910 or 1911 a small group of them committed small thefts in the fields at the mouth of the Gurupi Mirim River. The *Tembe* tracked them to the headwaters of the Gurupi Mirim. Although armed with powerful bows and arrows, the *Guaja* there surrendered meekly to their pursuers, who took them to the village. Here the captives soon died of intestinal ills attributed to the *Tembe's* cooked and seasoned food. The language of the two tribes was so similar that they understood each other with ease. In 1943, the botanist Ricardo Froes met a group of them on the upper Caru, a left tributary of the Pindare River.

Culture

The *Guaja* did not have any agriculture whatever, but at times stole from the plantations of the *Tembe, Guajajara,* and *Urubu.* When **caught** they were killed or beaten and imprisoned.

The *Guaja* built only temporary shelters, or merely camped under trees, sleeping on leaf beds on the ground.

Some *Guaja* bows and arrows were procured in by a punitive expedition against the then hostile *Urubu* Indians, who had massacred a *Guaja* camp. The weapons were carelessly made but were very large, the bamboo arrowheads being perhaps the largest known. Little is known of the Guaja today.

GUALE, now extinct, were once large, living in the Southeastern United States.

The word Guale probably means south, and the Spanish used the word to describe the area in which they were found. Their language was of Muskogean stock.

The Guale dwelt originally on the Georgian Coast between St. Andrews Sound and the Savannah River.

Little information exists on either the people or their culture but we do know that they were a mound building tribe. Earth was built up and gathered for tribal meetings. Other enclosures were formed into circles within which the tribe's dead were buried.

Physically the Guale were tall and quite agile. Some, notably the women, were considerably more light skinned than other tribes.

Guale houses were plain and adorned. As they used them solely for habitation, all houses, even the chief's, were small, built of pine and rough timber. Their economy generally revolved around food gathering.

They were met by Juan de Allgon in 1521. Within several years the Spanish established missions in Guale land for the purpose of converting the natives. In 1591 the son of a Guale chief lead a revolt against the missions and only one missionary escaped with his life. Ten years later the governor of Florida led a punitive expedition against the Indians and forced them into submission. The missions were re-established in 1604 and, though more insurrections took place in 1608 and 1645, they never rid themselves of the missions until 1704, when the British, with their Indian allies, crushed the missions in raids against the Spanish. Because of these attacks the Guale asked to be removed. Some were taken to Santa Cruz, others lived outside St. Augustine. Others still joined the Creole confederacy.

Though there were some 4,000 Guale in 1650, by the mid eighteenth century they were practically extinct, having merged with other tribes.

GUANO. Millions of birds on certain small Peruvian islands have formed huge deposits of guano, composed of excrement and the remains of dead birds. The guano was utilized by the coastal Peruvian aborigines for fertilizer, and the Inca enacted laws and exercised royal control for conservation purposes. This natural fertilizer had a large role in Peruvian aboriginal agriculture which was highly developed and which would not have been possible without guano. The exploitation of guano and the birds themselves for food in pre-Columbian times involved marine transportation (by balsa) and semipermanent camps were located on the guano islands. In the 19th century guano was the principal source of national wealth for the Republic of Peru, and until recently was exploited disastrously without conservation.

Garcilaso de la Vega recounted that:

On the sea coast from below Arequipa (south) to Tarapaca, a distance of more than two hundred leagues, they use no other manure than the droppings of sea birds,...(which) fly in such enormous flocks that it would be incredible to any one who had not seen them. They breed on certain desert islands on the coast, and the quantity of manure they make is also incredible. From a distance these heaps of manure look like peaks of snowy mountains. In the time of the Kings Yncas, such care was taken to preserve these birds, that it was unlawful for any one to land on the islands during the breeding season on pain of death; that the birds might not be disturbed or driven from their nests. Nor was it lawful to kill the birds at any time, either on the islands or elsewhere, also on pain of death.

Each island was, by order of the Ynca, set apart for the use of a particular province, or if the island was large it served for two or three provinces; and marks were set up to let the people of one province know their limits, and to prevent them from encroaching on those of another. More minute divisions were also made, to show the portions set apart for each village, which were again subdivided into portions for each individual, according to the quantity of manure that he would require. The inhabitant of one village was punished with death if he took manure from parts set apart for another; nor was he allowed to take more from within his own limits, than had been settled in accordance with the requirements of his lands.

Garcilaso especially mentioned fertilization with guano in the region from Arequipa south to Tarapaca (which is now the northern province of Chile) while the guano islands of today lie far north, from Chincha north almost to Tumbez. There are no coastal islands south of Vieja Island, Bay of Independencia, near Chincha, until one gets south of Valparaiso. Hence guano must have been imported in aboriginal times into these southern provinces. Guano was probably more extensively used from Chincha northward. However, in the middle 1800s, the guanay bird appeared to be a minor inhabitant and small contributor of guano on the northern islands and was found in larger numbers south as far as Tarapaca. This condition may have been existent in *Inca* times, and deposits of guano, now exhausted, may have been built up on the rocky headlands and utilized by the local inhabitants.

The accumulation of guano depends upon the presence of millions of birds, principally the guanay, crowded on small coastal islands.

GUARANI Indians are regarded as part of the Tupi-Guarani group of aborigines who, at the time of the conquest, occupied broad areas of central South America extending from present-day Asunción northeast to the mouth of the Amazon River. They also

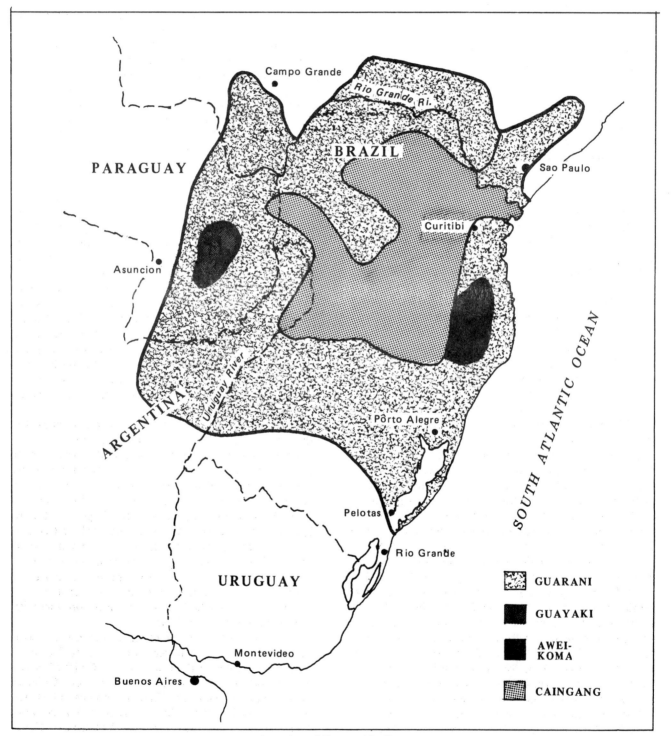

Location of Guarani Indians.

occupied an extensive strip along the eastern Atlantic coast of Brazil. The two complexes, designated respectively the Amazonian and the Coastal Tupi, comprised a large number of mutually related subtribes. Although they were basically of the same origins and cuture, the Guarani had relatively casual contacts with the Tupi to their north and east except for periodic tribal warfare, which marked the area for hundreds of years before the arrival of the Spaniards.

The Guarani are believed to have originated in the Paraguay River basin, centered in the area of the present site of Asunción. From here they spread over an extensive territory of eastern South America between the Rio de la Plata Estuary and the northern Orinoco River. Before the Spanish conquest they practiced a shifting cultivation of maize (corn) and manioc and supplemented their diet with fish and were a generally peaceable and friendly people, but they had a reputation for being formidable in battle. Their descendants still largely retain these qualities.

GUARDIAN SPIRITS, or spirit helpers, were actively sought out by individuals of at least half the cultures of the Americas for help in all important undertakings regarding hunting, warfare, and curing the sick. The seeking out of a guardian spirit sometimes occurred as early as age five, but more often it began at the onset of puberty. On the Plateau children engaged in vision quests and the concept of the guardian spirit was highly developed. In other areas the quest for a spirit helper was limited to boys. A child would go to an isolated spot that reportedly was an adobe for spirits. Usually this was a mountain, lake, or uninhabited forest. He would stay there for several days, fasting, naked, and engaging in self-mutilation to the point of bringing on a hallucination. He would beseech the spirits to take pity on him in his miserable and deprived condition. The first spirit seen usually was an animal spirit who would speak, teach the child a song, demonstrate designs for painting on the body, clothes and weapons for warfare. The youth would return to tell his story, and if he were convincing he might acquire a hunting following or comrades on a warring expedition. If the spirit told of knowledge that was helpful in curing diseases the youth might set himself up as a medicine man.

Quests for visions and the asking of help from guardian spirits was done frequently at intervals throughout the life of individuals to renew or increase the first power of youth. The guardian spirit often served the purpose of guaranteeing self sufficiency in the youth, encouraging initiative in war, hunting, and other activities. It was believed that the guardian spirit would protect from almost any predicament. A vision quest for a guardian spirit was part of the process of acquiring the mark of maturity. Throughout the Great Lakes area and the Mississippi Valley the vision of a guardian spirit was a necessary part of growing up and the first religious retreat, or ''hambeday,'' marked an important event in the life of a youth that could be compared to confirmation in Christian terms. The spirits sometimes were given names such as Canoe People or War Spirit. In some areas important spirits came only to chiefs or shamans. Commoners had less powerful guardian spirits. Among the hunter-gatherers, visions and the friendly help of guardian spirits were available to the average tribesman. The spirit could be contacted only through a vision that was reached after strenuous effort, but when reached he was sure to promise good luck throughout life.

South America

Shamans derived their power from their association with spirits whom they could summon at will to assist them in their many functions. As a rule, ordinary men did not enjoy any companionship with the supernaturals and, therefore, were obliged to resort to shamans when they needed the spirits' assistance. Nevertheless, the notion of the guardian spirit is not entirely lacking in South America; some references occur in the literature, but apparently the concept never was so clearly defined as among North American Indians.

The best instance of the quest for a guardian spirit in the North American manner occurs among the *Charrua* of Uruguay.

Some men went on top of a solitary hill where there was a pile of stones to fast in order to find a companion. There they inflicted on themselves many wounds and suffered a rigorous penance until in their mind they saw a living being whom they invoked in times of peril as their guardian angel.

Witoto myths collected by Preuss contain frequent allusions to protecting animal spirits captured during a hunting party. They advised their master when he was in danger and ran errands for him. There is also an allusion to a guardian spirit in a *Taulipang* myth in which a mutilated man sends his spirit in the guise of a bird to warn his wife.

A statement about the beliefs of the *Island Carib* may be construed as a reference to guardian spirits.

They believe that these good spirits, or gods, are many and every person believes that among them he has one all to himself; this is his particular spirit, his own familiar.

Yet spirits were invoked only through shamans, so that it seems these familiars were not guardian spirits in the strict sense of the word.

Every *Yahgan* was under the protection of a diminutive spirit assigned to him at his birth by a shaman.

The notion of the guardian spirit may perhaps throw some light on the nature of the mystic relationship between the *Inca* and his Wauki, or supernatural guardian, with whom he was united by a fraternal bond. The supernatural brother was represented by a statue. Still, there is little evidence that the belief in a personal guardian was widespread in Peru and even less that it was the soul of some ayllu ancestor.

GUATEMALA. The history of Guatemala is reflected in the composition of its population. To this day more than half the people still live within the Indian culture, and the physical characteristics of the large majority reflect their Indian heritage. The Spaniards who arrived in the 16th century dominated the country for over 300 years and established many of the political and social institutions which have remained until the present. The Spaniards and the Indians did not remain in separate worlds, yet neither did they fuse. Their imperfect blending comprises the history of modern Guatemala.

Guatemala has often been the hub of Central American history, and major historical events were focused within its territory. At one time or another the term Guatemala included all of the Central American isthmus. The area that is now Guatemala and Yucatan was for centuries the center of the Mayan empire. Colonial Guatemala was the capital of the Spanish government for all of Central America and, after independence in 1821, the most powerful state in a short-lived federation. During the 19th century it set the trends in Central American governments, often intervening politically in neighboring countries. It was the strongest proponent of reunification.

Guatemalan history through the 19th and into the 20th century was dominated by four major strongmen. Ruling with a mixture of paternalism and despotism, these men were supported largely by the landowners, the Army, and the Church. A constitutional structure existed but, in practice, the ruler defined the law in his own terms. In 1944, however, a rebellion ousted the last of these four dictators and ushered in a new social and economic order which the new president openly labeled "socialism."

This 1944 revolution was the product of the structural changes that were gradually taking place in Guatemalan society, but it also served to accelerate them. Originally designed as a means of social and economic reform, the movement was infiltrated by Communists who gained firm control of the unions, student groups, and parts of the government by 1954. After the anti-Communist reaction of that year overthrew the government and drove the Communists into hiding, the new government of the Liberation, as it was called, was strongly conservative. The pre-1944 balance was not restored, however, and the ideal, as well as many of the actual laws of the reformist period, was retained.

The deep cleavages between the heirs of the revolutionary decade, 1944-54, and those who opposed them under the banner of "The National Libera-

Location map, Guatemala.

tion'' have created a basically unstable situation. The years between 1954 and 1966 were marked, for example, by the assassination of one president, Castillo Armas; the forcible overthrow of another, Ydigoras Fuentes; and a period of military rule under Colonel Peralta. The latter cleared the way for the constitutional election in 1966 of President Mendez Montenegro, who succeeded in establishing a dialogue between the opposing camps and in reducing to some extent the political polarization of his country.

Pre-Columbian Era

The roots of the country's history are found in the preconquest world. More than half the population is directly descended from Indian tribes. The ruins of ancient cities are found in every part of Guatemala, and aspects of preconquest culture continue to influence and regulate Indian life and to have some bearing on the political, social, and religious structure of present-day Guatemala.

Pre-Mayan and Mayan civilization

Archaeological evidence reveals that the earliest tribes were nomadic hunters who wandered throughout Central America. Many of these later settled in the Guatemalan highlands, building sedentary agricultural communities based on the cultivation of corn.

Between 2,000 and 1,500 BC, similar farming communities began to appear in the El Peten rain forest area in northern Guatemala, and eventually created a corn economy which made the prosperity and growth of the Mayan Empire possible. Most authorities believe that these prehistoric farmers were immigrants from the highlands where traces of pre-Mayan cultures have been found. Others maintain, however, that they were late arrivals from Asia and brought many of their cultural patterns with them.

Whatever their origin, by 400 BC these people were building the foundations of Mayan civilization, one of the most advanced in the New World. They had devised the rudiments of their calendars, had begun the study of mathematics and astronomy, and had invented elementary hieroglyphics. Succeeding generations saw the florescence of this culture and its spread throughout Central America. The Mayan empire eventually covered 125,000 square miles and stretched from Yucatan to Honduras. It included all of Guatemala, with the heart of the empire located at Lake Peten Itza.

Attempts to decipher the Mayan chronology traditionally depended on translations of the calendric symbols found in the Mayan ruins and on clues provided by Bishop Diego de Landa of Yucatan in the 16th century. The various readings of the symbols, however, do not coincide. In the 1930's the Spinden and Makemson system, which placed the beginnings of the Mayan classic or golden age at AD 68, was the most popular. Since the 1940's a system called the Goodman-Martinez-Thompson calendar, which moves the date 250 years ahead to AD 317, has been dominant. A more recent method of establishing the chronology uses radioactive carbon tests which confirm the ages of wood found in Mayan artifacts. These tests, which have not been universally accepted, would strongly favor the Spinden and Makemson calendar.

Since the mathematical system was based on the number 20, the calendric computations divided the year into 18 months of 20 days each, with an extra month of 5 holy days. This same chronology is used in the highlands today and, as in the past, religious ceremonies tied to calendar observations are considered vital to the agricultural process. This veneration of numbers and yearly cycles, also found in the modern Guatemalan Indians, partly accounts for the supremacy of the Mayan priests who calculated and forecast the important dates.

The social life of the Mayas could best be described as a highly stratified theocracy. At the lowest level were the farmers who lived on their small plots surrounding the city, supported the priestly class, and supplied the labor for the temples and obelisks. At the next level were the priests, also accomplished mathematicians and astronomers, who conducted the religious rituals. These seasonal rites were tied to calendric counts and governed most social, economic, and political aspects of Mayan life. Information concerning the governmental structure is scarce and theories vary. If a hereditary nobility existed, it did not wield great power, and it appears more probable that the priests handled all political responsibilities.

Mayan cities were probably both religious centers and markets, which were busy on certain days and deserted on others. It is unlikely that even the priests lived within the city proper. The cities did contain, however, the tiered pyramids with temples located at the top and the dated obelisks which commemorated 10-year periods.

In a sense, the term Mayan empire is a misnomer because there was no central authority, and each city was a separate and autonomous state. These states were in rivalry with one another, but there was little warfare, and the Mayan culture remained remarkably homogeneous. Their language and religious practices were uniform throughout the empire. The ruins in Tikal, Piedras Negras, Copan and others all reveal a contiguous culture with a few regional variations.

About 500 years after the beginning of the golden age, a general decay began within the cities, and in a century the El Peten rain forest area was abandoned. This desertion has been attributed to the slash-and-burn farming techniques which eventually turned the forests into savannas. There is a possibility that the soil was exhausted through intensive use and the crop yield was no longer sufficient to support the cities. Other theories contend that disease, a revolt against the priests, or raids by less civilized groups from the north caused the disappearance of the El Peten

Smithsonian Institution, Bureau of American Ethnology.

Pottery cylinder from Yalloch, Guatemala.

Pottery vase from Yalloch, Guatemala.

civilization. To a considerable extent, the lowlands of Yucatan, the El Peten and the Guatemalan highlands returned to their pre-Mayan patterns, and the forests swallowed the ruins.

Post-Mayan civilization

The Yucatan cities which were built during the period of classic high culture were outposts of the Mayan civilizations and became the centers of a new florescence during the second millennium AD. This renaissance, however, was not pure Mayan but contained many elements of central Mexican culture. It is generally believed that an invasion from the north revived the waning Yucatan civilization and established new cities around the *cenotes* (natural wells).

Chichen Itza, Mayapan, and Uxmal, all ruled by families from the central valley of Mexico, became the main centers of this new empire. Mexican gods were imported, such as Kukulcan or Quetzalcoatl — a feathered serpent requiring human sacrifice on a large scale — and architecture and art assumed many Mexican characteristics. In time the Mexican elite lost most of their original heritage and were assimilated into the Mayan culture. This acculturation was not complete, however, and as the civilization became more secular, it also became more militaristic. Civil war erupted in AD 1200 and was won by the Mayapan dynasty. The Itza family, formerly the rulers of Chichen Itza, retreated to El Peten, and for over 200 years Yucatan was ruled by a centralized authority. In 1435 this central control was broken and, when the Spanish arrived, the cities were again fighting among themselves.

The history of Yucatan is paralleled somewhat in the highlands of Guatemala. Here too a group of Mexican invaders called Quiche conquered the local Mayan tribes and established their hegemony over surrounding areas. They eventually split into three nations, and the strongest, the Maya-Quiche, settled on the northwest shores of Lake Atitlan. The Cakchiquel took the northeast shore, and the Tzutuhil moved to the south. All three groups imposed the worship of Kukulcan and imported other Mexican traditions. They were, however, eventually assimilated and became more Mayan than Mexican.

The highlands had long been the destination of immigrating tribes, and the Quiches were only one of three great migrations. The Mam nation, which preceded the Quiche, migrated to an area of the Guatemalan highlands known today as Huehuetenango. The third nation, the Rabinal, settled in the present-day Departments of Alta and Baja Verapaz. These latter were fierce and invincible fighters who were never defeated by the Spanish armies, but were finally brought under Hispanic rule by Dominican priests.

Eventually, the Quiches became the ruling nation and held sway over most of the highlands. During the 15th century, however, when the Mayapan dynasty fell

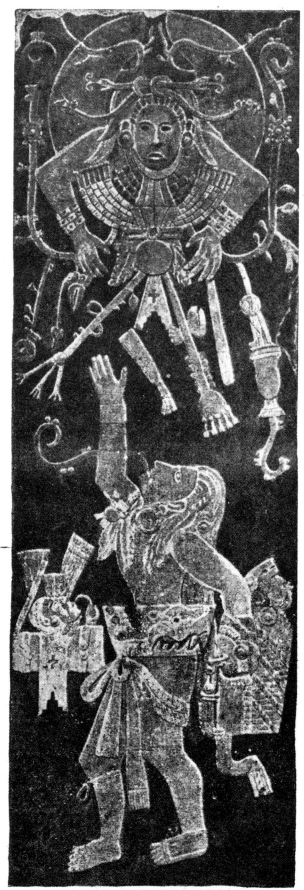

Guatemalan Symbols.

in Yucatan, the Quiche empire also collapsed. When the Spaniards arrived, internecine warfare characterized the area. Not even the threat of total defeat and subjugation by the Spaniards could end the tribal quarrels and create a united Indian army.

Preconquest Guatemala reveals a blending of several Indian cultures and groups dominated by a large Mayan strain. The Hispanic invasion destroyed many elements in this blend, especially the political and social structures. In other aspects, however, the conquest is only one event in a long and continuous history.

Conquest And Colonization

Subjugation of the Highlands

The Spanish conquest which began in the Caribbean area moved rapidly to the Guatemalan highlands. Only 32 years after Columbus landed in Santo Domingo, Pedro de Alvarado, the conqueror of much of Central America, crossed the Suchiate River into Guatemala. At this time the Guatemalan Indians were concentrated in the highlands, and the El Peten rain forest had long been deserted, except around Lake Peten Itza. These Indians first experienced the consequences of the Hispanic invasion when smallpox and other European diseases swept down from the north,

decimating the highland tribes. Pedro de Alvarado, however, brought the first Spanish army to the area.

Alvarado, a loyal and ruthless lieutenant under Cortes, was sent in 1523 to subdue the Maya-Quiche, the Cakchiquels, and the Tzutuhil tribes. His army consisted of 120 horsemen, 300 Spanish infantry, 4 small cannons, 40 reserve horses, and 300 Mexican allies. The Mexicans were responsible for renaming Mayan sites and, as a result, many cities and departments in Guatemala today bear Nahuatl titles.

The highland tribes might have defeated Alvarado's small force if they had joined together. They were, however, unable to forget their intertribal quarrels and many, such as the Cakchiquels, allied with the Spaniards to defeat their Indian enemies. The Spaniards eventually repaid this favor by turning against the Cakchiquels.

The first opposing native forces which the Spaniards met were the Quiche and the Soconusco of southern Mexico. The Spanish easily defeated these tribes and continued into the highlands. The Quiches, however, persisted and, early in 1524, met the invaders outside the city of Quezaltenango. Their chief, Tecun Uman, engaged Alvarado in personal combat and was killed. This ended not only the Indians' attack but the last army of the Quiche as well.

The remaining Quiche kings attempted to defeat Alvarado through trickery and invited him to their fortress. They planned to trap the Spaniards, burn the town, and kill them during the ensuing confusion. Alvarado, however, suspected the ruse and captured the kings instead, burning them alive for their treachery. Except for sporadic guerrilla attacks, this ended Quiche resistance.

During their war with the Quiches, the Spanish had been aided by the Cakchiquels, who also helped them to defeat other highland tribes. When the main Indian nations had been subdued. Alvarado began to demand tribute, both slaves and gold, from his former allies. The Cakchiquel leaders were killed by Alvarado as a lesson to their people, and thousands were literally worked to death attempting to fill the Spanish quota of gold. This situation was duplicated in every part of the Guatemalan highlands, setting the pattern for 300 years of subjugation and exploitation.

The scattered remains of the various Indian tribes finally joined together against the Spanish, but their effort came too late. Their armies were destroyed, their rulers were dead, and the Spanish were in control. Pockets of resistance existed, but these did not prevent the beginning of colonization.

Colonial political structure

Alvarado established the first capital of Central America in Guatemala in the old Cakchiquel fortress. It was called Santiago de los Caballeros, in honor of St. James, the patron saint of the conquerors. In less than a year, however, this site was abandoned, and the capital was moved to a valley between the volcanoes Agua and Fuego. This new community remained the center of Government until 1541 when it was destroyed by a flood. The capital was then reestablished in the valley of Panchoy and again called *Santiago de los Caballeros.* Today it is known as *Antigua.*

Alvarado was appointed *adelantado* (governor) of the Kingdom of Guatemala, but he lacked the capacity for administration. The dangers and rewards of exploration and combat were more to his liking, and he left the area on various expeditions. In 1541 he was killed during a search for the legendary Seven Cities of Cibola in northern Mexico.

The colonial era was virtually a static period in Guatemalan history. There were few outstanding events and little social or technological progress. Yet the Hispanic social, political, and religious institutions assumed their basic form during these 300 years.

In 1542 King Philip of Spain promulgated laws which organized the political structure of the colonies. Three *audiencias* (the supreme judicial bodies in the New World) were established, and one was brought to the Central American area in 1544. The capital of this court was moved to Guatemala in 1549.

Spain separated Central America from the viceroyalty of New Spain or Mexico in 1560, and a captain-general, the Crown's direct representative carrying the second highest rank of the colonies, was appointed for the area. The new captaincy-general was called the Kingdom of Guatemala and included the six provinces of Guatemala, Honduras, El Salvador, Costa Rica, Nicaragua, and Chiapas. It was theoretically subordinate to New Spain but, as its name implied, functioned as an autonomous state because of the lack of transportation and communication between Mexico and Guatemala.

Within Central America itself there was no strong central authority and, by necessity, each of the provinces had to govern its own affairs. Thus each State developed independently and evolved its own separate identity. The provinces had no history of functioning unity, even during the colonial era.

Although they controlled their own affairs, the provinces still looked to Guatemala as the center of power in the captaincy-general. It was the largest and most populous state, and set the trends for the area in most matters, from politics to fashions. Because of the captain-general's lower rank within colonial structure, however, he was closely checked upon by other Spanish authorities. Thus, the *audiencia* exercised more power here than in either of the viceroyalties of Peru or Mexico.

Aside from this stricter control, the governmental structure in Guatemala was similar to that found in all of Spanish America. The highest officials, such as members of the *audiencia* and the captain-general, were appointed by the king and were always *peninsulares* (persons born in Spain). The *criollos* (Spaniards who were born in the colonies) were allowed to hold only minor posts and occupied secondary positions in the social structure as well.

The remaining positions, local and national, which were not directly appointed, were sold by the Crown. This practice concentrated both power and wealth in a few hands. It also encouraged graft and corruption in public office, since the appointed official usually sought a return on what he thought of as his investment.

The provincial political structure included three levels of authority. At the lowest level the *regidores* (councilmen) who made local decisions were found in the Spanish towns. At the next level were the officers who ruled over the districts or larger towns. In the Spanish districts they were known as *alcaldes mayores* and, in the predominantly Indian areas, they were known as *corregidores.* There were also *gobiernos* (governors), who had been appointed before the *audiencia* existed.

In an effort to eliminate abuses and to bring the colonies under more direct control, the political structure was altered. In 1786 King Charles issued new laws reorganizing the colonial government by replacing the governors, *corregidores* and the *alcaldes mayores* with local administrators called *intendentes.* They were paid a better salary and were therefore less involved in petty corruption.

Guatemala remained isolated for much of its colonial era, both from neighboring provinces and foreign countries. Not only were communications and transportation extremely poor, but Spanish policy discouraged strong ties between the colonies. Nor did the area maintain contact with Europe through immigrants, for very few Spaniards were attracted to Guatemala. The early colonists were not looking for rich farming and grazing lands, but for gold and silver, and Guatemala had very little mineral wealth. Foreigners might have filled the gap, but the Crown passed restrictive laws against foreign immigration. A minority of wealthy Spaniards in the colonies sent for wives from Spain, although most married Indian women or *mestizas*.

Besides discouraging foreign settlement, the Spanish Government also legally forbade any trade with other countries. Originally this law included commerce with neighboring provinces and made Spain the only market for exports. This restriction on inter-colonial trade was eliminated in 1774. Laws against foreign trade, however, were never enforced, and in some areas the quanitity of smuggled goods became greater than that of legal trade.

The major sources of contact with foreigners were the pirates who ravaged the coastal cities. Guatemala, as a center of judicial, military, and governmental power, was obligated to provide protection against these raids. Poor communications, however, usually prevented knowledge of an attack from reaching the capital in time for effective action. Furthermore, the people within Guatemala made determined efforts to prevent the military force from leaving the capital unprotected. This contributed to deepened provincial separation in Central America.

The Indians played a very small role in the political process. In the early years of the colony, groups of Indians had been awarded to *conquistadores* in grants called *encomenderos,* promised to convert the natives in exchange for labor or monetary tribute. This system was greatly abused and was officially abolished in 1542. In practice, however, it continued throughout the colonial era, and became the model for forced labor systems imposed on the Indians by succeeding governments.

The *encomiendas* were officially replaced by a labor system called *repartimiento* which alloted a number of Indians to specific tasks, usually public works. Laws against malpractices existed but were seldom enforced, and the system became, in practice, slave labor. Women and children were not exempt from the forced-labor systems, and the Guatemalans were notorious for their exploitation of these two groups.

Those Indians who were not part of an *encomienda* grant were forced to move into towns around 1550. Both the Church and the Government preferred to have the Indian population under stricter control in these centralized locations. Some of these towns have since remained predominantly Indian.

Social and Religious Structure

The social classes in colonial Guatemala were rigidly stratified and clearly defined. The *peninsulares* occupied the highest level and controlled the most important positions in the Government. Wealthy *criollos* came next and were followed by craftsmen and artisans sent from Europe. At a much lower level were the populations of mixed ancestry and the Negro freedmen. The Indians and the Negro slaves occupied the lowest position in the class structure.

The two upper classes lived in relative comfort and luxury. Most owned country estates as well as large homes within the provincial capitals. These two groups, however, became increasingly hostile to one another because the *criollos* resented the higher status and the power of the *peninsulares*. This antagonism and the *criollos'* desire to replace the *peninsulares* eventually gave strong impetus to the independence movement.

The people of mixed racial origin usually lived in the urban areas and became merchants, craftsmen, or servants. It was during this time that the term *ladino* first came into general use. It was originally applied to the urban artisans but, as more and more *mestizos* moved into this class, *ladino* became synonymous with *mesitzo*. In the 20th century the term has been broadened by some to include all those who do not follow Indian customs.

During the latter part of the colonial era, the social structure became more flexible. Indians who moved to the urban areas, wore Western clothes, and spoke Spanish, became members of the *mestizo* class. A few *mestizos* acquired wealth and prestige and joined the *criollo* class. Social mobility existed to a certain extent in practice, but the rigid definitions of social classes remained.

The Roman Catholic clergy was one of the most powerful groups in the colonial structure and was at least as important as the secular officialdom. The first priests arrived with the conquerors and began the task of converting the Indians. Many became the Indians' protectors against the brutality and avarice of the *encomenderos* and continually fought for fair treatment of the native population.

Bartolome de las Casas, a Dominican priest, became the symbol of these missionaries. He first brought the plight of the Indian to the attention of Europe and the Spanish king through a book called *A Very Brief Account of the Destruction of the Indies*. This book and the influence which the priest had with King Philip were the reasons behind the New Laws of 1542 which abolished the *encomiendas* and made the Indians vassals of the Crown. These laws, however, had little practical effect, and the colonists continued their exploitive practices.

Shortly after the conquest, Las Casas arrived in the Kingdom of Guatemala as Bishop of Chiapas, and in 1537 reached an understanding with the Government officials. They promised to keep military force out of the territory of the Rabinal, the only major Indian nation which the Spaniards had not yet defeated. In return, Las Casas promised to convert the Indians to Christianity and to a peaceful way of life. Five years later, this conversion was accomplished, and the Crown changed the name of the area to Verapaz, or "the true peace."

Father Francisco Marroquin arrived in 1534 and became the first bishop of the Kingdom of Guatemala. He divided the area among the threee dominant orders, the Franciscans, the Dominicans, and the Mercedarians, granting each group one or more of the six provinces. These groups were later joined by the Jesuits who became the largest and wealthiest order in the New World. The orders became masters of huge tracts of land and large numbers of Indians, and their missions have often been described as autonomous kingdoms. The orders were self-sufficient and became increasingly wealthy, since they were exempt from taxes and received large incomes from their agricultural and industrial projects.

The clergy did not, however, confine its efforts to the Indians. Catholic churches were built in every Spanish town, where they were usually the largest and most beautiful buildings. The orders were in charge of education and established and operated the only schools in Guatemala. The first university, named the University of San Carlos, was founded in Antigua in 1676. The teachers were Dominicans, Jesuits, and Franciscans. In addition, the clergy built hospitals and supported the arts, such as painting, architecture, and literature.

As the Church became wealthier and more entrenched in the social and political framework of the colony, it also became more conservative. The ardent missionaries of the conquest were replaced for the most part by men who favored the status quo and a minimum of social upheaval. The Indians were still protected, but the Church began to agree with the colonists and considered forced labor necessary for the preservation of the colony.

Most of the native population was nominally converted to Catholicism, but their religion contained a strong indigenous flavor. The Mayan calendar was kept, and ancient religious agricultural festivals were still observed. In effect, the Indians practiced a highly syncretic faith.

Antigua, the capital of Guatemala until 1773, was the center of Church power. Native and Spanish stonemasons, silversmiths, and sculptors built magnificent churches. Paintings set with gold and silver told the stories of various saints, and opulent monasteries and convents were built. Antigua became a symbol of ecclesiastical wealth, prestige, and power.

In 1773, however, severe earth tremors shook the city and in July an earthquake partially destroyed the churches and palaces. The governor and the anticlerical party announced the political evacuation of the city. The priests strongly protested this move, and only an edict from the King finally ended the feud and established the new capital at its present site. There has been some conjecture that the quake was simply used as an excuse to limit clerical power. Both the destruction of Antigua and the expulsion of the Jesuits 6 years earlier seriously weakened the Church.

Economic aspects

From Spain's viewpoint, the colonies were a business venture and were expected to support the mother country. As a consequence, the colonial economic system was tightly controlled. Central America was no exception, although it was not one of the Crown's favored possessions. The area had little gold and silver, the colonial definition of wealth, and this was depleted in a short while. In lieu of minerals, the colonists sought crops which could be profitably traded.

Farming and grazing became large enterprises, and the Spanish were soon growing cacao, indigo, cotton, and tobacco. The first two, both indigenous products, became Guatemala's largest exports, especially to surrounding colonies when the ban against intercolony trade was lifted. Guatemala also exported balsam, sarsaparilla, quinine, gums, and resins. Some products were brought from Spain, both for profit and to remind the colonists of home. The mother country, however, was watchful of its own economy and wanted no competition from Spanish America. Laws prohibited the cultivation of mulberry trees, flax, and the production of wine within the colonies.

The forbidding of trade between the colonies and foreign countries simply increased the level of illegal trade with the Dutch, English, and French. This commerce monopoly, moreover, also encouraged piracy, and for decades the coastal cities were continually attacked by Dutch, English, and French pirates.

On the whole, the colonial economy was static. The Indians retained their traditional patterns of agriculture, and corn was still the largest crop grown in Guatemala. Even the Spaniards and Negroes accepted this food staple as they did the kidney bean, another indigenous contribution. Native fruits and vegetables were supplemented by imported varieties.

The greatest change in the economy was the introduction of domesticated animals. The pre-Columbian Indians raised for food no animal larger than a turkey, and employed no beasts of burden. The Spanish brought the horse and also imported and bred mules, cattle, and pigs.

On the whole, the colonial economy was a system of extremes. At the top were the few wealthy families who traded in cacao and indigo or bred cattle. At the bottom were the Indian or *mestizo* farmers who worked small corn plots and lived on a subsistence level. In between were the artisans and merchants who were closer economically to the Indian than to the wealthy.

Pictured gestures.

Cultural aspects

The cultural changes which occurred in colonial Guatemala were mainly the replacement of Indian with Spanish arts. The Mayan ball game disappeared, and the bullfight became popular. Indian plays and dances were largely forgotten, and Hispanic themes, such as the conquest of the Moors, were enacted. In Guatemala the struggle between the Quiche and Alvarado became a favorite theme for dramatic performance, but it was acted in the traditional Spanish style. Indian archetecture was neglected, but the Spanish churches and palaces in Guatemala were some of the most elegant and ornate in the Central American area.

Nevertheless, indigenous culture did not disappear. The Indians retained their language, much of their religion, many of their dances, and a great deal of their oral traditions. They accepted parts of the Spanish culture, but their own was not forgotten. In places, the Hispanic innovations were simply a facade for the indigenous customs. The colonial Spanish culture did not consciously incorporate any of the classic Mayan patterns and was only peripherally influenced by the 16th century Indian culture. Spaniards retained Europe as their model in art and intellectual thought.

Spanish paintings and sculptures were, for the most part, confined to religious subjects. Both Indian and European artisans were employed to decorate the religious and governmental buildings, but the style was European with few New World innovations. Since most of Guatemala's major buildings were found in Antigua, some of the best colonial art was destroyed in the earthquake.

Historical chronicles written by the conquerors and by Franciscan and Dominican priests constituted the earliest literature of the era. The best known of these is the story of the conquest of Mexico and Honduras by Bernal Diaz. The most distinctive literary

Cross from Guatemala.

A sculpterd head of the Maya Indians of Guatemala.

achievements, however, were written in the 16th century by Guatemalan Indians who were taught to write by the priests. *The Popol Vuh* is a Quiche document giving a vivid picture of the preconquest world. *The Annals of the Cakchiquels* records the events of the conquest and its immediate aftermath. The education of the Indians, however, gradually ceased and literary works were found only in the elite class.

The Church controlled the educational system in Guatemala and established various schools, both for the clergy and the laymen, throughout the province. During the colonial period the University of San Carlos, founded in 1676, was Guatemala's only institution of higher learning. The intellectual life of the colony was not, however, completely dominated by the Church and, in the 18th century, intellectual currents opposed to Church doctrine were especially strong. The French Revolution and its resulting philosophies and ideals had a powerful impact, especially in the capital, and laid part of the groundwork for the independence movement.

Independence And Dictators (1820-1944).

During the last decades of the 18th century, the political pace in Guatemala quickened and a new regional awareness evolved. The partial destruction of Antigua in 1773 disrupted trade and commerce and ruined many of the wealthy merchants. The more secular atmosphere in the relocated capital allowed the rise of new social and economic groups who were the precursors of Guatemala's political parties.

Juan Fermin Aycinena was one of the first men to take advantage of the economic opportunities and by doing so became very wealthy. He purchased the title of Marquis and was the only *criollo* holder of a noble title in the entire Central American area. With his wealth and claim to nobility, he and his relatives became the aristocracy of Guatemalan society and the head of a powerful economic and political faction known as "the family."

Though the Fermin Aycinena clan eventually lost its dominant position in Guatemalan society, it was representative of the conservative landowning oligarchy which would eventually form one of the most powerful classes in the nation. The elitist ideals of the family and of its peers became the major tenets of the Conservative Party in the 19th century.

The economic elite of the Central American area was not, however, a unified group, but was split by the rivalry between the capital and the provinces and between merchants and planters. The interests of part of the elite were represented in the *consulado* (merchants' guild), which was located in the capital. The planters in the provinces formed an indigo growers' society to combat the power of the merchants.

As indigo trade declined, the split between the *consulado* and the growers' society worsened. The official economic policy, since the merchants had trade contracts in Spain, usually worked to the disadvantage of the growers. Resentment between the two groups increased, and the economic wedge between the capital and the provinces was a significant element in the eventual failure of the Central American Union in the 19th century.

In addition to this rivalry, other situations were laying the foundations for independence. The first session of the Economic Society of Friends of the Country met in 1796 and discussed means by which the provinces could realize their full potential. This group disbanded 3 years later, but it left functioning the first newspaper, the *Guatemala Gazette,* which published debates and editorials on colonial matters.

Although conditions within the colony played a role in its preparation for independence, the first impetus came from Europe. In 1808 Napoleon invaded Spain and deposed Ferdinand VII. The royal court was held in exile, but a *cortes* (parliament) was established in Cadiz for all Spaniards, *criollos* or *peninsulares,* who were loyal to the Bourbon King.

This *cortes,* liberal in orientation, offered fuller representation to the colonies and a freer economic policy. Most Guatemalans supported these plans and sent the colony's representative to Cadiz in 1810. The Fermin Aycienena family was particularly vociferous in its support of freer trade, which would weaken the monopoly of the *peninsular* merchants in Guatemala.

This backing of the liberal *cortes* did not necessarily imply a desire for independence or decreased loyalty to the King. There was little, if any Guatemalan support for the insurrection in Mexico led by Miguel Hidalgo in 1810. In the years immediately following, however, sympathy for the independence movement increased in direct proportion to the suppression of proponents of more liberal policies by the captain-general and the returned King. Nonetheless, it is doubtful that Guatemala would have broken with Spain if Mexico had not taken the lead.

In 1811 a new captain-general, Jose de Bustamente, arrived and soon revealed his strong support of the Bourbon monarchy. During the next 7 years he repressed three rebellions on the isthmus and refused to honor concessions won by the *cortes,* including the Fermin Aycinenas, experienced political persecution.

By 1818 liberal policies were again in the ascendancy. A new captain-general was appointed, and in 1820 the Constitution of 1812 was restored. Freer trade policies were authorized and political discussions were prevalent. The elections, permitted by the Constitution, brought two political parties to the forefront.

The first, called Cacos, was a combination of certain members of the economic elite and liberal professional men. This alliance, originally founded on a shared hatred of Bustamente, began to advance the cause of an open economic system. Opposing the Cacos were the Bacos, or merchants and their allies. The Cacos won control of the provincial deputation, and the Bacos won the seats in the municipal government of the capital city.

The differences between and within the two became more acute when Mexico declared its independence from Spain. Many Guatemalan *criollos* decided that their interests lay with a break from Spain, and the loyalists, to prevent a civil war, conceded. The captain-general declared provisional independence on September 14, 1821, made himself head of the new government, and called for a regional congress. In short, the political structure remained intact but the power of the ruling *criollos* was increased. This group was now faced with the decision of complete independence or union with Mexico.

Augustin Iturbide, the military leader of the revolutionaries in Mexico, issued the Plan of Iguala, which called for unification of the colonies from California to Panama under the rule of a European king. Many isthmian provinces, which later became the Central American Republics, sought this connection in an effort to prevent Guatemalan domination. Within Guatemala itself, certain groups were also in favor of union with Mexico. The position of these groups was reinforced when Iturbide sent an army headed by General Vincente Filisola to the Central American area. He attempted to bring all the pro-

vinces under Mexican domination and in 1823 was in the process of subduing El Salvador when word came of Iturbide's fall. The annexation had lasted only 18 months, during which a regional government was never convened.

The final result of the episode was the loss of the province of Chiapas which elected to join Mexico. Guatemala, however, refused to acknowledge the loss, and the issue remained a problem for many years.

The Central American Nation

Filisola remained in Central America long enough to call a Congress which adopted a Federal Constitution in 1824. The United Provinces of Central America (Provincias Unidas del Centro de America) became the official title of the new nation, although in practice the Provinces were anything but unified. Within this federation were the Provinces of Guatemala, El Salvador, Honduras, Nicaragua, and Costa Rica. Additional turmoil and instability existed within the provinces themselves, and each was torn by factional strife between the two prevailing political parties.

Political divisions had begun with the old economic rivalries of the 18th century, but new philosophies had appeared, interests had changed, and the new political situation had altered alliances. By 1824 the Liberal Party was anticlerical, federalist, and states' rightist. Generally considered centralists, the members of the Conservative Party sought to preserve the status of the Church and the privileges of the elite. The Fermin Aycinena family had lost much of its power and had become a part of the Conservative Party during the Mexican intervention.

The first President of the weak federation of Central America was Jose Arce. Each province also had its own president who exercised considerable power. The influence and role of the Federation President depended upon the support of these provincial leaders. Arce attempted to win the Conservative Party following and, in doing so, alienated the Liberals. As a consequence, Central America became a battleground between the Conservatives and Liberals who attempted to depose Arce. Led by General Francisco Morazan, Liberal forces succeeded in capturing the Guatemalan capital in 1829. A year later Morazan was elected President of the Federation.

The next 9 years were characterized by anticlerical actions, liberal social politics, and civil insurrections. Morazan attempted to hold the union together, but divisive forces were too strong. At one time, dissatisfaction with the Liberal Government was so intense in the highlands of the country that they seceded from the rest of Guatemala. The Departments of Quezaltenango, Solola, Huehuetenango, and San Marcos formed the independent state of Los Altos.

Morazan was reelected in 1834, but 3 years later was faced with a full-scale Conservative rebellion in Guatemala. The *campesinos* joined a revolt led by Rafael Carrera, an illiterate Indian. The turmoil spread to all the provinces, and once more civil war erupted. Morazan rallied his Liberal forces, but Carrera won in Guatemala. Mariano Galvez, the Liberal President of Guatemala, was overthrown and, by 1839, the Conservative Party was in control of the government.

The Union still existed on paper, but it had lost all authority and power. Its dissolution was gradual, as first one and then another state declared its independence. Guatemala withdrew on April 16, 1839, and Morazan, the leading proponent of the Central American Union, was executed in 1842. The ideal of unity has survived, however, and is resurrected at intervals.

Conservative Era

In 1839 the Indian Rafael Carrera assumed control of Guatemala and maintained it, either directly or through puppets, for the next 26 years. He headed a Conservative Government which strongly suppressed the Liberals. In 1840 he subjugated the State of Los Altos and officially became president of the entire nation in 1844. Carrera became the first of Guatemala's dictators to rule as a *caudillo*. In Latin America this term is applied to those leaders who rule through the magnetism of their personality. They seldom rely on constitutional methods.

During Carrera's era the landowners and wealthy merchants were labeled the aristocracy and, along with the Church, were firmly installed in power. The Indians, who virtually worshipped Carrera and were his primary supporters, received little benefit from his rule. Except for military and road service, the demand for Indian labor had decreased. The native populations retreated into highland villages, building and syntheisizing their institutions, goals, and values. Contacts between the Indians and *ladinos* were at a minimum, and the cultural breach between the two widened.

Carrera's rule was characterized by harshness and cruelty, but he strongly upheld the legal system. In 1851 a conservative Constitution was promulgated which created a Congress controlled by the landowners and the Church. The primary duty of the Congress was the election of the president who legally exercised absolute power. When, in 1854, Carrera was chosen President for life, even this duty of the legislature was discontinued.

During the 26-year rule, Carrera made very little social or economic progress. His time was devoted to maintaining domestic tranquillity and protecting the privileges of the conservative class, both in Guatemala and in neighboring countries. Carrera supported a rebellion in El Salvador against the Liberal Party President, Gerado Barrios, and installed his own Conservative candidate in the office. He invaded Nicaragua in a joint Central American effort to oust William Walker, the North American adventurer who then controlled the Nicaraguan government. In all,

Carrera placed his own men in the presidency of El Salvador, Nicaragua, and Honduras, creating a conservative empire in Central America.

Carrera set the trend of autocratic government which characterized both Guatemala and her neighbors for the next 100 years. Although liberal governments would again assume control, the pattern of autocratic rule had been established and even liberal presidents continued the tradition.

One important aspect of Carrera's foreign policy which has had repercussions in the 20th century was a treaty signed in 1859 with Great Britain, defining the borders between Belize (British Honduras), an area between the Caribbean Coast and El Peten, and Guatemala. In colonial times Spain had granted Great Britain the right to cut dye woods in the area now called *Belize,* but the land itself was never ceded to the English.

Liberal Party dominance

Carrera died in 1865, but his government continued in the hands of Picente Cerna, his personally chosen successor. Cerna, however, lacked Carrera's power and personal magnetism and, at the beginning of his second term in 1869, a Liberal rebellion erupted led by Miguel Garcia Granados and Justo Rufino Barrios. The Liberals captured the city of Guatemala in 1871, and Garcia was declared provisional president. A moderate Liberal, he served only 2 years and was replaced by Rufino Barrios who ruled until 1885.

While Barrios professed Liberal ideals he ruled in the same autocratic style as Carrera. Although he took office in 1873, the country had no constitution until 6 years later. The new document was a model of Liberal doctrine and lasted for 66 years with minor amendments. It called for separation of Church and State, a 6-year term for the president, a unicameral legislature, and a bill of rights protecting the individual citizens. Nothing except the position of the Catholic Church, however, changed substantially.

The rise of coffee plantations had increased the need for Indian labor, and in 1877 debt peonage was legalized. This system allowed the landowners to demand the repayment of loans with certain amounts of work. Since wages were extremely low, the Indians were always in debt and sometimes were obligated for years of labor. Their children inherited their debts. Labor shortage continued, however, and in 1878 a vagrancy law was passed which required the unemployed to work 40 days on government projects. These laws destroyed the isolation which the Indians had created over the past 20 years.

Barrios did support schools within the Indian villages and, in fact, was an enthusiastic proponent of a better educational program for all of Guatemala. He disbanded the Church schools and replaced them with public schools under his direction. A university, a normal, and a military school were established as well as elementary and vocational schools throughout the country. He attempted to found free public schools which would require compulsory attendance, but the budget for this enterprise was less than one-quarter of that of the **War Department**.

Barrios' anticlerical laws were harsh and extensive. He expelled the Jesuits in 1871 and the bishops and the archbishops soon after. His campaign against the Church increased in scope and intensity, and in 1875 clerics were forbidden to teach. The government next confiscated all properties of the Church, destroying much of its political and economic power. Churchmen were prohibited from wearing clerical garb, public religious processions were banned, and civil marriage was declared obligatory. The institutionalized political power and prestige of the Church was weakened, but its influence among the Indians and the poor in general increased in proportion to the severity of the government measures against it.

The economic policies instituted by Barrios made perhaps his greatest permanent mark on the nation. He literally brought the industrial revolution to many parts of Guatemala and introduced railroads, river steamers, electric lights, streetcars, and other manifestations of modern technology. He accomplished this by granting concessions to foreigners, especially Americans, for mining, building railroads, establishing plantations, building ports, and installing telephone and telegraph systems. Because of his support and persistence, a railroad was constructed to connect the Pacific Coast and the capital, and one to the Caribbean was partially completed.

The agricultural system was also advanced as Barrios sought to expand the country's economic base. He encouraged the planting of coffee and offered free trees to those who could not afford to buy them. In addition, government officials were ordered to plant the crop in all suitable areas. Free land was offered to those who promised to plant rubber, sarsaparilla, and cacao, or to raise cattle. He was also influential in encouraging the banana industry on the north coast.

Barrios had little faith in the Indians' potential. He saw the slavation of the country in immigration and encouraged large colonialization projects. The Germans took advantage of these and established the coffee plantations, which became the basis of the Guatemalan economy in the 20th century.

In short, Barrios was a progressive dictator, harsh and despotic but an energetic leader. Little social progress took place during his era, but the economic gains were extensive, even though he was diverted by the old Liberal dream of a unified Central America and spent much of the nation's resources striving to achieve it.

Like Carrera, he frequently intervened in the governments of neighboring countries. The Liberal presidents of Honduras and El Salvador remained in power partly because of his support. Nicaragua felt his influence, as did Costa Rica. Only Honduras, however, fully supported his plan to recreate the Central American Union.

On February 28, 1885, Barrios issued a decree which placed Guatemala at the head of the proposed Union and made him Supreme Chief of the Armies. Confident of support from the people of all of Central America he set forth with the Guatemalan Army on March 23 to impose unity upon the region. El Salvador, though sympathetic to the ideal, did not approve of the creation of the Union by force and joined with Costa Rica and Nicaragua against him. The first battle took place at Chalchuapa, El Salvador, and Barrios was killed. Without his leadership, the Guatemalan Army was easily defeated, and the Union was stillborn.

The end of the Barrios regime also ended the normal form of party politics; the traditional Liberal and Conservative divisions lost all meaning. The labels remained, but the parties became vehicles for personalities rather than ideals. The landowners, the Army, and the Church hierarchy all joined to support men who would impose order and preserve the status quo. Lip service was paid to the Liberal Constitution promulgated under Barrios, but the men who followed him were Liberals in name only.

Two presidents held office for 6 years after the death of Barrios. In 1892 Jose Reina Barrios, nephew of the former president, became head of the government. After he was assassinated in 1898, his successor was Manuel Estrada Cabrera, who ruled until 1920.

Estrada Cabrera was thought to be a moderate and a Liberal, but the elections which extended his term were recognized as facades for his personal rule. The Constitution imposed by Barrios in 1879 was ignored, and the presidents word was law.

The lot of the Indian was particularly oppressive during these two decades. Schoolteachers received no salary and forced their students to work for them. Debt bondage was extensive and enforced by public officials. The labor laws promulgated under Rufino Barrios had been modified, but the forced-labor system was essentially the same.

Every male between the ages of 20 and 60 was considered a soldier. The standing army contained 15,000 to 16,000 men, and over 60,000 could be equipped and ready for battle in a short time. This gave Guatemala, relative to its population, an extraordinarily large army.

Estrada Cabrera continued to encourage foreign investors. Near the turn of the century, Minor Keith, vice president of the United Fruit Company, arrived in the country. The company had already purchased Guatemalan land, but needed railroads to transport the future banana crop. Keith contracted to finish the line between the capital and Puerto Barrios on the Atlantic coast, and did so in 1904. In 1912 he took over the remaining railroads in Guatemala and founded a corporation independent of the United Fruit Company called the International Railways of Central America. The system was extended over the years into neighboring countries and, by 1930, included about 887 miles of useable track.

Estrada Cabrera gradually lost the support of the landlords. On March 11, 1920, one of the members of an opposition group, the Central American Unionist Movement, was shot and killed in the National Congress. This caused a widespread outcry against Estrada Cabrera. He signed an armistice with the Unionist leader, allowing the return of all exiles, thereby strengthening the position of his enemies. On April 12 he was declared insane, and a broadly based revolt forcibly removed him from office.

The Unionist Party's candidate won the election that followed. Less than a year later, however, he was driven out by a revolt and was replaced by General Jose Maria Orellana. He and his successor, Lazaro Chacon, gave the country 9 years of relatively progressive leadership, though in the same tradition as their predecessors.

Orellana stabilized the currency and established the first central bank. He embarked upon an extensive program of educational improvement. New schools were founded, teachers' salaries were raised, and libraries were opened. Orellana also persuaded the United Fruit Company to take its complaints to the Guatemalan courts.

During his term the first labor organizations appeared. Influenced by the Mexican example, Central American laborers established the Confederation of Central American Workers in 1922 with local chapters in each of the countries. By 1927 this organization had moved far to the left. The Guatemalan chapter, known as the Regional Federation of Workers, withdrew and more conservative workers joined the official labor organization. It was banned, however, after 1931.

Orellana died in 1926, and Chacon, who became president, continued his predecessor's programs and added several liberal Amendments to the Constitution. He signed a 25-year contract exempting the United Fruit Company from all government duties and taxes.

Lazaro Chacon resigned because of illness and was followed by three presidents in the space of 3 months. The second imcumbent was deposed by a coup d'etat and two Army officers held power in quick succession. Elections were held again on January 2, 1931, and General Jorge Ubico became president.

The last Caudillo

The Ubico regime, which lasted for 13 years, personified the *caudillo* tradition while it set the stage for the social and political upheaval that followed. His economic policies were autocratic but progressive. His social policies, however, were conservative and his regime supported the privileges of the landowners. Nevertheless, for the first time, some concessions were awarded to the Indians.

When Ubico entered office the treasury was empty, but he reformed the national economic system and created a surplus. He paid most of the country's debts

and ran the government on a cash basis. The yearly surplus built new roads, buslines, sewers, and the like. He kept a close watch on his subordinates, and his Law of Probity subjected the income of public officials to periodic audit. At the same time, however, he became the largest landowner.

The depression of the 1930s created a severe economic crisis in the country. Ubico minimized its effects by signing a reciprocal trade agreement with the United States, which increased coffee exports, and by increasing cotton exports to Italy. In order to supplement revenue, he maintained friendly relations with foreign businesses. The Germans, who dominated the coffee industry, in practice received legal immunity. He exempted the United Fruit Company from import duties on its business materials and from real estate taxes.

In 1936 the United Fruit Company became a large stockholder in the International Railways of Central America. It became a preferred customer and was given preferential rates. Public rates were lower than in neighboring countries.

During World War II Ubico supported the United States, granted sites for United States Army bases, and had his government buy United States war bonds. He maintained close surveillance over the German community and, in 1943, permitted its removal to an army base in Texas. All of the German coffee lands were expropriated.

Ubico's efficient economic policies continued throughout the war, and he was able to prevent inflation. On the other hand, political organizations were prohibited. Censorship was extensive and strictly enforced. Any form of labor organization was made illegal.

Ubico liked to pose as friend and protector of the Indians. He even encouraged them to call him *tata*, or father. He canceled the debts of the Indians and abolished the system of debt peonage; he listened to their complaints in the National Palace, and enforced justice for them in the national courts. But they were commanded to give 2 weeks free labor annually on highways and were subject to a Vagrancy Law decreeing that every Indian must work a minimum of 150 days a year. The amount of worktime required was scaled down in accordance with the amount of land that the Indian worked for himself.

In practice, the remaining time had to be spent on the coffee or banana plantations. Wages were legally maintained at a very low level, and the *hacendados* (landowners) exercised absolute sovereignty.

Indian peoples

The population of Guatemala is composed principally of two major ethnic groups, officially designated as Indian and *ladino*. There is, however, great cultural and linguistic diversity among the Indians. The *ladinos* speak Spanish, the official language, but the Indians, who constitute almost half the population density has greatly reduced the available land. There are many regions which could support an expanded population, but this would require an increased pace in the official resettlement programs.

Guatemala is the most populous state in Central America and has one of the highest growth rates in the world. The extremely high birth and death rates produce a young population, over half of which is under 18 years of age. This situation has created some special educational, health, and economic problems. The age proportion is changing, however, and, with more effective medical facilities, the death rate is being held constant, thereby increasing the life span.

In recent years the Indian population has been declining as a result of large numbers leaving the Indian communities to join *ladino* society. The distinction between the two is based on cultural and social lines rather than racial differences. Ethnic differentiations include language, surnames, type of housing, location, literacy, and various social and religious customs. *Ladinos* generally carry European surnames, dress in the Western style, own homes with more than one room, and usually live in urban or semiurban environments. When they are found in Indian townships, they live in the *cabecera* (seat of local government) around the main plaza.

Social stratification among *ladinos* is based on lineage and wealth. At the top are wealthy descendants of European colonists who have little, if any, claim to Indian ancestry. In Guatemala they are not considered Indians, regardless of their racial heritage; they officially belong to *ladino* society, although the difinition of *ladino* changes from one area to another.

The Mayan culture was disrupted and partially destroyed during the Spanish Conquest. During the colonial and early republican years the Indians lived apart from the Hispanic settlements. Tribes disappeared and were replaced by *municipio,* or township, cultures, the smallest unit of local government, containing one or more villages. The Indians rebuilt their society, integrating many European elements, yet retaining most of their traditional customs. Each township evolved its own dialect, its particular clothing style, and its religious and social practices. In effect, each became a separate and distinct group.

A general Indian culture unites these communities. All Indians practice a syncretic religion composed of pre-Columbian beliefs and Catholicism, but gods and rituals differ from one town to another. Each community produces its particular economic specialty and most Indians participate in the market system which consists of extensive trade among the townships.

The only significant deviants from this general pattern are the Black Caribs. A population of mixed Indian and Negro heritage, they are late arrivals to Guatemala and were never part of the Mayan tribal structure.

Since Spanish is the official language and is spoken by the *ladinos,* Indian men employ it for trade and in social relations with the *ladino* group. Indian women seldom use Spanish, and it is not spoken in the Indian home. Over 40 percent of the population speaks a native language, and each township has its own dialect. There are over 17 different Indian languages and hundreds of township dialects.

Linguistic barriers hamper educational programs and inhibit a feeling of national solidarity. Most Indians continue to regard their township as the center of their world.

Population

The latest census recorded 4,284,475 inhabitants, over a million more than any of the country's Central American neighbors. Between 1778, when the first census was taken, and 1950 the population doubled every 37 years. Between 1950, when the census recorded 2,790,868 inhabitants, and 1964, the population increased by more than 50 percent.

This rate of growth resulted almost entirely from natural increase, rather than immigration, which has been minimal.

The high birth rate is accompanied by a high mortality rate. In 1964 the birth rate was 47.7 births per 1,000 inhabitants, and the mortality rate was 16.6 per 1,000. Because of increased health facilities, the mortality rate has been steadily declining; it has decreased by 5.2 deaths per 1,000 since 1950. The in-

Mayan Indians, Guatemala, 1960.

fant mortality rate fell from 106.8 to 92.4 per 1,000 between 1950 and 1964. If this trend continues, the growth rate could rise even higher.

In 1966, however, the birth rate declined by 3 per 1,000 to 44.2 per 1,000, and the death rate remained the same. This reduced the rate of growth to 2.8 percent. There is some debate concerning the accuracy and completeness of these figures.

The majority of the population is young: 56.6 percent is under 20 years of age, and 4.8 percent, over 60. The highest percentage within an age group is between the ages of one and five, comprising 17.6 percent of the population. The median age is 17.8.

This age composition creates special health problems and requires medical and health facilities geared to a young population. Ideally, it would demand an extensive educational program; however, most children leave school at an early age to join the work force. This increases the percentage of those who are economically active, although the majority are employed by their families in household or farming tasks.

There are slightly more men than women in the overall population. Women predominate in the urban areas because the urban environment offers better employment. Men are in the majority in the rural areas, especially in the Escuintla, Retalhuleu, and Santa Rosa Departments, the centers of commercial agriculture.

In 1964 the population density was 102 inhabitants per square mile, a figure exceeded by only six countries in the Western Hemisphere; however, density varies widely from area to area. The Department of Guatemala contains 991 inhabitants per square mile while the Department of El Peten, approximately 17 times as large, has only two persons per square mile.

The majority of the people are rural, accounting for 65.9 percent of the population. Over a third of the rural population is found in the Departments of San Marcos, Huehuetenango, El Quiche, and Alta Verapaz. These four departments are located in and around the central plateau which is the demographic center.

In the 1950 and 1964 censuses the population was divided into two groups, Indian and non-Indian, or *ladino*. The official distinction is made on the basis of social status as defined by local standards. In 1950 the Indians were in the majority, with over 53 percent of the population. This figure has been steadily decreasing as more and more Indians are acculturated into *ladino* society. In 1964 only 43.3 percent of the population was classified as Indian.

The growth rate of the two groups is different. The Indian population increased by only 1.4 percent between 1950 and 1964, while the *ladino* rate of growth was 4.4 percent.

The Indian population has become more mobile since 1950. Although there has been a large migratory movement to El Peten from the highlands, distribution has changed only slightly. The departments can be divided into three distinct types, according to the percentage of Indian inhabitants. Those with over 70 percent are considered Indian departments; those with less than 30 percent are considered *ladino;* and five are Indian. The Indian areas form a block in the northwest region while the *ladino* departments are found in central, southern, and eastern Guatemala.

Immigrants, who are mostly urban dwellers, account for a very small portion of the population. According to the 1950 census, 1.1 percent came from neighboring countries and 12 percent, from other parts of the Western Hemisphere. Only 5 percent had immigrated from Europe, predominantly Spain and Germany. Asians constitute a very small percentage; the Chinese, numbering approximately 600, form the majority.

The immigrants from surrounding countries simply cross the border from one rural area to another; they usually settle in the departments nearest their previous home. The border departments each contain approximately 1,000 immigrants.

The small foreign colony has been active in the country's economic life. The Germans, until World War II, and the British played a vital role in coffee production, while companies from the United States have been important in the railroad and banana industries. Chinese merchants are influential in the eastern and coastal towns.

Ethnic groups

Groups other than *ladinos* and Indians either have been absorbed into or form only a minute section of the population.

The terms, *ladino* and Indian, do not take into account the diversity which exists within each group. The *ladino* classification is applied to those persons who adopted or inherited a European or Western style of life, and to those who may have European ancestry. There are objections to applying this term to the upperclass descendants of Spanish and other European colonists. Some authorities prefer to use *ladino* interchangeably with *mestizo* (a mixture of Indian and European ancestry.) It is generally accepted that, although there are great differences between urban and rural as well as between rich and poor *ladinos,* the group share a similar cultural orientation toward Western values.

Someone who is accepted as a *ladino* in a rural environment may, nevertheless, be classified as an Indian in an urban milieu. Ideally, an Indian with no European ancestry can assume the habits and dress of the *ladinos* and become a member of that group. In some regions, however, only his children can successfully change cultures. In still others, transitional or acculturated Indians must move from the area to change their Indian status.

Indians are relatively homogeneous in their physical characteristics, whereas *ladinos* are not. Many have

Indian physical traits, while others are predominantly or completely European. In the 1950 and 1964 censuses anyone who was not culturally Indian, including Europeans and Asiatics as well as pure Indians, was classified as a *ladino*.

Indian culture

Guatemalan Indians are originally descendants of the highland Mayas although they possess some Mexican traits. Historically, their culture can be traced to the classic Mayan empire which evolved in El Peten and surrounding areas. After the empire's decay the highland tribes came under the sway of various Mexican conquerors who were gradually assimilated. The tribes of the area which is now Guatemala were not united before the Spanish Conquest, and no homogenous culture existed even within individual tribes.

Present divisions among the Indians date from colonial times when the authorities divided the native population into townships, either arbitrarily or on the basis of existing delineations. Tribal groupings were replaced by approximately 315 townships. As a consequence, the Indian ethnic group is composed of hundreds of communities with cultural similarities; however, each Indian township is a distinct social and, often, linguistic entity.

The inhabitants of the townships consider themselves a separate people with distinct customs, economic specialties, patron saints, and special festivals and market days. Because of endogamy, certain physical features tend to predominate in a particular community. Although the people may share a native dialect with a neighboring township, there are minor differences in pronunciation, vocabulary, and grammatical usage.

Inhabitants of townships which speak the same general language can communicate with one another regardless of slight differences. In fact, as contact between linguistic areas is extended and intensified, some uniformity may become apparent in religious beliefs, costumes, and social practices. The Chorti language, for instance, is spoken in the Department of Chiquimula in four townships, each having distinct characteristics and communal loyalty. There are, however, strong ties and cultural similarities among them, a possible sign of incipient regional culture.

The township is the primary unit of cultural homogeneity except where migration and acculturation have altered the traditional pattern. The Indian's community is the center of his world since he seldom recognizes it as an integral part of a larger national entity. For him it is a closely integrated society bound by strong ties of religion and tradition which mitigate against social change. These township groups fulfill an important function in the subculture within the dominant *ladino* society. Although most Indians would prefer to remain aloof from *ladino* society, they are forced to interact on social, economic, and political levels.

Technology

Indian technology has three levels. At the most primitive level are the pre-Columbian tools and techniques important in agriculture, the production of textiles, and cooking. Only war implements and stone tools have been completely lost from the original Mayan technology. Corn (Maize) is still the major crop and is occasionally planted with a sharpened stick and a Mayan hoe. It is ground on a *metate* (grinding stone) and baked on a griddle. Clothes are woven on a backstrap loom with one end attached to a high support and the other to the weaver. Several of these elements are part of the *ladino* culture as well.

Most *ladino* technology, however, is derived from 16th century preindustrial Spanish influence. The Indians have also accepted some of the European methods. Wool technology, domesticating animals, metal tools, and distilled liquor have all been incorporated into Indian culture. Indians have no shoemakers, however.

Modern technology has influenced Indian communities only peripherally. Indians are acquainted with buses and trains but use them infrequently. Although few own radios, most have had some experience with them. A small percentage of the wealthier Indians have electric lighting. The manual sewing machine is well known and is one of the few

Indian mother with firewood, Guatemala.

STONE METATE, GUATEMALA

mechanical devices the Indians have accepted. This acquaintance with modern technology has accelerated the process of acculturation in some areas, but it has not significantly altered the traditional pattern because those who accept modernity tend to leave the Indian culture and become *ladinos*. The Indian customs and philosophy have remained remarkably unchanged.

Costumes

The three technological levels are typical of all the Indian communities, but their use is dependent upon the cultural values of each group. For example, clothing is generally made on the backstrap loom, but both men's and women's clothing styles were evolved in the colonial era. Each township has a different mode of dress. In the Cubulco township of the Department of Baja Verapaz the men wear dark blue wool coats, straw hats, rubber sandals, white shirts, and pants with a fringed apron. In Chichicastenango the men's costume is also made of wool and consists of a pullover jacket and knee-breeches cut in a 17th century style. Silk embroidery, fringes, and a red sash brighten the apparel. In Panajachel men wear plaid wool kilts reminiscent of Mayan loincloths.

Men's clothing is usually very colorful, regardless of the township; embroidery and jaspe cottons (spot-dyed yarns) are used extensively. Since the current styles were copied from the clothing of Spanish colonists, most men have adopted trousers, shirts, and hats. These basic articles, however, have been re-designed in an Indian manner, giving each costume an indigenous character. There is a recent trend toward factory-made clothes, which may replace these local costumes.

Like the men, the women of each township are known for their distinctive style and take particular pride in their community's costume. Very few Indian women wear factory-made clothing.

In Cubulco the women wear brightly embroidered blouses and ankle-length wraparound skirts. In the highlands the *huipil* (a sleeveless blouse made from a rectangular piece of cloth) is more common and, in the township Santiago Atitlan, the women wear a tightly bound skirt, a narrow *huipil*, and a small scarf over one shoulder.

Indians buy their clothing at local markets, adding the embellishments which make it peculiar to a community. Most weaving is done in the Department of Quezaltenango.

Economy

Each township has an economic specialty consisting of particular crops, handicrafts, trades, marketing, or labor. The choice of a specialization is often determined by the variation in altitude, natural resources, or the quantity and quality of land; however, similar geographic components do not produce the same economy, and the specialty in many communities derives simply from tradition or inventiveness. An economic specialty is a basic part of each community's individuality.

Townships within the same region do not necessarily specialize in the same general occupation. All communities grow corn, but some, such as Santiago Atitlan, and San Pedro, are corn exporters. San Pablo, which is nearby, specializes in ropemaking and must import most of its corn and other foodstuffs. Panajachel is known for its onions, whereas the people of San Antonio, a neighboring community, grow anise.

Handicrafts are also characteristic of particular townships. The people of Totonicapan make high-quality pottery, although their neighbors in the township of Chichicastenango make none. Both communities have large forest reserves, but the former porduces furniture, and the latter sells the wood as lumber. Chichicastenango makes a specially designed blanket while the weavers of the townships of Momostenango and San Francisco make another type. All grinding stones used in the country originate in the township of Nahuala.

A few communities specialize in trades, usually for service to the *ladino* society. Because Indians build their own homes by means of reciprocal labor, some persons in each township have a basic knowledge of carpentry, masonry, and adobe and tile making. The construction of *ladino* homes. The Atitecos of Santiago Atitlan are skilled navigators and practice this specialty along the shore of Lake Atitlan.

Pottery Jar, Guatemala.

Some of the communities, such as Chichicastenango and Atitlan, buy local products and transport them to other areas. Others, such as Solala and Sacapulas, distribute their own goods.

Indians, in contrast to *ladinos,* place a high value on manual labor. The number of communities involved in this migratory labor specialization has been steadily increasing since 1950, probably one reason for the growing number of acculturated Indians.

The system of economic specialties is characteristic of most Indian townships. It is particularly well developed in the western highlands, the area with the highest density of Indian population. It also occurs in the Departments of Chiquimula, Guatemala, and other eastern regions with large Indian groups.

Some communities specialize in one item while others produce three or four. This depends on the available resources and the inventiveness of the people. Whatever its specialty, however, virtually everyone in the village grows or manufactures the item, and internal specialization does not exist. Interdependence among the townships produces a market economy and trade centers. *Ladinos* purchase the specialties produced by the Indian townships but do not otherwise participate in their system of economic specialization.

Each community has a special market day and participates in the marketing routine of a particular region. There is usually a main market, supplemented by smaller markets, which serves as the center for an area. The system was not consciously planned, nor is it regulated. It is simply the traditional response to the economic conditions of the Indian life.

Markets are based on a money economy, and barter is rare. Pricing is completely competitive, and value is determined by supply and demand, not custom. In fact, the whole system is guided by economic rationality rather than rigid tradition.

The market is also a social institution, and a day or more is spent there each week. Only Indians sell in the marketplaces, although both Indians and *ladinos* are customers. Sundays are the favorite market days, especially in the smaller towns. If a township is large and is situated on a prominent trade route between two areas of production, markets will probably be open 2 or 3 days a week. During a fiesta the local market is called a fair and stays open for a week or more. More people participate, and buyers and sellers come from all parts of the country.

In the neighborhood markets the sellers are mainly women, and local men are seldom seen. When a family carries its goods to a distant market, however, the men not only carry the items but sell them as well. The men also generally deal in the heavier goods, such as stones used for grinding corn, and in the more important commodities, such as livestock.

The marketplace is located in the center of a town, in the main square, and is usually known for a particular commodity which is cheaper there than in any

other town. Thus, Tecpan is the place to buy lime; Chichicastenango, to buy pitch pine; and Atitlan, to buy bananas. These evaluations are taken into account when an Indian wishes to purchase large quantities of a product, and he will visit these markets if necessary. On the other hand, a seller knows which products are scarce in a certain area and may bring his product to a more profitable market.

Some townships duplicate one another's specialties, but the value placed on their commodities may not be the same. For instance, in Quezaltenango, the potatoes grown in Nahuala are considered better than those of Todo los Santos. In searching for a favorite type of produce, the buyer will look for the distinctive costume of a certain township; this serves as identification of the desired commodity.

These economic specialties, however, are only supplements to the main Indian occupation. The Indians have been part of a rural, agricultural society since pre-Columbian days. The major Indian occupation is still agriculture, and much of the social and religious life is an integral part of the cultivation cycle. Land is the Indian's most prized possession, and no one feels secure unless he has a small plot, or *milpa,* to work. The ownership of land and its use are tied to the definition of manhood, and the ideal goal of any male is to own a *milpa* and grow corn. Land is the symbol of respect.

Land is privately owned, since communal lands disappeared for the most part in the 19th century. Some forest areas are still owned by communities in the Department of Huehuetenango and, in one or two villages, such as San Antonio Huista, the tradition of communal landholding still persists. Nonetheless, in the majority of the townships, land is owned by individuals.

The Indian is deeply attached to his land. He will sell it only if absolutely necessary, and extra money is invariably spent on the acquisition of new land. In the cultivation and care of his property, a man acquires a feeling for his relation to the universe. Without land, he feels basically insecure and rootless.

Many *ladinos,* particularly in the eastern regions, are also rural agriculturalists, but their style of life and use of technology differ from those of the Indians. The Indians are concentrated in the central and western highlands where, because of greater density and less available land, the farms are smaller. According to the 1950 census, the average farm size for an Indian was 7.6 acres, as compared to 60.7 acres for the *ladino.* The latter figure included the large plantations but, in general, even the smaller *ladino* farms are larger than the average Indian plot.

The staple is corn, supplemented by beans and squash. All of these are often grown on the same plot. Few Indians own livestock or any implements more advanced than hand tools. *Ladinos,* unlike the Indians, rarely serve as seasonal labor for the coffee plantations. *Ladino* communities do not produce the economic specialties common to the highlands, nor do they practice the complex of religious rites associated with Indian agriculture. These have been an integral part of Indian life since pre-Columbian times, and they are considered just as vital to the successful planting of the crops as the mechanics of cultivation.

Religious and social practices

Agricultural rituals are only one part of the religious complex which influences almost every aspect of Indian life. Officially, both the Indian population and the *ladinos* are considered Roman Catholic, but ancient Mayan beliefs are retained in Indian culture in syncretic form with Catholicism. In practice, each township pays homage to its own pantheon of gods, ranging from Catholic saints with locally acquired attributes to the ancient nature spirits and devils.

Each community has a religious structure which incorporates political and civil functions and influences both the economic and social life of the town. The religious organization maintains the traditions and customs binding the township together and sustains the vital feelings of exclusiveness and matuality.

The primary unit of this religious structure is the *cofradia,* a religious brotherhood and hierarchy of approximately 24 men. The brotherhood has custody of a particular saint and is in charge of its fiesta and other religious celebrations. The number of these groups within a town differs from one area to another, as do their duties, rituals, and composition. Smaller towns have only one; larger ones have four or more principal brotherhoods.

In Chichicastenango there are four major positions within the brotherhood, and the highest is an official called the *alcalde* (mayor). In another community, Chinuautla, there are six positions at each level, and their leader is called the *majordomo* (manager). Young, unmarried men of the village fill the lower offices and gradually work their way up the hierarchy, serving 1-year terms in each position. To attain the higher offices, they must be married, since this is visible proof of their stability and sense of responsibility.

The lower offices of the brotherhoods are principally civil. Those who fill them are likely to be young men who work as policemen, messengers, street cleaners and market cleaners, and minor assistants during official ceremonies. The higher posts carry more authority and involve the care of the church and images of the saints, the preparation of the fiesta, and the celebration of rituals. Those who hold them also have considerable secular responsibility and often make administrative and political decisions for the community.

The hierarchal religious structure also stratifies society. Not only do economic barriers prevent some people from serving, but in a large community there are simply not enough positions for every male. The pyramid structure of the brotherhood insures a position form many men at the bottom but few at the top.

Some communities, such as San Luis Jilotepeque, separate the political and religious functions into separate brotherhoods. This often occurs in a predominantly *ladino* town; as an Indian community becomes acculturated, it tends to separate the two duties.

In a few townships the women have parallel organizations in which the office of the woman is determined by her husband's corresponding position. In Chamelco and Nebaj women occupy the highest offices of the hierarchy and are equal with the men. In other communities women serve only peripherally, if at all.

The higher officials are in charge of the saint's fiestas and must pay for these annual celebrations. Candles, fireworks, and new clothes for the saint's image must be bought and a large quantity of food and liquor provided. The cost is partially sustained by the earnings from communal land, if any, and by donations from the village families. The largest share of the cost, however, is provided by the sponsor of the celebration who serves as the annual head of the saint's brotherhood.

The fiestas often cost over 80 quetzales (Q1 equals US$1), the average annual income of an Indian. The sponsorship of these celebrations is an effective leveling device within the Indian community and prevents the accumulation of excessive wealth. A wealthy individual is socially obligated to hold many of these religious offices, thereby channeling a large amount of his riches into community activities.

A poorer man can bypass the more expensive posts, but even he is expected to serve the community in some capacity.

The festival of the patron saint is not the only fiesta held during the year; some kind of celebration occurs in almost every month, especially in the larger towns. Some of them are conducted by religious groups to commemorate the lesser saints, and others are related to the agricultural process. The highest concentration of fiestas among the indigenous communities occurs in February, July, August, and December.

There are usually secular and religious aspects to these celebrations. The religious side is primary in the Indian townships but secular activities dominate in the *ladino* areas. Even in the Indian ceremonies, however, the secular has its place. Music, dancing, races, and fights are part of the fiestas.

Native dances are prominent during the fiesta and are a blend of Mayan and European influences. Only a few of the original pre-Columbian dances and dramas remain. One of these tells the story of a young Rabinal warrior who kills a Quiche man in combat; he is captured and sacrificed to 12 priestly anthropomorphic eagles and 12 jaguars. The Deer Dance of San Marcos and the Pole Dance also have pre-Columbian origins but these exhibit many European traits. Certain steps and musical rhythms and instruments have been borrowed from Spanish sources.

Most of the fiesta dances and dramas have a religious character. These are called *Loas* and consist of European-influenced morality plays, the reenactment of scriptures, and stories of the village people themselves. The Dance of Saint George, the Conquest of Jerusalem, and the Conquest of Antiqua are all popular. Women seldom participate in these dances, and men and women never dance together. In a few communities the women have separate dances which are performed on special occasions.

A distilled liquor, *aguardiente,* is necessary to any fiesta and is used for both religious and social purposes. Most Indians get drunk during the festivities and consider this a normal and desired effect of the celebration. Fiesta is the only time that women are allowed to be drunk in public. Social and moral principles are relaxed, and the sexes intermingle freely. Emotional and violent outbursts and fights are common.

The fiestas and other social, economic, and religious customs form a pattern which is different in each township, although they exist within a common framework. They bind together both the community's and the individual's social and cultural roles.

Acculturation and government policy

Since 1950 the Indian population has decreased by over 10 percent, implying that large numbers of Indians have abandoned the traditional Indian customs and joined the *ladino* society. This tendency has been evident since the Spanish Conquest. The Indian tribes in the eastern regions of Guatemala were never able to reconstruct their society after the devastation of the conquest, and became *ladinos* almost by default. The western tribes retreated into the highlands, isolating themselves both physically and culturally from the Hispanic society concentrated at lower altitudes. Gradually, however, Western customs have been penetrating the Indian communities, and marginal individuals, as well as whole communities, have adopted *ladino* ways.

Two of the most potent forces accelerating the process of acculturation have been the establishment of plantations and the influence of the Industrial Revolution. When President Rufino Barrios established the debt peonage and the vagrancy laws in 1875, he destroyed the isolation of the Indian communities and began the tradition of migratory labor. To supplement their meager living, and in compliance with national laws, Indian families temporarily left their townships and worked on the large plantations, or *fincas,* in the lowlands.

Plantation life weakened the strong religious and family ties which sustained the highland communities, and the permanent residents on the plantations became partially acculturated to European ways, or transitional Indians. Others who returned to their highland townships continued living as Indians but brought with them a wider knowledge of the modern world.

The Industrial Revolution also influenced and disrupted the traditional Indian pattern. Factory-made clothes are cheap and comfortable and, in many areas, are replacing the more expensive, although distinctive, Indian costumes. Some townships have been unable to compete with the factories, and a few handicrafts have almost disappeared; palm leaf raincoats, for instance, have been replaced by cheap plastic tablecloths worn as ponchos.

Better means of transportation have reduced the distances between the *ladino* and Indian townships, thus increasing the amount of contact. Better communication, especially the widespread use of transistor radios, brings the Indians a more complete knowledge of the nation and the world. With increasing knowledge and interaction with the *ladino* society, more and more Indians are moving away from the traditional customs.

The degree of acculturation which an Indian must undergo before he is considered a *ladino* is dependent upon his location. In the midwestern highlands an Indian, theoretically, changes ethnic groups if he acquires *ladino* ways; however, even the maintenance of one or two Indian customs may undermine his *ladino* status. In the Department of Chiquimula there is no ethnic change unless an Indian moves to a town, acts like a *ladino,* and conceals his indigenous past. If his ancestry becomes known, only his children are considered fully *ladino.* In Agua Escondida an Indian can pass as a *ladino* If he was raised as such.

Recently, the government has been encouraging the integration of the Indians into the national society, and has sponsored various programs toward this end. The 1964 census cited the official literacy programs and better communication and transportation as some of the reasons for the decreased number of Indians.

The government-sponsored literacy campaigns, one of the main projects of which is handled by the army, have evidently been successful. A common language not only facilitates interaction between the two ethnic groups but also opens new avenues to Indians who have previously been excluded from many opportunities.

The Indians were largely ignored before 1944, but participation and concern on the part of the government have been evident since that time. During the colonial era and the early republican years the Indians remained in their townships, building and integrating their culture. The Liberal Party, in the 1870s, passed debt peonage and vagrancy laws which required Indians to work for the government or landowners between 4 to 6 months of the year, thus forcing them at least peripherally into *ladino* society. The Indians were, theoretically, freed upon the cancellation of their debts by President Jorge Ubico (1931-44). Ubico, however, replaced the old labor laws with new ones forcing the Indians to work for a certain period each·

year. In 1944 the official policy was altered again, and the government became actively involved in the welfare of the Indian.

The townships were declared autonomous in 1945, and illiterates were given the vote, thereby bringing politics to the local level. In many places Indians were elected to positions of authority. In the 1950s illiterates were disenfranchised, but *ladinos,* by this time, were more responsive to Indian problems and needs.

The local involvement in politics is undermining the civil role of the brotherhoods and the respected position of older men. Youths are recruited by the political parties and are elected to administrative posts. They bypass the traditional channels of authority, and many no longer feel compelled to join the brotherhoods.

Black Caribs

Small numbers of Negroes were brought as slaves to Guatemala, but they disappeared as a separate racial group toward the end of the colonial era. The Black Carib Indians along the Atlantic Coast in Livingston, Izabal Department, are descendants of runaway African slaves who intermarried with the Carib Indians of St. Vincent Island in the Antilles.

This group arrived in Central America in 1797; the British had deported them from the Antilles, because of the loyalty to the French, to Goatan in the Gulf of Honduras. The majority crossed over to the mainland, and their descendants are now found in the coastal areas of Honduras, Guatemala, and Belize (British Honduras). They are predominantly Negroid, but much of their culture, including the language, is Antillean (Carib Indian). They live in small villages along the coast and depend on agriculture and wage labor for their livelihood. Rice, cassava, and plantain cultivation are supplemented by fishing. Since 1900 wage labor positions held by the men have been the major economic prop of the communities.

Since Livingston is an isolated town, many men leave home for extended stays in places where work is available, generally in the large cities of Guatemala, but some travel as far as New York or New Orleans. They are usually gone for 2 or 3 years, returning to their communities at intervals. Formerly, they remained tied, both socially and emotionally, to their homes in Livingston, often maintaining wives and families there.

Such labor migrations brought an awareness of the outside world to the men and, consequently, to the community itself, as evidenced by the popularity of such magazines as *Tan* and *Ebony* and by the influence on dress styles of United States mail-order catalogues. The Black Caribs value especially their knowledge of and experience with Negro culture in the United States.

The primitive culture, which still exists, was originally based on slash-and-burn agriculture, supplemented by fishing. Basketry and wood handicraft are the principal skills. Certain dances and musical rhythms can be traced to their African origins. Religious customs are still in practice. Replacing some of these is the adoption, from *ladino* culture, of the use of almanacs and astrology manuals for guidance in personal and economic matters.

Since the mid-1950s, however, many of the migrants are rejecting their traditional cultural patterns as well as their rural ties. The number coming to the national capital has increased, and most intend to stay permanently. Some of the men have married *ladino* women, and many no longer speak their native language. They have not rejected all of their cultural heritage but have simply adapted to an urban environment.

Those remaining in Livingston retain portions of the cultural tradition, and many migrants still regard Livingston as home; however, the influence of other mores is steadily undermining the older ways.

Languages

Spanish is the official language and is spoken by a majority of the population. It is the language of government, schools, newspapers, and radio. Most Indians know at least a few Spanish words, and the social and economic relations between *ladinos* and Indians are usually conducted in this language. Economic and social transactions between Indians who speak different Mayan languages are also conducted in Spanish. Only a small percentage of the Indian population is bilingual, and most Indians speak one of the approximately 18 native languages.

Spanish was brought by the Hispanic conquerors and perpetuated by their descendants and the colonists who followed them. Since it was the language of the dominant group, a knowledge of Spanish was necessary for anyone who wished to participate in Hispanic society. The *mestizos* and acculturated Indians accepted and learned it, rejecting their own tongues.

Language has, consequently, been one of the key items in the definition of ethnic groups. In 1950, 59.4 percent of the population spoke Spanish in the home, 78 percent of whom were *ladinos*. The remaining 22 percent were Indians who had not yet adopted enough *ladino* traits to be classified as members of this group. The rest of the population spoke Indian dialects.

Despite the acceptance of Spanish by some, the native languages remain a vital and integral part of the Indian culture. This has presented the government with a distinct problem, for it is very difficult to create a literate populace within the mainstream of national life when no linguistic uniformity exists. The government has started literacy campaigns in Spanish in hopes of abolishing language barriers.

The Indian's attachment to their languages is very strong, however, and there is little indication that the native dialects are becoming obsolete. Men may learn some Spanish for economic purposes, but the women continue to speak the Indian languages in the home.

Spanish is considered a secondary language. Many express the belief that, someday, everyone will learn their dialect because it is the language of God.

Before the Spaniards arrived there were four distinct linguistic families. The Aztec family, represented by the Pipil language, was spoken near Salama, Baja Verapaz. The Mixe family, Pupuluca, was found along the western border and is still spoken in Mexico. Only the Maya and the Carib families now exist in Guatemala.

The languages of the existing Maya family were originally spoken by the post-Mayan tribes which occupied the Guatemala highlands before the Spanish conquest. Physical barriers prevented regular communication and transportation between the different regions, and warfare further divided the tribes. As a consequence, language differences were created and perpetuated. Each language has a separate, although similar, alphabet and a special rhythm varying with the rise and fall of tone. In all of them the stress falls on the final syllable of each word.

There is some debate concerning the number of Mayan languages now spoken in the country. The 1950 census listed approximately 15, whereas other sources have placed the number at 17. These are located principally in the western and central highlands with a few native languages found in Izabal Department and southern El Peten. This corresponds to areas of the highest concentration of Indian population.

The Quiche language has changed very little since the Spanish conquest, and the historical Quiche document, the *Popul Vuh,* written at that time, can still be understood by modern Indians. The Kelchi, the Quiche, the Cakchiquel, and the Mam are the four major Indian linguistic groups in Guatemala and, based on the 1950 census, they account for the majority of native speakers. The speakers of Kelchi are found among the least acculturated Indians in the country.

Carib is unique in that the men and women have a different vocabulary and, at one time, spoke different languages. This is a Carib Indian trait, a consequence of the fact that, historically, many of the women were Arawakian (South American Indians) slaves and did not know the Carib language. Most of the distinctions between the two have now disappeared and, although separate vocabularies are maintained, the same grammatical structure is used. Each sex now understands the other's language.

Because they have been subject, at various times, to British, French, and Spanish rule, their language incorporates many foreign words. The present number system, beginning with the word for "4," is French, while the English and Spanish have provided common household and economic terms. This process continues today with the introduction of many technical terms, such as *radio.*

Because of the small number of immigrants, few people speak a foreign language. According to the 1950 census, foreign speakers accounted for only about 0.2 percent of the population, or 4,128 persons. Over three-fourths of these spoke English and resided mainly in Izabal Department.

LANGUAGES OF GUATEMALA

Language	Speakers	Departments
Quiche	300,000	El Quiche, Totonicapan, Quezeltenango, Retalhuleu
Cakchiquel	170,000	Guatemala, chimaltenango, Sacatepequez, Escuintla
Mam	170,00	San Marcos, Quezaltenango, Huehuetenango
Kelchi	150,000	Alta Verapaz, El Peten
Kanjobal	40,000	Huehuetenango
Poconchi	40,000	Alta Verapaz
Ixil	25,000	El Quiche
Tzutuhil	18,000	Solola, Suchitepequez
Achi	14,000	Boja Verapaz
Jacaltec	13,000	Huehuetenango
Uspantecs	12,000	El Quiche
Chorti	12,000	Chiquimula
Chuj	10,000	Huehuetenango
Aquacatecs	8,000	Huehuetenango
Central Pocomans	6,000	Escuintla, Chimaltenango
Eastern Pocomans	5,000	Guatemala
Mopan Maya	3,000	El Peten
Carib	1,000	Izabal

Religion

The religious orders brought a form of primitive Catholicism to the New World; stripped of many European folk customs, it contained only the essentials of the Catholic faith. As a consequence, the priests were able to impose a fairly uniform religion, except where modified by native beliefs from Mexico to Chile. It contained an emphasis on reverence for God, and his son Christ, a veneration of the same saints, a similar Mass performed each Sunday, and a deep trust in the intercession of the Virgin Mary. Even churches were constructed in the early Christian manner with only one nave, as opposed to the three of medieval Gothic cathedrals.

Priests attempted to superimpose basic Catholic beliefs upon the native Indian beliefs without destroying the deep spirituality of the Indian. They hoped to remould and reconstruct the spiritual culture without creating a vacuum. This was done on the assumption that after Christianity was firmly established, remnants of the old religion would wither.

This plan was not entirely successful, mainly because there were not enough priests and not enough time to fully accomplish the conversion. When Christian saints were placed in native shrines, the Indians confused the two religions and attributed characteristics of the old deity to the new saint. In most areas the priest did not remain in residence long enough to eliminate syncretism; thus native religious teachers were only partially converted themselves.

Maya religion was localized and closely associated with agriculture. There was a supreme god, but he was remote and unapproachable. The more popular deities were tied to the cultivation cycle. The *chaacs* (rain gods), the *pauahtuns* (wind gods), and the *bacabs* (sky bearers) were of prime importance as were the sun god and moon goddess. Except for the sun and moon deities, the gods were thought of in terms of groupings of four, representing the four sacred directions, which were depicted symbolically as a cross, and the four sacred colors. Thus, the *chaacs* could either be represented as four gods or worshiped collectively as one. The concept of duality was also important, and each god had both a malevolent and benevolent disposition. The essence of religion was to offer sacrifice to the gods in the hope of propitiating them; in return the gods would extend their good will and prevent illness.

The sacred Maya calendar was central to these beliefs and to the ceremonies and rituals that symbolized them. According to the religion, each day and each calendric period were ruled by a different god. Thus, a knowledge of the calendar was necessary in the reading of omens, in preparing sacrifices for the *milpa* (small plot of land), and in divination. A person's fate was believed to depend upon his relationship to the calendar, determined by his date of birth.

These beliefs remain at the core of present-day Indian religion; however, partial conversion to Chris-

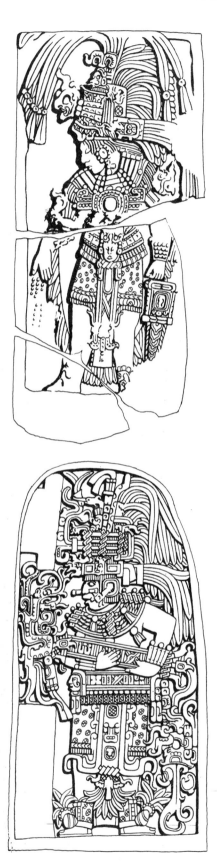

Stelae depicting Mayan deities.

tianity occurred as resistance weakened. Catholic doctrine has been adapted and incorporated within this faith. The process of syncretism first began when Indians accepted Christianity to escape the *encomienda* system and to receive the protection of the priests. The process was accelerated by the receptivity of the Indians to new gods as long as they could continue to worship and respect the old pantheon. In addition, many elements of the Catholic faith, such as the cross, baptism, confession, communion fasting, pilgrimages, continence, and visual representations of sacrifice, have parallels in the Maya religion. Often the Indians simply exchanged one set of terms for another.

Hence, in choosing between the representation of Christ as a young man or as a suffering figure upon the cross, the Indians chose the latter because it fit into their previous religious framework in which sacrifice played a role.

The result of fusion is a syncretic faith in which the Indians do not recognize the distinct origins of their two sets of beliefs. They practice Catholic rituals in the local church and Maya customs in the *milpa* or at ancient shrines, but they consider the whole complex of beliefs as one religion.

On the whole, the present-day Indian religion exists within a broad framework of Chatolicism with a strong pre-Columbian underpinning. It is highly localized as rituals, favorite saints, Mayan gods, and sacred days vary from one township to another. Whatever the location, however, religion permeates almost every aspect of Indian life from the cultivation cycle to social activities to personal ethics.

Supernatural beings

In most Indian towns God and Christ now reside at the top of the aggregate of supernatural beings, but are considered too remote to be approached directly. Catholic saints and Maya nature gods populate the descending hierarchy and are classified as lesser deities acting as intermediaries between God and man. The lesser gods usually are visualized as anthropomorphic beings, but are also considered to have supernatural power.

The separation between the Catholic and Maya deities is often vague, for in many areas a Catholic saint has assumed the powers and duties of a Maya god. In the Department of Chiquimula, for example, the gods of rain are collectively referred to as *chicchans,* but individually bear the names of Catholic saints. In some places the two sets of deities are so closely interwoven that they perform integrated tasks. In one township St. Michael Archangel is in command of the four Maya rain gods and gives orders for them to ride across the sky, pouring water from their gourds. They are often accompanied by the Virgin Mary who, for some, has become the guardian of the maize.

There have been many confusions about the concept of the Virgin Mary. Because Spanish paintings always show her standing on a crescent moon, she has become associated with the moon goddess; however, she is also variously represented as Mother Earth, guardian of the corn, and the wife of Christ. Every Indian is expected to have a wife, so it is logical that they expect the same of their gods. Most village churches contain at least one of her images, but each individual image is considered a separate person with distinctive characteristics.

In most townships the Christian deities are worshipped principally in the villages; and Maya gods, in the fields. In a prayer to the wind gods in preparation for burning a *milpa,* an Indian always addresses both sets of gods.

On the whole, however, the local church is considered the center of the Catholic faith, and all the images of Christian saints and of the holy family are kept here in places of honor. The images are brought out of the church into the village for religious festivals and if the *cofradia* system is strong, the statues of certain saints may be moved to the homes of leaders of the brotherhoods for special rituals. The images seldom leave the boundaries of the village.

Most Indians consider the images themselves divine and not mere representations of a spiritual being. The statues of the holy are dressed in Indian clothing and, like the images of the holy family are considered local personages. Two townships may have saints of the same name, but they are not considered the same person. The two are more like relatives.

The saints are perceived as very influential and powerful beings, yet they are also believed to have human weaknesses and desires. In the township of San Miguel, St. Ann is thought to be the wife of Santiago (St. James), the patron saint. Some time ago, she was supposedly unfaithful to him and, consequently, he beat her and threw her into jail. A very similar story, involving the sun and the moon, can be traced to pre-Columbian origins.

Each township has its own patron saint, who is considered the personal god of each member of the village. He cares for his people and watches over their crops and their health. The religious brotherhood devoted to him is the most important, and his name is invoked in almost every ritual. Most of the villagers pray directly to him because it is believed that he readily intercedes with God on their behalf. The patron saint is so vital to the community that often the township is named for him, as in San Gregorio or Santo Tomas. It is illustrative of the syncretic and localized character of their religion that often an Indian name is added, as in Santo Tomas Chichicastenango.

Townships in the Northwest value their patron cross as much or more than the saint. The cross is an intermediary deity whose roots lie in both Maya beliefs and Christianity. In pre-Columbian times the cross symbolized the four sacred directions. When the Spaniards arrived more emphasis was placed on this symbol, and it gained great significance in the new syn-

Maya gods and saints adorn many of Maya art forms. Above is a painted vase, below is a stone lintel.

cretic religion. Today crosses are personalized and, according to many Indians, can see, hear, and speak to certain shamans. They are often dressed in Indian clothing and are found at the four entrances of a village.

Another supernatural being that has been taken from Christian theology is the devil. The early friars saw the Indian religion as communication with Satan, and they attempted to convince the Indians of this. The Indians did not completely accept this belief, but they did assimilate the concept of the devil. Maya religion had many malevolent spirits, but the Christian devil, being in charge of the underworld, became the dominant one. It is generally believed that his powers are extensive and that anyone who wishes to become a witch or sorcerer must first make a pact with him. He is usually depicted as the early Spaniards visualized him — with horns, a tail, and cloven feet. In many of the dramatic presentations performed by the Indians, the devil plays a role and is inevitably converted by the Virgin Mary.

Many of the supernatural beings found in present-day Indian religion can be traced directly to the ancient Maya religion or to Spanish folk beliefs. These spirits and deities are usually invoked in the *milpa* or by shamans at ancient shrines, but many comprise the superstitious beliefs, which indirectly affect daily activities, and are not worshiped. They form the legends and folk beliefs that belong to no organized religion.

The Maya nature gods are still influential and are propitiated throughout the cultivation cycle. The rituals vary with the township, but in many towns a turkey is taken to the field at the beginning of planting and sacrificed, his blood poured upon the ground to feed the earth. Incense is burned, and prayers are said to the various gods. These rituals are continued throughout the cycle with seasonal variations. In choosing the proper day on which to commence cultivating or harvesting, a farmer generally goes to the shaman, who consults the sacred Maya calendar or, at least, surviving portions of it. The calendar is also used in divination and in setting the dates of agricultural feasts. Most Indians know of the existence of the calendar, but only the shaman understands how to use it.

In addition to the nature gods, there are many supernatural beings who are mixtures of Spanish and Indian spirits. Their appearance, powers, and names vary from one township to another, but the pattern of beliefs is similar. Many of the malevolent spirits such as Juan Noq, Don Avelin Caballero Sombreron, and the Duende are depicted as *ladinos*. The first two are in charge of witchcraft and those who practice it. The last-mentioned is a dwarf who, in some townships, seduces women, causing them sadness and sometimes death. In other towns he distributes favors.

The majority of spirits, however, retain the appearance and power that they had in the Maya legends. The Sigvanaba and Llonona are phantom women who lure men to their destruction. The first of these appears to a man as a beautiful woman, but turns into a skeleton or a figure with a horselike face if he follows her. The Dueno de los Cerros (Lord of the Hills) is particularly influential in the northwestern highlands and, supposedly, guards all the resources of nature within his domain. Some townships consider him a protector of the village as long as he is appeased with offerings. To others, however, he is a malevolent being causing disease and destruction.

The most widely known supernatural concept is that of the *nagual*. The term is the subject of much debate and confusion for it is used differently throughout Central America. Basically, however, it concerns two phenomena. The first is derived from an ancient Maya belief that every person is born with an animal counterpart that serves as his protector. The fate of both is interwoven, and when one dies, so does the other. This animal can be discovered from the sacred calendar or by scattering ash around the home in order to clearly record the animal's prints.

A second definition of the *nagual* phenomenon is a sorcerer who by the power given him by the devil, can transform himself into an animal. An evil individual who wishes to make this pact with the devil sleeps in the cemetery for nine nights, and on the tenth the devil appears. The two fight, and if the man wins, the devil teaches him how to change himself into an animal. If the man loses, he dies. The purpose of this transformation is to perform evil deeds, usually against virtuous people. It is believed that his most common act is nocturnal thievery.

Intermediaries

Indians may approach the gods individually, but in the majority of cases they appeal to religious specialists to intervene in their behalf. One of these intermediaries is the Catholic priest; however, he seldom visits the highland villages. Over the centuries, the Indians have evolved religious practices that do not require the services of a priest. When he does come, his time is primarily occupied with baptisms, a few marriages, and with the annual Mass of the patron saint, all of which occur within the church. The priest is not expected to intervene in other areas, and one who attempts to change the traditional beliefs is labeled a Protestant.

Because of the scarcity of priests Indians have never placed much faith in them. Instead, ceremonies, and *fiestas* are sponsored and conducted by the religious brotherhoods. Composed of local men, these groups are responsible for the care of the Church and particular saints, for the sponsoring of *fiestas*, and the celebration of various Catholic holy days. These duties are performed in the name of the whole village so that the saints, in turn, will bless all its inhabitants with good fortune. The offices in the brotherhood are rotated annually, and all men assume the responsibility and honor of serving both the saints and the village.

In the more isolated areas, which almost never see a priest, older men who have passed through all the offices of the brotherhoods become unofficial native priests. They maintain the adherence to folk-Catholic ceremonies, conducting many of these, since they have amassed a vast knowledge of religious and magical ritual; however, they seldom administer the sacraments other than baptism. These native priests are found primarily in the north in Verapaz and Chiquimula Departments.

One of the most important religious specialists is the *chiman*, or shaman. His duties and powers vary from one township to another, and in some areas he maintains strong ties with the official Roman Catholic structure, working closely with the brotherhoods and conducting a large part of the ceremonies. In these areas the shaman has wide knowledge of Maya lore and is similar to the native priests, but usually has not passed through the offices of the brotherhoods. This type of shaman is found mainly in the eastern part of the country.

In most townships, however, the shaman is associated with supernatural beliefs and rituals, which exist outside of the formal religious organization, and is more involved with personal and family problems rather than village ceremonies. Although he consults and pays homage to Catholic saints, he usually propitiates and appeals to the nature gods or supernatural spirits of legends and folklore. He is the prime user of the ancient Maya calendar, or at least portions of it, employing it for selecting sacrificial days in the cultivation cycle and for divination.

Two of the shaman's greatest abilities are divination and curing. Most possess a bundle of red beans, called *miches,* which were supposedly given to them by God. With these they can predict the future, discover the cause of an illness and, in conjunction with the calendar, pick a good day on which to conduct rituals. Some shamans, however, do not use the beans exclusively, but rely on the twitching of their leg muscles, which can be read either as a positive or negative answer to a question asked of the gods.

In solving personal problems, the shaman uses both his power of divination and his supposedly direct contact with the spirit world. Indians claim that he can find lost articles, discover if a wife or husband has been unfaithful, predict the sex of an unborn baby, and other similar matters. He can also intercede with the gods on behalf of someone who has offended them. If a man's crop is not doing well he can go to a shaman, who will offer sacrifices to the proper gods in the man's name.

Most of the divination and curing process is based on set rituals, which are performed the same way each time. Many of the shamans contend that their knowledge of these rituals comes directly from God, who speaks to them in dreams. Others admit that they acquire the knowledge informally by early and constant attendance at ceremonies and rituals conducted by older shamans. There appear to be no instances of formal training, although this may occur covertly.

It is sometimes hard to separate the witch or sorcerer from the shaman, for in certain areas one man performs both roles. Generally, however, the shaman seeks only to help the individual, whereas the sorcerer deals primarily in black magic. This sort of witchcraft has been officially outlawed; nevertheless, it still does exist and is considered quite powerful. Although the definitions vary in most places the sorcerer is considered a practitioner who sells his knowledge of witchcraft to clients wishing to cause bodily harm to, or to place a supernatural curse on, an enemy.

The sorcerer is an ordinary man who supposedly has learned magic formulas and rituals from another sorcerer. It is doubtful that this type of training is done formally, but many *ladinos* insist that schools of witches and diviners exist in the highlands. The knowledge of black magic is fairly common though in legends and folk beliefs, and anyone who wants to practice these rituals can obtain the information with little trouble.

The sorcerers usually make their victim ill by allegedly casting animals into his body. As a rule they need some possession of the victim, and often the client must participate in the ritual.

It is also believed that many sorcerers do not sell their knowledge; rather they practice witchcraft against their own enemies and against anyone they envy. For this reason Indians do not wish to flaunt their good fortune, as this would be inviting witchcraft against themselves. When a man's luck goes bad, he immediately suspects witchcraft from an enemy and will seek out a shaman or a sorcerer to counteract the curse.

Ceremonies

Various stages of the life cycle are marked by religious ceremonies, involving a blend of Catholic tradition and ancient superstition. Childbirth is accompanied by ritual bathing, sweat baths and ritual foods for the mother. The umbilical cord has magical significance and, in some townships, it is burned to prevent sickness. In other towns, if the newborn is a girl, the cord is buried under the hearth to keep her from wandering; if the child is a boy, the cord is hung in a tree to ensure his diligence.

Baptism is of vital importance and has its origins in both Christianity and pre-Columbian practices. In many villages the Indians believe that this act changes the child from an animal into a human being and will insist upon the ceremony even if the child is dead. In other places the practice supposedly prevents death and is received as early as possible. If the child dies without being baptized, it is believed that he goes to limbo and returns to haunt the village. Godparents hold the child during the ceremony, thus sealing the ritual tie between the families.

There are no puberty rites, and confirmation occurs

infrequently. Religious sanctions regarding marriage are taken lightly. Common-law marriages are prevalent, and divorce is socially acceptable. Even when a religious ceremony does occur, the secular events that accompany the vows are prominent.

Death is surrounded by numerous superstitions and traditional practices. Often it is attributed to sorcery, but it is also accepted as the inevitable fate of man. If a shaman predicts a patient's death, the patient will stop eating in preparation for his fate; however, he will seek to avoid this if the shaman considers recovery possible and will follow the prescribed rituals and cures.

The actual burial ceremonies are conducted by laymen, although in some places a shaman may participate. The wake follows the traditional Catholic pattern with a night watch, prayers, and lighted candles. Alcohol is a prominent feature, and people may become intoxicated as the night progresses. The wails of the women characterize the proceedings.

The corpse is dressed in his best clothes, and many of his belongings are placed in the coffin. If the deceased is a child, he is buried with his toys; and adult is buried with his old clothes, household tools, and food. Supposedly, these will ease his journey to eternity. In addition, drinking water and pitch pine to light the way are buried with the coffin. In many townships stones are placed inside the coffin to prevent future deaths in the family.

The corpse is removed feet first from his home, and the pallbearers walk around the house so that the dead can say a last goodbye. He is carried to the cemetery in a long and solemn procession and buried with his head toward the west. If he died violently, the corpse is brought to the cemetery in a special litter and buried face downward; a ceremony is performed at the site of his death.

Beliefs about afterlife vary and are generally a blend of Christian doctrine and Maya superstitions. In most places there is no concept of hell, although it is believed that some lesser gods have kingdoms inside of mountains and recruit souls of the dead as workers. If a soul is taken by God he lives a very pleasant afterlife with much leisure time and many fields of corn. Some believe that the place of God is located in the sky, whereas others insist that it is below the earth. In many townships there is no concept of punishment for evil, but in others it is believed that those who led an un-Christian life cannot enter heaven and must wander the earth as spirits. Purgatory exists in the Indian mind as a spiritual jail where the soul remains until its fine is paid by his surviving family who contribute pennies to the Church. If released, the soul will then seek to repay its family and intercede on its behalf with God.

Religious ceremonies involving the *milpa* are of vital importance and are conducted throughout the cultivation cycle. A shaman usually chooses the propitious day and often conducts the ritual. These ceremonies vary with the locale and the time of year, but have many common elements. They may occur in the *milpa* on the spot where a small animal is sacrificed while candles, incense, and copal are burned. Some of these rites are held at ancient shrines surrounded by pieces of broken pottery that have been used as offerings. Here copal, candles, and incense are also burned, and alcohol is poured on the altar. The highland Indians have introduced the worship at ancient shrines to the lowland Indians, and in the Department of Escuintla the monuments receive a steady stream of petitioners.

Social customs

Kinship terminology among Indians varies with the regions but, as a rule, names exist for only three generations, although older ancestors may be remembered. Only one kinship system, the Jacaltec, has names for the brothers and sisters of grandparents. On the horizontal level, most Indians recognize second and third cousins, who are favored marriage partners in some areas but excluded in most. Generally, descent is traced through the families of both father and mother.

Indian kinship patterns are most influential in choosing a spouse, and close relations are usually regarded as improper and illegal partners; however, kinship outside the nuclear family or, in rare cases, the extended family does not occupy the important position that it holds in *ladino* culture. Members of the kin group rarely maintain close social ties and see one another infrequently at weddings, baptismal ceremonies, or fiestas. As a rule, the women maintain closer kin relationships than the men. An individual may call upon members of the group in time of illness, but financial and economic problems are usually handled outside the kin circle. Granparents offer moral guidance to their grandchildren, but never punish or discipline them. This is the parents' sole responsibility, and they do not welcome infringement in this area from any relatives. In short, the kindred is recognized as a special group, but no close bond is maintained unless an individual actively seeks one. Intimate friendship between two relatives is based more on mutual interests and compatible personalities than on kinship.

Compadrazgo

The *compadrazgo* (godparenthood) system is a form of ritual kinship first brought to Latin America by the Spaniards. It is still present in *ladino* culture and has been adopted by Indian society, where it performs a vital integrative function. Two relationships are created by this system, one involving the child and his godfather *(padrino)* and godmother *(madrina),* and the other consisting of the godparents and the parents, who address each other as *compadre* (comother). The whole complex is formally begun at the baptismal ceremony, but may be reinforced or actually initiated at confirmation. It may also be initiated as part of an effort to effect a cure if the child is seriously ill.

Parents choose a couple whom they consider responsible, welloff, or lucky, who can offer their child protection and assistance. If the couple agrees to accept the position, they take the child to them. A bond exists between the two families, theoretically providing a second set of parents for the child and a close set of friends for the natural parents.

In *ladino* culture the position of godparent is primarily honorary, and many of the social and economic motives have been lost; however, the system establishes a set of intimate friends who will provide assistance or loyalty if needed and who often perform the role of a surrogate family. In short, it is an extension of the kinship circle and performs the same functions. *Ladinos* may act as godparents to Indians, but never the reverse.

In the Indian culture ritual kinship performs a more vital and influential role. The form which it takes varies from one township to another, but it is almost always present. The most important set of godparents are those who are chosen at the baptismal ceremony. The relationship which this establishes is characterized by a set of patterned activities and reciprocal duties involving all members.

In some townships the godparents are expected to provide moral and religious guidance to their godchildren, initiating them into many cultural activities. They are the only persons outside of the nuclear family who are allowed to discipline or reward the children. They also assume the expenses of the burial if the child dies, and will usually provide part of the cost of his wedding.

For his part the child is expected to demonstrate complete obedience and respect for his godparents, bowing his head when meeting them. He generally takes them gifts at specified times and goes to them for advice and guidance. He considers their children his sisters and brothers, on the same level as his own natural siblings. The bond between them is so strong that often the child will request that his same godparents serve at his confirmation, marriage, and the birth of his first child.

The relationship between the two sets of parents *(compadres)* is equally important and provides a means of extending the kinship circle. In many townships it is more influential than the kin relationships, involving extensive reciprocal duties. Parents always consult the godparents in major decisions regarding the child and on private and public matters involving financial, religious, and political problems. In addition, the godparents are supposed to act as mediators in arguments between the father and the mother of the child. Both sets of adults turn to each other for mutual aid, and a man prefers to borrow money from his *compadre* than from kindred. They greet one another with formality.

In choosing godparents, the father and mother generally ask people outside the kinship circle. Occasionally, however, the parents may choose relatives, and some believe that one will only meet parents in the afterlife if they have served as godparents to their grandchildren. Usually, the choice of godparents is made among people with whom one has amicable but distant relations. In many towns the closest friends are excluded, since the existing intimate and informal bond would have to be replaced with a relationship of respect.

Indians sometimes seek *ladinos* to act as godparents to their children because this enables the Indian family to establish a special bond with at least one *ladino* in the community. This means that their child can expect small favors, and if the parents die he will be cared for. More importantly, however, the family itself now has access to a *ladino* household and will usually receive financial assistance in case of need, protection from the law, or even preferential treatment in the renting of land. Thus, a bridge is formed between the two cultures and, even though the equality between both sets of parents is missing, the advantages are numerous enough to maintain the bond.

Childhood and youth

In the *ladino* home, and particularly in middle and upper class families, children are more carefree and irresponsible than in Indian society. *Ladino* children are expected to attend school for as long as possible and to engage in games and other social activities with their companions. Among lower-class rural and urban *ladinos,* however, children are a necessary economic asset and are taught farming and household tasks at an early age. Nevertheless, the ideal of an irresponsible childhood remains, and lower-class parents indulge this pattern for as long as they are financially able to support a noncontributing member.

Discipline for *ladino* children is characterized by extremes of permissiveness and authoritarianism. The mother generally serves as the indulgent parent who is expected to spoil her children, ideally with the help of the maids and nurses. The father is the central authority and disciplines the children. Severe discipline supposedly inculcates the right kind of behavior in the child, but it also, at times, causes the child to demonstrate more loyalty to the mother, while exhibiting fear and even hostility toward his father.

Boys are given much more freedom than girls, and among the middle and upper class families they are usually supported. In lower-class families, however, the boy must often work for his family or as a wage earner. In all social classes boys usually marry later than girls, but are expected by their peers to have had premarital affairs in order to prove their manhood. Marriage is seldom undertaken unless the boy can support his wife and is able to accept the responsibilities of adulthood.

Girls lose their freedom of activity as they grow older and generally do not attend school as long as boys. They are kept close to the home, learning the duties of a woman commensurate with their status. At adolescence upper-class girls are considered marriageable and are continually on display at picnics, weddings, fiestas, and religious ceremonies, always heavily chaperoned. Lower-class families cannot supply the clothes for these events or the time away from household duties.

In the last 10 or 15 years the social pattern of a girl's behavior has been changing, and many are now attending more years of school and taking jobs in the business world; however, a girl is still watched more closely than her brother, and freedom is not as complete. In lower-class families girls often work in factories or as maids to help support the family, continuing their work after marriage. Although acceptable and sometimes necessary, education and a job for a girl are still considered deviations from the ideal.

In Indian homes the smallest child is the center of attention, and only he receives public displays of affection. He is usually nursed for about 15 months, which may extend to 3 years if another child is not born in the meantime. Walking and talking are encouraged but not forced; he is generally allowed to develop at his own pace. Both mother and father play with the infant, and the older children care for him. He is never left alone without some supervision. Usually a boy is given more attention than a girl, and his needs are satisfied first.

At approximately 4 years of age this permissive and lenient pattern ends, and parents begin the process of socialization. The child no longer receives immediate attention and is expected to entertain himself or play with his brothers and sisters. He is no longer carried and is not comforted if he falls or hurts himself; he is expected to develop endurance and emotional restraint. Obedience is demanded, but requests to children are usually given in a conversational tone of voice. The authoritarianism of the *ladino* household is missing. There are no organized games, and play usually consists of imitating the activities of adults. Most toys are miniature versions of household and field implements.

Festivals and markets

While most people use the Western calendar for daily and business activities, two other calendars are significant in the lives of particular Indian groups. One, used in parts of Huehuetenango, is the old Maya "vague year" calendar of 365 days divided into 18 months of 20 days each. The extra five days, which come after the end of one year and before the beginning of the next, are the "evil days" or the days of the "five women." The most important event in connection with this calendar, and perhaps the oldest Indian rite still practiced, is the Year Bearer's ceremony on the first day of the new year. This ceremony has been best preserved in the *municipio* of Jacaltenango. The old calendar was constructed so that the first day of the new year could fall on only

Alvarado marching upon Guatemala.

four day names. The deity of the first day of the new year is the Year Bearer. Prayer-makers begin their duties days in advance in anticipation of the ceremony. They burn incense, make offerings of red flowers, and burn candles.

The Tzolkin calendar, which has 260 days divided into thirteen months of 20 days each, is important to the Indians of Momostenango, Totonicapan. Each day of the month has its own name. In addition, each day is numbered from one to 13, so that each month the same name day will have a different number from the one that it has in any other month. The ancient Maya used the sacred Tzolkin calendar simultaneously with the "vague year" calendar. The most important celebration in connection with this calendar is also the first day of the year. The occasion is called the *Ceremony of Eight Monkeys*. Those who live in the village, and those who were born there but live elsewhere, take part in the ceremony, for it is considered very bad luck not to attend.

All towns throughout the country celebrate their saint's days, a Spanish contribution, with a characteristic mixture of solemnity and festivity. The emphasis is somewhat different in Indian and *ladino* towns. Among *ladinos* a novena may be held before the feast day. On the day itself, Mass is held.

The saint's day in an Indian town is similar in many ways. Masked dances, however, such as the Dance of the Moors and the Christians and the Dance of the Conquest, play a prominent role in the Indian town. Sacred *costumbres* (customary religious rituals), sacrifices, and prayers accompany these performances. The flavor of the Indian fiesta is more religious than that of the *ladino*.

The market is usually a relatively local affair, held once or twice a week in the cabacera of a *municipio*. Traders are usually residents of the *municipio,* though there may be some itinerant peddlers who come from farther away. The products sold at these frequent markets are necessities such as fruits, vegetables, and locally made textiles.

A fair, usually held in connection with some other occasion such as a fiesta, goes on for several days. It is a larger version of the market and attracts people from many parts of the country. Sections of the marketplace are set aside for particular products. Most Guatemalan *municipios* are known for a particular craft or product. The men from Chinautla, laden down with water jugs, go to the pottery section where they rent space; those from Momostenango carry their woolen blankets to another section. In recent years sections have been set aside for inexpensive factory-made items, such as combs, soap, and flashlights. Goods are usually bought and sold for cash after much bargaining.

GUAYAKI of eastern Paraguay are one of the least-known tribes of South America. The *Cainguá* and the *Guarani* once waged a war of extermination against them.

The Guayaki lived in the forests of eastern Paraguay where hills and mountains separate the tributaries of the Paraguay River from those of the Paraná River. They were distributed from the Monday River in the north to the outskirts of the forest in the south and west, and to the Paraná River in the east. The constant encroachments of lumber camps and farms forced them to retreat to the less accessible mountains and hills of the Caaguazú. A smaller group lived near the Paraná River, between two of its tributaries, the Monday and Nacunday Rivers. The southernmost Guayaki inhabited the region of San Juan Nepomuceno, and wander in the forested plains between the Tembey and Teyucuaré Rivers (near Encarnación).

On the basis of ethnological evidence, some maintain that there are two different kinds of Guayaki. The total number of the Guayaki was 800 or 1,000 in 1910. In 1920 only 500 were left after a severe influenza epidemic.

Northern and southern groups spoke the same dialect but differed in minor aspects of material culture. Although the former keep equally aloof from civilization, their material culture has been slightly affected by indirect contact with whites. They discarded stone axes for steel hatchets and used iron pots and tin cans instead of wax-smeared baskets.

Guayaki warrior, 1897

GUAYANÁ. *See Guaraní.*

GUAYMI are still a numerous people of western
Panama, in pre-white times existing from the Chagres
River basin near what is now the Canal Zone to some
parts of southwestern Costa Rica. At the time of the
conquest they included possibly 6-9 separate nations,
each headed by a high chief, and were noted warriors,
having come up out of South America as conquerors
many centuries ago. The name Guaymi is possibly
derived from the Guaymi word "Gua," which means
"to flog," something the Guaymi still do to each other
in their famous Stick Games (called *Balseria* by the
Spanish).

Subsistence and economy. Deer and other large
animals were hunted mainly with bows and arrows, but
small animals and birds were often hunted with blow
guns, throwing hard clay pellets instead of darts. The
Guaymi were extremely clever at making traps,
deadfalls and covered pits, the latter with sharpened
stakes; also even bows and arrows were set up to be
tripped as traps, a trick used against human enemies.

Cone-shaped basketry traps and large nets were
used in rivers and streams to catch fish, including W-
shaped dams with traps at the points. A peculiar
method to catch fish was to line up people along a
stream to shout so loudly that fish were frightened into
jumping into mats held in canoes! Fishing in the large
rivers and the sea was carried out in small to large
dug-out canoes, sometimes using sails for locomotion.
Fish were shot with single or three-pronged arrows,
large ones harpooned, others caught with hand nets or
floating nets, or with fish hooks made of shell. Sea food
was very important along the coasts.

Inland agriculture produced the main bulk of the
food eaten, with corn, beans and edible gourds being
most important, but papaya, yucca (or sweet manioc),
sweet potatoes and peach palm nuts were also common. Farming was done by the tropical slash and burn
method, the men cutting down and then burning the
brush and trees, the women then planting and tending
the crops over a period of three to five years, to be
followed by moving to a new location to repeat the
process.

Dogs were the main domesticated animal, packs
being used for hunting, but peccaries and tapirs were
sometimes tamed to be raised for meat. Many other
wild pets were kept for entertainment.

Almost all foods were boiled; meat, when not eaten
right away, being salted and smoked. Corn was hulled
in a mortar, boiled and then ground on a metate to
make flour, from which mush was made, or it was
formed into cakes, wrapped in corn husks and then
steamed.

There was much trade between different areas, and
barter prevailed instead of money even though gold
was much used in ornaments. Sea food was traded
inland, and smoked meat and hides came down from

the interior to the coast. The greatest source of salt was
from the Burica Indians of the Panama-Costa Rica
Pacific Coast border.

Technology and arts. Square or round steep-
roofed houses were the rule, though rectangular were a
later development, each house with a well-built frame
of strong poles covered with thick palm leaf thatching,
and usually with an upper floor or attic for storage and
where the children slept. Walls were thatched too and
inside were hung with weapons, utensils and dried or
smoked foods. Platform beds were built along the
walls, with leaves and skins used to form mattresses.
Benches of two horizontal poles or of split logs, plus
stools that were carved out of single blocks of wood or
sometimes with legs, formed seats. In the center of
every house floor near the cooking fire there was
placed a large wooden trough for making chicha, the
national corn drink. Grain was stored in the house loft
in circular bark bins or in large baskets.

A breech-clout made of a six foot long strip of bark
cloth wrapped between the legs and around the waist
was the principal clothing of men, while women not
only had the breech-clout, made of softer bark, but
also a knee-length wrap-around bark or cotton skirt.

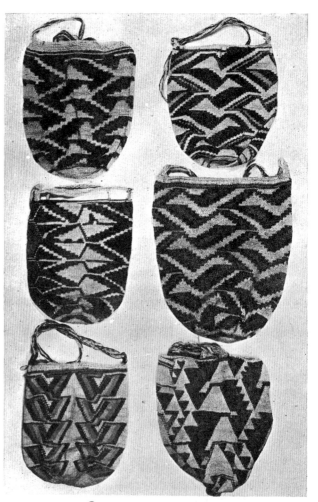

Guaymi bags, Panama.

Some wore a scant shirt or jacket, and, in bad weather, all might use a blanket with a hole in the center as a poncho. Rawhide sandals were more rarely used. In the old days there was much painting of the body and face, especially by the men, including a paint made from crushed cockroaches, to which various plant, charcoal or other dyes were added to give color. Beautiful circles of feathers of tropical birds were used as head decorations at dances and ceremonials, but more striking still and peculiar were stuffed skins of animals, carried on the back with the nose pointed skyward, a stuffed jaguar skin marking a great warrior or hunter.

The old way of making and weaving cloth out of wild or cultivated cotton has almost been forgotten because of store-bought clothing. A two bar loom was used. Also far back in time were the famous and elaborate gold ornaments, once worn by nearly all the people, but which the white man's lust for gold soon induced the Indians to hide. The gold was probably cast by the lost wax process, producing such intricate and beautiful work as diminutive skeletons, flowers and spiders.

Pottery of the Guaymi included large, pointed or round-bottomed jars, often with restricted necks. Most was plain, but some were decorated with simple designs, more commonly so in ancient days. Much artistry was shown in the production of carved stone pipes. Some with animal and human figures, or incised with geometrical designs. Collars of bone beads and necklaces of perforated teeth wre also common, while the Guaymi are famous to this day for their basket bags that are often attractively decorated with various designs.

Social organization. There was a strong family life among the old time Guaymi, with some men, however, having more than one wife. Marriage was generally made by purchase. In the old days there were a number of feudal governments, each headed by a powerful chief. Wars with the Spaniards often welded such units together for mutual defense, and the mountain Guaymi were able to keep their independence down to very recent times. The Guaymi character seems more oriental and self-controlled than with most Indians, the Guaymi cleverly masking their thoughts behind stone-like faces and being masters of subtrefuge and camouflage, all very useful in defeating the white man or avoiding conflict with him.

Social and cultural boundaries and subdivisions

Culturally the Guaymi were divided into two main subdivisions, the Southern Guaymi, who lived in the foothills, plateaus and lowlands along the Pacific Coast, which was comparatively dry, with often open savannahs and not so much forest, and the Northern Guaymi of the mountains and the Caribbean coast areas of the north half of western Panama where there was much thick rain forest. The Northern Guaymi were a more primitive and hunting type people, though they did have agriculture, while the Southern Guaymi did extensive agriculture, had less hunting and developed more artistic and civilized qualities, living in larger towns with well-constructed fortified walls. They were bound on the northwest by the Caribs, in the western mountains by the related Dorasques and Talamancans, along the Pacific Coast west by the Burica, and to the east by the Cuna.

Language

The Guaymi belonged to the large Chibchan

Guaymi shelter and loom weaving.

language family, prevalent in northwestern South America, where it included peoples who built stone temples and had well-organized city states. The Guaymi language has been divided by Jijon y Caamano and J. Alden Mason, in the *Handbook of Southern American Indians*, into nine dialects: Murire, Muoi, Move, Valiente, Penonomen, Changuena, Dorasco, Chumula and Gualaca. (But Lucien Adams allows only six dialects.)

Life cycle. Using sympathetic magic, special herbs, etc., to give her child useful characteristics, a pregnant woman retired to a small separate house to give birth, usually assisted by her mother or a mid-wife. The child, after being washed in the river, usually had smoke blown on it by a medicine man to purify it.

At puberty boys went through a secretinitiation ceremony and received an official but secret name. They also often suffered several kinds of torture to prove their stamina and endurance before entering manhood.

Some Guaymi after death were left in a special place to decay, and then later their bones were collected with great ceremony and buried.

Traditions, folklore, religion and tribal medicine. Perhaps the greatest tradition of the Guaymi is the story of the *Ngobo Ulikron*, a messenger from the Great Spirit and also called the "Son of the Virgin," who came to the Guaymi long ago out of the north, bringing a message of love and harmony, and left them to take the same message to the people of the south. They said war was ended for centuries because of his coming. How much of the Guaymi religion came from him and how much from the old nature gods and spirits of the far past we do not know. We do know that many of the Guaymi believed such things that if you had a bad dream you would die unless this was soon counteracted by the magic of a medicine man. They also had to call on such a man to ward off the influence of evil spirits. But he could act as a healer too, using herbs and other cures for sickness and wounds. A common method of getting rid of sores was to hold the injured part of the body in the smoke of a fire made of termite nests.

In the old days there were several ceremonies, but the one great ceremony and festival remaining to the Guaymi today is the *Balseria* (Spanish) or *Krunkite*, of which the main part sees two lines of men formed, one with their backs turned, the other with sticks that they whirl and then throw at the legs of their competitors. Hits were counted as points, bets were made, and even wives were sometimes lost in the gamble!

Summary of tribal history and contemporary condition

After the wars, which ended with most of the Mountain Guaymi still independent, white civilization nevertheless continued its inroads on these people, with traders bringing in metal goods, manufactured cloth and injurious foods and alcoholic drinks. Recently many of the Guaymi have taken up cattle rais-

ing, which has put more of a burden on the land and the people, especially the women, than they expected. Though many of the old ways are dying, new religious impulses have begun to reawaken an interest in and pride in the best of their past, and give them an aim of greater harmony and economic independence. This rugged people, great fighters and wise knowers of jungle life and ways, need such a new hope and a new life.

VINSON BROWN

Men in ceremonial dress.

Hip-roofed house of the Guaymi. *Top:* Completed. *Bottom:* Framework.

GUAYUPÉ of the llanos and forests on the eastern slope of the Andes south of the *Chibcha* had a general Tropical Forest culture with perhaps a few Sub-Andean traits. They were farmers and lived in palisaded villages of multi-family houses arranged around a plaza that had a ceremonial building. They had no class system, but old men apparently had superior status and formed a council. Chiefs were elected, and their prestige is indicated only in their use of stools and feather blankets and their claim to half the bride price paid at each marriage. A deceased chief was cremated, and his ashes were ceremonially drunk in chicha by his successor.

There was much warfare, but slave taking, cannibalism and human trophies are not reported. At their initiation boys were whipped and pricked with lances to make them good warriors.

The special religious house was perhaps comparable to that of the Tropical Forests rather than to the Andean temple. The sun and moon, who were man and wife, were the gods, and the jaguar and other animals were evil beings. No ceremonialism is mentioned except shamanistic curing, which was accomplished by sucking out the disease-causing object.

Subsistence was based on farming, bitter manioc probably being one of the crops. The technology is now well known, but cotton was grown and must have been woven, though feather instead of cotton blankets are mentioned as articles of clothing. Except for these blankets and some gold, shell, and feather ornaments, people went naked. They used hammocks, wooden stools, dugout canoes, spears, lances, clubs, bows and arrows, slings, and shields. They took coca and tobacco to obtain visions.

GUINN, NORA (Inuit; Nov. 11, 1920–   ), was the first Inuit woman judge in the U.S., and her interests have also involved her in projects with Native American youth and mental retardation. Born at Akiah, Alaska, she entered a public service career after her marriage. She worked at a medical facility at Tununah on the Bering Sea and then moved to Bethel, Alaska, where she served two terms on the city council. Nora Guinn holds court in many places throughout her judicial district, which covers 100,000 square miles, and she conducts court in many different languages, since she speaks several Eskimo dialects and tries to use the appropriate language in the courtroom. She also serves as a parole officer and counselor.

GUIRIGRAMA (Nahua; fl. 17th century), was chief of a tribe of Nahua Indians in the Duy Valley of western Panama before 1605, when the Spanish conquistador Diego de Sojo y Peñaranda invaded the region. Guirigrama was captured and punished for his resistance to the colonizing efforts. Shortly thereafter, Diego de Sojo founded the modern city of

Nora Guinn

ᵤuretka, Costa Rica, just across the Panama border. Guirigrama was a close neighbor of the Tarica Indians.

GUIRILL (Yaqui; fl. early century), was an Indian chief who, along with his allies Torin and Potam was killed in May 1927 by a Mexican army detachment in the command of a General Zertache. 1927 was the last year of concerted Yaqui violence in Mexico's Sonora state.

GUMS AND RESINS. From humble beginnings, the chewing-gum industry has become big business, built on *chicle* (chee-klay). This principal ingredient of "gum" is from a tree, also named chicle, that yields one of the finest white resins in the world. This is in Middle America, where, during the rainy season, the Indians extract the resin by a process similar to that for obtaining rubber. The Indian name in the Nahuatl language is *chictle*.

Incidentally, the wood of the tree is of remarkable value. The Maya carved logs of it into beams for their vast temples, where it has withstood the ravages of time for a thousand years.

GUNS, primarily shoulder weapons, were first acquired by Indians on the North Atlantic Coast in the seventeenth century through trade with the French, English, and Dutch. As guns diffused along with the migration of whites throughout the rest of North America during the next two centuries, they became a significant factor in the drastic enviromental, cultural, and economic changes experienced by the Indians during those times.

The early smooth-bore muzzle-loading muskets were not immediately adopted by the Indians in preference to traditional weapons. Compared to the bow and arrow they were more awkward and time consuming to load and less dependable. Gradually, however, improved forms of the musket and later the rifle were developed until in the nineteenth century the breech-loading rifle, cartridge ammunition, and finally the repeating rifle came into use. In hunting and warfare the improved guns, for Indians who could obtain them, rendered the bow and arrow and the lance largely obsolete.

In warfare the use of rifles and cannon by whites put Indians using native weapons at a tremendous disadvantage. The use of guns in war was one of the major factors contributing to a much higher proportion of combatants killed than generally had occurred in earlier traditional forms of Indian warfare.

Hunting by the Indians before aquisition of guns

Mexican Indian holding gun, 1934.

had been primarily for subsistence purposes. It had been a limiting factor on the animal populations hunted but generally had not seriously depleted them or threatened the survival of any species. The efficiency of the gun coupled with the tremendous growth of the fur trade was a major factor in producing excessive hunting pressure by both Indians and whites. The diffusion of guns throughout North America was repeatedly followed by serious depletion of game populations on which most Indians depended to a significant extent for food. Probably the most well known example is that of the buffalo on the Plains, where the use of the gun and horse made possible the reduction of a population ranging from Canada to Mexico to near extinction within about eighty years.

GUYANA. Present-day Guyana was first recognized by Europe in 1498 when Columbus sailed along the coast during the last of his three voyages. Little attention, however, was paid to this area until the last decade of the 16th century and the arrival of Sir Walter Raleigh. Searching for El Dorado — the mythical city of gold — Raleigh and the Dutch explorers who followed him mapped the coastline and established friendly contact with the primitive Amerindian natives. Efforts by these early adventurers to stimulate the colonization of the Guianas finally produced a Dutch expedition in 1616 that formed the settlement of Fort Kijkorveral on an island in the Essequibo River at its confluence with the Cuyuni and Mazaruni. In 1621 the colony was placed under the direction of the newly-incorporated West Indian Company of the Netherlands. This group of Dutch commercial concerns administered the settlements known as Essequibo and Demerer for 170 years. Although it was under the general jurisdiction of this private group, the other region of present-day Guyana, Berbice, was governed separately as a patroon.

Dutch expansion into the interior of Essequibo, Demerara, and Berbice made it clear that the good will of the Amerindian population was necessary for both the profitability of trade and the safety of Dutch settlements. In addition, early attempts by the Europeans to enslave the Amerindians had proved uneconomical and reinforced the tendency to treat these nomadic hunters as allies and not as subjugated natives.

Although the settlements engaged in the cultivation of crops, such as tabacco, cotton, and coffee, agriculture remained at the subsistence level. Moreover, Guianese production of these commodities on a commercial basis was hurt by the development of the southern region by the United States. Unable to compete, Guiana gradually shifted away from these crops toward sugar cane. First grown in the pomeroon settlement in 1658, sugar became the dominant commodity in both Essequibo and Demerara. Berbice continued to specialize in coffee and cotton.

The rapid growth of sugar production in the first quarter of the 18th century brought a movement

Sioux using guns, 1915.

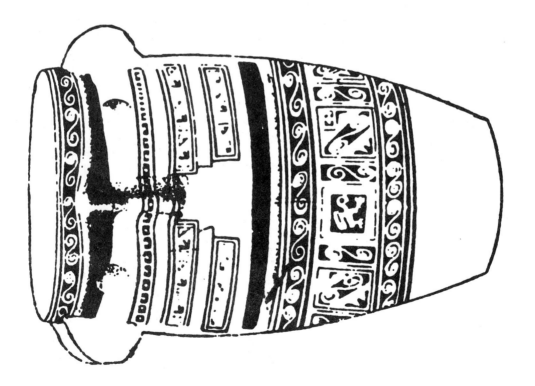

Pottery jars from Guyana.

BASKETRY

BRITISH GUIANA

BEAD APRON

BRITISH GUIANA

toward the coastal strip. The migration from the interior occurred over an extended period of time as the soil along the rivers was progressively exhausted. This trend was officially recognized in 1738 by the transfer of the Dutch administrative center from Fort Kijkoveral to Fort Island at the mouth of the Essequibo River.

The appointment of a new secretary to the West Indian Company of the Netherlands, Laurens Storm van's Gravesande, also occurred in 1738. Four years later he was elevated to Commandeur, the colony's highest office. Gravesande opened the Demerara region to settlement in 1746, and it grew so rapidly that by 1750 a separate Commandeur had to be appointed to govern its affairs. Gravesande was thereupon named to the newly-created post of Directeur-General of Essequibo and Demerara, thus retaining his position as the Company's chief overseer in Guiana. Berbice continued to be administered separately.

For the next 30 years, Gravesande governed Guiana with little interference from the Company's headquarters in the Netherlands. His energetic and

enlightened rule established his place in history as probably the single most important figure in Guiana's early development.

The promise of fertile, virgin lands in Demerara was attractive to the English planters of the West Indies. Concerned by the depletion of the soil on the Carribbean islands, British citizens migrated to Guiana in large numbers. The influx was so great that by 1760 the English constituted a majority of the Demerara population. As a further inducement to colonization, new settlers were offered a 10-year tax exemption and an initial grant of 250 acres of land. Situated on the coast, these plots had a sea-frontage of 400 yards and a depth of 3,000 yards. When the new colonist had cleared his original 250 acres, he was allowed to expand his plantation inland. The sugar estates consequently developed as long, narrow strips of cultivated land extending from the coast to as much as 10 miles inland.

Although the colony was experiencing rapid economic growth, strains began to appear in the relations between the planters and the West India Com-

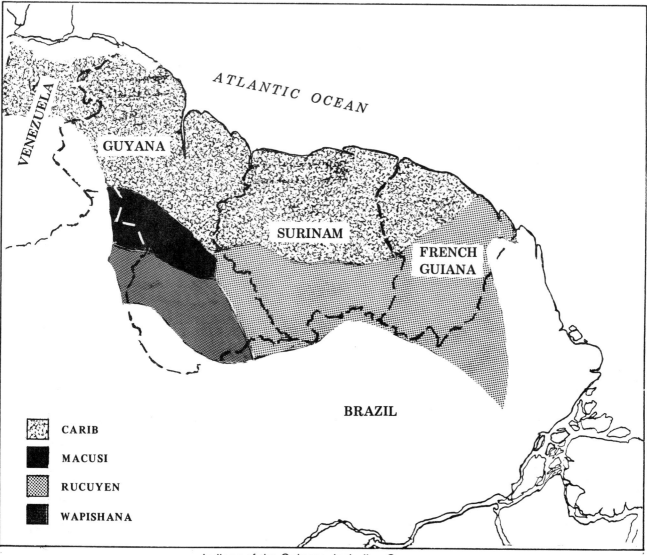

Indians of the Guianas, including Guyana.

pany. Administrative reforms during the early 1770s vastly increased the cost of government. The Company periodically sought to raise taxes to cover these expenditures and thereby provoked the resistance of the planters. In 1781 war broke out between Holland and England and resulted in the British occupation of Berbice, Essequibo, and Demerara. Some months later, France, allied with Holland, seized control of Guiana. The French governed for 2 years during which time they constructed a new town, Longchamps, at the mouth of the Demerara River. When the Dutch regained power in 1784, they decided to move their colonial capital to Longchamps and renamed it Stabrock, later known as Georgetown.

The return of Dutch rule reignited the conflict between the planters of Essequibo and Demerara and the Company. Rebelling against plans for an increase in the slave tax and a reduction in their representation on the colony's judicial and policy councils, the colonists petitioned the Dutch government for consideration of their grievances. A special committee was appointed in response to these protests and proceeded to draw up a report calling for a "Concept Plan of Redress." This document called for far-reaching constitutional reforms which later became the basis of the British governmental structure. The primary policy-making body was the Court of Policy, consisting of the Directeur-General, the Commandeur of Essequibo, the Company's chief fiscal officers of Essequibo and Demerara, and two colonists from each of these adminstrative districts. The judiciary was divided into two Courts of Justice, one serving Demerara and the other Essequibo. Each of these courts was composed of eight members — six colonists and two Company officials. The colonists who sat on the Court of Policy and the Courts of Justice were appointed by the Directeur-General from a list of nominees submitted by the two Colleges of Kiegers. In turn, the seven members of each College of Kiegers were elected for life by those planters possessing 25 or more slaves. Though their power was restricted to nominating colonists to fill vacancies on the three major governmental councils, these electoral colleges became the nucleus of political agitation by the planters.

The Dutch commission assigned the responsibility of implementing this new system of government returned to Holland with extremely unfavorable reports concerning the West India Company's administration. The Company's charter was therefore allowed to expire in 1792. Rechristened the United Colony of Demerara and Essequibo, the area then came under the direct control of the Dutch government, although Berbice maintained its status as a distinct patroon.

Following the opening of the Demerara region in 1746, the number of English planters migrating from the West Indies to Guiana was so great that by 1786 the internal functioning of this Dutch colony was effectively under British control. The French Revolution, however, was the final catalyst that produced a complete British take-over. Defeated by the French in 1795, the Prince of Orange fled Holland and sought refuge in England. The Netherlands then became the Batavian Republic, allied with France. Though the colonists of Demerara and Essequibo were unenthusiastic about the new republic, they neither supported the ousted Prince nor aligned themselves with Britain against France. The British consequently sent an expeditionary force from Barbados in 1796 to occupy Guiana. No resistance was offered, and the Dutch administration was permitted to remain in office governing the colony under the constitution provided by the Plan of Redress.

After 6 years of British occupation, the colony was returned to the Batavian Republic in accordance with the Treaty of Amiens (1802). When the war between England and France was renewed less than a year later, the United Colony was again seized by British troops. This time the occupation proved to be permanent, making the former Dutch territory the only British possession on the continent of South America until the 20th century, when it became independent.

Amerindians

The aboriginal inhabitants of Guyana are the least assimilated of the ethnic groups. They rarely participate in the coast-centered life of the country, although they are entitled to vote and have done so. Most of them live in the interior where they practice a mixed agricultural and hunting economy. They have been in contact with European colonists for 200 years and have been the focus of intensive missionary activity during the last century. It has been estimated that about half of them are literate in English, but their own languages survive.

The Guyana Amerindians form three linguistic families: Warrau, Arawak, and Carib. Representatives of all three groups live in widely scattered settlements along the lower reaches of the rivers from the Barima on the west to the Courantyne on the east. These coastal groups have mixed physically and culturally

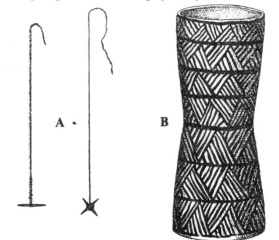

A. Waiwai fish gorges made of palm spines. B. Waiwai wooden mortar.

Shallow carvings in Guiana.

with the local populations. Some groups have been strongly influenced by missionaries during the past 100 years, and some of the young coastal Arawaks no longer speak their own language.

Six Carib-speaking groups (Carib, Akawaio, Patamona, Arekuna, Makusi, Waiwai) and the Arawak-speaking Wapisiana live on the upper reaches and tributaries of the interior rivers. Many of these interior groups maintain their identity while others are becoming rapidly acculturated. Missionary activity is widespread, and working for wages is becoming more common on the cattle ranches. Many Indians also collect balata, and some produce a small surplus of cassava flour for the local markets.

At the extreme southern end of Guyana live the Waiwai, one of the most colorful groups of Amerindians in South America. Intensive missionary activity and influence are rapidly changing their traditional ways of life.

In general, the Amerindians of Guyana are typical representatives of what anthropologists call Tropical Forest culture. The primary characteristics of this culture, which differentiate it from the ways of life in neighboring areas, are the cultivation of manioc, extensive use of canoes, hammocks used as beds, and pottery making.

Men and women wear loincloths or aprons, and san-

Warrau burial.

BEAD APRON, BRITISH GUIANA

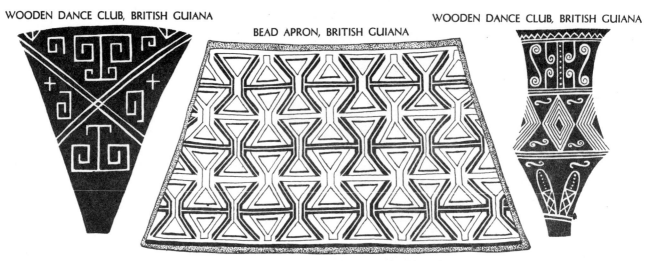

dals. They decorate themselves with brightly colored feathers and other ornaments inserted through holes in the lips, nose, or ears. Most men pull out their facial hair, and tattooing is practiced by many people. Body and face painting with vegetable dyes and animal oils is common. Hair styles vary from group to group. Arm and leg bands, necklaces and rings are worn everywhere.

The Tropical Forest Amerindians live in small settlements of 30 to 40 related individuals. These settlements are only semi-permanent because the people must move whenever the soil has been exhausted by their agricultural techniques. The basic house form is rectangular with a pitched roof supported on a ridge pole. Some people build large circular houses up to 50 feet in diameter, but the basic dwelling is for a single family. Savanna people usually build walls for their houses, but the forest people do not. Houses contain little furniture. There are logs and carved wooden benches for sitting, and hammock for sleeping and relaxing. Household tools are often hung from the roof.

The economy of the Tropical Forest dwellers is based on a combination of farming, hunting, gathering and fishing. The principal farming method is to cut down one or two acres of forest and burn the slash in place. Ashes fertilize the field for the first crops, but the soil then is depleted rapidly. Planting may be done by men, women, or both, but weeding and harvesting are women's work.

The basic crop is manioc; both "bitter" and "sweet" varieties are grown. The Amerindians also raise pineapple, papaya, gourd, sweet potato, cotton, tobacco, pepper, avocado, and maize. They also grow plants introduced by Europeans; these include banana, plantain, yam, sugarcane, and citrus fruits.

The Amerindians collect a wide variety of wild fruits, honey, insects and reptiles to supplement their diet, but they have not developed any specialized techniques for collecting. Hunting is a more important activity, and many forest and river animals are taken. Hunters use blowguns, bows and arrows, spears, harpoons, traps, and dogs. The hunters usually work alone or with one partner and they rely on their ability to stalk their prey.

Fishing is a major activity of all the Amerindians. The principal techniques include the use of hook and line, poisoning, traps, nets, and shooting with arrows and spears.

The staple food, manioc, is peeled, grated, squeezed in a tube made of basketry, and baked. Surplus meat is dried and smoked. Meat and vegetables are cooked together continuously in a stew pot. Soft drinks are made from many fruits and fermented, intoxicating drinks are made from manioc bread, maize, sweet potatoes, pineapple, cashew, sugarcane, and bananas. Tobacco is smoked or chewed everywhere.

Land transportation is limited to whatever an individual can carry. Water transportation, however, is provided by many varieties of dugout canoes, bark canoes, and rafts.

The Guyana Amerindian men have highly developed the techniques and arts of basketry. The basic methods are wickerwork, checkerboard, and twilled weaving. A great variety of products ranges from mats and baskets to fish traps and manioc presses. Cotton thread is spun into cord for such things as hammocks and fish lines. Hammocks, belts and aprons are woven on looms.

The Amerindian settlement is supervised by a headman with the advice of older men in the group. There are no formal tribal organizations, however, and groups are related only by marriage and language. Married couples frequently live with the bride's family, and a man may have more than one wife.

Amerindian mothers are separated from their families or communities during childbirth. Fathers' movements outside the settlement also are restricted. This practice is based on the idea that the well-being of the child's spirit depends on the presence of the father.

Education is informal and imitative. There are puberty ordeals for both boys and girls. The dead are mourned in a variety of ceremonies, and usually buried under the floor of the house which then is abandoned.

The drinking spree is the most common form of

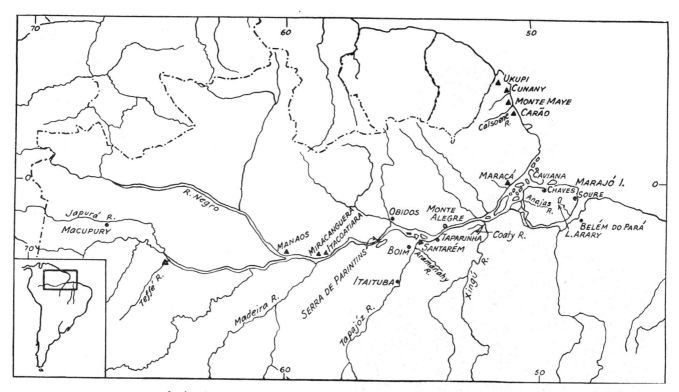

Archeological sites of the lower Amazon and the Guianas.

social recreation. Sprees last many days and are marked by dancing, athletic competitions, and sex play. Musical instruments include woodwinds, drums, and strings.

The Amerindians believe the world was created by a man-like heroic figure. They also believe there is a "boss spirit," but he is not worshipped. Animals with magical powers populate their medicine man, or shaman, is found in every community, and he usually serves as an advisor or curer.

Intensive missionary activity among the Amerindians has been only partially successful. All of the Protestant denominations which had missions among the East Indians and the Africans sent ministers into the interior. The Anglican and Presbyterian Churches have had the most success among Amerindians, but the Roman Catholic Church also maintains missions had developed among the Carib-speaking people. It combines certain elements of Christianity with indigenous beliefs.

Many Amerindians feel hostile and cheated, in part because of missionary disapproval of their traditional beliefs and customs and the missionary emphasis on concepts and customs which could not easily be absorbed into the old framework. The general cultural disorientation had outweighed other benefits, with the possible exception of vastly improved health.

Air travel has brought medical care (and missionaries) within reach of nearly all the Amerindians, and their population is expanding as a result. The colonial government made plans for reservations, but they never were implemented. The policy of the new government is to encourage the "absorption" of Amerindians into Guyanese society. The government hopes to do this by providing professional and technical training through the use of mobile schools, hotels, and other facilities. The success of this plan remains to be determined.

GUYON, JOSEPH N. (White Earth Chippewa; 1892– Nov. 27, 1971), was an outstanding football player who was inducted into the National Professional Football Hall of Fame in 1966 and was one of the original inductees into the American Indian Athletic Hall of Fame in 1972. Born at White Earth, Minnesota, he attended Carlisle Indian School (1911– 14) and Georgia Tech University (1917– 18). He was selected to the All-American, All Indian football team in 1913 and 1914; and to the All-American football team in 1917 and 1918. He played both professional football and professional baseball with several teams (1919– 27), including the Canton Bulldogs and the New York Giants.

Guyon, Joe

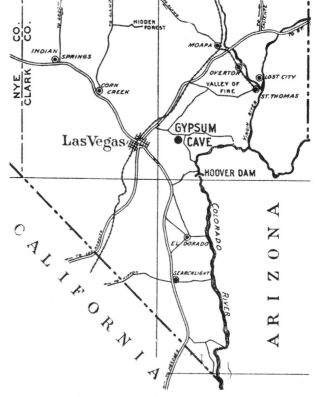

Location of Gypsum Cave.

GUZMÁN, (DON) DOMINGO de (Mixtec; 1510–1558), was a 16th-century Indian chief of Yanuuitlán, southern Mexico. Born in 1510, Don Domingo was apparently the chief tried by the Spanish Inquisition in 1544 for practicing native religion. He ruled during the minority of his nephew Don Gabriel, and died in 1558.

GUZMÁN, (DON) GABRIEL de (Mixtec; ?–1591), was a 16th-century Indian king of Yanhuitlán, southern Mexico, and the son of the rulers Doña Maria Coquahua and Diego Nugh. He inherited his title from his mother, but his uncle Don Domingo ruled during his minority. Don Gabriel ruled from 1558 till his death in 1591.

GYPSUM CAVE, about twenty miles northeast of Las Vegas, Nevada, saw important excavations carried on in 1930 and 1931. This cave had been discovered about the time white men first began to settle in Nevada but had attracted attention merely because of its gypsum deposits until someone began to dig down through the many layers of deposits on the floor of its five deep chambers. The upper layers revealed relics of fairly recent Paiute occupation; farther down relics of earlier cultures were found — the Pueblo III and, lower, the Basketmaker. Eventually the excavators reached layers of excrement deposited by the long-extinct ground sloth. There among fossil remains of

the ground sloth — bones, claws, and wisps of coarse, yellowish hair — were found charred pieces of wood, worked flint dart points, and primitive ropes of twisted sinew — sure evidence of man's presence in the cave during the lifetime of the prehistoric beast. Of especial interest was the discovery of short, painted wooden shafts, possibly primitive *atlatls,* or spear-throwers.

HABITATIONS. *See* DWELLINGS.

HACHO, DON SANCHO, was a direct descencant of an Inca Indian family from the Latacunga region of central Ecuador. After the Spanish conquest, the colonial governor Rodriquez Nunez de Bonilla (in office 1560-61) recommended Sancho Hacho for a title from the Spanish, crown, which gave him estates in the Panzaleo Indian country and various other privileges.

HACIENDAS.

Although, in time, the *encomienda* and the *hacienda* became confused, at the start, there were radical differences between the two institutions in Latin America. In general, these lay in (1) form of ownership, (2) labor employed, and (3) type of production.

With respect to the first, ownership of the *encomienda* was insecure, whereas that of the *hacienda* was definitive; that is to say, the latter might be bequeathed, transferred, or sold, without restriction.

The second difference also was fundamental. Whereas the *encomendero* had forced native labor at his disposition, the *hacendado* was obliged to hire help—although, upon occasion, the Indians might give him manual labor by means of a *repartimiento*. The *hacienda* gave rise to a new social stratum: the peon, composed in part of Indians and in part of imported Negro workmen.

The third distinction lay in the fact that the *encomienda* tended, as a rule, to preserve ancient crops and ancient methods of cultivation, whereas, under the *hacienda,* a different type of economic activity generally was developed—in Totonacapan, particularly stock raising and sugar cane production.

Late sixteenth-century records mention numerous authorizations for Spanish colonists to establish ranches *(estancias)*. Undoubtedly, the lands were indigenous property, either abandoned by the occupants or taken from them. At the time of the Discovery the great Totonac center of "Cempoala" is credited by one source with between 20,000 and 30,000 *vecinos* (heads of families) by another with "more than twenty thousand houses." But by the end of the sixteenth century, it was reduced to 12 taxable individuals and a few years later, to 8 heads of families (*indios casados*). The greater part of its lands were converted into cattle ranches and stock raising became of considerable importance.

Haciendas dedicated to sugar cane and its elaboration also flourished, contributing to the reduction in numbers and to the dispersal of the native population, and at the same time stimulating the introduction of Negro slaves.

HACKENSACK

consisted of a number of *Munsee Delaware*-speaking groups which inhabited the coastal lowlands of northeastern New Jersey to the east of the Watchung Hills from the Hackensack-Passaic River drainage south to the lower reaches of the Raritan River. The Hackensack, who were extinct as an identifiable socio-political organization by the mid 1700s, are today known almost exclusively through the surviving documentation of the successive Dutch (1609-1664), English (1664-1782), and American

(1782-present) regimes. Archaeological activity in the area has failed to establish a connection between any known site and a historically known Hackensack settlement.

The first documentary record of aboriginal occupation in Hackensack territory occurred in a 1616 Dutch reference to a group located along the west bank of the Hudson River opposite Manhattan Island. Identified as the *Machkentiwomi*, this group may have been people "dwelling over against the Manhattans" who were decimated by epidemic disease and dispersed by the *Wappinger* sometime before 1628.

A number of "aboriginal proprietors" later identified as Hackensack *sachems,* or leaders, participated in a series of land sales to the authorities of the Dutch colony of New Netherland in 1630. Among the native signatories were a number of "Virginians." The terms Virginian and "Southern Indian" referred to native people from groups that inhabited lands to the south of the Delaware River, the southern boundary of New Netherland. The presence of Virginians, along with the dispersion of the earlier Native population of the Hackensack valley clearly point out the enormous changes that wre occurring among the Native groups during the opening years of European intrusion into the region. These data also indicate that the group later known as the Hackensack was made up of a number of different peoples from several regions.

The 1630 land sales conveyed the Bayonne Peninsula and Staten Island to the Dutch. The Dutch soon established trading posts and plantations on these lands, which were located close to the centers of Hackensack settlement. The major Hackensack communities of the period were *Ahasimus*, on the Bayonne Peninsula, *Hespatingh*, in the city of the same name, and the *Hackensack Castle*, situated in the highlands to the northwest of Hackensack.

The Dutch settlements became a source of friction between the Hackensack and the Dutch soon after their establishment during the early 1630s. Sharp trade deals, defective trade goods, and liquor defrauded many of the Native people who frequented the Dutch traders. The fatal shooting of a Dutchman by a "Hackingsack" man at Pavonia, now Jersey City, in 1642 marked the first time the Hackensack were mentioned by name in the Dutch records. This and other incidents led the Dutch to meditate retaliation against the lower Hudson River Native groups. The Dutch got their opportunity when a large *Mahican* war party attacked the *Wiechquaeskeck* of the east bank of the lower Hudson River during February, 1643. The Wiechquaeskeck claimed and received refuge from the Mahican under the walls of Fort Amsterdam in lower Manhattan and at Pavonia across the river in Hackensack territory. Both camps were subsequently simultaneously subjected to Dutch surprise attacks during the night of February 25-26, 1643. The lower Hudson River groups were outraged by this massacre. Many Hackensack reportedly perished along with some 120 Wiechquaeskeck people at Pavonia. The lower Hudson River groups immediately burned the outlying Dutch settlements throughout the region and drove their inhabitants to the shelter of Fort Amsterdam.

The conflict was ruinous for both sides, dependent as they were upon each other. New Netherland was a trading colony, and the Native people of the area provided the furs that were the raw material of the commerce. The Dutch on their part supplied the metal tools, cloth, muskets, and other trade goods that had become an indispensible part of aboriginal life. The Hackensack sachem *Oratam* accordingly agitated for peace, and succeeded in arranging a truce with the Dutch on April 22, 1643 on behalf of "the savages living at Ackinkes hacky...and...Tappaen, Rechgawawanc, Kichtawanc, and Sinsinck." Oratam continued to play a major role in negotiations between the remaining Native belligerents and the Dutch. Two years later, on August 30, 1645, Oratam signed the general peace treaty that ended the conflict, known thereafter as "The Governor Kieft War," after the Director of the Colony of New Netherland. The Wiechquaeskeck and their allies did not participate in this treaty. Finally, following pressure from the powerful *Susquehannock* group and under Hackensack sponsor, the last remaining hostile groups pledged to keep the peace with the Dutch on July 19, 1649.

The Hackensack were again split into pro- and anti-war factions during the brief "Peach War" of 1655-1656. A report dated November 10, 1655 noted that the Hackensack and Tappan groups did the most damage to the Dutch. Oratam's speaker *Pennekeck* served as a key intermediary between the warring groups, and assisted in ransoming a large number of white captives during the conflict.

These wars resulted in extensive changes in native life. Large numbers of native people living near the center of Dutch settlement immigrated to more hospitable regions. The Hackensack accepted a substantial number of Western Long Island, Staten Island, and Wiechquaeskeck immigrants. The nature of Hackensack settlement also changed at this time. The natives of the region found that their large fortified towns were easy targets for Dutch armies. Population losses caused by the wars and epidemics made such large settlements even more vulnerable. The Hackensack and their neighbors accordingly chose to settle in small hamlets scattered throughout their territories. These were more difficult to surprise, easier to escape from, and gave the impression of a sizable native presence on their territories.

Oratam and the Hackensack served as intermediaries between the hostile Esopus groups of the mid-Hudson valley and the Dutch during the "Esopus Wars" of 1659-1664. Favoring the Esopus pro-peace faction, Oratam secured asylum for their sachems, ransomed white captives, and gave the Dutch intelligence of Esopus activities. Other Hackensack sided

with the hostile Esopus, and supported their operations. Dutch military successes and Hackensack diplomacy brought the contending parties to the conference table, and a treaty was signed by the Esopus and the Dutch on May 15, 1664.

The Hackensack swiftly allied themselves with the English following the capture of New Netherland by the forces of the Duke of York on September 6, 1664. The English quickly embarked on a series of land purchases that increasingly crowded the Hackensack out of their traditional territories along the lower reaches of the Hackensack and Passaic rivers. Relations with the English remained peaceable, however, and the Hackensack submitted to English jurisdiction. The Hackensack responded to English territorial demands by selling small parcels and demanding the right to remain in their small settlements. Relentless English pressure gradually drove them northward to the headwaters of the northeastern New Jersey river drainages by the turn of the eighteenth century. The records indicate that the Hackensack increasingly became involved with the Tappan, their northern neighbors. Sachems like *Mindawassa* and *Jan Claes* came to represent both groups, and the Hackensack and Tappan were effectively merged by 1700.

The Hackensack and Tappan were last mentioned by name on April 19, 1693. The people that made up these groups did not, however, disappear along with their name. They remained in small communities scattered throughout the upland portions of the Passaic watershed during the first half of the eighteenth century. Their leaders, *Memshe, Memerescum, Taphow*, and others often signed documents as sachems "of all the nations on Romopuck, Sadle, Pasqueek, Narashunk, Hackinsack rivers and Tapaan."

The Northern New Jersey Indians became increasingly connected with their *Minisink* neighbors to the west along the upper Delaware River Valley. Most of them either joined the Minisink or moved further south to the settlements at the "Forks of the Delaware" at Easton, Pennsylvania. Both groups finally sided against the English during their last war with the French over control of North America, known as the Seven Years, or French and Indian War (1755-1762). Not all of the native people of the region chose to oppose English dominion, however, and most of the remaining groups still in New Jersey signed a treaty with the English at Crosswicks on January 8-9, 1756. A number of otherwise unidentified "Indians in the County of Bergen," the heart of traditional Hackensack territory, claimed English protection under the provisions of the Crosswicks treaty on March 16, 1756. They and other natives living north of the Raritan River were confined to an area between the Hudson River and the western limits of the Passaic and Raritan valleys for the duration of the conflict. The "Bergen County Indians" and their neighbors were unable to wait the conflict out, however.

On October 23, 1758 the Minisink sold their last

claims to land in northern New Jersey from the Raritan River north to the N.Y.-N.J. line. They and their allies then moved into the western Susquehanna and Allegheny River valleys of Pennsylvania. by June 15, 1759 it was reported that "the Indians in the northern parts of the Province (of New Jersey) have entirely quitted it & are going to Sesquehannah." The descendents of the Hackensack were among those westward immigrants, and today reside in the surviving *Munsee* communities in Wisconsin, Oklahoma, and Ontario.

ROBERT STEVEN GRUMET

HAGBERG, A. E. "BUD" (Inuit; 20th century), is an airline executive who has been active in civic affairs in his home state of Alaska. He worked his way up from an after-school job to become, in 1969, a vice president of Wien Consolidated Airlines. He was president of the Alaska Chamber of Commerce, chairman of the 1967 Alaska Centennial, and co-founder of the annual World Eskimo Olympic Games held at Fairbanks, Alaska.

HAIDA. The dense forests, sparse in game, in the interior of the Queen Charlotte islands, and the deeply indented coast-line frequented by shoals of salmon and halibut, by sea-otters, sea-lions, and fur seals, made the Haida ("People") almost wholly dependent on the sea for their livelihood. Their villages lay on the coast near halibut banks, and the forested hills behind them were little valued except so far as they provided timber for houses and canoes. Of land animals the Haida killed only a few black bears that came out to the coast to feed on berries and on the dead salmon along the edges of the streams. Yet they were mighty hunters on the sea, and captured more fur seals and sea-otters than any other tribe along the Pacific Coast. Every nobleman kept a stock of the skins of these sea mammals to distribute at potlatches and to trade with the Tsimshian, so that when the fur traders of the late eighteenth century began to frequent the northwest coast it was from the Haida that they gathered their richest harvest.

The isolation of their home and their dependence on the sea made the Haida great voyagers, and, as is commonly the case with maritime peoples, keen imitators of the tribes with which they came into contact. In their dug-out canoes they raided the mainland as far as Sitka in the north, and to the lower end of Vancouver island in the south. Naturally they encountered most-frequently the Tlingit and the Tsimshian, and it was from these tribes that they borrowed most extensively. They copied with indifferent success the basketry of the Tlingit, and derived from the same source most of their shamanistic paraphernalia and songs. Their phratries bore the same names as the Tlingit phratries, Raven and Eagle, and were similarly divided into a number of clans, with subdivisions into family groups or "houses" each governed by its own chief. From the Tsimshian, with whom they traded canoes and sea-

HORN SPOONS' HAIDA

CARVED SLATE DISH, HAIDA

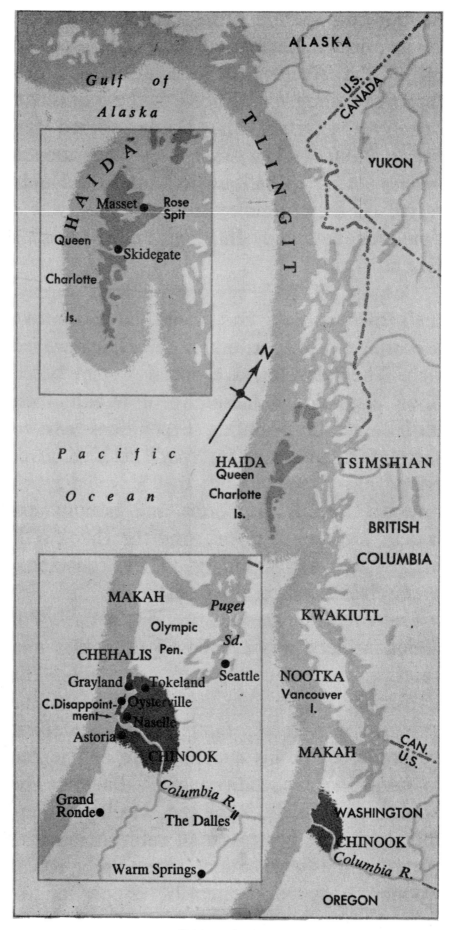

Haida territory.

otter skins for Chilkat blankets and the oil of the oolakan or candle-fish, they derived the majority of their dance songs, and the beginnings of a secret society that the tsimshian had themselves taken over from the Kwakiutl.

The shamans or medicine-men of the Haida and other west coast Indian tribes, like medicine-men elsewhere in Canada, claimed to have received special powers from the supernatural world in answer to prayer and fasting; but the passion of the west coast people for ritualism made them elaborate the fasting process, and distinguish their medicine-men by certain peculiarities in appearance or dress. Diseases were treated in much the same way as elsewhere, e.g., by massage, sucking over the afflicted part through a tube, application of herbs, etc., all to the accompaniment of much drumming, shaking of rattles, and the singing of medicine-songs. Peculiar to the medicine-

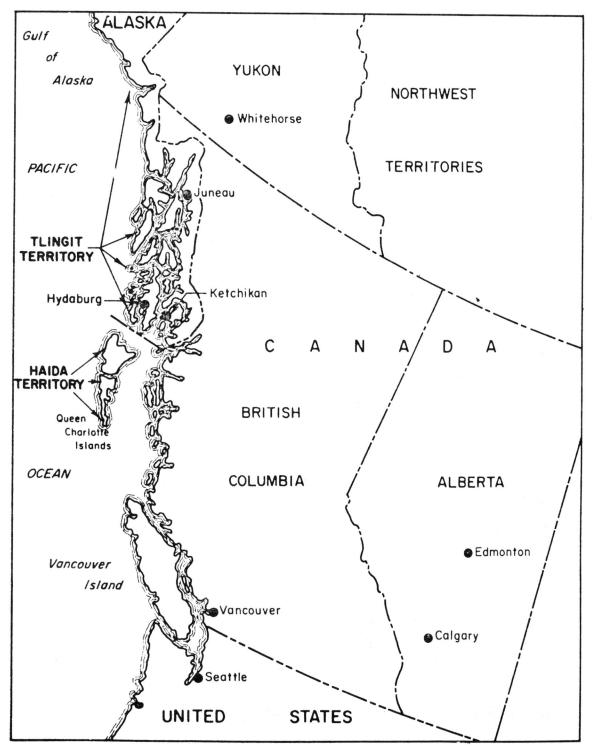

Tlingit and Haida Territory.

men of the Haida, Tlingit, and Tsimshian was the use of a special "soul-catcher" a bone tube, generally carved, for capturing the wandering souls of the sick and restoring them to their bodies. Since the souls of even healthy people often wander, especially when the body sleeps, every Haida war-party carried at least one medicine-man to capture and destroy the souls of enemies, whose bodies would then be slain in the approaching battle. Dread of the medicine-man af-

flicted the Haida Indians even after his death, impelling them to deposit his body in a special grave-house overlooking the water which none but other medicine-men had the courage to visit.

The secret society of the West Coast Indians probably originated among the Kwakiutl. Its members were men and women who underwent prolonged and usually arduous initiation rites in order to gain the favour and patronage of certain supernatural guar-

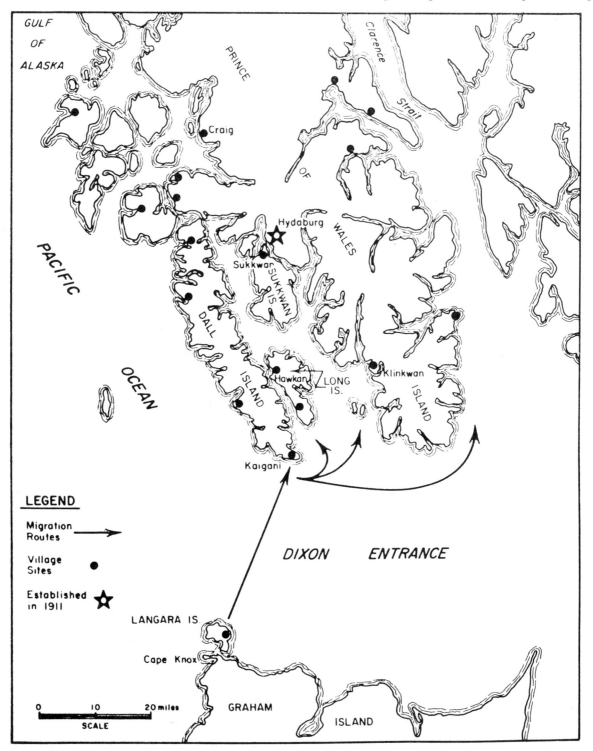

Early Haida migration into Tlingit territory.

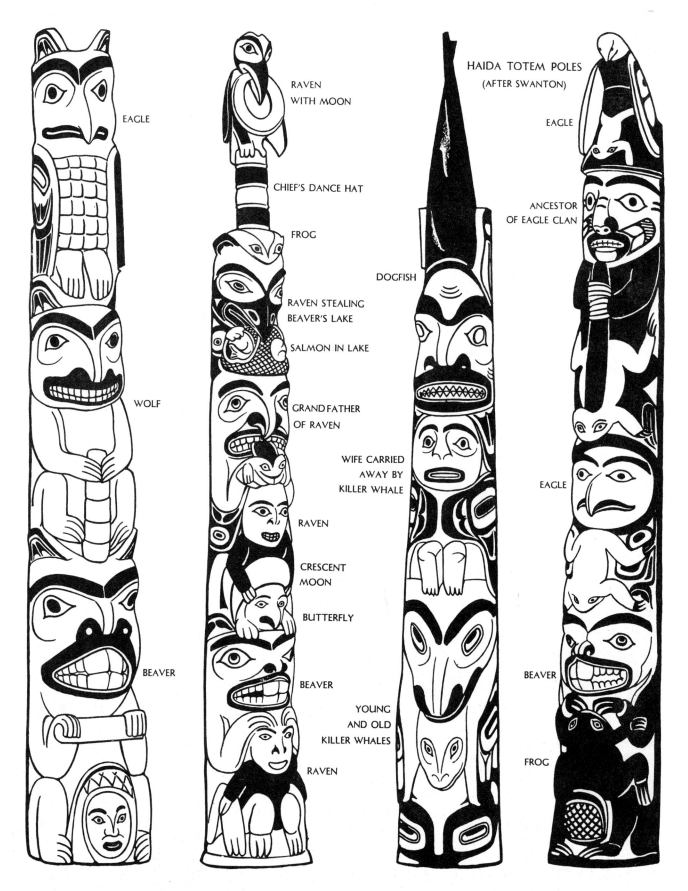

Haida totem post.

Haida Totem Pole.

dians. Those who had the same supernatural guardian sometimes formed a fraternity that acted as a separate unit within the society and held its own public ceremonies and dances. Among the Kwakiutl there were a number of these fraternities, and the society was so powerful that when it conducted its ceremonies during the winter months it suspended the normal organization of the communities and practically controlled the lives of the people. The chiefs of the Haida, however, would not tolerate such usurpation of their authority and prestige. When they borrowed (or bought) the institution from the Tsimshian they retained all rights to initiation in their own hands, restricted membership to near kinsmen, permitted the dances only at potlatches, and prevented any union of initiates into groups that might usurp the control of the villages. Strictly speaking, therefore, there was no secret society among the Haida, only an unorganized body of initiates who vaguely imitated the dramatic ceremonies of the secret society to the east and south in order to glorify their "houses" and clans.

The dependence of the Haida on the sea reflected

Killer whale, Haida.

Wasco and mythic raven, Haida.

Haida gambling stick.

Haida Wooden figure.

itself in their religion. They believed, like other Indians, that supernatural beings surrounded them on every side; and the more philosophic among them postulated a being on high, a "Power of the Shining Heavens," as the ultimate source of the power that resides in both the supernatural world and the world of the senses. Yet it was to the "Ocean-Beings" that they offered most of their prayers and sacrifices, because they considered that these beings could embody themselves in fish and sea mammals and, in consequence, affect the main food supply of the people. So the Haida offerd them grease, tobacco, and the feathers of the flicker, either by burning these ofjects in the fire (which released their souls), or by throwing them into the water.

The ceremonial life of the Haida closely paralleled that of the Tlingit; in both there was a succession of feasts and potlatches to mark every event from childhood to the grave. The Haida, however, were more addicted to tattooing than any of the other West Coast tribes, and as the process was very painful, they performed it in three stages, each of which required the assumption of a new name and the holding of a potlatch. Cremation, common among the northern Tlinkit, was comparatively rare among the Haida, who sometimes deposited their dead in caves, but more frequently laid them in the coffin on the top of a carved post or in a niche in its side. Occasionally the body of a prominent chief lay in state within his house for a whole year before removal to its final resting place.

Contact with Europeans wrought a speedy change in the lives of these islanders. Potatoes, introduced by the early voyagers, took the place of the vanished sea-otter skins in purchasing oolakan oil from the Tsimshian. Steel tools gave a tremendous impetus to sculpture, for the Haida, though inferior to the Tlingit in basket-making, far surpassed them and all the other west coast tribes in painting and wood-carving. Enormous totem poles that only the highest chiefs could afford in the days of stone adzes now stood before every house, and Haida carvers found their services in demand up and down the coast of the mainland. A few turned their talents to metal-work, and from the large United States dollar wrought silver bracelets and brooches beautifully engraved with the highly conventionalized bird and animal designs so typical of west coast art. Potlatches became more frequent when money could purchase the Hudson's Bay blankets that replaced skins as the currency, and whole villages flocked to Victoria to gain quick wealth by lending their women to white men. But smallpox at the end of the eighteenth century, and both smallpox and venereal diseases in the nineteenth, took their toll of the population, which rapidly dwindled from perhaps 8,400 in 1800 to less than 1,000 (including the Haida on Prince of Wales island) a century later. Today there are but two inhabited villages on the Queen Charlotte islands, Skidegate and Massett, and their combined population numbers barely 1,000.

HAIGLAR (Catawba; ?– Aug. 30, 1763?) was a principal Catawba chief in South Carolina during the mid-1700s. He was a staunch friend of the English colonists, who called him King Haiglar, and helped protect them during the French and Indian War.

Haiglar lived on the Catawba lands near where Lake Catawba touches the North Carolina border. He probably became chief in 1748. During his chieftainship, the Catawba were engaged in intermittent warfare with the Iroquois, the Shawnee, and the Delaware. In acquiescence to the wishes of Gov. James Glen of South Carolina, Haiglar tried negotiating with his enemies instead of fighting them. He signed a treaty with the Iroquois in 1751 at Albany. But the peace was not dependable, and in December 1754 Governor Glen sent the Catawba arms and ammunition to fight off an Iroquois war party. He signed a later treaty with the Iroquois in 1761 at Charles Town (Charleston), S. Carolina.

A life-long friend of the English, Haiglar was well-known to the colonial governments in both the Carolinas and Virginia. His warriors scouted for George Washington against the French in 1756. He helped Col. James Grant significantly in his defeat of the Cherokee at the Battle of Etochoe in 1759. Although occasional friction did develop between the English and the Catawba, Haiglar always tried to settle it in council. His one continuing problem with the colonists was their sale of liquor to the Indians. This, he felt, would in the end hurt relations between them, and he wrote Chief Justice Henley of North Carolina on May 26, 1756, asking that it be stopped.

In 1759 nearly half of the Catawba tribe was destroyed by an attack of smallpox, and after that they ceased to play a prominent part in history. Haiglar was killed when a Shawnee war party ambushed him on his return from a Waxhaw settlement near his home, probably on August 30, 1763.

HAIR AND HAIRWORK made from animal, and occasionally human hair were widely used as textile material. Animals which provided hair were the horse, deer, moose, buffalo, mountain goat, sheep, dog, rabbit, beaver, and others.

Hair was used as decoration in many areas. Indians of the Eastern Woodlands embroidered moose hair onto a deerskin, cloth, or birchbark base which they made into garments, pouches, and moccasins. They frequently dyed the deerskin black to contrast with the soft colors of the vegetable dyed moose hair. Midwest Indians wove spun buffalo hair into pouches which were used to store medicine bundles or were presented as gifts. By the middle of the 19th century they used commercial yarn instead of buffalo hair. Fringe made of dyed deer hair decorated these bags. Plains Indians decorated hides of deer, elk, or buffalo, which were sometimes painted, with dyed horsehair or porcupine quills. In the Southwest, horsehair was used on Kachina masks and dolls by the Hopi and Zuni Indians. In the 20th century Papagos have made miniature baskets of horsehair. Among the Northwest Coast tribes the Tlingit wove goat hair into abstract animal designs on a cedar bark base to make clothing such as shirts and shoulder blankets, which were worn by the wealthy.

Hair was used not only for decoration but also for utilitarian purposes. It was sometimes braided into cord and used as rope. Horsehair has been used as stuffing for items such as pillows, dolls, and drumsticks. Some Plains Indians used cowskin pads stuffed with animal hair instead of saddles. Hair was sometimes combined with other fibers in weaving textiles and baskets.

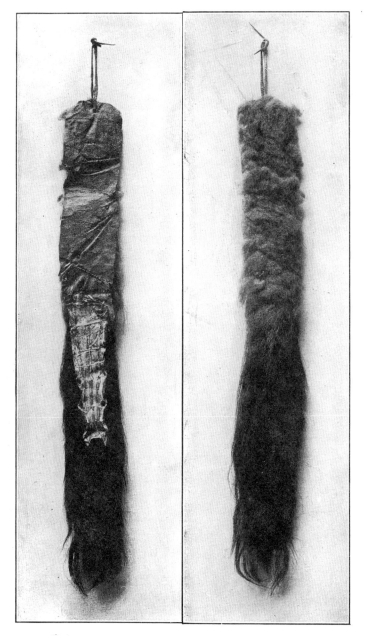

Hair ornament of Buffalo hide worn in sundance.

BRAIDS

Utes, Hualpai Taos

LOW KNOT
Pima

HAIR KNOT
Havasupai, Papago

BRAID-DOUBLE CHONGO
Pueblos

BRAIDS
Plains Indians
(note scalp lock)
(Notice Scalp Lock)

LOOSE HAIR
(WITH BANGS)
Cocopah, Havasupai, others

LOOSE HAIR
(WITHOUT BANGS)
Yuma, Maricopa Mohave

Three hair styles.

CHONGO

PUEBLO

NAVAJO

HOPI
maiden

Hair cord

BRAIDS
Utes, Apaches, others

BRAIDS
San Lorenzo, Taos

LOOSE HAIR
(WITHOUT BANGS)
Apache, Papazo, others

BASKETMAKER

PUEBLO II or III

PUEBLO II OR III

BASKETMAKER

BASKETMAKER

BRAIDS
Tesuque, San Ildefons
Jicarilla Apaches

Pre-columbian Indian hair-dos.

Manner of wearing the hair.

Fragment of plain-twined pliable bag with pattern of human hair.

Hair ornament worn by elk dreamer.

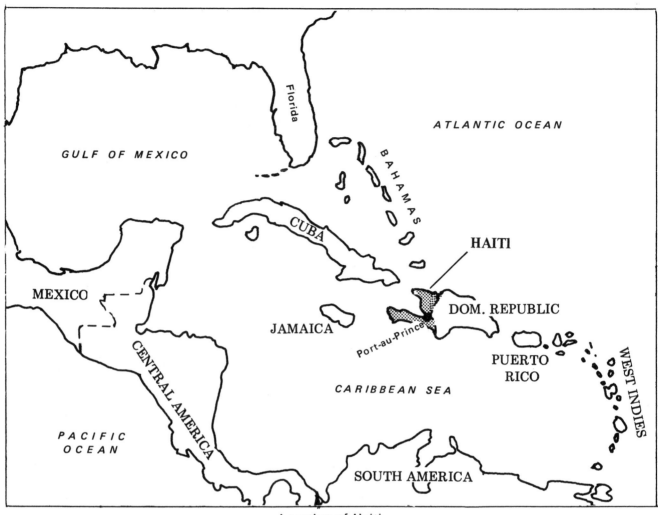

Location of Haiti.

HAITI was discovered by Christopher Columbus in 1492 when, in the course of his first voyage in search of a route to Asia, he landed on the northern shore of the island, which he named La Isla Espanola, later known as Hispaniola. This island became the first permanent European colony in the Americas (Santo Domingo). The western part of the colony of Santo Domingo was to become a French colony (Saint-Domingue), which in 1804 became the Republic of Haiti, while the eastern part eventually became the Dominican Republic.

It was in Hispaniola that Columbus conceived a colonial policy for Spain that left a lasting imprint on the life in the New World. Finding friendly Taino Indians who wore golden ornaments, Columbus predicted that Europeans would gain "profitable things without number," and he speculated on the great opportunity for spreading Christianity that would result from his discovery.

After founding the town and fortress of Navidad on the northern coast, Columbus returned to Spain, leaving about forty men with instructions to avoid trouble with the Indians, to seek gold, and to explore the island. After an enthusiastic reception in Spain,

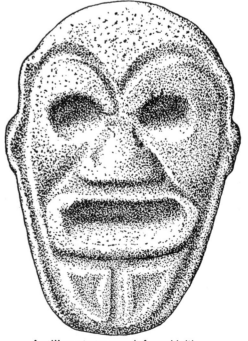

Antilles stone mask from Haiti.

Columbus sailed with seventeen ships: 1,500 settlers; soldiers and missionaries; and supplies of agricultural implements, cattle, and seeds. He found Navidad deserted. The settlers, who had treated the Indians ruthlessly, had been killed.

Columbus then founded Isabela on the northern coast of what is now the Dominican Republic. The settlers suffered from disease and fought off attacks by Indians, thousands of whom were killed. In an effort to build a handsome city, Columbus ordered his followers to perform manual labor—a command deeply resented by men who considered themselves gentlemen. These malcontents plotted against Columbus and denounced him to the authorities in Spain. The Spaniards' cruel treatment of the Indians generated revolts that were mercilessly crushed, and many Indians fled to the mountains.

Isabela, where Columbus' brother Bartolome was serving as Columbus' deputy, was in a virtual state of anarchy, and the prospects for the colony were gloomy. In June 1496 Columbus, intent on defending himself against his detractors, returned to Spain, where he waited two years before obtaining ships for a third voyage.

When Columbus arrived at the town of Santo Domingo, a new settlement founded by his brother, many Spaniards in the northern part of the island were openly revolting against Bartolome. In an effort to mollify the rebellious colonists, Columbus established a system of exploitation that was to become a basis for social institutions throughout the Spanish colonies in America. This was the sceme of *repartimientos,* under which a settler was granted a large tract of land, along with the Indians who lived on it, to exploit as he pleased. In order to rid themselves of a gold tribute that the Spaniards had been demanding, the Indian chieftains turned their subjects over to the colonists.

News of dissension among the colonists, however, had prompted the Spanish king and queen, Ferdinand and Isabella, to name Francisco Bobadillo chief justice to investigate conditions in the colony. On his arrival at Santo Domingo in August 1500 he found a number of colonists, who had revolted against Columbus, swinging from the gallows and several others about to be hanged. Bobadillo ordered the arrest of Columbus and his brother Bartolome and sent them to Spain in chains.

Columbus was released six weeks after his arrival in Spain and was received by Ferdinand and Isabella; but, without consulting Columbus, the monarchs sent Nicholas de Ovando to Hispaniola as governor. Ovando imported the first blacks into Hispaniola, fought Indians who had managed to maintain their independence, and built up the city of Santo Domingo. Columbus, however, persuaded Ferdinand and Isabella to furnish ships for a fourth voyage, in the course of which he coasted the shores of Central America, was wrecked on the island of Jamaica, and was rescued by Ovando. The man who, in the words of Hubert Herring,

had made the Caribbean Sea "a Spanish lake" returned to Spain and died in 1506.

The *repartimiento* system failed to improve the lot of the Indians, and in 1503 the Spanish crown instituted the *encomienda* system, under which all the land theoretically became the property of the crown, but the colonist to whom land was granted was entitled to certain days of labor from his Indian tenants. He was obliged to look after their physical well-being, to instruct them in Christianity, and to pay a tribute to the crown. Although the *encomienda* did not involve actual possession of the land, grantees were able in one way or another to become owners of the tracts assigned to them and to reduce the Indians to a state of virtual slavery.

Although it was to persist for many years in the Spanish colonies on the mainland and was not outlawed until the end of the eighteenth century, the *encomienda* system in Hispaniola did not last long. By the middle of the sixteenth century the Taino population, estimated at about 1 million in 1492, had been reduced to about 500. The need for a new labor force led to the importation of increasing numbers of Negro slaves, principally for the cultivation of sugarcane, and by 1520 Negro labor was used almost exclusively in Hispaniola.

Throughout the island each landowner exercised virtually complete authority over his estate, and there was little contact between the Hinterland and Santo Domingo, the capital city. Santo Domingo was principally concerned with its relations with Spain, which furnished supplies, administrators, and settlers for the colonies, and with the continent, which provided treasure for the crown. It was a way station for traffic between Sapin and continental America, and a jumping-off point from which the Spaniards explored the New World.

In 1509 Columbus' son, Diego, was appointed governor of the colony. With a view to curbing the power of the governor, the crown in 1511 established a new political institution called the *audiencias,* in many parts of the Spanish Empire, which became the continuing core of royal authority; but the failure of some to carry out administrative and disciplinary duties assigned to them led to the appointment of viceroys, who personified the power and the prestige of the king. In 1535 Hispaniola became part of the Viceroyalty of New Spain, which included Central America and much of North America.

After the conquest of Mexico by Hernan Cortes in 1521 and the discovery in Mexico and Peru of great wealth in gold and silver, the prestige of Santo Domingo began to decline. Alluvial deposits of gold were depleted, and the Indian labor force was dying off. Large numbers of colonists left for Mexico and Peru, and the population of Hispaniola declined sharply. Agriculture was neglected, and Spain became pre-occupied with the larger and richer colonies on the mainland. According to the Haitian historian, J. C. Dorsainvil, the population of the colony in 1545 amounted to no more than 1,100 persons.

HALCHIDHOMA (Halchadhoma) of southern California at one time an important tribe, suffered in the course of their history, and at last completely lost their identity among the Maricopa, although there are probably survivors today with that tribe.

The Halchidhoma lived along the river at Parker, about halfway between the Mohave and Yuma territories. This was subsequent to 1776, when the missionary Garces found the Halchidhoma. Evidently they found living too uncomfortable in the turmoil of tribes below the confluence of the Gila in California. (Mohave indicate they lived at Aramsi on the east side of the stream below the Yuma and were troubled by the latter. They, too, followed the Halchidhoma to the fertile but unoccupied bottom lands farther up).

HALF KING (Huron; fl. latter half of the 18th century) was a Wyandot chief in the area of Sandusky, Ohio, who joined the British during the War of Independence to fight against American encroachment on Indian territory west of the Allegheny Mountains. During the Revolution he commanded Ottawa, Chippewa, Shawnee, and other tribes of warriors in addition to his Huron followers. He won particular recognition for the firm discipline he exercised over this unusual composite force. To assure the good behavior of his warriors, Half King took special pains to prevent their access to alcohol. The result was that Half King's Indian army behaved well in combat and avoided the temptation to spill white blood indiscriminately.

The primary beneficiaries of Half King's efforts were the Moravians of Lichtenau, an evangelical Protestant sect that settled in Ohio. At times during 1777 as many as 200 warriors camped immediately outside of Lichtenau, and—since it was largely antisettler sentiment that motivated many of the Indians to fight on the British side—the Moravians could have been massacred easily. Half King kept the mixed assemblage of warriors from making the Moravians the victims of their wrath.

Nevertheless, Half King did insist upon the removal of Christianized Indians from the Sandusky area. This was done not so much out of hostility to Christianity as from concern that such Indians were not safe among their unconverted brethren. He continued to protect the Moravians and their converts after the Revolution, even when the Protestants abandoned his domain and went to Detroit.

On March 6, 1782, two Indian families were wantonly killed by a settlers' militia. The northern Ohio area tribes, even those supporting the colonies, arose to seek revenge. On June 4, about two miles from his village, Half King met the militia under Col. William Crawford. With the aid of Butler's Rangers (British reinforcements), and warriors sent from the Delaware and Shawnee tribes, Half King overwhelmed the colonial militia and caught

and executed Crawford. After the Revolution, Half King signed the Treaty of Fort McIntosh (January 2, 1785).

HALF KING (Oneida; c. 1700– Oct. 4, 1754) was an important chief in the area of Logstown, Pennsylvania, who was a trusted ally of both Gov. Robert Dinwiddie of Virginia and George Washington.

Half King seems to have come into notice about 1748, at which time he lived in or near Logstown, an important trading rendezvous on the right bank of the Ohio River about 18 miles below present Pittsburgh. At Logstown most of the official visitors to the Indians of the Ohio region sought out Half King for information, advice, and assistance. He was a prominent figure on the Indian side in the treaty with the Virginia commissioners in 1752. For this and for various services he was decorated by Governor Dinwiddie and was given the honorary name "Dinwiddie," which, it is said, he adopted with pride.

In late 1753 Half King accompanied Washington on his journey to warn the French to stop their encroachments on the Ohio Valley lands claimed by the English. The following year he was again with Washington on an expedition against the French. Half King claimed that he killed Coulon de Jumonville, the French commander, during the skirmish at Great Meadows on May 28, 1754. Half King died later that year in the house of John Harris at the site of Harrisburg, Pennsylvania.

HAMMER is an ancient and common tool fashioned with a wide variety of forms and purposes by the North American aborigines. Hammers ranged in size from small finger-held stones to large sledges. They were either hafted or unhafted, and the heads were made primarily of stone, but also of bone, ivory, shell, antler, and copper. Wooden mallets were probably used to some extent from ancient times but are difficult to detect archaeologically.

The most simple, common, and ancient hammers were unhafted stones having little or no shaping. They ranged from the size of walnuts to large rocks requiring two hands to lift. These hammerstones are often nearly indistinguishable from ordinary stones except for signs of wear, but some were fashioned in a thick discoidal shape with shallow depressions in each side for gripping. As well as being of general utility, hammerstones were commonly used for pecking and flaking in fashioning other stone implements.

Pounding tools with both a head and handle fashioned from a single piece of stone were widely distributed. They are of a wide range of craftsmanship and variety of forms, and their history is not well known. The majority are in the shape of large pestles consisting of a heavy base with a curved or flat bottom face, and of a thinner upper section, sometimes knobbed or ridged, for the handle. Many of these apparently served as pestles for grinding and mashing food; others served hammering functions such as driving stakes and quarrying and working stone. They were common on the Atlantic and Pacific coasts and the Prairies, but also have been found in many other areas.

The more familiar type of hammer, hafted with ivory, bone, or wood, was used widely and ranged in size from small tapping hammers to large sledges. Some forms were designed as clubs for use in warfare. Hafted stone hammers were used in many areas and usually consisted of a roughly ovoid head, sometimes with a flat face, lashed to a wooden handle. Most heads were grooved for hafting, and some were provided with a pit to fit the end of the handle. The maúl common on the Plains usually had rawhide wrapped around the handle or the entire hammer with only the faces exposed. It was used primarily for mashing food, breaking bones, and driving tent stakes.

Large sledge hammers were commonly used in rock quarries and copper mines. They were roughly fashioned, some had grooved heads, and the wooden handle was generally attached by a withe. On the northwest Coast sledges were commonly used for driving large stakes and wedges. These were generally more finely crafted, and the handles were sometimes ornamentally carved.

HAMMOCK, an Indian invention, has wide distribution, with concentration in the Orinoco-Amazon region of South America.

Hammock materials are chiefly leaf fibers, bast, and cotton. Inner barks are pulled off, split into small strands and dried (*Tule*); pinnate leaflets of the tucum palm are shredded with thumb and forefingers. Thigh spinning combines singles into double-ply cord (*Witoto, Tucano, Yagua*).. Palm fiber is commonly used for hammocks throughout the Guiana region, and balls of spun fiber are an important trade item in some districts (*Tucano*); caraguata fibers (*Bromelia*) are used by the *Lengua* ; maguey (*Agave americana*) by tribes in Central America. Smaller *Carib* hammocks are sometimes made of aeta palm wraps and cotton wefts; similar combinations are reported from the *Aueto, Mojo,* and some *Arawak*-speaking tribes on the upper Xingu. The idea of using cotton has spread among bast using tribes (*Guianas, Bacairi, Chane*) chiefly through the *Carib* and *Guarani.* Tribes that have not completely substituted cotton for bast still use both materials. Cotton hammock cord must be strong. Ordinarily, two or more spinnings are given to reduce the size and make the strand more uniform (*Tule*). The *Arecuna* grow, spin, and distribute spun cotton in a district where hammock making is very important. Twine is offered for sale or exchange in big balls of sufficient size to complete one hammock. The *Paressi* and *Mundurucu* also make fine cotton hammock twine. Among the *Central Arawak* there is much trade in hammocks with the whites; the makers vary the sizes,

textures, and qualities. Provisional hammocks were fashioned by Guiana Indians from bush rope and lianas; the *Apinaye, Eastern Timbira,* and *Sherente* make only this type by plaiting together tips of buriti palm leaflets. The hammock length includes that of the bed plus the length of suspension cords. Guiana Indians set their poles from 5 to 7 feet apart; bamboo supporting frames may be from over 6 to nearly 10 feet in size (lower Xingu); the ordinary *Paressi* hammocks are often more than 10 by 4 feet; the regulation length of hammocks on the Rio Negro reaches 15 feet.

Hammock techniques include the following:

(1) True weaving by interlacing warp and weft elements as in cloth making. *Tule* and *Cuna* weave on a frame of poles bound together with vines. Each *Tule* village has several of these, communally owned. There is no heddle arrangement: weft is put through with the fingers; the battening sword is the only tool. Thick clothlike hammocks are made among tribes in Venezuela and Columbia; in northwest Brazil they are woven on *Arawak* looms equipped with shed roll and heddle stick with pendent loops. The weaver has bobbins and a weaving sword. Although there is some doubt regarding the technique employed by lower Xingu tribes, their hammocks are clothlike in texture.

(2) In the Guiana region hammocks with twined "bars" are made on frames consisting of two upright poles sunk in the ground, on upright frames without or with head sticks like the ordinary *Arawak* loom, and on special contrivances for holding warps taut (*Cubeo*). Warping is done by different methods; women in some Guiana tribes walk around and around two poles carrying big balls of cotton string in their hands. Warps are spaced and slack is eliminated as work proceeds.

The warp skein in barred hammocks is crossed at regular intervals by two twining weft elements or by two pairs of countertwined weft elements. Wooden gages maintain uniform distances between the bars. The side of the *Paressi* hammock edges are broken by small tassels formed by knotting the ends of the weft elements.

Simple twining appears in hammocks from *Tupi* groups, from *Mojo, Chiriguano, Bacairi,* the Guapore River, etc.

(3) *Cayapa* hammocks are netted with coarse pita string. No mesh gage is used, since the meshes are from 4 to 6 inches on a side. The term netting may have been used more often to indicate appearance than technique. The *Warrau* make "purse net" hammocks on square wooden frames raised up from the ground; the hammock cord is a continuous length. Held in a long skein, it is stretched to make a warp element between the end-bars, then is returned to enclose it and the previously stretched warp in a wrapping coil. *Witoto* procedures corss strings "knotted" from one edge string to that on the opposite side. The hammock frame consists of two posts driven into the hut floor; the only tools are the women's fingers. Finely netted bases of palm string are characteristic of the feather-decorated hammocks of northwest Amazon tribes; *Tupi-Cawahib*

Loom for manufacture of thick hammocks. Columbia, 1906.

Hammocks of the whole family among the Waiwai Indians living along the headwaters of the Trombetas.

net small hammocks. Women on the upper Xingu in netting hammocks use a wooden needle. "Looped" bast-fiber hammocks are reported from the *Tule* and *Choco;* "coiled netting" for the *Guaymi.*

Guiana tribes use three shuttles to enclose each long hammock warp in a unit of three-strand braid; cross bars are spaced.

Men and women make hammocks. The latter frequently make the bed, and men add the heavier suspension cords, which are adjusted to make the hammock hang evenly. Men and women work on the same hammock in Guiana tribes; among the *Bora* it is woman's "light work."

Hammocks are colored in various ways: by painting while yet on the loom (Guianas), and by striping with colored string prepared before the fabrication is commenced. The *Aueto* alternate dark blue and white bands of cotton weft on tucum warp; the *Tucano* set up blue, yellow, and red stripes; the *Arekena* set up multicolored stripe patterns.

HAMPTON INSTITUTE. This private school is primarily significant in the growth of black education and culture in the United States, but for many years it also educated small groups of Indians. (Founded as the Hampton Normal and Industrial Institute in 1868 by Gen. Samuel C. Armstrong, a white whose interest in black education was stimulated while leading a black regiment during the Civil War, it became a model for the numerous black normal and industrial schools subsequently established. It also influenced Lt. Richard H. Pratt in his founding of Carlisle Indian School, Pa.)

In 1878 a group of about 17 young Indians who had been released as prisoners of war from Fort Marion, Fla., began to attend Hampton, the only school that had responded to Pratt's appeal for their further education under government auspices. That same year Pratt recruited 49 additional Indians in the West, including 9 girls. Indians attended the school until 1923, though the government discontinued appropriations in 1912. Hampton's distinguished alumnus Booker T. Washington returned to his alma mater in 1879-81 as secretary to Armstrong, and among his duties in 1880 took charge of the Indian dormitory.

Numerous buildings on the campus date from the 19th century. Pertinent to Indian education is the Wigwam, erected in 1878 to house the students from Fort Marion. A museum in the Administration Building is devoted to Indian cultural displays, contributed mainly by ex-students.

HAN are an Athapascan-speaking people who live in the region of the Canadian Yukon and are members of the Western Subarctic culture area. Their nearest neighbors are the Tutchone.

The word "Han" means "those who dwell along the river."

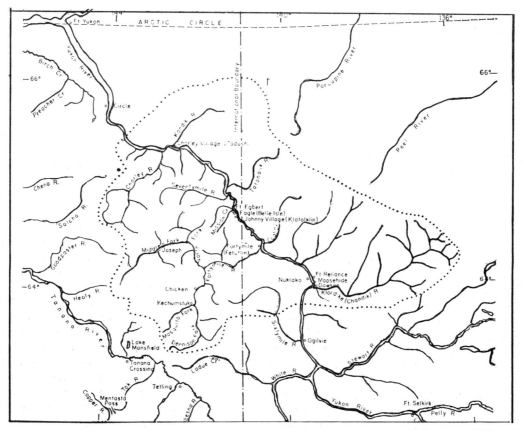

The Han territory.

HANDSOME LAKE (Seneca; *c*. 1735– Aug. 10, 1815) was a chief and a religious leader who developed an ethical code which became the basis of a new religion for the Iroquois people — known as the Handsome Lake religion or the Longhouse religion.

Handsome Lake, or Ganioda'yo, was born at Ganawaugus, New York, at the end of the era of power and prosperity for the Seneca nation. During his youth and early manhood, he watched his society and his culture disintegrate while he fought as a warrior against the British in Pontiac's Conspiracy, then against the Cherokee and Choctaw, and during the Revolution against the Americans. At the council with the British at Oswego, New York, in the early summer of 1777, Handsome Lake supported the position of his brother Cornplanter (*q.v.*) that the Iroquois should remain neutral in what was a civil war among white people, but the warriors voted to go to war and Handsome Lake fought with his people.

Handsome Lake took an active part in the drawn-out negotiations between the Iroquois and the Americans following the war. After several disasterous treaties, the Seneca sold all their lands, with the exception of a few reservations, at the Treaty of Big Tree in 1797.

After a period of prolonged whiskey drinking, Handsome Lake became seriously ill in 1799 and was near death. He recovered and declared that he had been visited by three spirits who revealed to him the will of the Creator. More visions followed, and from 1800 Handsome Lake became an itinerant preacher of the religion that he called Gaiwiio ("good message"). His message was predominated by three apocalyptic themes: the imminence of world destruction, the definition of sin, and the prescription for salvation (*i.e.*, following the practices he recommended). He condemned the drinking of whiskey and the practice of witchcraft and magic, and he urged his people to confess their sins and abandon their evil ways. His message was a combination of traditional Iroquois beliefs with Christian ethics. It provided the Iroquois with a faith that revitalized their civilization at a time when it was threatened with extinction.

In 1801 Handsome Lake accused Red Jacket (*q.v.*) of witchcraft. The confrontation was precipitated by an argument over land. Red Jacket favored the sale to the State of New York of a strip of land along the Niagara River, which was a favorite fishing place of the Seneca. Handsome Lake was a leader of the opposition, and his "slanders" against Red Jacket for a time cost him his status as a Seneca tribal speaker and prevented his elevation to the position of sachem.

Beginning in the fall of 1801 and increasingly in the years thereafter, Handsome Lake emphasized a social message—temperance in daily life, peace, land retention, domestic morality, and accultura-

tion. In the winter of 1801– 02, he led a delegation of Seneca to Washington and met with President Thomas Jefferson. Although his political power waned in his later years, Handsome Lake always remained a triumphantly successful evangelist. He died on a visit to Onondaga, New York, and was buried there in the center of the council house.

HANDSOME LAKE, RELIGION OF. *See* CHRISTIANITY.

HANGING MAW (Cherokee; ?– 1795) was a prominent chief of the Upper Cherokee in the late 18th century who was noted for his efforts to maintain peace with the whites. He was particularly friendly to William Blount, the U.S. governor of the "Territory South of the Ohio." In June 1793 a party of whites invaded Hanging Maw's town of Coyatee (meaning "sacred old place"; in present Loudon County, Tennessee), wounding the chief and killing his wife. Despite this incident, Hanging Maw continued to seek peace and led the Upper Cherokee in a series of cooperative endeavors with the whites during 1794 to punish various raiding parties of Creek and Cherokee.

HANNAHVILLE RESERVATION, in Menomenee County, Michigan, is 3,400 acres of Potawatomi Indian land. There are an estimated 200 Indian residents. All land is individually held by Indians in allotments. There is no tribally-owned land. The land was purchased by Congress, June 30, 1913, except for 39 acres later added in 1942 with the Indian Reorganization Act funds.

When the first Europeans arrived in the Upper Great Lakes area, they found the Potawatomi, a numerous and powerful tribe, living along the shore of Lake Michigan. Their Chief, Onanquisee, saved a band of LaSalle's men from starvation in 1680. When the Potawatomi ceded their lands in 1833 and agreed to move to the Iowa Territory, about 400 remained in Wisconsin. After the Black Hawk War in 1833, they lost the Nottawaseepe Reservation which amounted to over 73,000 acres. Several of their chiefs became famous. Chief Simon Pokagon became a lecturer of note in the 1850's. Chief Sawauguette, who sold his tribe's reservation in 1833 for $10,000, was poisoned by his people when he attempted to persuade them to leave for the rich hunting grounds promised in Kansas. For years the survivors led a poverty stricken existence. Their last properly-designated chief died in 1934.

The Potawatomi shared the culture patterns of the Ottawa and Chippewa. They lived in agricultural groups in the summer and traveled in hunting bands in the winter. The bands appear to have been politically independent, each ranging through its own territory. The society was organized according to clans which carried animal names. Clothing was of deerskin and fur. They have continued to be isolated due to lack of transportation routes and facilities and the poor resources of the reservation. Hunting and fishing rights do not exist compared to other Indian reservations.

The tribe was organized under the Indian Reorganization Act. A council composed of three council officers and nine council members govern the community. Elections for all members of the governing body are held annually.

HANO is the only pueblo inhabited today that exemplifies the shifts of the Native New Mexican population resulting from Spanish pressures. During the first part of the 17th century, the Tewa-speaking people of Hano lived in the Galisteo Basin south of Santa Fe. During the Pueblo Revolt of 1680-92, they moved to a new pueblo near Santa Cruz. In 1696, they rebelled again, burned their church, killed two padres, and abandoned their pueblo, Tsanwari, as they fled west, as had other Rio Grande groups during earlier periods of unrest.

To help protect Walpi from Ute inroads, the Hopi Indians at that pueblo invited the Tewas to settle to the north, at the head of the trail leading from First Mesa. As time passed, other Rio Grande groups that had taken refuge in Hopiland returned to New Mexico, but the people of Hano remained. They still retain their language and ceremonies, although their kivas and some other aspects of their culture have been influenced by contact with the Hopis. They are noted as producers of pottery. Their population is more than 300 today.

HARE Indians of Canada lived west and northwest of Great Bear Lake, extending in the east to a little beyond the Anderson River, and in the west to the first line of mountains west of the Mackenzie River. Although they hunted caribou in the vicinity of the Eskimo lakes, they did not descend the Mackenzie itself much below the Ramparts through fear of the Eskimo, and Yellowknife.

Their mode of life did not differ greatly from that of the Dogrib and Slave. Woodland caribou, moose, and beaver were scarce in their territory, but a few musk-oxen and many herds of barren-ground caribou roamed the tundra north of Great Bear Lake. The Hare hunted these caribou in April, and again in August and the early part of September; but they seem to have been less skilful in the chase than other Indians, and throughout the greater part of the year relied on fish, supplemented by hares during the winter months. In seasons when hares were scarce — every seventh year or thereabouts — they suffered great hardships, and generally some of them perished of starvation. It was, indeed, to their dependence on the hare that they owed their name. It furnished them not only food, but clothing, for though they preferred garments of caribou fur, not all families could secure enough hides,

especially families that clung to the banks of the Mackenzie River and rarely wandered east into the barren grounds.

The costume of the Hare resembled that of the Slave and Dogrib except for the extensive use of rabbit fur and the rarity of ornamentation. In summer they wore a shirt, leggings, and moccasins, possibly also a breech-cloth; in winter they added a robe, and in lieu of a cap, attached a hood to the shirt after the manner of the Kutchin and Eskimo.

Their implements and weapons were the stone-bladed adze, knives, daggers and ice-chisels of caribou antler, whittling knives with beaver-tooth blades, bows and arrows and babiche snares for hunting, nets of willow bark, and probably spears for fishing. The dwelling was the usual rectangular hut of poles and brush with a gabled roof and covering of spruce boughs; during the summer they often contented themselves with simple lean-tos. In the nineteenth century many families possessed tipis covered with caribou hides, later replaced by cloth; but tipis were probably rare in pre-European times. Like all other northern Athapaskans, they made fire with pyrites, cooked in water-tight baskets of interwoven spruce roots and willow, and served up their food in dishes of wood or bark.

Their social life also contained very little that was remarkable. The tribe comprised several independent, semi-leaderless bands, each controlling a definite territory; there were five in the middle of the nineteenth century, but these may not have corresponded exactly to the pre-European alinement. The hardships of life caused frequent desertion of the aged and the destruction of female infants. Male prisoners taken in raids were staked to the ground, and their quivering hearts given to the women to devour, a custom that savoured more of the Plains' tribes and the Iroquoians than of the Athapaskans. Alone of all the Canadian Indians, the Hare seem to have practised circumcision. Medicine-men permitted themselves to be suspended in the air to facilitate communion with their guardian spirits. There were two ceremonial feasts; a memorial feast to the dead a year after burial, and a lunar feast on the occasion of each new moon. The latter was celebrated by most Athapaskan tribes, but at eclipses only. The memorial feast, and indeed all the burial customs of the Hare, were identical with the Dogrib rites. Some Hare death chants greatly resemble the corresponding chants of the Tahltan.

The Hare have experienced all the epidemics that have ravaged the other tribes along the Mackenzie River. The Hare population today is several hundred.

HARPOON is a spear with one or two detachable heads to which a retrieving line is connected, used by many North American aborigines for hunting fish, aquatic mammals, and sea turtles. Its primary advantage was that once the point was embedded, the line

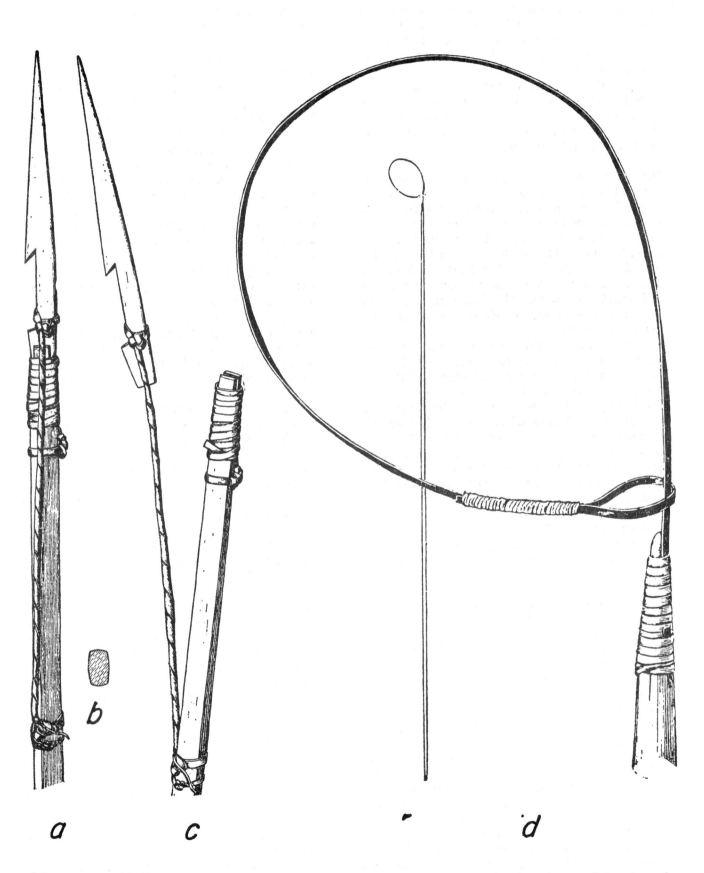

A, harpoon assembled for casting; B, cross section of harpoon shaft; C, position when dragging through water; D, two views of bird snare.

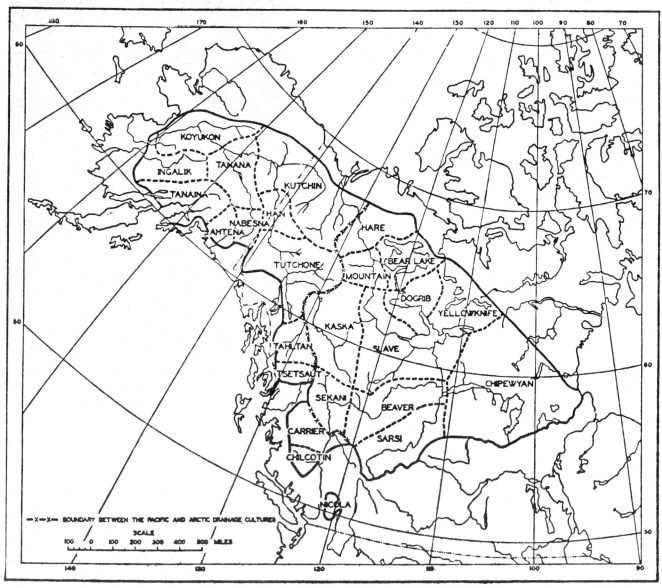

Distribution of the Northern Athapaskan Indians.

was much more effective than a spear shaft for holding, playing, and retrieving the prey, especially larger species. Harpoons were used throughout most of the Arctic, eastern and western Subarctic, Great Lakes region, Northwest Coast, southern California, and in parts of the Plateau, Great Basin, northeastern United States, and possibly on the east coast of Florida. They are still an important hunting weapon of the Eskimos.

Before iron and steel were readily available, harpoons were made of wood, bone, ivory, shell, stone, sinew, and hide. The detachable harpoon heads were of two general types: a barbed head with the line attached near its butt end, the barbs serving to hold it fast in the prey; a toggle-head, which was slightly elongated, with the line attached near its center to cause it to hold fast by turning sideways in the wound when the line tightened. Many harpoon head designs utilized characteristics of both types. The line was

commonly strung through holes or eyelets in the shaft or tied to it so that it would not be lost and would act as a drag to tire the prey.

Harpoons for hunting fish were commonly used in conjunction with fish traps and weirs. In hunting whales and other large sea animals, the Eskimos commonly tied mechanical drags and inflated bladder or seal skin floats to the line to tire the animal and keep it near the surface. When iron and steel became available to the Eskimos, these replaced the older materials used for fashioning the harpoon heads and foreshafts. Today the harpoon, with modern modifications such as the harpoon gun and explosive head, is still the basic weapon in whaling.

HARRINGTON, VIRGIL N. (Choctaw; 1919–   ), was a career official with the U.S. Bureau of Indian Affairs (BIA), serving as director of the Muskogee (Oklahoma) Area Office from 1963 until his retirement in the mid-1970s. He was born in Kiowa, Oklahoma, and received his B.A. in agriculture from Oklahoma A and M College in 1942. He served on the board of directors of the Five Civilized Tribes and has been active in child welfare programs.

HARRIS, CYRUS (Chickasaw; Aug. 22, 1817–*c.* 1886), was governor of the Chickasaw Nation 1856–64 and was a most respected leader of his people. Harris was born near Pontotoc, Mississippi, and lived with his mother until 1827, when he was sent off to a series of missionary schools. He left school in 1830 and—after spending some time near Memphis, Tennessee, where his mother had moved—he eventually returned to Pontotoc, where he became an interpreter for a land speculating firm. In the winter of 1837–38, Harris emigrated from his homeland to Indian Territory.

Soon after arriving in Indian Territory (present Oklahoma), Harris entered politics. He served as a delegate from the Chickasaw Nation to Washington, D.C., in 1850 and 1854. In 1856, after the Chickasaw constitution was adopted, he was elected governor of the nation, serving four two-year terms. Harris was defeated in a bid for re-election as governor in 1876. Then again in 1880, contrary to his wishes, his friends made him a candidate for the office. He was pronounced elected by the legislature, but a questionable recount of the votes gave the election to B. C. Burney, a friend of Harris. He died at his residence on Mill Creek in the Chickasaw Nation and was deeply mourned by his nation as an "uncorruptible" man who, "despite his progressive ideas, . . . was an Indian in the truest sense, a patriot and a leader of his people."

HARRIS, DAVID ADA (Catawba) born in 1872 was also known as *Toad* and lived on the Catawba Reservation, South Carolina.

HARRIS, IRVING A. (Schaghticoke; Dec. 9, 1931–), was elected chief of his tribe in September 1968 and has been instrumental in organizing and obtaining recognition at the state level for the four Connecticut Indian tribes. Born in Bridgeport, Connecticut, Harris was in 1973 elected chairman of the Connecticut Indian Affairs Council, which he helped create, and he has worked to obtain restitution of Indian lands.

HARRIS, LADONNA C. (Comanche; 1931–), who is the founder and executive director of Americans for Indian Opportunity (AIO), has been one of the most prominent Indian leaders in the United States in the 1960s and 1970s. Born in Oklahoma, she was raised by her grandparents because her parents separated soon after she was born. She married Fred Harris, who was later U.S. Senator from

Harris, Davidada

Harris, Ladonna

Oklahoma, chairman of the Democratic National Committee, and a candidate for the Democratic Party's nomination for President in 1976.

LaDonna Harris was active among the Indian peoples of her home state, especially in the protest movement against the U.S. policy of termination of Indian tribes and tribal lands. In June 1965 she was one of the organizers of a gathering of Oklahoma Indians called to discuss their common problems. Two months later she chaired a statewide meeting attended by more than 500 Indians. At this meeting, Oklahomans for Indian Opportunity (OIO) was formed and LaDonna Harris was elected president. That same year she was voted the Outstanding Indian of the Year in the United States.

In 1968 she resigned her position with OIO to become chairperson of the National Women's Advisory Council of the War on Poverty. Also in March 1968 she was named by President Lyndon B. Johnson to the National Council on Indian Opportunity. Because of a variety of political events, including the U.S. national elections of 1968, the council did little. Finally, on January 26, 1970, Vice President Spiro Agnew called the first meeting of the council at the angry insistence of Mrs. Harris.

In 1969 LaDonna Harris founded AIO and under her direction the organization, which is based in Washington, D.C., has worked at community, regional, national, and even international levels as a liason, advocate, catalyst, and information resource for Native Americans.

HASINAI. *See* CADDO.

HASKELL INDIAN JUNIOR COLLEGE. Established in 1884 as the Indian Training School, Haskell was one of the nonreservation Indian schools modeled after the Carlisle Indian School, Pa., and within a few years attained an importance second only to it. Of all the nonreservation schools set up in the late 19th century, when many reformers believed that Indian education should be provided at off-reservation boarding schools removed from the pervasive influence and restrictions of reservation life , Haskell is one of the few surviving today. Its history mirrors the changing governmental philosophy of education for Indians — which has ranged from vocational education and the inculcation of white values to preprofessional and precollegiate training and recognition of the richness of the Indian heritage. The major goal today is to aid students who return to their tribes to improve their own social and economic conditions, as well as that of their people and to aid all students to take their place in national life.

The institute opened in 1884 with only 22 pupils, but by the end of the second year enrollment numbered 220 from 31 tribes. In the early years the educational program stressed vocational training and elementary education, for many of the students had to be taught to speak, read, and write English. By 1906, however, when enrollment numbered 921 from 60 tribes, emphasis had begun to shift toward academic training. Although agriculture, handicrafts, and home economics continued to be taught, the curriculum came more and more to resemble that of standard elementary and junior high schools. Later the program was broadened to equal a standard high school course. In 1931 enrollment reached a peak of 1,240. In 1965 the school ended its academic program, created new curricula and facilities, and became the first Indian school offering vocational and technical training exclusively at the postsecondary level.

Administered by the U.S. Bureau of Indian Affairs, Haskell Institute today resembles a typical small American college. Most of the buildings are modern structures, but several recall the school's early years: Keokuk Hall (1884), a boys' dormitory; the hospital (1886), today housing school employees; Hiawatha Hall (1898), a girls' gymnasium; Winona Hall (1899), a girls' dormitory; and Tecumseh Hall (1915), a boys' gymnasium.

HASTINGS, WILLIAM W. (Cherokee; 1866–1938), served nine terms in the U.S. Congress as a Democratic representative from Oklahoma (1915–21 and 1923–35). He was educated in Cherokee tribal schools in Indian Territory (present Oklahoma) and graduated from the Cherokee Male Seminary in Tahlequah in 1884. He taught for a while in Cherokee schools and then received his degree in law from Vanderbilt University in 1889.

Hastings served as attorney general for the Cherokee Nation for four years and, after Oklahoma became a state in 1907, he was attorney for the tribe for another seven years. After taking his seat in Congress in 1915, he served for a total of 18 years, being defeated for reelection only once, in 1920. He retired from politics in 1935 and died three years later.

HATATHLI, NED (Navajo; 20th century), was president of the Navajo Community College in the 1970s. He was born and raised on the Navajo Reservation and later graduated from Northern Arizona University. He was instrumental in the founding of the Navajo Community College in 1969 on the reservation near Many Farms, Arizona. It was the first institution of higher learning to be operated by an Indian tribe. Hatathli succeeded Robert A. Roessel, Jr., a white man who had taught the Navajo for many years, as president.

HATCH, VIOLA (Cheyenne; 20th century), has served as a field worker for Oklahomans for Indian Opportunity (OIO), developing youth programs and organizing Indian leaders to solve local Indian problems. In addition, she has worked with Indians moving into the cities, acquainting them with health and job opportunities.

HAVASUPAI. Hidden in the depths of Arizona's Grand Canyon lies the Indian reservation of the Havasupai which means "Blue-Green Water People", a name suggestive of the clear waters of the Havausu Creek along which they live. Their homes and fields are hemmed in by sheer perpendicular walls of red sandstone, 2,000 feet below the desert forest. Since the descent into the canyon is only by foot or horseback— each a day's journey— or by helicopter— an 8-minute flight, the Havasupai are now and always have been well proteted from unwanted visitors.

The tribe is a particularly interesting one, since of all the Yuman tribes it is the only one which has developed or borrowed a culture similar to the Pueblo peoples. According to legend, the Havasupai once built and occupied villages of a permanent nature on the Colorado Chiquito east of the San Francisco Mountains. As a result of war with other Indian tribes, the village dwellers moved first into the San Francisco mountains and then to their present site, where they have lived for the past 800 or 900 years. The first recorded white person to visit the Havasupai was Coronado in 1692. Padre Francisco Garces, a Spanish missionary, contacted them in 1776; it was another century before other exploring expeditions entered their domain. In 1880, General O. B. Wilcox, commander of the Department of Arizona, secured the present reservation for the Havasupai. General Wilcox wanted to give them lands on the desert plateau where more space was available, but their chief, after much thought, refused. "White man will likely some day want the desert and take it from us; he is not ever likely to want this land in the canyon so we can keep it," reasoned the chief.

Frank Cushing lived with the Havasupai in the early 1880s and described them as well built, short in stature with broad shoulders, long arms and small hands that were hardened and short nailed from work. Their hair was long, abundant, and a beautiful raven. They did not have as keen eyesight as the Plains Indians. Partial or total blindness was common.

The Havasupai were skilled in the manufacture and use of impliments, excelling in the preparation of raw hide and weaving of baskets. As long as the buffalo roamed the Plains, they depended upon them and deer for their winter food, growing corn, sunflowers, melons, pumpkins, squash, peaches, apricots and figs for their summer food. After the buffalo disappeared, the Havasupai lived in destitute conditions for sometime. Floods have devastated the area on numerous occasions and the U.S. government has had to help. In the early 1930s the Indian Service constructed small cottages for them. At first the Indians, especially the older folks, refused to use the modern abodes, preferring their traditional mud and brush hogans. They used the cottages for storage. Younger members of the tribe adapted themselves more readily to the ways of white man, so today most of the Havasupai occupy the houses. Agriculture is still their main industry. Through the use of the helicopter, their present homes have modern conveniences, like electricity and refrigerators.

By tradition, the Havasupai have no descent or organization among them. Society is consanguineally patriarchal. As late as 1880, they were polygamists, limited only by the number of wives he could procure or by his means of supporting them. Marriages were constant; the only grounds for divorce was unfaithfulness. Betrothals by purchase or stipulation were common— a girl of 7 or 8 years being frequently promised to a man as old or older than her father. Consequently the women were monopolized, with or without their will, by the wealthier or more influential men of the tribe. Children belong to and inherit property through the father. Until recently all dead were cremated as in other Yuman tribes; today they bury in shallow graves in the rocks at the foot of the cliff.

The head chieftainship is hereditary. In the absence of a son, the chief's nephew on the father's side is chosen as successor. All subchiefs were named by the head chief according to his personal preference, wealth or influence. There was no distinct order among the warriors. In case of hostility, all able-bodied males fought for the very existence of the tribe. A war chief, because of his valor, had influence as the keeper of the war medicine. Civil and martial affairs were more closely allied than was the case of most Indian tribes.

In 1903, the Havasupai numbered about 250 but in 3 years disease reduced them to 166. Today, 1978, there are about 425 (325 living on the reservation) which may be the largest number they have ever been.

The head chief combines his political life with a kind of high priesthood. He not only presided at the councils, made treaties with other tribes and the United States and comdemned criminals but also prayed in the ancestoral manner for rain, good crops and a good hunt. He received pay for his offices and was usually as wealthy as any member of the tribe. However, he was not exempt from labor in the fields.

Aside from the head chief, other members of the ecclesiastical order were well-paid medicine men whose duties include the keeping of the songs, dances and old traditions. In the 19th century, they were were responsible for the healing of the sick. The medicinemen used no herbs but relied wholly on incantation, believing that power to heal came to them in childhood through dream-songs. Women in childbirth were attended by four women, not necessarily medicinewomen, although they used medicine songs. Today the ill receive the benefit of both the prayers and songs of the medicine-men and the services of white man's medical knowledge.

Both sexes work in the fields: the men plow and plant the field, the women help with the weeding and harvest. Today the Havasupai possess tractors that makes all work much easier. Inasmuch as they have little tillable land (about 3,000 acres in the entire reservation), and that must be irrigated, many of today's male population supplement the income by working

The canyon of Havasupais, is accessible only by foot or by horseback. This picture shows the area occupied by the old Agency; the stone buildings are government work. On the right is a Havasupai house, with flat roof and thatched walls. Honduras stone sculptures.

Winter dwellings of the Havasupai.

for the general United States public as guides or the United States government as foresters, lumbermen, road repairmen or park laborers. The women do the food preparation, care for the children and weave baskets for sale or trade.

The record shows the Havasupai being called by at least 50 different names, most of which are variations in spellings or various attempts to put into a known written language that which was spoken and unwritten in an entirely different language. Havasupai as spelled by Cushing in 1882 easily could have been Aqua Supais, Ah-Supai, Ăk-ba-sü-pai, A kuesú-pai, Ava-Suapies, Avěsú-pai, Supais, Supies, Supis, Suppai, Tonto Comino, Yabipais Jabesua, Yavai Suppai or Yuva-Suapi with only a slight variation in accent and a knowledge of English, Spanish or German as the writer's background. Coconinos (also Cushing's spelling) is his interpretation of the word the Hopi called the Havasupai. Variations of this word include Casinos, Casnino, Co-a-ni-nis, Cochineans, Cochnichnos, Coconinos, Cohoninos, Cojonina, Cominas, Cominos, Coninas, Conninos, Cosninas, Cosninos, Cuesninas, Cuismer, Cuisnurs, Culis nisna, Culisnurs, Kochninakwe (Zuni) Kochonino, Kó-hni-na, Kóhonino, Kokoninos, Konino, Kox-ninákve, Koxniname, Kuchnikwe, Kuhni-kwe and Ku-ni kue. Nation of the Willows, People of the Blue Waters and People of the Willows are descriptive terms applied.

The Havasupai live in a verdant paradise where the spring begins early and the fall extends late, where one feels the desert sun only a few hours during the day, where three majestic waterfalls defy Hollywood to duplicate, and where a happy community life revolves around a school, church, grocery store, clinic, post office and other buildings.

JANELLE WALKER

HAVASUPAI RESERVATION, in Caconino County, Arizona, is 3,000 acres in size and home to more than 200 Havasupai Indians. All the reservation land is tribally-owned. The reservation, which lies at the bottom of the Grand Canyon, 3,000 feet deep, is surrounded by Forest Service and parkland. An 1880 executive order created the reservation of 60 square miles. This area was reduced to 518.6 acres in 1882. Because of this land loss, the tribe was granted grazing rights on 245,760 acres of federal land.

The Havasupai have for centuries made their home in the bottom of this extremely rugged section of the Grand Canyon. Their reservation lies 3,000 feet below the canyon rim and averages one-quarter mile in width.

The "People of the Blue-Green Water" were a sedentary tribe living along the Colorado River. They practiced agriculture with a planting stick similar to the pueblo method, irrigated their fields, and made baskets and pottery. They are probably related to the basin culture rather than to the rancheria or pueblo,

but they have adopted some farming methods and ceremonies from the Hopi. Havasupai social organization was simple, the family being the sole unit. Chiefs were hereditary and patrilineal. Havasupai religion was shamanistic, and there was an absence of organized religious rites. The people have a very peaceful disposition. They are closely related to the Hualapai.

The Havasupai Council is composed of seven members, four selected and three hereditary chiefs. The chairman and vice-chairman appoint a secretary from within the council. The constitution and bylaws were adopted in 1939, and the tribe incorporated under a corporate charter in 1946. The council assisted by a general manager, tourist enterprise manager, trading company manager, and stock-tender manager.

HAVERSTRAW, also known as the *Remahenonck* and *Rechgawawanck*, were a small *Munsee Delaware*-speaking group that lived upon a stretch of shoreline along the western banks of the Haverstraw Bay reach of the Hudson River in southeastern New York. Closely hemmed in by the steep walls of the northernmost escarpment of the Palisades Highlands, the *Haverstraw* settlements were bounded on the south by the territories of the *Tappan* group and by the slopes of the Hudson Highlands to the west and north. The village of Haverstraw, New York today occupies the central portion of the traditional *Haverstraw* country.

The *Haverstraw* were named after a prominent sachem, or leader like many other *Delawaran* groups. A manuscript dated March 6, 1660 documented the fact that their chief was named "Rumachenanck alias Haverstroo." This practice has long contributed to the misidentification of the *Rechgawawanck* as the *Manhattan Indians* of central Manhattan Island and the adjacent southwest Bronx. The Reverend Robert Bolton, a prominent early nineteenth century student of local native ethnohistory in Westchester County, New York, first made the latter connection. He noted that a sachem named *Rechgewac* signed over a number of tracts of land upon Manhattan and the Bronx to Dutch purchasers. He further noticed that several place names on Manhattan, most notably Rechewas Point and Rechewanes, seemed to suggest a relationship with *Rechgewac*. It only took a small leap to name the otherwise unlocated *Rechgawawanck* of the colonial literature after this sachem.

The problem with this interpretation is the fact that many place names based upon the Delaware words *lekau* "sand" and *lechauwaak* "fork, branch" occur widely throughout this region by virtue of the extensive presence of sand and complex river systems. Further, the *Rechgawawanck* were repeatedly mentioned in company with the *Tappan* and *Hackensack*, neighbors of the *Haverstraw*. The Hudson River was a formidable boundary, and the other ethnohistoric data do not support extensive connections between the down river groups fronting its shorelines. Finally, the only known

Rechgawawanck sachem was listed as *Sesekemu*, which was another spelling for *Sessikout*, an influential *Haverstraw* paramount sachem.

The *Haverstraw* first appeared in the Dutch documentation of their New Netherland colony in 1642 when some chiefs from "Ackinghsack and Reckawanck" reported that the murderer of a Dutchman in the Hackensack area had fled into the interior. A number of them were later victims of the Dutch massacre of the fugitives from the *Mahican* raid on Manhattan and at Pavonia, now Jersey City, New Jersey during the night of February 25-26, 1643. They were among the groups represented by the *Hackensack* sachem *Oratam* in the subsequent peace negotiations with the Dutch. *Oratam* concluded the peace on April 22, 1643 on behalf of his own people and for "the savages of Tappaen, Rechgawawanc, Kichtawanc, and Sintsinck." The latter two groups lived along the eastern banks of the Tappan Zee and Haverstraw Bay reaches of the Hudson River opposite the Tappan and *Haverstraw* groups. The sachems *Sesekemu* (*Sessikout*) and *Willem* of "Tappaens and Rechgawawanch" signed the final peace of August 30, 1645 that ended the Governor Kieft War (1640-1645) on behalf of their people. These friendly relations were reaffirmed on July 19, 1649 by the group, then identified as the *Remahenonck*.

The *Haverstraw* were first mentioned by that name on the 1656 Adriaen van der Donck map of New Netherland. Documents related to the events of the Esopus Wars (1659-1664) indicated close relations between the *Haverstraw* and their *Esopus*, *Tappan*, and *Hackensack* neighbors. On July 10, 1657 a *Haverstraw* chief named *Keghtackcean* sold out his land holdings to the Dutch. He thereupon moved north among the *Esopus* of the lower Wallkill River valley. On March 15, 1664 it was revealed that *Sessikout* was the brother of an *Esopus* sachem. An earlier document dated March 6, 1660 noted that *Corruspin*, often mistaken for the chief sachem of the *Haverstraw*, was actually the brother of *Sessikout*. Both citations clearly demonstrate the principle of matrilineal descent commonly found among the native peoples of the mid-Atlantic Coast. This kinship principle held that leadership was inherited not by a person's son, but by brothers and sisters, and then by sisters' children.

Many *Haverstraw* chose to support the *Esopus* and their allies in their struggle against the Dutch. Confused by *Haverstraw* intentions and lacking direct evidence of their participation in the war, the Dutch attempted to obtain confirmation of war or peace from their sachems on April 21, 1664. The Dutch were put off at that time, but "Ses-Segh-Hout, chief of the Rewechnongh or Haverstraw" placed his mark upon the May 16, 1664 treaty that ended the Esopus War.

The English takeover of New Netherland on September 6, 1664 did not immediately affect the *Haverstraw*. *Corruspin* signed the April 13, 1671 deed to lands along the Palisades in Hackensack territory as "Croppun, sackima of Haverstroo." This land conveyance did not, however, concern any part of the traditional *Haverstraw* homeland. It did serve to emphasize the connections between the *Haverstraw* and the *Hackensack*.

English interest finally focused directly upon the *Haverstraw* territory during the following decade, and two land cessions dated July 13, 1683 and September 10, 1684 completely sold off their homeland. A number of *Haverstraw* families removed north to the Esopus, though most moved among their *Tappan-Hackensack* neighbors in the upper Ramapo and Pequannock River drainages in northern New Jersey. Known during the following century as part of the *River Indians*, the present day descendents of the *Haverstraw* today reside in reservations in Ontario, Canada, Wisconsin, and Oklahoma.

ROBERT STEVEN GRUMET

HAWIKUH. The now-abandoned Zuni pueblo of Hawikuh was once the largest of the fabled "Cities of Cibola," at which the early Spanish explorers hoped to find wealth. Probably at Hawikuh, or possibly Kiakima, the Negro Estevan died at the hands of the Indians in May 1539, and Fray Marcos de Niza viewed one of these pueblos from a distance. In July 1540, Coronado and his army arrived at Hawikuh, the first pueblo they visited. After a sharp skirmish with the inhabitants, during which a few Spaniards were wounded and a few Indians killed, Coronado stormed the pueblo and took possession. The ill treatment that he and his men accorded the Indians set the pattern for Spanish-Indian conflict in the Southwest for the duration of Spanish rule.

From Hawikuh, Tovar and Cardenas journeyed to the Hopi country and the Grand Canyon; Alvarado, north and east to Taos and Pecos. Coronado made his headquarters at Hawikuh for several months during the summer and autumn of 1540 before moving east to winter on the Rio Grande. Subsequent Spanish explorers, including Chamuscado and Rodriquez (1581), Espejo (1583), Onate (1598 and 1604-05), and Zaldivar (1599), also visited the pueblo.

In 1629, the Spanish founded a mission, La

Purisima Concepcion de Hawikuh, at the pueblo. The Zunis in 1632 murdered the resident priest, Fray Francisco Letrado, and fled to another pueblo. They returned in 1635, when the mission was reestablished as a *visita* of the mission at Halona Pueblo. In 1672, Apaches raided Hawikuh, killed the priest, and burned the church. The church was rebuilt, only to be destroyed during the Pueblo rebellion of 1680, in which the Zunis participated wholeheartedly, and during which they abandoned the pueblo. When they submitted to Don Diego de Vargas during the reconquest of 1692, they returned to the Zuni country but reoccupied only one of the six pueblos, Halona. Hawikuh has thus been abandoned since 1680.

The ruins of Hawikuh cover the top of a long, low ridge on the Zuni Indian Reservation. The site was excavated during the period 1917-23 by an expedition of the Heye Foundation under the leadership of Frederick Webb Hodge. Sandstone rock walls in places several feet high, outline the foundations and rooms of part of the pueblo; and mounds of earth littered with rocks mark the locations of other portions. Mounds of eroded adobe, 2 or 3 feet high, are all that remain of the mission church and part of the monastery.

HAYES, IRA (Pima; 1922–Jan. 24, 1955), was a decorated U.S. marine in the Pacific Theater during World War II who became famous when he was among a group of marines who were photographed raising the American flag at Mt. Suribachi on Iwo Jima Island. Following the war, he settled in Chicago. He found the adjustment to peacetime life difficult and became an alcoholic. Hayes returned to the reservation in Arizona, where he was found dead in the desert in January 1955. A screenplay based on his life, *The Outsider*, was produced shortly after his death.

HAYFIELD, BATTLE OF was an 1867 Cheyenne attack on Fort C.V. Smith. The Sioux, under Red Cloud, and their Cheyenne allies were determined in their efforts to close down the fortified Bozeman Trail. Since 1865 they had vigorously opposed this route through their hunting lands, lands reserved to them by treaty. While the Sioux attacked Fort Phil Kearny (The Wagon Box Fight), 500-600 Cheyenne moved north of Fort C.F. Smith.

The Cheyenne had previously captured or killed most of the soldiers' horses and anticipated an easy victory. On August 1, 1867, they trapped 30 men in a hayfield near the fort. Equipped with new repeating rifles, the soldiers held their ground and only one Cheyenne penetrated the corral. The Cheyenne then set fire to the high surrounding grass, a fire which cascaded toward the encircled soldiers at magnificent heights. About 20 feet short of the corral, it suddenly stopped and the wind blew dense smoke back at the Cheyenne. Under the smoke cover the Indians collected their dead and wounded and retreated.

Although they were not victorious, through this and other continuing incidents, the Indians of the Powder River country caused the U.S. government to abandon the Bozeman Trail in 1868.

HEADMEN. *See* CHIEFS AND HEADMEN.

HEAD SHRINKING was a practice not unknown to some Indian tribes of South America. The *Jivaro* owe their fame to the shrunken heads, or *tsantsas,* which they still prepared in modern times and which have been sought after by collectors.

In pre-Columbian times the act of shrinking heads was widespread in the Andean area. Early chroniclers have given us descriptions of shrunken heads and of the methods of their preparation among the Indians of the Ecuadorian Coast. Vases in the shape of shrunken heads and representations of heads reminiscent of the tsantsas may be assigned to the Nazca, Ica, and Tiahuanaco Periods, but shrunken heads themselves have not been found in Peru. It is a moot question whether the countless heads with skewered lips painted on Nazca vases actually were reduced or were prepared like the specimens described by Tello.

Trophies of a manhunt in interior Equador.

In the 17th century, the neighbors of the *Jivaro,* the *Maina, Chebero,* and *Cocama,* also prepared tsantsas from the heads of their enemies.

HENDRICK (Mohawk; *c*. 1700– Sept. 8, 1755) was an influential chief who fought with the British during the French and Indian War. After the French defeated the British forces under Gen. Edward Braddock at Fort Duquesne on July 9, 1755, the majority of the Indians sided with the French. Hendrick, however, joined the British force under Gen. William Johnson, a long-time friend of the Iroquois Confederacy and fought for him at the Battle of Lake George, New York, on September 8, 1755. At that battle, while separated from the main British force on a scouting mission, Hendrick unexpectedly met the much larger French force under General Dieskau and was killed.

Some sources claim that Hendrick had objected to the separation of the forces as bad military strategy, but he was overruled by General Johnson. When viewing his Indian force before the battle, Hendrick is reported to have stated: "If they are to fight, they are too few. If they are to be killed, they are too many."

HENSLEY, WILLIAM L. (Inuit; 1941–   ), served two terms in the Alaska House of Representatives (1967– 71) and in 1971 was elected to the Alaska State Senate. Born at Kotzebue, Alaska, he attended the University of Alaska and graduated from George Washington University. He has been active in state and national organizations of Native Americans, serving as vice chairman of the Alaska Federation of Natives and as vice chairman and then executive director of the Northwest Alaska Native Association. He was active in the successful six-year effort to get the Alaska Native Claims Settlement Act passed by the U.S. Congress (December 18, 1971).

In March 1968 he was named by President Lyndon B. Johnson to the National Council on Indian Opportunity. In 1969 he delivered a paper at an international meeting in Paris on the future of the Inuit people, and he has also traveled in Poland and the Soviet Union under a John F. Kennedy Memorial Award, studying the living conditions in those countries.

HESSING, VALJEAN McCARTY (Choctaw; Aug. 30, 1934–   ), is an artist and a book illustrator. Born at Tulsa, Oklahoma, she was reared by her mother's parents. While in elementary and secondary schools, she received numerous awards for her artwork and a scholarship to Mary Hardin-Baylor College. She married Robert C. Hessing in 1954 and devoted most of her time during the next ten years to raising a family. Since 1964, Valjean Hessing has been painting and exhibiting her work regularly.

Hewitt, John Napoleon

HEWITT, JOHN NAPOLEON BRINTON (Tuscarora; Dec. 16, 1859– Oct. 14, 1937), was a noted ethnologist with the Bureau of American Ethnology (BAE) at the Smithsonian Institution, who became an expert in Native American linguistics, mythology, and sociology, particularly of the Iroquois peoples.

Born in the neighborhood of Lewiston, Niagara County, New York, his mother was of Tuscarora descent and his father was a physician of Scot ancestry. In 1880 he was employed by Mrs. Erminnie A. Smith to help her collect myths among the Iroquois tribes of New York. He was associated with her in this work from 1880 to 1884 and, after her death in June 1886, Hewitt was called to the BAE to take up her work. He continued in that same institution until his death, becoming regarded as the leading authority on the organization of the Iroquois League and the ceremonials, customs, and usages of the tribes composing it.

Although he contributed to many publications, including the famous *Handbook of American Indians North of Mexico* edited by Frederick W. Hodge (1912), he was painstakingly conscientious in his work and only a small part of his research was actually published.

HIACOOMES (Wampanoag; *c.* 1610–1690) was allegedly the first Indian in North America to be converted to Christianity and the first to be ordained a Christian clergyman. Information about his life is largely unsubstantiated, but apparently he lived on Martha's Vineyard (Massachusetts) near Thomas Mayhew, Jr., who settled there in 1642. Hiacoomes was Mayhew's first convert in 1643. He began preaching in 1646; was ordained on August 22, 1670; and died in 1690 at about the age of 80. For some years before his death, he was unable to preach.

HIAWATHA (Mohawk or Onondaga; *c.* 1525–*c.* 1590) was an apostle of peace and brotherhood, who devoted his life to ending the bloodshed among the Mohawk, Oneida, Cayuga, Seneca, and Onondaga and to uniting these five tribes into the League of the Iroquois (the Confederation of Five Nations).

Possessing exceptional oratorical powers, Hiawatha was a medicine man and magician among the Onondaga, and—like them—he probably practiced cannibalism. Distressed at the constant warfare and never-ending feuds among the five tribes, though, Hiawatha emerged as a reform leader, advocating the unification of the tribes and the cessation of blood revenge. His bitter opponent, the Onondaga chief Wathatotarho (*q.v.*), did all he could to prevent the reformers from achieving their objectives, including having one of Hiawatha's daughters murdered. Unable to overcome Wathatotarho's opposition, Hiawatha left the Onondaga to preach his message of peace and brotherhood to the Mohawk, Oneida, and Cayuga—all of whom agreed to unite and abandon bloodshed among fellow Iroquois on the condition that Wathatotarho and the Onondaga did likewise.

Apparently defeated in his reform efforts once again, Hiawatha was about to abandon hope when he fell under the influence of a mystical peacemaker and prophet named Dekanawida (*q.v.*). The latter converted Hiawatha from cannibalism and convinced him that the obstinate and evil Wathatotarho could be won over to what would later be called The Great Peace. Together, Hiawatha and Dekanawida persuaded the Onondaga chief to join the league. During the negotiations Wathatotarho won certain concessions, but the League of the Iroquois became a reality, cannibalism was outlawed (except in times of war), and blood revenge was ended among the five tribes.

Hiawatha now turned missionary, carrying Dekanawida's confederation ideas and moral principles to other tribes. He roamed far from his home territory, traveling as far away as Lake Superior and the Mississippi River. Although he had some success in winning converts to the Great Peace, no other tribes joined the confederation until the white man had advanced so far that various tribes were forced to seek sanctuary on the lands of the Five Nations. The remnants of the conquered Tuscarora, for example, became the sixth nation in the league about the year 1715.

Meanwhile, the Iroquois were committed to warring against tribes who rejected their overtures of peace and brotherhood, with the ironic result being that the whites came to know the Confederation of Five Nations only as cruel and bloodthirsty warriors—the very antithesis of the pacifistic principles to which Hiawatha had devoted his life. The apostle/missionary himself probably spent his last days as an elder statesman among the Mohawk. The confederation he had helped to forge, however, lasted until the American Revolution, inspiring the colonists in their dream of creating a stable federal union.

In the second quarter of the 19th century, Henry R. Schoolcraft, an early U.S. ethnologist, collected some of the Iroquois legends and published them in such a way that Hiawatha became identified as the greatest of the Iroquoian gods, Teharonhiawagon ("The Master of Life"), which Schoolcraft apparently assumed was just another way of spelling Hiawatha. He went on to identify this same god with the chief deity of the Chippewa (Ojibwa) Indians, who lived farther west in the Great Lakes region. The ethnologist referred to the Chippewa deity Manabozho as Hiawatha in a series of Chippewa myths which he published. This error was compounded by Henry Wadsworth Longfellow. Fascinated by Schoolcraft's Chippewa legends, Longfellow based his famous poem, written in 1855, on them, and the name Hiawatha became identified with a fictionalized Chippewa god and hero.

HICKS, CHARLES (Cherokee; ?–1827), was a mixed-blood who became one of the leaders of the Cherokee Nation in the turbulent period before the tribe's removal to Indian Territory (present Oklahoma). During the 1790s he was an interpreter between the Cherokee and the whites, and he was greatly relied upon by the Indian leaders. He rose in power and by 1822 he was the assistant principal chief and treasurer of the nation. In 1827 he succeeded Path Killer as principal chief, but he died shortly thereafter. Hicks was the first Cherokee convert to the Moravian Church.

HICKS, WILLIAM (Cherokee; fl. early 19th century), was a leader of the Cherokee Nation who favored removal to Indian Territory (present Oklahoma) in 1835. He was defeated by John Ross in the election to fill the office of principal chief of the nation left vacant by the death of his brother Charles Hicks in the fall of 1827. Recoiling from this blow to his ambition, he was a prey to the enticements of the U.S. government to support emigration. In December 1833 he was elected principal chief of the emigrating faction.

HIDATSA Indians were a horticultural tribe living in earthlodge villages in the Missouri valley in present-day North Dakota. The tribal name was derived from the largest village and is supposed to mean "willows." They are also known by their Mandan name, *Minataree* (variously spelled), meaning "they crossed the river," a reference to the tradition that they joined the Mandan on the west bank of the Missouri. A third name for the tribe is Gros Ventres, or Big Bellies, derived from a misunderstanding of the Plains Indian sign language symbol for them. Sometimes they are referred to as the Gros Ventres of the Missouri, to distinguish them from the Atsina, known as the Gros Ventres of the Prairie.

The historic Hidatsa tribe represents an amalgamation of three politically autonomous but culturally and linguistically allied groups: the Hidatsa proper, the Amatiha, and the Amahami. These divisions persisted well into historic times. Lewis and Clark, for example, recognized the Amahami as a separate tribe in 1804-6. Only minor differences existed between their languages, however, and from that of the Crow, an offshoot of the Hidatsa.

The Hidatsa shared in the cultural tradition of the village Indians of the upper Missouri, a tradition best exemplified by the Mandan (q.v.), by whom they were strongly influenced. Although they were less sedentary than the Mandan and left their earthlodge villages for long periods of time, they depended for subsistence on a combination of horticulture—corn, beams, sunflowers, and squash—and hunting, mainly of the bison. Food-gathering and fishing contributed in a limited way also.

Like the other village tribes, the Hidatsa used implements of bone and stone, made pottery, wooden bowls, and horn spoons, and lived in earthlodges except on hunting expeditions. Their summer villages were typically located on bluffs overlooking their fields; in the winter they moved to protected sites in the timbered

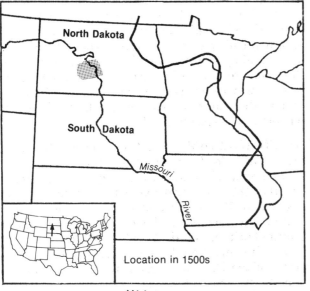

Hidatsa

bottomlands and lived in smaller earthlodges. Until the advent of trade blankets, their clothing consisted of skins. Besides utilitarian dress for everyday wear, they had elaborate ceremonial costumes for special occasions. Prince Maximilian of Wied-Neuwied characterized the Hidatsa as the most "elegant" Indians on the upper Missouri.

The original components of the historic Hidatsa tribe maintained separate political organizations until their amalgamation in a single village in the 1840s. Each village had its clan system and a number of age-grade societies. These merged when the villages were united, and eventually the clans and societies were equated with the corresponding divisions in the Mandan tribe. In early times Mandan influence was preponderant, but in the nineteenth century, when the Mandan tribe was almost destroyed, the convergence of the two into a combined Mandan-Hidatsa tribe was accompanied by Hidatsa dominance.

Because of the long association of the two tribes, it is difficult to distinguish between Hidatsa and Mandan beliefs and rituals. The Hidatsa seem to have adopted the open ceremonial plaza from the Mandan, and their major ceremony, the Naxpike, may owe some of its salient features to the better-known Mandan Okipa. Similarities between the creation myths of the two tribes suggest borrowing, but there is no agreement on who borrowed specific elements from whom. The major cultural traits shared by both tribes are discussed under the Mandan.

Native tradition and archeology do not agree on when the components of the Hidatsa tribe reached the Missouri. Tribal legends have them arriving in the late prehistoric or protohistoric period, whereas archeological evidence suggests a longer tenure in the valley. In all probability, they came from the northeast, from the Devils Lake area, where they already practiced horticulture. The Amatiha were probably the earliest to arrive on the Missouri, followed by the Amahami and later by the Hidatsa proper. The last group, though cultivators of the soil in their old homes, had "lost their corn" by the time they reached the Missouri and had to relearn the techniques of horticulture from the Mandan.

So close was the relationship between the Hidatsa and the Mandan that early European visitors made no distinction between the two tribes, and the former do not appear as a separate tribe until the very end of the eighteenth century. By that time they and the Mandan were living in five or six villages near the mouth of the Knife River; some villages included members of both tribes. They resided there until the smallpox epidemic of 1837.

After the epidemic some of the Hidatsa remained at or near their old village sites, others joined the Crow, and still others became nomadic. In 1845 the bulk of the tribe, together with most of the Mandan, re-established themselves in a single community, known as Like-a-Fishhook village, adjacent to the fur trading

Hidatsa dancers bearing exploit marks.

post of Fort Berthold. Although nominally under the jurisdiction of the Bureau of Indian Affairs, the village peoples actually saw very little of the Bureau's representative, who commonly visited them once a year after steamboats began plying the upper Missouri. Until the later 1860s, when a resident agent was appointed, white contacts were largely restricted to the fur traders, who exerted a powerful influence on the Indians.

In 1851, at Fort Laramie, the three village tribes—Hidatsa, Mandan, and Arikara—were acknowledged to have a valid claim to a triangular segment of territory extending southwest from the Missouri to northeastern Wyoming. Most of this was embraced in the reservation established for them by executive order in 1870, along with a small area on the left bank of the Missouri including the site of their village. The Fort Berthold reservation was subsequently reduced by executive order in 1880 and by acts of Congress in 1891 and 1910.

The Mandan, Hidatsa, and (after 1862) Arikara continued to live together in Like-a-Fishhook village until about 1885, when pressure from government agents, together with the exhaustion of the local timber supply, caused them to abandon the village and scatter over the reservation, where they were allotted farms by an agreement negotiated in 1886. Their efforts to farm were not wholly successful, however, the Indians gradually settled in communities, usually centered about a church and school, and leased most of their farming and grazing lands to white operators.

In the 1930s, when the Fort Berthold people accepted the Indian Reorganization Act and officially became the Three Affiliated Tribes, there was a partial return to farming and ranching. Off-reservation employment during World War II, however, followed by the construction of the Garison Dam and the flooding of most of the best farm land, again reversed the economic development of the Fort Berthold people. In the 1960s and 1970s there was some increase in the proportion of land used by the Indians themselves, but greater emphasis was placed on the industrial development of the reservation, whose population was again concentrated in villages.

Because early white observers failed to recognize the Hidatsa as a separate tribe, it is impossible to estimate their population at the time of the first European contacts. Modern educated guesses have placed the com-

Hunting antelope.

bined Mandan-Hidatsa population anywhere from 12,000 to 16,000 around the middle of the eighteenth century. Just prior to the 1837 smallpox epidemic the Hidatsa were said to number 2,000 to 2,500. Although they lost less heavily in that catastrophe than the Mandan, their numbers were sharply reduced. Further declines in later years brought their population to about 500 in 1876, when the first reliable census was taken. After the turn of the century their numbers gradually began to rise, until by 1946 there were 897 who identified as Hidatsa. Since then the Three Affiliated Tribes have customarily been enumerated as a single group.

ROY W. MEYER

HIDES AND SKINS were one of the most important and versatile natural materials utilized by North American Indians. They were used to some extent by all tribes but most commonly in the Arctic, Subarctic, northeastern United States, Prairies, and Plains, where tribes depended primarily on hunting for their subsistence.

Among hunting tribes, tanned hide was the commonest material used for clothing. Buckskin, because of its softness and pliability, was favored for articles worn next to the skin. Other hides, such as those of

Hunting buffalo.

buffalo, elk, moose, bear, and caribou, were used for robes and other outer garments. Skins of smaller animals such as sea otter and rabbits were sewn together or cut into strips and woven into fur robes and blankets in many areas.

Hide was used for tipi coverings throughout most of the Plains. It was the most common covering for dwellings, used either alone or in combination with other materials, in most of the Arctic, Subarctic, Prairies, and parts of the Northwest Coast, Plateau, Great Basin, and Southwest. Many storage and transport containers were made of hide, which was one of the most practical materials for this purpose among nomadic tribes. The Eskimos used seal or other skin as the covering for the kayak and umiak, and other hide boats were used in parts of the eastern and western Subarctic, Northwest Coast, Plains, Great Lakes region, and Southeast. Hide was also one of the most widely used materials for defensive armor. The most common shield was a circular hide type characteristic of the Plains and several other areas. Hide was the material most frequently used for body armor, the commonest form consisting simply of an untailored hide wrapped around the body under one arm and tied over the opposite shoulder. One of the most indispensable and universal uses of hide was for lashing, either alone or in combination with natural cements, in the construction of boats, dwellings, tools, weapons, religious objects, and many other articles.

Colonists and early Anglo-American frontiersmen often adopted Indian methods of utilizing hides and skins. The growth of the fur trade and the introduction of the gun and steel trap, however, eventually led to serious depletion of game populations. Game shortages and introduction of mass-produced textiles and other European materials and technology largely eliminated the role of hides and skins in Indian culture.

HIEROGLYPHICS. A postclassic phase of Mayan civilization flourished in Yucatan, heavily influenced by contact with Mexican (i.e. Aztec and Toltec) culture, until the Spanish conquest. Major sites include Chichen Itza and Uxmal. At the time of the arrival of the Spaniards, this civilization was still partly alive, and a system of hieroglyphic writing, on bark paper and in stone, was still in use. This writing, and the religious and calendrical systems represented by means of it, must rank among the highest cultural artistic, and intellectual achievements of aboriginal America. The decipherment of the writing system began in the latter part of the last century, and relied at first especially on materials from Yucatan, including the three surviving Mayan codices, painted in many colors on bark paper, and pleated accordion-fashion. These codices, known as the Dresden, the Madrid, and the Paris, for the libraries where the originals are kept, were interpreted with the help of a document prepared by the first Bishop of Yucatan, Diego de Landa (1524-1579) containing much information on the knowledge and practices of the Yucatec Mayas which the Spanish were then energetically suppressing. An edition of this document, *Landa's Relacion de las cosas de Yucatan,* translated into English and heavily annotated by A. M. Tozzer, remains an excellent source of information on the culture of Yucatan at this period, and contains precious information on the writing system given to Landa by Mayas who still knew it. The system consists of several hundred signs, some used as word signs, some used as syllable signs, to "spell out" or to remind the reader of pronunciations, and some used as "affixes" in a variety of ways in combination with main signs. The interpretation of the arithmetic and calendrical signs, explained more fully in Landa, is essentially complete, and most signs for deities have been reasonably well identified. Landa was less helpful with the textual uses of the glyphs, however, since he seems to have considered the system as alphabetic in principle, which it certainly is not. With the aid of studies of earlier inscriptions, however, the content of textual passages is slowly becoming clearer, though much remains to be learned.

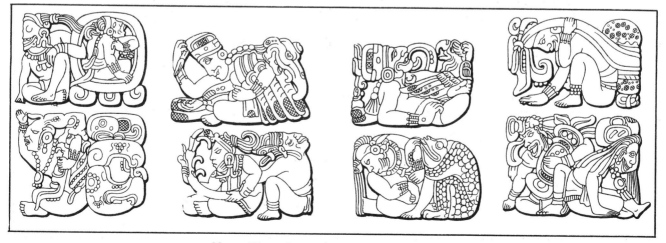

Maya Hieroglyphs (carved on stone stela).

nnshinen
Our Father

Wajok
in heaven

ebin
seated

tchiptook
may

delwigin
thy name

meguidedemek
be respected

Wajok
in heaven

n'telidanen
to us

tchiptook
may

ignemwiek
grant

ula
thee

nemulek
to see

uledechinen.
in staying.

Natel
There

wajok
in heaven

deli
as

chkedoolk
thou art obeyed

tchiptook
may

deli
so

be

chkedulek
obeyed

makimiguek
on earth

eimek
where we are

Delamukubenigua
As thou hast given it to us

echemieguel
in the same manner

apch
also

neguech
now

kichkook
to-day

delamooktech
give it

peneguunenwin
our nourishment

niluaen;
to us;

deli abikchiktakachik
we forgive those

wegaiwinametnik
who have offended us

elp
so

kel
thou

nixkam
O God

abikchiktwin
forgive

clweultick
our faults

melkeninrech
hold us strong

winnchudil
by the hand

mu
not

k'tygalinen
to fall

keginukamkel
keep far from us

winnchiguel
sufferings

twaktwin.
evils.

N'delietch.
Amen.

The Lord's Prayer in Micmac hieroglypics.

Glyphs and diety figures from the Maya codices.

Glyphs of the month Kayab
and turtle figures.

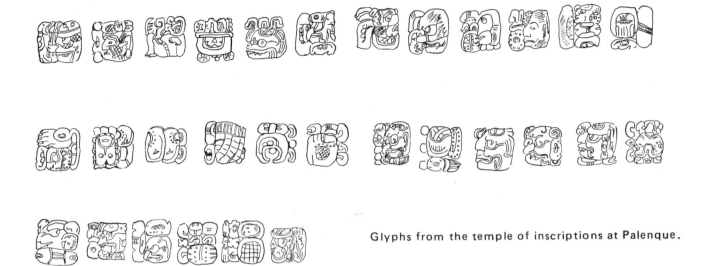

Glyphs from the temple of inscriptions at Palenque.

Figures and symbols of Maya and Mexican deities.

HIGHTOWER, ROSELLA (Choctaw; 1920–   ) is an internationally famous ballerina. Born at Ardmore, Oklahoma, she was taken to Kansas City, Missouri, when she was still an infant. After early ballet training in Kansas City, she studied under several private tutors and received an appointment to the Ballet Russe de Monte Carlo after auditioning before the great Leonide Massine. Two years later she returned to the United States to become a soloist with the Ballet Theatre (later American Ballet Theatre) of Lucia Chase.

After a tour of North and South America with the original Ballet Russe, she became the grand ballerina of the newly formed company of Marquis de Cuevas in France. At the request of the U.S. government she rejoined the American Ballet Theatre and toured for two years.

Following this tour, which included performances in the Soviet Union, she returned to France, eventually forming her own Center of Classical Dance in Cannes. In 1967 she was one of the four Oklahoma ballerinas who appeared in the world premier of *The Four Moons* in Tulsa.

HILL, JOAN (Cherokee-Creek; Dec. 19, 1930–   ), is an artist who is considered by some art critics to be the most talented and most versatile contemporary female American Indian painter in the United States. Joan Hill, whose Cherokee name, Chea-se-quah, means Redbird, was born in Muskogee, Oklahoma. Numbered among her ancestors are chiefs of the Cherokee and Creek tribes. Her family settled in Indian Territory (present Oklahoma) in the mid-1800s and played a major role in forming the history of the region.

Joan Hill graduated from high school in 1948; received a B.A. in education at Northeastern State College, Tahlequah, Oklahoma, in 1952; and then became an art instructor at the secondary level in the public school system in Tulsa, Oklahoma. In 1956 she left teaching to become a full-time, freelance painter.

In the late 1970s, of her numerous works, 74 were in public collections, an additional 19 were owned by the U.S. Department of the Interior, and nearly 500 were in private collections. Her wide variety of styles and media have been seen in more than 250 juried and nonjuried exhibitions throughout the world and in many one-woman shows. In 1973 she received the Waite Phillips Trophy, the Philbrook Art Center's highest award presented to an Indian artist.

By 1975, Joan Hill's special commissions had included 36 portraits and 14 paintings recording Cherokee history in her realistic style. Other styles in which she has worked are abstraction, impression, and the flat style known as traditional Indian painting. She has been judged to be equally competent in any of her approaches to painting.

Hill, Joan

HILLIS, HADJO (Seminole; ?–1817) was a noted Seminole leader in the early 19th century who was known to whites as Francis the Prophet. He first came to notice in April 1814 when he escaped from Gen. Andrew Jackson's camp at the confluence of the Coosa and Tallapoosa rivers while being held prisoner. Led by some English traders to believe that the Treaty of Ghent in 1814, which ended the War of 1812, had a provision for the restoration of Seminole lands, and in the hope of obtaining help for his people against the Americans, he went to England, where he received considerable attention. His mission, however, led to no practical result.

In late 1817, during the First Seminole War (1817–18), Hadjo ordered the execution of a captured American named McKrimmon. The pleas of Hillis Hadjo's daughter, Milly, saved McKrimmon. Shortly after this incident, Hillis Hadjo was captured by the Americans and hanged.

HINDS, PATRICK SWAZO (Tesuque; March 25, 1929–   ), is an artist, a silk screen processor, and a teacher of art. Born at Tesuque Pueblo, New Mexico, the artist was adopted in 1939 by Dr. Norman A. E. Hinds, an honorary member of Tesuque who was a professor of geology at the University of California at Berkeley for 45 years. Shortly after he was adopted, Hinds moved to California where he has resided ever since, usually returning to Tesuque for summer vacations. He served in the U.S. Marine Corps, 1945–46 and 1950–51, receiving two Purple Heart awards.

Hinds works as a silk screen processor in Berkeley, California, and is active in the Society of Western Artists, the Berkeley Arts and Crafts Cooperative, and the American Indian Artists Association. He has won numerous awards for his work, including the Walter Simpson Grand Award at the Scottsdale National Indian Exhibition in 1966.

HISHKOWITS (Southern Cheyenne; 1867–after 1912), known to whites as Harvey Whiteshield, was an interpreter and assistant teacher at the Mennonite mission school for the Cheyenne at Cantonment in Indian Territory (present Oklahoma) from 1893 to 1897 and afterwards helped the Rev. Rudolph Petter, missionary-in-charge at the school, to prepare several translations and a manuscript dictionary of the Cheyenne language. Hishkowits was born in western Indian Territory, the son of Chief White Shield.

HISTORY. The earliest immigrants brought with them to this continent the cultural traditions of the upper Paleolithic of the Old World. Within America the diversity of environmental conditions, operating as limiting or stimulating factors, combined with the effects of historical forces. These produced, in the course of some 25,000 years, a wide variety of cultural types. In 1492, these ranged in scale from the low level of hunters and gatherers (such as the groups in Lower California or Tierra del Fuego) to the advanced civilizations of Mexico and Guatemala or of Peru and Bolivia.

American history before the Discovery and the Conquest constitutes one kind of human experience; its world-wide significance is clear. It raises cultural problems which trancend the American framework. Thus, the areas of the American Continent where plant cultivation and the domestication of a few animals was begun and where these formed the basis of agriculture in some regions, are isolated from the Old World. It is probable, as a result of this isolation, that the change from ways of life based on gathering-hunting-fishing to ways of life based on agriculture took place in the New World independently of corresponding revolutionary changes in the Old World. Later, civilizations emerged in Mesoamerica and the Andean area which were comparable — from the point of view of cultural types, and without implying historical connection — to the ancient civilizations of Mesopotamia, Egypt, Pakistan or China, and which were also independent American developments according to our present knowledge.

But Columbian history has special significance, within that of American history. This is true apart from its importance *per se,* as the experience of a considerable part of humanity, and as indispensable information for theoretical formulation of the problems of cultural causality. The existence of very diverse cultural forms at different levels of development was a factor of supreme importance in the genesis of the events of discovery, conquest and colonization. They determined the diversity of situations of cultural clash in different areas of the Continent, the nature — and even the mere existence — of biological and cultural mixture, the racial conflicts, the different features of the colonial societies and the peculiar characteristics of the modern nations.

Native history acquires full significance within that of the History of America when it is considered from this point of view. This is by no means to say that it would not be possible to write a unified general history of pre-Columbian America, independent of Pan-American unity on a different plane — as a part (with different degrees of assimilation and greatly varied shades) of the civilization which formerly was European and now is Atlantic that was produced by the discovery and the European conquest and colonization.

If, then, we consider American history prior to 1492 as a sequence of human experience parallel to that of the Old World, and the clash of cultures produced by European conquest and colonization as well as the continuing interaction of the two worlds — American Indian and the Western European — from the first encounter in the Antilles up to the present time, the significance of Native American History goes beyond the purely historical to pose problems of causality and cultural laws. These problems arise with reference not only to the question of internal developments but also with regard to the contact of differing peoples and cultures and their effects on the dynamics of cultural change. The analysis of the factors at work in the cultural revolutions of pre-Columbian America and their comparison with the corresponding revolutions of the Old World would permit a better understanding of the relationships of cause and effect which determine cultural progress, as well as stagnation and retrogression. The available documentation on four and a half centuries of interchange between the European (and also the African) cultures transplanted to American soil and the indigenous cultures constitutes a rich but largely untapped reservoir of information for the study of the phenomena of acculturation.

Man first entered the North American continent by way of the Bering Land Bridge which connected Asia with North America during the Pleistocene Glacial Age.

There are several reasons for considering the Bering Strait a natural crossing-point from Asia to North America. Today the Strait is only 120 feet wide and 56 miles wide, and with many small islands, such as the

Diomede Islands dotting the Strait, there is a maximum of only 25 miles of open sea. During the Glacial Age the oceans were considerably lower than their present levels, and it is generally assumed that a bridge or bridges reached from Asia to America. Even if the Strait had been frozen, man could easily have walked across it.

Early Pleistocene man was primarily a hunter and seed gatherer. During the Pleistocene there was a general shift in animal populations throughout the world. This was, undoubtedly, his motive, for there are many excavations where the bones of animals have been discovered — at Rosey Creek, near Fairbanks, what appears to be an entire herd of mammoths. Throughout the Alaskan valleys, these bones, as well as many kinds of points such as Eden points of Asian origin, are present.

Cultural factors

The process of cultural diffusion, by which features of a culture become a part of neighboring cultures, usually took place through migrations of people from one region to another, though contacts made by travelers, or though trade. Among the North American Indians, virtually every tribe traded with other groups and often possessed at least a few objects from other cultures. The only exception known are the Polar Eskimos, and before they were discovered by John Ross in 1818 they had thought themselves to be the only people on earth.

The diffusion of cultural objects may have unexpected consequences. For example, a hunting society dominated by male hunters may relegate women to the relatively unimportant task of farming. But agriculture may become much more important with the introduction of maize, and a rise in the status of women would in such a case follow as a matter of course. In fact, the whole fabric of a society may be affected. Patrilocal residence, for example, may give away to matrilocal residence, or property may come to be inherited through the women of the tribe instead of through the men. Such shifts seem to have occurred in parts of the Oasis, Prairies, and Eastern regions of North America.

Many North American cultures borrowed extensively from the cultures of Central and South America, beginning early in the prehistoric era. One of the earliest and greatest of North American cultures, the Hohokam, possessed styles of jewelry and pottery, pyramids, and ball courts, all of which were borrowed or adapted from Central American peoples. The Hohokam even used rubber balls that were imported from Central America.

Political systems organized around chieftainships, mound-building, and elevation in social rank on the basis of achievement in war, are cultural elements that appear in many North American societies, including, for example, among the Natchez Indians and other southeastern tribes. These traits are similar to those found in many cultures situated around the Caribbean Sea, the Gulf of Mexico, and the South Atlantic coastal plain. Many southern Indians are known to have been excellent seamen, and the similarity between the Natchez and southern cultures can clearly be traced to their influence. The Arawak Indians, for example, lived on the northern coast of South America and are known to have sailed to islands in the West Indies and even to parts of Florida. As is typical with the process of diffusion, the similarities grow more attenuated the farther cultural features disperse from their points of origin. Thus, the farther north and east one goes, the fainter the resemblance of specific cultural features to the societies where they originated. And, although the influence of one culture may be seen in development of another, additional factors must be taken into account. Similar environments, for example, could play a part in the development of social institutions along parallel lines. Likewise, the inherent dynamics of chieftainships may themselves lead in certain more or less predetermined directions. Or, similarities between distant cultures may be due simply to coincidence.

Almost anything that can be named can be spread by means of cultural diffusion. Dentalia shells, for example, served as a medium of exchange from the Northwest Coast to as far east as the Missouri River and the Dakotas. Most Dentalia used by North American Indians originated on the western side of Vancouver Island and spread by means of trade. Corn, which does not survive in the wild, also spread over large portions of North America by means of trade. Tribes acquiring corn for the first time not only obtained a new crop, but created a new crop as well — by cultivating corn from another region until it was adapted to its new environment. Even methods of building tipis spread from tribe to tribe. Whether three or four poles are used for support, for example, does not effect the stability of the tipi. There being no practical reason to prefer one method over the other, one would expect the two methods to be about equally popular. But three poles were the most widely used in the East, while in the West four poles were the common pattern. This regional preference for one method or the other indicates that methods of building tipis spread, within particular regions of North America, by means of cultural diffusion.

Geographic factors

The large oceans which surround the Western Hemisphere constituted, without doubt, effective barriers to the diffusion of cultural influences until the development of navigation converted them into means of inter-continental communication. Before that time, America was a "cul-de-sac" of the oikoumene and practically constituted a separate world. It should be noted, however, that the obstacle presented by the Atlantic Ocean to communication between Europe and Africa, on the one side, and America, on the other, was not overcome, apparently, until the end of the tenth century of the Christian Era, with the arrival of the Norsemen in Greenland and Labrador. This even had no effect on the later development of native cultures, since it took place in a peripheral zone. The obstacle was thus not really overcome until 1492. The Pacific Ocean, on the other hand, could have been a route of diffusion between Asia and America and between South America and Polynesia, if we can go by certain indications whose historical significance, however, is not yet certain. It is not sufficient to point to more or less specific similarities as proof of contact, thus excluding the possibility of parallel developments. The historical fact of transmission must be demonstrated — so that it seems reasonably certain — for each factor considered. Whatever may have been the contacts by this route, it seems evident, keeping in mind both the first peopling of the Continent and the arrival after the first migrations of cultural influences emanating from the Old World, that the principal port of entry, and perhaps the only one, was by way of the Bering Straits. If influences arrived across the Pacific, it seems very doubtful that they had decisive effects on the development of the native civilizations.

Nevertheless the American Continent constitutes a geographic unity only from the point of view of its almost complete isolation from the Old World. A second general factor which has to be taken into account in studying the pre-Columbian past is that America is divided into two almost isolated continental masses united only by the narrow corridor of the Central American isthmus and a chain of islands which do not appear to have been used as a frequent means of communication between North and South America. If, in addition to the distribution of land masses, we take into consideration the ecological conditions — especially the distribution· of tropical forest zones which effectively bar the dispersion of certain forms of life — the situation described becomes even more pronounced. After the first waves of immigrants, and especially since the beginning of sedentary life based

on agriculture in the entrance funnel of South América, the influences emanating from Asia and introduced by way of the Bering Strait do not appear to have affected appreciably the cultures of inter-tropical America or of the southern part of the Continent. On the other hand stimuli radiating from the nuclear zone — between Mexico and Bolivia — as a result of cultural developments which occured there (such as the introduction of agriculture and the later growth of civilization in Mesoamerica and in the central Andean area) extended in divergent forms into northern and southern America.

The environmental medium is a variable factor. In the course of time environmental conditions on the Continent have changed both intrinsically (climatic changes, etc.) and extrinsically, from the point of view of their significance for man in relation to the technology available for the use of existing resources. Since man was undoubtedly present on the Continent since the Upper Pleistocene, the different ecological situation which existed then and the changes brought about as a result of climatic fluctuations which marked the transition to the present must be taken into account in a study of the conditions of life among the oldest Americans.

In addition to the greater climatological changes, lesser fluctuations or climatic cycles may produce very important disturbances in the zones of environmental transition. One must also take into account the fact that exploitation of natural resources by man produces environmental changes (for example: extermination of game animals or their reduction in number, formation of grasslands as a result of the negative effects of the slash and burn system of cultivation in tropical forest zones.) Although their effects may be on a local scale, their consequences on the history of the people are likely to be transmitted by means of chain reactions.

Consider, for example, the possibility that the Chichimecan invasions in the northern zone of Mesoamerica were related to modifications in en-

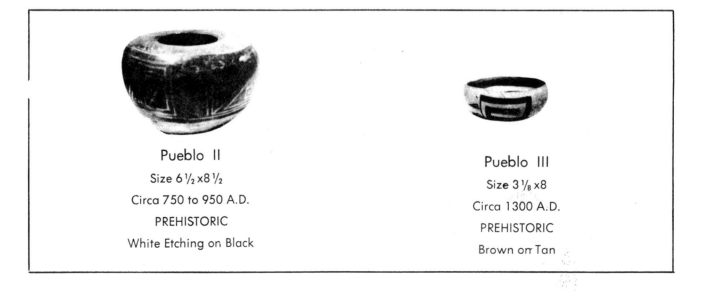

Pueblo II

Size 6 ½ x 8 ½

Circa 750 to 950 A.D.

PREHISTORIC

White Etching on Black

Pueblo III

Size 3 ⅛ x 8

Circa 1300 A.D.

PREHISTORIC

Brown on Tan

vironmental conditions, either due to minor climatic fluctuations (related to changes of circulation in the upper atmosphere) that produced displacement of the limits of the arid zone of northern Mexico, or by aridity caused by excessive exploitation of marginal agricultural zones, or both causes combined; it would have caused the withdrawal to more favorable agricultural regions of the cultivators established in marginal zones in eras of expansion and would have left frontier territories open to gatherer-hunter nomads. The resettlement of the former would be represented by the traditional invasions of the Chichimecan cultivators; groups of Chichimecan hunters would thus find routes open to reach even the center of Mexico. In fact the causes of these movements have not yet been investigated but their effects on the history of Central Mexico are sufficiently well-known.

With respect to extrinsic environmental changes it is important to note the fact that natural resourses are resources only when adequate techniques to exploit them exists. Technological changes in pre-Columbian history produced significant changes of environmental factors in their relation to man. The most important of these were without doubt the invention of agriculture, the acquisition of plant varieties adapted to environmental conditions different from those peculiar to the original habitat of the forest ancestors of the cultivated plants, and the development of systems of cultivation that permitted the efective exploitation of the potentialities of very diverse geographic media. The introduction of the techniques of the Old World since 1492 produced new changes which brought in their wake the displacement of key economic areas and of the cultural centers of gravity. The use of transportation techniques far superior to the pre-Columbian ones altered the significance of distances and permitted easier access to previously marginal regions. The spread of diseases previously nonexistent in America wrought havoc among the population (also in regions not directly affected by the impact of the Conquest) and changes in the geographical distribution of diseases, etc.

It is necessary to pay attention to paleo-geographic studies in order to emphasize the changes which occurred in America both intrinsically and from viewpoint of man's dominance over his environment.

It is necessary to place the different developments of the native cultures in space and time as historical events. It is not enough merely to draw up a description of cultural situations or an abstract analysis — lucid though this could be — of the dynamics of development and cultural change. But it is possible to assign each group its place in relation to general perspectives arrived at in the reconstruction of history, when specifically historical information is lacking. The same should be done with cultural areas within the general outlines of a program of continental scope.

In writing the general history for Native America,

the problem of establishing general periods was expecially complex, for the following reasons: a) the continental scope of and the great differences in the rhythm of the development of native cultures in different parts of the Continent; b) the lack of historical depth in the information available for large areas. A system of cross sections on horizontal segments of historical development serves to tie together at certain time levels the necessarily separate individual histories into Pan American panoramas. (This was much more practical than the attempt to enclose the different regional histories — whose chronology is in many cases indefinite or very doubtful — in chronologically rigid comparative outlines.)

The cross sections set up in following out this idea have been the following: I) up to 3,000 BC, coinciding with the probable beginnings of cultivation in intertropical America — between Mexico and Bolivia — while the rest of the continent was populated by gathering-hunting-fishing groups of various cultural types. In the light of our present knowledge we must assign that minimum antiquity to the beginnings of cultivation in this Hemisphere. It is expected that future discoveries or the confirmation of earlier dates which are still doubtful (for corn in the deepest strata of Bat Cave in New Mexico) would cause the limit to be fixed somewhat earlier. II) around 500 BC, characterized by the appearance of the first definite symptoms of civilization in Mesoamerica and in the Andean area. III) up to AD 1500, empires in Mexico and in Peru, semi-civilized peoples in the intermediate zones; village-dwelling cultivators, of various types and cultural levels, occupying peripheral positions in relation to the nucleus of civilized and semi-civilized groups; marginal cultures of gatherers-hunters-fishers, including in this classification the interior marginal groups pushed back into unfavorable zones, and the outer marginal groups of the Great Plains, the Great Basin, the Pacific region, the northern forests and the Arctic zone (in North America), the Gran Chaco, the Pampas, Patagonia and the Chilean archipelago (in South America). Discovery and the beginning of the era of European-Native interaction, complicated by importation of Africans into the tropical and subtropical regions. IV) Up to AD 1800, marked by the Euro-American (in Haiti, Afro-American) independence movements, the disruption of the colonial systems and the constitution of new socio-political structures, which affected not only the situation of the native groups previously incorporated into the European dominions but also those who had remained free though maintaining some relations with them, and the opening of a new cycle of colonization which affected the Indians in areas that until then had remained outside the compass of European expansion.

Cultural anthropologists recognize various revolutions in the historical development of culture — passage from the state of gathering-hunting-fishing to that of village-dwelling cultivators, from this to

The hunt (drawing by Jaw)

Scenes from Jaw's Sioux childhood.

civilization, and, finally, the change in the character of civilization produced by the Industrial Revolution — whose effects radically change the destiny of mankind. The first revolution is characterized by the cultivation of plants and the domestication of animals (apart from the dog which was domesticated earlier) and by the development of new processing techniques; production of cutting tools made of polished stone, textiles, pottery. The beginnings in some regions of the Continent of ways of life based on cultivation mark the beginning of the first cross-section.

The second revolution — which gives rise to what is called civilization in the strict sense — seems to be associated with increases in productivity due to the development of the techniques of intensive agriculture and to other technological changes. When the Spaniards arrived there was irrigation and terracing both in Peru and in Mesoamerica; archeological data on irrigation on the coast of Peru go back to some centuries before the beginning of the Christian era; the documentary and archeological evidence on irrigation in Mesoamerica are more recent, but that is due to a lack of research on its origins; the beginning of the construction of terraces for cultivation could be equally ancient — from before the start of the Christian era — in both areas. Metallurgy is ancient in Peru, but more recent and less developed in Mesoamerica, where it appeared — according to actually known data — more than a thousand years after the beginning of civilization.

Nevertheless, the most notable changes that characterize this revolution are produced in the economic, social, political and intellectual fields. These are: agrarian production beyond the level of the subsistence and reserve needs of the producers, to produce a surplus, and a social system for the concentration of surpluses; full-time specialization, both in artisan and other activities (government, religion, commerce, war); formal markets, money, external trade, professional traders; social stratification on an economic basis, with domination of the upper class over the means of production (land, water, labor force); political government with concentration of power (instead of tribal democracy), organized war as a political instrument, in order to increase the concentration of surpluses, resulting in the formation of empires; theistic religion, temples, sacerdotal hierarchy; legal system and judicial organization; writing, mathematics, astronomy, calendar (and the monopoly of this knowledge as an instrument of domination); urban centers (political, religious, commercial) sustained by revenue from the land, tribute and income from trade. This revolution changed the moral order — the relationships between men and the attitude toward the Universe.

With regard to writing, it should be noted that it was hieroglyphic in Mesoamerica; although in Incan Peru writing was not known, Quipu, and other mnemonic aids were used as a substitute to register data. The question of pre-Incan writing is debatable. Authors consider the figured beans found on the northern coast and their painted representation on the Mochican ceramics as ideograms possibly used for divinatory purposes, but not as evidence of a true system of writing. In the art of the Paracas-Necropolis culture of the southern coast and later in the Tiahuanaco style symbols similar to the painted beans on the Mochican ceramics were used as decorative elements. The representation of isolated ideograms does not constitute a system of writing and, consequently, the evidence inferred to date is not sufficient proof of the existence of pre-Incan writing.

The cultural phenomena mentioned appear to be associated with the birth and development of the ancient civilizations of Mesoamerica and Peru, as with that of Mesopotamia, Egypt, the Valley of India, and China. The appearance of these diagnostic elements defines the state of civilization, as an evolutionary development from the barbaric state. Suffice it to say that we do not have archeological data on the appearance of some of these cultural phenomena either in Mesoamerica or in Peru; although they were present in the civilizations at the time of discovery, we cannot trace the history of their origin and development. Nevertheless, archeological evidence does exist on the antiquity of many of them and these traits permit us to date the appearance of civilization in America. The functional interrelation between the different traits which define the degree of civilization aid in the hypothetical reconstruction of the history of those who did not leave material testimony. The appearance of traits of civilization in Mesoamerica and in Peru serves to mark off the second cross-section.

The decision to take the cultural revolutions in nuclear America as the basis for making these cross-sections is justified by the fact that each of these revolutions generated processes of acculturation (through diffusion of ideas, material diffusion or movements of peoples) that influenced the later cultural development of large areas of the Continent.

The selection of the approximate date of 1500 for the third cross-section appears to be in contradiction to the comments made during the meeting of collaborators of the Program held in Havana in January 1953. These observations were related to the undoubted fact that the first contact between European civilization and the native cultures occurred at very diverse epochs in different regions of the Hemisphere. Nevertheless, it seems very important to establish a cross-section for 1500 for the following reasons: the particular cultures of the native peoples of America — technology and economy and their effects on the people in forms of social and political organization — exercised a decisive influence on the events of discovery and conquest, more than did geographic position or historical accident. Francisco Hernandez de Cordoba would not have had immediate followers if he had not discovered in Yucatan peoples more civilized than any

Battle scene from Mexican painting, Aubin-Goupil collection.

of those found up to that time in the Indies, and Hernan Cortes would not have undertaken the journey to the Mexican altiplano had it not been for the fame of the riches and power of a great man called Moctezuma. Along the Pacific, Peru was conquered at an early date, after countless difficulties had been overcome in order to reach it, while a region such as California, discovered early, accessible by sea from New Spain and situated on the return route from the Philippines, remained outside the currents of colonization until very recent times, in spite of the attractions it offered for European settlement. The difference is based on the fact that in Peru there was a rich empire to conquer as the prize for adventure; in California there were only groups of fishermen and gatherers from whom nothing could be obtained. Again with reference to Peru, the news of the voyage of Alejo Garcia and the reports of the Guaranis about a fabulously rich empire in the west promoted the interest of the Spaniards in the prairies of the Gran Chaco as a route of access to that empire, resulting in early exploratory expeditions across inhospitable regions which did not in themselves offer attractions for the conquistadores. French penetration by way of the Saint Lawrence River and Dutch penetration by way of the Hudson was based on the existence of the Algonquin hunters of the forests from whom fine pelts were obtained. The presence of the warlike Botocudo on the natural route of access from the coast to the interior altiplano of southeast Brazil, the valley of the Rio Doce, impeded the use of this route by the Portuguese colonists, and that, as a consequence of the Indian raids on the Portuguese and mestizo settlements during the Colonial epoch, the section of the coast between Campos and Bahia is still sparsely populated today. Let these examples suffice; It is unnecessary and would be tiresome to enlarge further on this point.

In addition to the different influences (positive and negative) brought to bear by the diversity of aboriginal cultures on the conquest and colonization — and even on the events of discovery — European penetration in some parts of the hemisphere resulted in very active changes and movements. Of course, in the zones affected by early colonization the processes of acculturation began immediately. Nevertheless, with reference to the unsubdued Incas of Vilcabamba, even resistence to the conquest brought about acculturation which in this case was more active than that experienced by the subdued Indians. Moreover, the effects of these changes and movements made themselves felt in regions far away from the first European settlements long before direct contact between European civilization and local cultures took place. It is necessary to take into account also the fact that the internal dynamics of the cultures and the processes of acculturation between native groups were operating at the same time, independently or in addition to those external disruptive forces. If we wish to present a panorama of aboriginal America which faithfully reflects the situation prior to the disruption of the independent development of the aboriginal cultures which resulted from the discovery, we must adopt 1500 for a cross-section.

To be sure, at the present state of our knowledge it would be impossible to present an integral and truthful picture of the American cultural situation at the time of Columbus, but that should serve to stimulate research oriented toward reconstruction of the earlier condition of those cultures known only in a form already modified by direct impact, indirect influences or factors independent of the European expansion. This should be done by combining archeological and ethnological-historical methods, and inquiries.

The fourth cross-section (about 1800), that is, in the epoch of the movements for independence, is based on the fact that the situation existing at that date represents the results of the Indian policies of the colonial powers; of the varying effects of a more or less lengthy period of acculturation or at least of reception — directly or through intermediaries — of cultural influences emanating from the centers of colonization; and of all kinds of disturbances which had affected even the native groups on regions not yet included at that time within the areas of European colonization. Moreover, this situation affected the characteristics (Euro-American, Indian-mestizo, or Afro-American) of the developing nationalities, almost all of which received from the colonial powers the legacy of various "indigenous problems" which persist to our day and have affected to different degrees the national integration of the new states. In the area of nuclear America, where three centuries of colonial rule had resulted in relative stabilization insofar as the position of the Indian is concerned, the completion of independence unleashed new forces which affected the socio-economic situation of the natives and the processes of acculturation. At the same time, the effects of the Industrial Revolution on over-populated Europe, the subsequent influx of European immigrants to North and South America, and the increasing demands for food and raw materials for the peoples and industries of Europe motivated the expansion of the zones of cultivation and of stockraising and mining. This produced colonization movements toward areas not directly affected during the 1500-1800 cycle. From the point of view of its effects on the native groups, the new cycle of colonization is especially evident in those countries where there remained ample extent of territory cultivable with European techniques or suitable for stockraising, principally Canada, the United States and Argentina, or mineral resources not yet utilized in 1800. But to differing degrees it affected even the countries with an ancient colonial tradition.

These cross-sections divide the history of pre-Columbian America into three stages. A fourth is constituted by native history during the colonial and national periods. We thus obtain the following divisions: 1)Pre-agricultural stage, from the arrival of the first immigrants on American soil — certainly more than 12,000 years ago, possibly more than 25,000 — until the beginning of plant cultivation about 3,000 , or earlier, in inter-tropical America. 2)Proto-agricultural stage, from about 3,000 to 500. Village dwelling cultivators in the nuclear zone; expansion of cultivation from the original centers toward the Southwest and west of the United States and undoubtedly also toward South America, although there we do not know the historical details apart from the Peruvian coast and the central Andes. (The carbon 14 dates referring to the beginnings of agriculture in South America outside of the Central Andean area date the Saladero culture, which marks the appearance of cultivation and ceramics in the lower Orinoco, between *c*. 950-600 (dates Y-42: 2860 ± 130, 2880 ± 30; Y-43: 2700 ± 130; Y-44: 2570 ± 130). Contemporary dates for the Ortoire culture of Trinidad, still preceramic, confirm what was supposed, that these skills were spread from the Continent to Trinidad with some delay (Y-260-1: 2750 ± 130; Y-260-2:2760 ± 130). From the appearance of the civilizations of Mesoamerica and the Andean area, about 500 until 1500. Development of the civilizations mentioned to the point of empire formation, in both Mexico and Peru; diffusion of cultural elements which originated in the civilized areas outward to their periphery. Expansion of the village dwelling cultivators until they occupied nearly all the remaining regions cultivable without the plow. 4) Colonial Period. Progressive reduction of independent territories. Demographic changes of great magnitude occurred not only in the regions occupied by Europeans and their African slaves but also outside of them. Populations decreased in size or were exterminated, owing to the transmission of diseases, cultural readjustments or the fact of the conquest itself. Because the elite in the areas of native civilization (Mexico-Guatemala and Peru-Bolivia) was destroyed or assimilated, many aspects of the higher cultures disappeared, but the rural sub-cultures in the same areas were affected less and influenced the formation of the regional variants in the culture of the conquerors. In general, the tendency, from the indigenous point of view, was that of cultural impoverishment. There was, of course, acculturation, but also "de-culturation," that is to say the loss of cultural elements or complexes without compensating substitution, and cultural disintegration. In addition to the changes occurring in the colonized regions, European impact influenced history in the areas situated outside of the zones dominated by the conquerors, producing phenomena such as the formation of the equestrian cultures of North and South America. 5) National Period. Demographic recuperation of the indigenous groups in some zones of the hemisphere, which had old colonial tradition and opening of a new cycle of Euro-American expansion which resulted in the destruction (in some cases to the point of extermination) of Indian populations until then

relatively unaffected, both in North and South America. Important modifications in the situation of the native communities incorporated into the national states as a result of the application of the philosophy of liberal, egalitarian individualism, and later of the policy of directed *indigenismo* attempted in some countries in the twentieth century.

During the pre-Columbian period the differences in rhythm of historical development in different parts of the hemisphere are very notable. The suspension of the most backward marginal peoples on a paleomesolithic cultural level contrasts with the advanced degree of civilization reached in some areas. Between these extremes we encounter differentiation along an extremely varied range of cultural types. The fact that impulses arising in the western regions of inter-tropical America were the principal agents of cultural transformation in much of the hemisphere justifies the designation "nuclear America" applied to this zone. The cultural areas in which the pre-agricultural stage persisted to the time of European discovery and conquest are located in a marginal position with respect to the necleus. In the nuclear zone, with advanced native civilizations, the colonial systems were established on the basis of exploitation of the Indian, while outside of it the conquest meant his expulsion or anihilation and substitution by European immigrants or African slaves. As a consequence, it has been in nuclear America that the native peoples have persisted as a predominant component of the population, either segregated — in Indian communities or in various forms of peonage — or forming the large popular masses, physically and culturally mixed. That is to say, the importance of the nuclear zone in the indigenous history persisted, although with different significance, throughout the colonial and national periods.

To conclude these considerations of method, it is necessary to note that the history of the stages prior to 1500 was reconstructed with materials which differ greatly from those utilized in writing colonial and national history, since outside of Mesoamerica and Peru the American Indian remained "pre-historic" until the time of discovery. Even in the areas where a developed historical consciousness existed, the methods used to record history, including the hieroglyphic writing of Mesoamerica, were mere mnemonic aids to assist the oral transmission of historical traditions. Moreover, as a logical consequence, the greater part of the data recorded by these means and which have reached us refer to times shortly before the discovery. The history of pre-Columbian America has to be reconstructed by archeological and ethnological techniques with the aid of very diverse sciences: historical linguistics, geology, paleontology, paleo-climatology, nuclear physics, etc. Because of the dissimilarity of methods utilized by the historians of the colonial and national periods, who work on the basis of the written documents that form the raw materials of history, and the pre-Columbian period, more emphasis is placed on the study of material culture for the stages prior to the European discovery and conquest. This is necessary since data on the moral and intellectual aspects of culture obtainable by means of archeology are less abundant and precise. In the majority of cases, features of these aspects have to be deduced on the basis of the material remains or by applying the method of comparative ethnology, which does not always guarantee certainty in the inferred conclusions. On the other hand, for the post-Columbian period we have at our disposal more studies on the history of the non-material aspects of culture — religious conversion, changes in the socioeconomic structure, etc. — than of the changes which have taken place in the material aspects of daily life — usages, techniques, etc.

The chronological framework of pre-colonial history is based on data which differ from those which can be utilized by the historians of the later periods. The pre-Columbian chronology is based on the following: a) geological and paleontological evidence, which demonstrate the presence of man in America during the Pleistocene and the relationships existing between the cultures of the most ancient hunters and gatherers, species of extinct fauna, glacial phenomena (from the last glaciation) and the ecological changes that took place at the beginning of the post-glacial epoch. b) the carbon 14 method of dating based on the content of this radioactive element in organic matter that has in the space of the last five years revolutionized our knowledge of the absolute chronology of pre-Columbian history; c) the method of dating by annual tree rings (dendrochronology), first applied to prehistoric dates in 1928, which has furnished an absolute time scale for the archeology of the Southwest of the United States (now reaching back to 58 BC) and has been used also to date the "culture of the Arctic forests" in the interior of Alaska; in the Southwestern United States dendrochronology is based on the effects of annual variations of moisture, in Alaska on variations of temperature; d) pre-Columbian written history, only in Mesoamerica where the hieroglyphic inscriptions of the Mayan Long Count — principally preserved in monuments, such as sculptured stelae, lintels, etc. — furnish us dates for the history of the development of civilization in that area during the greater part of the first millenium of the Christian era, although the correlation between this count and our calendar has not yet been determined with unassailable precision, and where there were also some historical books which have been preserved to our day and data contained in others which have been destroyed or lost since the Spanish conquest were incorporated in written histories at the beginning of the colonial period; e) traditional history, transmitted orally in many cases by means of epic songs and transcribed in the colonial chronicles both in Mesoamerica and in the Andean altiplano and the Peruvian coast; the believable chronology contained in them covers only a few generations before the arrival of the Spaniards, but, it

is very important insofar as it refers to the origins and expansion of Mexico and Inca empires; and f) relative chronology established by means of typology or stratigraphic series where there are no dates obtained by some other method or in conjunction with them where they exist. Chronologies based on systematic analysis of archeological evidence were first set up at the start of the first decade of the twentieth century for Peru, in the last years of the second decade for Mexico, in the third for the Southwestern United States, later for the Eskimo areas, and beginning in 1940 for western North America and California. In recent years much progress has been made in the formulation of a chronological outline for the circum-Caribbean area. There still remain some areas of this Hemisphere where we completely lack time scales; in such cases we have to apply ethno-historical methods and utilize the data furnished by linguistics or by physical anthropology — which are also scarce — to try to reconstruct the general lines of history, while yet unable to arrive at a precise chronology.

HOBOMOK (Wampanoag; fl. early 17th century) was a Wampanoag chief who was a life-long friend of the English at Plymouth Colony from the time he met them in 1621. He was a great favorite of Massasoit (q.v.), and with Squanto (q.v.) he became the colonists' guide to the surrounding Indians. In August 1621 he was captured together with Squanto and another Indian by Corbitant (q.v.) as part of a plot to weaken both the colonists and Massasoit. Hobomok escaped, however, and warned the colonists who, under the command of Myles Standish, captured Corbitant and smashed his conspiracy.

HOHOKAM culture, which is dated 300BC-AD1400, refers to the ancestors of the Pima Indians of present-day Arizona. The people of the "Hohokam" (A Pima Indian word meaning "those who have gone") culture, farmed their arid lands by means of extensive canal irrigation. Some of these canals were five feet wide and five feet deep. Corn was grown as the staple food, supplemented by wild beans and cactus.

Both basketry and pottery were highly developed by the Hohokam people. Most villages had a large ball court of hard packed earth, similar to those used by the Maya Indians of Central America.

HOH RESERVATION, in Jefferson County, Washington, is 443 acres of land which belongs to several dozen Hoh Indians.

All the reservation land is tribally-owned. The Hoh tribe has shared in an awarded claims judgment for the Quileute and Hoh Indians amounting to $112,152.

The Hoh Reservation was established by Executive order of September 11, 1893. The Hoh are considered to be a part of the Quileute Tribe, but are recognized as a separate tribal group. Funds from cutting timber on the reservation are in deposit for use in tribal development programs.

The Hoh Indians were part of the Coastal Indian culture of the Pacific Northwest which flourished in the moist coastal strip, their lives built around a natural abundance of fish and forests. Many coastal tribes made fine basketry and wood carvings, and Indians of the Juan de Fuca Strait were famed for blankets loom-woven of dog hair. Salmon was the foremost food and many tribal beliefs and ceremonies centered around salmon. The second most important natural wealth was wood, particularly the western red cedar. Although strong and durable, it was easily worked with primitive tools. In the highly materialistic culture of the Pacific Northwest, the skillfully crafted gabled lodges helped proclaim the prestige of the owners. Steamed and bent cedar was fashioned into boxes, buckets, serving dishes, and utensils. Cedar bark supplied clothing, mats, furnishings, and rope. Wealth determined leadership in this property-conscious culture, and the elaborate social structure included a hereditary nobility, a middle class, and a slave class of war captives and their descendants.

As a result of Public Law 89-655 providing for a basic role of the tribe, a constitution was adopted on May 24, 1969, and approved on July 1, 1969. This constitution authorized the election of a tribal business committee.

HOH. A tribe living on the Lower Hoh River Reservation located on the Pacific Coast of Washington's Olympic Peninsula at the mouth of the Hoh River. Historically one of the three principal bands of Quileute (q.v.) speakers (along with the Quileute River and Goodman Creek communities), they include the rainforested slopes of Mount Olympus and the entire Hoh River drainage in their aboriginal area. The reservation was established by executive order in 1893 and had a population of 76 in 1977.

HOKAN-SIOUAN (Hokan-Coahuiltecan). This phylum (group of languages related more remotely than those of a family or stock) consists of rather diverse groups of languages which may stem from an original strain. Yet the affinities between the Hokan groups (California, Lower Colorado, Texas Coast, possibly Iroquoian), Coahuiltecan (Gulf languages), and Siouan (Plains) are less easily discerned. Communication .

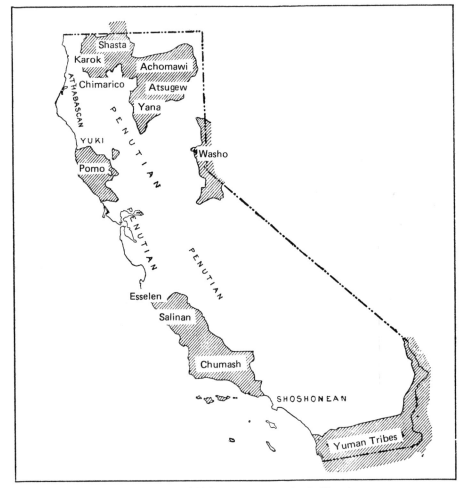

Distribution of Hokan Language in California.

HOLAPPA, THEODORE R. (Chippewa; Feb. 28, 1945–), was the administrator of the Comprehensive Health Service Center of the Keweenaw Bay Indian Community on the L'Anse Reservation at Baraga, Michigan, and chief judge of the tribal court in the late 1970s. Born at Zeba, Michigan, he graduated from Wisconsin State University at Eau Claire in 1968 and did graduate work at the University of Colorado.

HOLE IN THE DAY (Chippewa; ?–1846) succeeded Curly Head as war chief of the Noka (Bear) clan in 1825 and continued the ancient feud with the Dakota (Sioux). He had already been recognized as a chief by the U.S. government for his bravery and fidelity to the Americans during the War of 1812. He spent the rest of his life fighting with the Dakota, and he ended the struggle that had lasted for centuries over the possession of the fisheries and the hunting grounds of the Lake Superior region by definitively driving the hereditary enemy across the Mississippi River.

Hole in the Day threatened to plant his village on the Minnesota River and chase the Dakota even farther into the western Plains, but the U.S. government intervened and compelled the warring tribes to accept a line of demarcation. At Prairie du Chien, Wisconsin, he acknowledged the ancient possession by the Dakota of the territory from the Mississippi to Green Bay and the head of Lake Superior, but he claimed it for the Chippewa by reason of conquest. George Copway (*q.v.*), who valued the friendship of Hole in the Day and once ran 270 miles in four days to warn him about a Dakota raid, related how he almost converted the old chief to Christianity. According to Copway, Hole in the Day promised to embrace Christianity and to urge his people to do so also "after one more battle with the Sioux." He was succeeded as head chief of the Chippewa on his death in 1846 by his son, who bore his father's name.

HOLE IN THE DAY (Chippewa; *c.* 1825–June 27, 1868) succeeded his father as head chief of the Chippewa in 1846 and pursued the same aggressive policy against the hated Dakota (Sioux). At the time of the Sioux uprising in Minnesota in 1862, he was accused of planning a similar revolt. He was murdered by men of his own tribe at Crow Wing, Minnesota in 1868.

HOLLOWBREAST, DONALD (Northern Cheyenne; May 17, 1917–), is an artist and an editor. Hollowbreast, who is also known as Maxhebaho (Big Black), was born at Birney, Montana. Interested in painting since he was a child, he began to paint with oils in 1950. Subsequently, he began experimenting with other media. Since

Hole In The Day.

1959, Hollowbreast has been the editor of the *Birney Arrow*.

HOLLOW HORN BEAR (Brulé Dakota; March 1850– March 15, 1913) was a chief who first became famous in the Plains Wars of the 1860s; he later negotiated settlements with Gen. George Crook and then became something of a favorite in Washington, attending two inaugural parades and getting his picture on a 14-cent postage stamp and a 5-dollar silver certificate.

Hollow Horn Bear was born in Sheridan County, Nebraska. At the age of 16, he was raiding the Pawnee with Dakota war parties. In 1868 he helped attack U.S. troops, first in Wyoming, then in Montana; in 1869 he began to raid Union Pacific Railroad laborers. After hostilities died down, he was appointed captain of the police at the Rosebud Agency, South Dakota. To him fell the duty of arresting Crow Dog for the murder of Spotted Tail. He resigned his post later because of illness.

Hollow Horn Bear was also a famous orator, and because of this he was chosen by his tribe in 1889 to negotiate with General Crook at the Rosebud Agency. In 1905 the chief attended the presidential inauguration of Theodore Roosevelt, and in 1913 he led the Indian contingent in the parade down Pennsylvania Avenue for the inauguration of Woodrow Wilson. On that visit to Washington, he caught pneumonia and died there on March 15, 1913.

HOLLYWOOD RESERVATION, in Broward County, Florida, is 481 acres of land belonging to nearly 400 Seminole Indians. All land is tribally-owned. In addition to the three Seminole federal reservations, the State of Florida has set aside approximately 104,000 acres adjoining the Big Cypress Reservation called the Florida State Indian Reservation, jointly administered by the Seminole Tribe (northern portion) and the Miccosukee Tribe (southern portion). The Seminoles enjoy hunting and fishing rights on this land, most of which is swamp.

The people who came to be known as "Seminole" (the name means "wild people") were Yamasee, driven from the Carolinas in 1715, Hitchiti-speaking Oconee from the Apalachicola River, and Creeks from the Chattahoochee River area, all of whom moved into Florida to excape the whites. Their ranks were swelled by fugitive slaves who found refuge and freedom among the Indians. Attempts by owners to recover these fugitives led to Andrew Jackson's campaigns in 1814 and 1818. The Seminole were united by hostility and fear they felt toward their common foe, the young United States. In 1821 Florida was annexed by the United States, and pressure by white settlers for the Seminole lands and farms led to an attempt in 1832 to remove the Indians west of the Mississippi by force. Chief Osceola's wife was seized as a fugitive, and bloody warfare followed as the Seminoles, under the leadership of Osceola, fought bitterly. When Osceola was captured under a flag of truce, some of his warriors fled into the Everglades. Later a portion of the tribe was transported to Oklahoma where they formed one of the Five Civilized tribes. A truce between the Florida Seminoles and the United States was finally concluded in 1934, and another such treaty in 1937.

With the withdrawal of troops, yet in constant fear of being captured and sent west, the Seminole lived in scattered locations and pursued a nomadic existence mostly by hunting and fishing. They lived in small houses built with cypress poles and thatched with palmetto leaves. On the Hollywood Reservation, however, modern dwellings have replaced the old shelters. Deerskin leggings have been replaced by cloth trousers. The clothing is colorful and difficult to make. Tunics and overblouses are laboriously made of different strips of colored cloth sewed into long rows and stitched together. Seminole folk arts, including dollmaking, are an important source of income. The turban, once the headdress of every Seminole brave, has been replaced by the 10-gallon hat. Seasonal Green Corn and Hunting Dances are still performed and are occasions for meetings and festivities.

The Seminole tribe's constitution was ratified in 1957. The tribe has an elected five-member tribal council as its governing body. All problems relating to government, law and order, education, welfare, and recreation are handled through standing committees. Authority for the development and management of tribal resources has been delegated to the council.

HONDURAS. Centuries before the arrival of the first Spaniards, the area of western Honduras harbored the Old Mayan Empire, one of the hemisphere's most advanced civilizations. This culture apparently arose toward the end of the fourth century AD and flourished until the eighth or ninth century. Among other things, its people charted the movements of the sun, moon, and planets, devised methods of writing, constructed elaborate religious centers, and traded over wide areas. Actually composed of semi-independent villages and religious centers, this so-called empire's major works were concentrated in an area near the modern village of Copan.

Around the time of Charlemagne, however, the more advanced parts of this culture forsook Honduras and shifted some 250 miles northward to Mexico's Yucatan Peninsula. When the Spaniards arrived in the early sixteenth century, they found some relatively advanced Indians but scant trace of the Mayas' former glory. Jungles had long since covered over the major cities, and it was not until the nineteenth century that archaeologists began the slow process of restoration that has made the Copan region a major center for scholarly investigation and one of modern Honduras' foremost points of interest to foreign visitors.

The major Indian groups present when the Spaniards arrived showed features of four major cultures. In the western and central highlands, concentrated around the Comayagua and Ulua valleys, lived tribes who were strongly influenced by the Maya and who traded extensively with remnants of Mayan culture to the north. Southern Honduras contained an

ALABASTER VASE, HONDURAS

enclave of peoples speaking Nahuatl who owed their language and probably some of their cultural patterns to advanced civilizations from other parts of Mexico, while the tribes along Honduras' north coast had their roots in the Carib-Arawak culture that dominated the islands of the Caribbean Sea. To the east, centering on the Valley of Olancho, were warlike tribes showing some characteristics of cultures influenced by the Chibcha civilization of northern Columbia.

Compared to the Old Maya or Chibcha cultures,

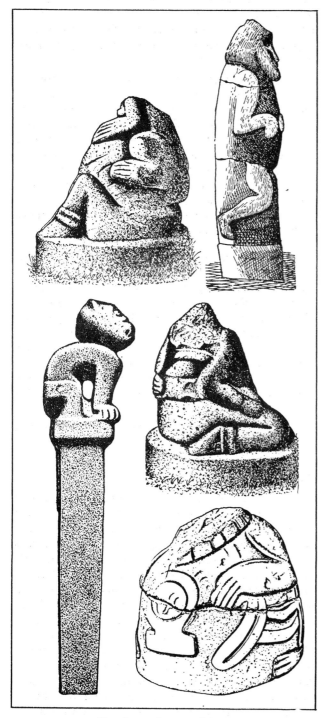

Honduras stone sculptures.

none of the Honduran tribal groupings were particularly advanced; most of their villages were only tenuously tied into federations owing loyalty to a regional chief. This lack of effective organization tended to prevent immediate resistance to the Spanish expeditions that roamed the territory in the first quarter of the sixteenth century.

DISCOVERY AND CONQEST

Christopher Columbus discovered Honduras in 1502 during his fourth and final voyage, in the course of which he stopped at one of the small Bay Islands (Islas de la Bahia) off the Atlantic coast and then crossed over to the mainland. The Spaniards made no attempt to occupy the area until the 1520s, however, after the conquest of Mexico by Hernan Cortes, the establishment of a permanent colony in Panama, and exploration by Gil Gonzalez Davila from Panama up to the Bay of Fonseca in 1522 and 1523.

In 1524 four competing expeditions set out to seize Honduras. One was led by Gonzalez Davila, who sailed from Spain with royal permission to take over the regions already explored; another, loyal to Pedro Arias de Avila (known popularly as Pedrarias), the governor of Panama, set out from Nicaragua. Hernan Cortes dispatched a third expedition from Mexico, but its leader renounced his authority, whereupon Cortes dispatched yet another party.

Ferocious fighting ensued between these four groups and prompted Cortes to personally lead a fifth expedition into Honduras in 1525. He arrived at what is now part of extreme northeastern Guatemala just in time to replenish the supplies of the few remaining Spaniards there; he then moved them to the mouth of the Ulua River, site of the modern Honduran town of Puerto Cortes. Pushing on, Cortes found about forty more colonists at the only other settlement, that of Trujillo, on the northeast coast. His presence quelled most disputes and established a measure of peace among the Spaniards until his departure in 1526.

Honduras' first royal administrator, Diego Lopez de Salcedo, was installed as governor of the territory in 1526. Although his leadership was uninspired, the mere presence of a royally appointed official helped maintain stability in the area. From this time on, rivalries were generally limited to territorial disputes between neighboring areas or conflicts between two or more persons claiming royal authority to govern. Such disputes occurred frequently but tended to produce involved legal controversies rather than the bloodshed of the first few years.

Meanwhile, Indian problems helped unite the Spanish colonists. The natives along the north coast had offered little opposition, but the more advanced and better organized tribes in the hinterlands were determined to resist subjugation. A Spanish attempt to establish permanent centers in the western highlands culminated in a major war from 1537 to 1539. This resistance was directed by a powerful young chieftain known to the Spaniards as Lempira, or "Lord of the Mountain." The colonists estimated that he dominated about 200 towns and commanded up to 30,000 warriors; his followers believed him to be invincible.

Lempira's uprising centered on a stronghold constructed by his forces about fifteen miles south of Gracias a Dios. Known as the Penol de Cerquin, it proved impregnable to the Spaniards until they arranged for a truce to conduct negotiations. Instead of negotiating, however, they killed Lempira and launched a successful all-out attack on his stunned followers in the Penol. The great fortress' fall was the turning point of the revolt, though fighting continued for several months.

Suppression of this revolt consolidated Spanish control over the area and paved the way for establishment of the *repartimiento* and *encomienda* systems throughout the interior. These Spanish institutions were used to obtain a work force for the colonists, who regarded themselves as an upper class and were generally unwilling to engage in routine manual labor. *Repartimiento,* a system of dividing up Indian groups and apportioning their members among individual Spaniards as slaves was employed in many parts of the New World. Though it caused severe hardship among Honduras' Indians in the first years of the Spanish conquest, the combined opposition of many local officials and the Spanish crown caused the use of *repartimiento* to decline after about 1530.

Instead, what predominated in most parts of Honduras was the *encomienda* system, which granted individual Spaniards the right to a certain amount of labor from Indians living on a given parcel of land. Such Spaniards were theoretically responsible for the well-being of their charges, but the system was widely abused.

Because of this treatment, diseases brought from the Old World, and extreme hardships associated with the rebellion of 1537 to 1539, the Indian population declined precipitously. Precise figures are not available, but there may have been as many as 500,000 Indians in the area when the Spaniards arrived. Robert Chamberlain in *the Conquest and Colonization of Honduras* suggests that this Indian population may have been reduced to 36,000 by 1547. This devastation seems all the more remarkable when account is taken of the tiny number of Spanish colonists involved. As of 1542 the total population of Honduras appears to have included less than 250 Spaniards.

Indians

When the Spaniards arrived, they encountered many Indian tribes; the strongest and most numerous were the Lenca, who occupied much of the central and southwest territory extending into El Salvador.

Two general groupings were present at the time of the conquest; each comprised numerous Indian tribes. The settled agricultural peoples, including the Lenca and groups related to the Maya of Guatemala, inhabited the southwest and western highlands. Seminomadic peoples, who depended primarily on hunting and fishing and only secondarily on agriculture for their livelihood, inhabited parts of the central highlands and the northern lowlands; their culture was related to that of the South American rain forest peoples. Moreover, the north coastal area came under English influence early and remained remote from Honduran government control until the mid-nineteenth century. Some of the settled highland agricultural peoples were the ones with whom the Spanish made contact and who contributed to the present *ladino* culture. Their culture was more advanced than that of the lowlands, and the people were less isolated and, for the most part, more amenable to acculturation.

For these reasons official government policy toward the two groups has been different since independence. The Indians of the southwest were treated more liberally than those of the northern lowlands; with some notable exceptions, no special separate laws were designed to govern them. These Indians, in contact with *ladinos,* were subject to acculturating processes. The Indians still remaining in the southwest, though more numerous than those of the northern lowlands, are subject to continual erosion of what little remains of their traditional culture.

The so-called Forest Indians of the northern lowlands, on the other hand, were subject to a more aggressive program, particularly after control of the area was relinquished by the English in 1860. The clergy played an important role in establishing schools and permanent settlements among these seminomadic peoples in addition to converting them to Catholicism. This policy was particularly successful among the Jicaque Indians of the department of Yoro, most of whom were to a great degree absorbed into *ladino* culture. A small band of them retreated into the highlands, however, where they have maintained many of their traditions.

The Lenca

In the 1970s the Lenca constituted about 70 percent of all the Indians in the country. They were concentrated in the mountainous region of the southwest in the departments of Intibuca (the only department in which Indians constituted a majority of the population in the early 1970s), La Paz and, to a lesser extent, Lempira. When the Spaniards arrived, they were also found farther north in what is now Francisco Morazan, but these inhabitants either contributed to the *ladino* culture of Honduras by mixing with the Spaniards or retreated to the southwest. The origins of Lenca culture are somewhat uncertain; some scholars hypothesized that they were of South American origin. Nevertheless, Middle American influences had affected the Lenca area by the time of the conquest, and they were culturally similar to the Maya.

Northeast coast Honduras pottery types.

In the 1970s they were a modified Indian group; that is, the traits that served to distinguish them from their *ladino* neighbors were important, but their similarities were many. They were not unified as a group, however; municipal cultures had developed since the conquest, and each had its own amalgam of traits. Lenca migrations to the banana plantations of the north coast, to the coffee areas, and the mines are common. Moreover, the Lenca are in constant contact with the *ladinos* who live among them, and they are changing as a result.

Certain aspects of their economy served to separate the Lenca from their *ladino* neighbors. Most of the Lenca lands were owned by the community; their distribution varied from muncipality to municipality. Such lands were often parceled out for lifetime use to individuals who were, in effect, owners although they held no formal titles. Sometimes, as in the case of the municipality of Guajiquiro, the land was worked in true communal fashion. This system was introduced by the Spanish but taken over by Indians, as was the case with many aspects of Spanish culture.

In the 1970s exchange labor between Lenca men was common. Most Lenca used the digging stick to sow seed, a practice not common among *ladinos,* who have adopted the plow and other more sophisticated agricultural techniques. Moreover, Lenca women work in the fields, uncommon among *ladinos.* The Lenca grow corn, wheat, plantains, and beans, among other crops. Traditional taboos are practiced at various times in the agricultural cycle.

The Lenca have retained handicraft industries and depend on regional and local markets throughout their area for distribution and acquisition of goods. The production of nets, baskets, and pottery is still important; the spinning and weaving of cloth have disappeared, though women still make by hand their characteristic costume, an adaptation of nineteenth-century colonial style dress, consisting of a wide skirt and loose blouse. Most towns that had markets held them on Thursdays and Sundays; some attracted only local people, whereas others were attended by traders from throughout the Lenca area and from El Salvador. Most of the Lenca traveled on foot and carried their produce on their backs; the topography may have prevented their adopting more modern methods, the southwest highlands being the highest and most rugged in the country.

Some towns retained an only slightly changed form of their ancient political organization and had in them certain vestiges of the ancient tribal organizations; in some towns as late as the 1960s, the headman inherited his office. In most towns, however, the setup was much the same as in *ladino* towns, including a mayor, councilmen, and others. Nevertheless, there was evidence that in some towns a group of village elders in consultation with a few other men of the municipality actually chose the officials, and their choices were merely confirmed in the election.

The Lenca are Catholic, although they have retained many of their aboriginal beliefs in syncretic form with Catholicism. The religious and political organizations in Lenca municipalities were kept separate, a situation patterned on that of the *ladino.* The *ladino* and Indian religious organizations were similar, although they were kept separate. In Intibuca religious brotherhoods were responsible for raising money to pay for their respective fiestas and to guard religious property; reliable information was not available for other towns.

The fiestas are an important part of the town's activities; most important is the fiesta of the town's patron saint. In Intibuca this fiesta for the Virgen de la Candelaria lasts for nine days in February. An unusual ceremony was an integral part of this fiesta. The town was visited by the patron saint of Yamaringuila, a neighboring town. In turn, the patron saint of Intibuca visited Yamaringuila during its patron saint's day in December. *Guancasco* is the term for this reciprocal visiting of patron saints, which is carried out between other towns in Honduras. Religious ritual also accompanies the crucial activities of the agriculturally oriented lives of the Lenca, such as the planting and the harvest. At such times much *chicha* (an alcoholic beverage) is drunk; copal incense is burned; offerings are sometimes made to the sun, which is revered among the Lenca as a powerful life force; and dances are performed.

The social structure and family life were similar to those of *ladinos,* with important exceptions. In most Lenca towns the people were divided into an upper and a lower class, the upper class being composed of the village headman, his family, and the elders. Marriages were most often arranged by the parents, though the couple would not be forced into an unwanted union. A period of trial marriage in the home of the girl's parents sometimes preceded the actual marriage. Most newly married couples established residences apart from their parents, although it was not uncommon for them to move in temporarily with either the girl's or the boy's family. Men were permitted to have more than one wife, and polygyny was not uncommon.

The acculturated Indians of Santa Barbara and El Paraiso

In the early 1970s in the departments of Santa Barbara and El Paraiso there existed numerous pockets of highly acculturated Indians who retained only a few distinct traits, but these were sufficient to set them somewhat apart from the *ladinos* even though many of their members were racially *mestizos.* The antecedents of the two groups are uncertain; no Indian languages were spoken in either area. The Indians of Santa Barbara are probably descendants of the Lenca, although they may be related to the neighboring Jicaque or Chorti. The Indians of El Paraiso are probably descendants of the Matagalpa.

The Indians of Santa Barbara lived in the east-central part of the department, most of them in municipalities located along two tributaries of the Ulua River. In the early 1970s the largest group of these Indians was found in the municipality of Llama, but their numbers there probably did not exceed 2,800. Unlike most Indian areas, this one was not located in an isolated area. On the contrary, it was located along one of the country's main transportation routes, between San Pedro Sula and the department capital of Santa Barbara, that is, in turn, connected by major roads with Tegucigalpa.

It was considered unusual that Indians in such an area had not been completely absorbed into *ladino* culture and had retained remnants of their Indian culture. Most of their lands were community owned, although they were usually worked as if they were privately owned; the worker could even rent out his plot if he so desired. Exchange labor was common in some areas. Most of these Indians used horses and mules for carrying goods. The Indian men's dress was indistinguishable from that of the *ladinos,* but Indian women still wore the wide skirt patterned after Spanish colonial dress. A *guancasco* was carried out between two of the towns, though it varied somewhat from the one held in the Lenca area.

The Indians of El Paraiso were situated in the southwest corner of that department along the border with Nicaragua in a rough highland area accessible only by traveling on foot or horseback. Many of the people are racially *mestizo* though they are culturally Indian. Two of the four principal Indian municipalities of the area retain the customs of *guancasco* and communal landownership.

Other Indians of the West

Two modified Indian groups whose cultures were similar to those of the Lenca lived in the western part of the country. The larger group was the Chorti, numbering several thousand in the early 1970s and inhabiting the forest-covered hills of western Copan Department. They are part of a larger Chorti group that lived in the adjacent department of Chiquimula in Guatemala. The Honduran Chorti are descendants of the Maya Indians who long ago moved into the area from Guatemala. Ruins of one of the greatest centers of the ancient lowland Maya culture are found in this area.

A small isolated group of Pipil Indians was still intact in the municipality of Dolores in Ocotepeque Department on the border with El Salvador; most of the remaining Pipil inhabit the southwest highlands of that country where they constitute the major Indian group. The Pipil are of Mexican origin. They arrived in El Salvador and Honduras sometime after the eleventh century when they were driven out of Mexico by wars that broke up the Toltec Empire there.

The Jicaque of Yoro and the Montana de la Flor

The origins of the Jicaque Indians are not clear. For many years their language was regarded as an isolated

one or one related to Chibchan, spoken in northern South America. In the mid-1950s, on the basis of further research, other scholars classified it as belonging to the Hokan-Siouan language group, primarily spoken by Indians of Mexico and the United States.

In the eighteenth century Christianizing missions were established in the territory of the Jicaque (or the Torrupan, as they are also sometimes called), which extended along the north coast from the Aguan River westward to the Sierra de Omoa and inland to the Lenca territory. The coastal lands of the Jicaque were taken from them when the Black Caribs settled there in the nineteenth century and the Jicaque retreated to the southern part of what is now the department of Yoro.

The absorption of the Jicaque was advanced by the efforts of Father Manuel Jesus de Subirana in the nineteenth century, who gained their confidence, collected them from their scattered settlements into villages, and introduced them to corn agriculture. Their new concentration in the villages, however, made them easy prey to the government's demand for forced labor. Those few who did not become Hispanicized under these influences retreated westward into the highlands in the 1860s and established a remnant colony in the region of Montana de la Flor, which still existed in the 1960s.

By that time the Jicaque of Yoro, much more numerous than those of Montana de la Flor, had been almost completely absorbed in *ladino* culture. Most were bilingual in Spanish and Jicaque. In most other respects, they were culturally similar to poor *ladinos* of the area.

The roughly 300 Jicaque who inhabited a 1,900-acre reservation in Montana de la Flor had few contacts with outsiders and retained a distinctive culture. Most of them spoke only their own language and were descended from the heads of two families that had formed the original colony. Their ruler was an elder who had been appointed by the previous ruler and who had the power to choose his own successor. As a concession to government authorities there was also a mayor with aides, but their power actually was minimal.

Families lived in scattered dwellings, made of planks tied together with vines and roofed with palm leaves. Each household maintained its own garden; various tubers, including *yuca* (starchy root,) potatoes, taro, and yams, were the principal crops grown and constituted the main food staples. Agriculture was supplemented by hunting small game; the preferred weapon was the blowgun loaded with clay pellets. Bows and arrows and traps were also used. Corn and coffee were grown as cash crops on community-worked fields. Group labor for tree cutting, housebuilding, communal planting, and the maintenance of the two roads leading to the reservation was customary.

Some of the religious beliefs showed elements taken from Catholicism probably learned before the migration to the Montana de la Flor. Priests were not allowed on the reservation, however, and baptism was prohibited. These Jicaque believed the sun to be the Supreme Being and feared an evil female goddess named Tsii. The dead were wrapped in bark cloth and buried in an enclosed cemetery. At the foot of some graves crosses were implanted. On top of each grave was a clay pot with a hole in it that, the people believed, permitted the dead to see the sun.

Polygyny was permitted but, because of a shortage of women, was uncommon. Marriages were prearranged at birth, and the girls went to live with their husbands when very young, sometimes under eleven years of age.

Folk remedies for illnesses were the common property of the people; there were no medicine men who had sole access to cures. A form of divination was also common property, by which all manner of things could be ascertained.

Both men and women wore distinctive costumes, although some men dressed in the manner of *ladinos*. The women wore either a long wrapped piece of cloth tucked in at the waist or a blouse and wide skirt, as was worn in colonial times by Spaniards. Men wore a bark cloth or cotton tunic tied at the waist and reaching below the knee.

Lowland Indians of the Northeast: Miskito, Sumo, and Paya

The northeast lowlands, called the Mosquitia, have always been sparsely populated. Small groups of Indians who had relatively few contacts with other peoples populated the area in the 1970s. The Miskito and Sumo Indians inhabited parts of the departments of Colon and Gracias a Dios, the Miskito living nearer to the coast and the Sumo living farther up the rivers of the area that drain into the Caribbean. The Miskito, who may at one time have been a subtribe of the Sumo, showed some Negro traits. In the 1960s these two groups together numbered several thousand. In the mid-1950s the Paya, who inhabited the river towns of Dulce Nombre de Culmi and Santa Maria del

Carbon in the department of Olancho, numbered only a few hundred.

Like the tropical forest people of South America, they lived seminomadic lives in the lowlands where they cultivated tubers and spoke languages related to those of northern South America; the language of the Paya had not been definitely classified by 1960 as had the others, but it was thought to lean toward the same linguistic affiliation.

Before European contact the lowland peoples lived as small, separate groupings, only sometimes sharing a common dialect. They were constantly at war with one another. The Miskito were not a cohesive people before the conquest. The Spanish were not much interested in the Mosquitia because of the climate and the absence of precious metals, although it was considered part of crown property. The British were interested in establishing trading contacts in the area and, to rationlize their dealings with the coastal peoples that were considered illegal by the Spanish, they created a Miskito king in 1687 who applied for British protection.

The Miskito were armed by the British, and as a result other Indian groups, including the Sumo and the Paya, retreated into the interior. The Miskito, unlike the Sumo, intermarried with Negroes from a wrecked slave ship in the seventeenth century. By the mid-eighteenth century, a leader known as General ruled the Miskito, the Sumo, and the Paya, his authority having been bestowed by the British.

The Miskito served as middlemen in the illegal trade being carried out between the British and the Spanish settlers and the interior Indians. The British traded such things as cloth, machetes, and other European manufactures for the tortoise shell, animal skins, canoes, and forest products of the Miskito, Sumo and Paya. The Miskito often raided the territories of the interior to acquire goods of trade.

The trade relationship gradually declined after 1860 when the British relinquished claims to territory in the Mosquitia. Nevertheless, tribes in the area maintained trading contacts with one another. In the 1970s,

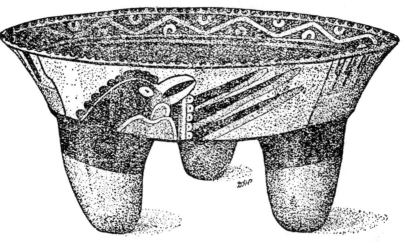

Pottery vessel from Tenampua, Honduras.

however, this Indian area was in economic depression because of the few trade and labor opportunities available.

The cultures of the groups were similar in the mid-twentieth century. All of them lived along rivers or on the ocean, using dugout canoes and rafts on the rivers and large canoes at sea. Miskito communities were usually populated by 100 to 500 people; Sumo villages were smaller, and Paya villages, even smaller.

All practiced slash-and-burn agriculture. Their principal food crops included sweet and bitter manioc (the bitter variety probably introduced by the Carib Indians) and plantains. The men cleared the lands while the women did the planting, cultivating, and harvesting. Men did all the hunting; their weapons included bows and arrows, blowguns, and guns. Both men and women fished, which was important among those people who lived on the water. Fish were taken either by spear or by poisoning the water. Handcrafting still played a part in the local economy. Wicker baskets, bark cloth (made by pounding the bark of a particular tree to make it soft), cotton fabric into which feathers were sometimes incorporated, pottery, and other items were produced.

European styles of clothing were slowly being adopted, particularly among the men. Most men, however, wore a breechclout and poncho tied under the arms and belted, while the women wore a knee-length wraparound skirt of bark cloth.

All three groups believed in a remote deity who had little control over events on earth and in numerous other spirits that inhabited caves, ponds, and hills and who were responsible for the many misfortunes that men suffered. It was the duty of the shamans, who had special powers, to placate these demons. It was also their duty to cure the sick.

Polygamy was practiced, particularly among the leaders and shamans. Young persons generally chose their own marriage partners, although on occasion the girl's parents arranged for the marriage without her consent. Marriage between certain cousins was common. The bridegroom had to pay the bride's family an agreed price before the ceremony. A man could abandon a woman who was barren. Divorce could be arranged by making payments to the offended person's family.

Black Caribs

The Black Caribs (sometimes called Garif or Morenos), who were of mixed origins, live along the north coast, from about Trujillo west to La Ceiba and in parts of the Bay Islands. In the late 1950s their numbers were estimated to be about 12,000, and presumably there were more by 1970. They are descendants of runaway African slaves who intermarried with the Carib Indians of Saint Vincent Island, one of the Windward Islands in the Antilles.

In 1796 the English deported the Black Caribs from Saint Vincent to Roatan, one of the Bay Islands. The

Spanish invited the Black Caribs to move to the mainland. Most of them, along with some other Antillean Blacks, made the move and were eventually converted to Catholicism.

Some Black Caribs work for wages on the docks, as seamen on modern ships, and on the plantations. Others live in small villages and practice a subsistence slash-and-burn agriculture. The women do much of the planting, cultivating, and harvesting. Crops grown include bitter *yuca,* sweet potatoes, taro, plantains, and pineapples. The vegetable diet is supplemented by fish and shellfish caught by the men. The men also build dugout canoes and plank vessels, used for transportation along the coast.

The Black Carib are Catholic but retain elements of an aboriginal religion. Each community holds a fiesta for its patron saint. Two specifically Black Carib celebrations were held on Christmas and New Year's Day. The *jugujugu,* performed on Christmas Eve and New Year's Eve, is a dance in which men and women dance separately all night. The *yancunu,* danced on Christmas and New Year's Day, is performed by men wearing masks. Black Carib music is reminiscent of that played in West Africa, but the dance steps, done in a cirlce, recall those of the South American rain Forest Indians.

Many of the Black Carib rituals revolved around deceased ancestors. Spirits of the dead were considered very powerful, capable of helping or hindering in curing the sick. Two kinds of sickness were thought to exist: that brought on by dead ancestors and that induced by evil spirits. Much attention was given to propitiating spirits. Shamans also produced cures with their herb medicines and special powers.

Polygyny was practiced, and it was not uncommon for a man to have wives in separate villages. The man was responsible for providing fish and a house for each wife. Housebuilding was usually a community affair.

Languages

Spanish is the official language and is spoken by most of the population. It is the language of the government, schools, newspapers, and radio. Many of the Indians, particularly those in the departments of Santa Barbara and El Paraiso, speak only Spanish.

Spanish was introduced by the conquerors in the sixteenth century and was perpetuated by their descendants and other colonists. Because it was the language of the dominant group, those who wished to benefit from association with the Spaniards and the *ladinos* had to learn it.

Nevertheless, even in the 1970s a number of other languages continued to be spoken. Estimates were not available for the number of speakers of these other languages.

English was spoken by the Bay Islanders, few of whom spoke any other language, even though Spanish was required in the schools. English was also spoken

Ceremonial cache and urn skull burials, Honduras.

Bay Island polychrome pottery, Honduras.

by the Negroes from various Caribbean islands who worked on the north coast plantations and in the port towns, although they were often bilingual in Spanish if they had been there for some time. Some of the Black Caribs were trilingual, speaking English as a third language after their Carib language and Spanish.

Because the country lies in the area of contact between Middle and South American cultures, the languages spoken by the indigenous peoples represent both areas. Many are dying out. The Lenca language had not in the 1970s yet been definitely classified with relation to other languages; its origins were obscure, but it was thought to belong to the Chibchan group of South American origin. The Jicaque language (although it had been related to South American languages) was part of the Hokan-Siouan language group, of North American affinity, and most prevalent among tribes in the United States. The Chorti language belongs to the Mayan stock and is related to many of the indigenous languages of Guatemala. Pipil, though no longer spoken in Honduras, belongs to the Aztecoid subfamily and is related to many Mexican languages.

Languages belonging to two South American language groups were still spoken in the 1970s. Carib, spoken by the Black Carib, belongs to the Ge-Pano-Carib group and has borrowed many terms from French, English, and Spanish. Men and women have different vocabularies and at one time spoke different languages, though they now understand one another's vocabularies. This is owing to the fact that historically many of the women were Arawakanian slaves and did not know the Carib language. The Miskito and Sumo languages (and perhaps also the Paya, although its origins are uncertain) belong to the Macro-Chibchan group. There are several mutually intelligible dialects, on the other hand, are often not mutually intelligible.

HOOKER JIM (Modoc; ?–1879) was one of several temporary war leaders of Kintpuash's band of Modoc Indians during the Modoc War in Oregon in 1872–73. He, together with Curly Headed Doctor, Boston Charlie, and 11 other men retaliated against U.S. army threats to their camp by raiding ranches around Tule Lake in November 1872. After 12 white settlers had been killed, Hooker Jim and his band went to Kintpuash (Captain Jack) for protection. The chief felt compelled to provide sanctuary, but this forced him to defy U.S. orders that the guilty Modoc be handed over for trial.

Hooker Jim then vehemently opposed Kintpuash's plans for surrender. After unsuccessfully attempting to turn himself in as a prisoner of war (so that he would not be subject to state law), he shamed Kintpuash into a promise to assassinate Gen. Edward R. S. Canby if the general refused the Indians' request for a reservation on Lost River. When the Modoc position was desperate, Hooker

Jim quarreled with Kintpuash and led his followers out of the beseiged Modoc camp. This left the chief with only 37 fighting men to oppose more than 1,000 U.S. troops.

Subsequently, Hooker Jim's band surrendered to the U.S. forces and offered to act as scouts against their fellow Modoc in exchange for amnesty. On May 27 they located Kintpuash and told him to give up the fight. In reply the chief stated: "You are no better than the coyotes that run in valleys."

Together with Schonchin John, Boston Charlie, and Black Jim, Kintpuash was captured and charged with murder. Prominent among the witnesses against them was Hooker Jim, now given his freedom for betraying his tribesmen. In his closing speech, Kintpuash, who was given no defense attorney, said simply: "Hooker Jim is the one that always wanted to fight and commenced killing and murdering. . . . Life is mine only for a short time. You white people conquered me not; my own men did."

After Kintpuash's execution, Hooker Jim and other former combatants and their families were removed to the Quapaw Agency in Indian Territory (now Oklahoma), where he died in 1879.

HOONAH RESERVATION, in Southeast Alaska, is a native Tlingit community of nearly 750 Indians. Hoonah is incorporated as a town in Alaska. The term ''Indian Reservation'' has been applied generally to any lands in Alaska set aside for the benefit of Indians. The lands in established native townsites are held in trust by the Federal Government for disposal as provided by the 1926 Alaska Native Townsite Act which authorizes the townsite trustee to issue a restricted deed to an Alaskan native for a tract of land occupied by and set apart for him in a townsite established under the 1891 Townsite Act.

The Tlingit were formerly one of North America's more powerful tribes, crossing the mountains from Canada to seek the seacoast. Russian explorers found them in 1741 and exerted a harsh, oppressive rule over them. The Tlingit continued to live in this area, dividing into villages, each with hunting and fishing grounds. Today they participate actively in Alaska's political affairs.

Social status among the Tlingit depended on elaborate feasts called ''Potlatches'' at which the heads of families or clans vied in destroying or giving away vast quantities of valuable goods. The goat wool and cedar bark ceremonial blanket has always been in great demand as a trade item with each clan house having its own design. Totem poles were important to the culture of the Tlingit, serving as the decorative record of outstanding events of a family or clan. The Tlingit developed a rich economy based largely on the abundant resources of the sea and coast. War captives from other tribes were enslaved. The tlingit contructed seaworthy boats and canoes, and seem to have carried on active trade with the Orient.

Hoonah was incorporated in 1946 with a mayor and council form of government. Primary income is from sales tax and revenue from electricity and water collections.

HOOPA EXTENSION RESERVATION, 7,000 acres in Humboldt County, California, has 150 Yurok Indians residing there. The reservation was established by an Executive order of October 16, 1891 adding the Klamath strip, a tract 1 mile in width on each side of the Klamath River, from the Hoopa Valley Reservation to the Pacific Ocean. The tribal land is checkerboarded with a considerable amount of non-Indian land. The Hoopa Extension has a claim filed in the U.S. Court of Claims to be included as a part of the Greater Hoopa Valley Reservation. The Yurok Tribe still practice traditional hunting and fishing, and many of the people speak their native language.

HOOPA VALLEY RESERVATION, in Humboldt County, California, is 87,000 acres of land belonging to nearly 1,000 Yurok (Hoopa band) Indians. Much of the reservation land is owned in a complicated heirship pattern. Several non-Indians have inherited undivided interests in the property. Due to the land status, the members of the tribe are unable to establish homesites.

The Hoopa Reservation was established on June 23, 1876. The tribes placed here included Huntsatung, Hoopa, Klamath River, Meskeet, Redwood, Raiaz, Sermolton, and Sish Langton. The Hoopa Valley lies along the banks of the Trinity River in Humboldt County. The Hoopas are of Athapascan language stock.

The Hoopa Indians have maintained their culture to the extent of performing their cultural dances such as the White Deerskin Dance and the Jump Dance which is held every two years. The Brush Dance is held annually. The Hoopa still practice and encourage basket weaving and beadwork. Tribal members hunt and fish, and prepare native foods such as acorns.

The constitution and bylaws were adopted by the tribe on May 5, 1950, and approved by the Commissioner of Indian Affairs on September 4, 1954. The seven-member Hoopa council is elected from tribal membership by referendum vote of the members over 21 years of age. The council members select their chairman. The council votes on all resolutions presented to them; however, any resolution passed by them must have final approval by the Bureau of Indian Affairs. Five members constitute a quorum.

HOPEHOOD (Narridgewock; ?–1690), properly Wahowa, Wahawa, or Wohawa, the son of a chief known as Robinhood, was a late 17th century Norridgewock, Maine Kennebec chief. At the end of King Philip's War in which he fought, Hopehood participated with four other chiefs in the 1676 meet-

ing at Taconnet, Maine with Abraham Shurte and Sylvanus Davis, who, representing traders in the area, wished to see raids on the settlements and trading posts stopped as well as hostilities among the Indians. Nothing came of the meeting except a war party Hopehood formed shortly thereafter. Nine years later he was willing to sign a treaty, but only because Gov. Edward Cranefield of New Hampshire promised that the English would protect the Maine tribes from their enemies the Mohawk.

This treaty, signed 1685 at Portsmouth, New Hampshire, lasted only until the outbreak of King William's War (1689–97). Under French influence, Hopehood joined the raids on the New England settlements, and on March 27, 1690 killed 14 people at Fox Point, New Hampshire where he himself was wounded. Mistaken for an Iroquois, friends of the English, he was killed while in Canada by pro-French Indians.

HOPEWELL CULTURE. In the Mississippi basin the culmination of the cultural pattern of mound-building (*Middle Woodland* or Burial Mound II period) is represented by the Hopewell culture, whose principal centers are found in the central section of the Ohio valley (southern Ohio, northern Kentucky) and in the valley of the Illinois. Various carbon 14 tests date the climax in those places at between 550 BC and the beginning of the Christian era.

The Hopewell culture shows continuity and development of the pattern established in the preceding period. There is somatic evidence and also evidence furnished by certain cultural traits which indicate population movements from the north and northeast; the immigrants mixed with the peoples of the Adena cultures in Ohio and the Morton culture in Illinois. There is evidence of agriculture (maize) but its economic importance in relation to hunting, fishing and gathering is not precisely known. On the other hand, a considerable increase of population is evident, with permanent villages, some of them of large size. Terraces were constructed in order to form habitation and ceremonial districts on level ground and also on hills and promontories (on these sites, sometimes they were enclosed with stone). Burial mounds, frequently with burial chambers constructed of logs were used for the burial of prominent personages. Burial in cists and especially cremation and burial of the ashes were the usual means of disposing of bodies. There was active trade of raw materials, largely for sumptuary and ceremonial purposes with remote regions: copper from the Lake Superior region, sea shells from the Gulf of Mexico and from the coast of the Atlantic, mica from the Carolinas, obsidian (probably from the Rocky Mountains or perhaps from Mexico).

The emphasis on the religious-ceremonial aspect of this culture suggest the differentiation of a specialized priesthood. The quality of the artistic products of stone, bone, copper, shell, mica, etc. probably indicates incipient specialization of artisans. While, the cultural roots are found in the tradition existing in the earlier centuries and while part of the population and certain stylistic traits must have arrived from the north and northeast, the origin of corn and possibly some ideas (manifested by terra-cotta figurines, ear adornments, and perhaps also the use of obsidian) indicate the arrival of influences emanating from Mesoamerica.

The burial mound cultural pattern spread, with temporal and regional variations, through the Mississippi basin from the Great Lakes to the coast of the Gulf, the Missouri basin and the Atlantic watershed lowing stage.

HOPEWELL, TREATY OF was the Cherokee's first treaty with the newly independent United States. It was signed in 1785 and recognized the sovereign status of the Indian nation.

The Cherokee had previously (Sycamore Shoals, 1775) sold a large tract of land to the Transylvania Land Company. Frontiersmen and squatters overran remaining Cherokee lands and a frontier battle led to much Cherokee suffering during the Revolutionary War.

President George Washington sent a peace commission to Hopewell, South Carolina on November 18, 1785. Old Tassel was the major Cherokee leader in attendance. At the Treaty of Hopewell the Cherokee ceded more land but, in return, the United States agreed to the permanent boundary of the Cherokee nation and promised that white settlers would never intrude on their lands. In the 12th article, the Cherokees were allowed to send an agent to Congress.

The treaty made no provision for expelling the thousands of white settlers who were already in illegal residence on Cherokee property between the French Broad and Holston rivers. Frontier warfare continued as Dragging Canoe and his followers, the Chickamaugans, attempted to push the settlers and speculators off Cherokee lands.

HOPI. Though generally small in stature, the men not much over five feet, the Hopi tribe of what is now northern Arizona stand high in their strength of character and their devotion to ancient ideals and aims. Their struggle for independence from the smothering grasp of our civilization and from the warlike Navajo who surround them, has been threaded by near disasters as well as creeping corruption from outside. They have indeed been a culture in crisis ever since they saw the first white man, but their staunch determination, born of many centuries of living in difficult desert country and of facing and conquering social and and ecological disasters in their past, still stands them in good stead to prevail against all odds.

The name *Hopi* is derived from the longer name of "Hopi-tu Shin-u-mu", meaning "People of Peace."

Two Hopi maidens, 1898.

Another name by which they have been frequently called is *Moqui*, which is actually a Zuñi epithet towards a stranger tribe, meaning "people that need handkerchiefs," possibly because the Zuñi may have seen some Hopi with runny noses.

Social and cultural boundaries and subdivisions

In ancient times the Hopi came to occupy four satellite mesas of the Great Black Mesa of northern Arizona. These four from east to west were Antelope Mesa, with such towns as Amatovi, Kawaika and Chakpahui (now all extinct); First Mesa, with Walpi, Sichamovi, Hano, Terkinovi and Sikaki; Second Mesa, with Shongopovi, Mishangnovi, Shipaulove and Toreva; and Third Mesa with Oraibi and Bakabi. In modern times, the villages of Antelope Mesa were wiped out by war or abandoned, while in Third Mesa both conservative and liberal dissidents from Old Oraibi formed the modern villages of New Oraibi and Hotevilla.

The U.S. government in 1882 recognized the Hopi claim to about 3920 square miles of mesa and desert, but, by 1943, the Navajo had considerably encroached on this area, and the government changed its mind, recognized the Navajo squatters rights to the land they had taken, and gave the Hopi a final settlement of 986 square miles, so increasing the crisis of the Hopi economy. It should be noted that Tewa-speaking Pueblos of the Rio Grande Valley in New Mexico sent some of their people as migrators to found the village of Hano on the First Mesa and Payuphi on the Second Mesa in the early eighteenth century, but the latter village moved back to the Rio Grande in 1742. The Hano Tewas learned to speak Hopi and are now well-integrated with them today.

Language

Hopi is a Shoshonean language of the great Uto-Aztecan language family, which extends from the primitive desert dwellers, like the Shoshones and Paiutes of Nevada, to the civilized Hopi and the still greater civilization of the Aztecs in Mexico.

Summary of tribal material culture

Subsistence and economy. For many hundreds of years the Hopi have been farmers, living in permanent villages, and farming fields of corn, beans, squash and sunflower seeds, also cultivating cotton for clothing, in the areas around them. Recently white civilization has brought them such fruits as peaches, apricots and apples, while potatoes and other vegetables such as carrots and tomatoes have also been brought in to grow. The planting was done mainly by digging sticks in the old days, supplanted somewhat by horses drawing plows in modern times. However, we can recognize that the Hopi method of planting and raising crops was very scientific and well-organized because of its success in desert and semi-desert surroundings where a rainfall of usually less than 12 inches yearly and the existence of only a few springs that gave permanent water made food-raising most difficult. They did have available some peculiar type sand dunes that held water for a long time and they knew exactly when and how to plant to take advantages of these. They also worked on their arroyos with small temporary dams of rocks, brush and dirt to catch flash floods and redistribute the water to help their crops. Plants were often protected by carefully constructed windbreaks to preserve them against the fierce desert winds. Soil was very precious to them and they knew how to conserve and rebuild it whenever possible. The use of their religion and its ceremonies and prayers to influence greater powers to help their crops are laughed at by some white people, but experts fromthe U.S. Department of Agriculture who came to Hopiland to show the Hopi how to raise crops found their knowledge not as effective as that of the supposedly primitive Indians. Planting was also based on the use of a quite accurate calendar, based on careful measurements of the sun's places of rising day by day and by an exact knowledge of the winter and summer solstices. A sign of great Hopi intelligence and fore-sight is shown by their ingenious ways to dry and store agricultural crops for future times of drouth or cold, with every home having its special place for storing such food.

Hunting for deer, antelope, rabbits, buffalo, quail and other creatures was much more prevalent in pre-white times before the larger game was killed off. Hopi still make annual surrounds of jackrabbits, with men and boys forming a great circle, which is tightened to drive the jackrabbits into a central place where nets and pits help hold them to be killed with curved sticks. Bows and arrows were used on most of the other game, aided by elaborate and careful stalking. Quail were trapped in nets and snares.

The were also very industrious about collecting

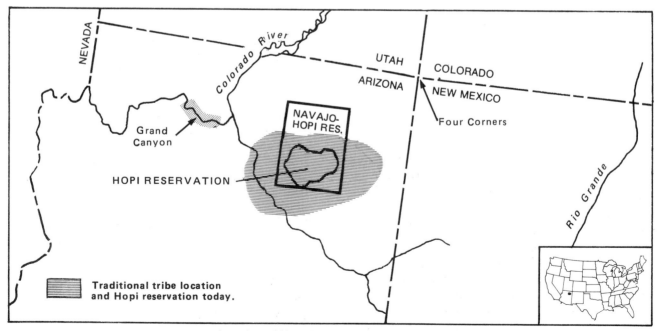

Location of Hopi Reservation, 20th century.

many wild and semi-cultivated plants, of which they knew at least 200 different species. Many plants and their parts were dug up with sharp digging sticks. Women and children did most of this gathering.

Turkeys were raised for food and fathers, with dogs being the main other domestic animal, sometimes used in hunting. Recently the Hopi have acquired chickens, also horses, sheep and cattle. The last two, however, have caused them considerable trouble because of overgrazing that has ruined much land by starting erosion, but they are learning better range management.

Technology and arts. The stone and adobe homes of the Hopi were and are erected in apartment-like clusters on the tops of the mesas, sometimes three or four stories high, for defense against enemy tribes. The one modern element that the Hopis have been glad to add to their homes has been glass windows for protections against the cold and winds. Plumbing is still absent in most cases, and human wastes in the old days were usually dropped or dumped from pottery jars over the edges of the mesas. A simple stone hearth formed the basis for cooking, though some homes had adobe stone ovens.

Fired pottery vessels have been made for the last few hundred years, an evolutionary development from the times of the ancient Basketmaker Culture of the Southwest. Men more often than women made these pots and men more often than women did weaving. Cotton thread was used to weave blankets and clothing. In the old days cotton blankets were made as a major part of the clothing, with a lin cloth being the basic covering of the men, and a simple sack-like dress that of the women. But blankets and capes were also made out of the woven strips of rabbit fur, and the skins of deer, antelope and buffalo when greater warmth was needed. When the Hopi began to be influenced by white culture the main thing they took up with considerable fervor was the weaving of wool blankets on looms, the wool taken from their own sheep, and woven with the aid of colored vegetable dyes into many beautiful designs. They much appreciate the greater warmth of wool in winter.

Hopi art was generally asymetrical, except in the

Hopi storage container.

Hopi bowl for food storage.

Swing type water jar, Hopi.

Hopi seed storage container.

Old Hopi food bowl.

The Hopi house, Grand Canyon, Arizona.

designs on clothing, and was very sophisticated in its balance between different objects and different shades of color, with a square balancing with a circle, for example, and a red area balanced with a black one of different shape, yet the whole giving a feeling of harmony. Little attempt was made to do realistic drawings of animals, birds and people, but rather symbolic designs meant these items. Interesting geometric designs formed in intricate inward-moving or outward-moving whirls were symbolic of the Hopi view of our needed harmony with ourselves, with all life, and with the Spirit World. Much of their art can be thought of as prayers rendered into design and beauty.

Hopi art appeared most dramatically in the Kachina dolls and Kachina dance costumes, and in the symbolic designs on sacred objects, such as the dance rattles, sometimes telling in such designs the sacred legends of their past, as when the symbol of the lightning indicated the beginning of life. The kachina dolls and dance costumes allowed for a great deal of imagination, each being a distinct form with special colors, facial features (such as big noses or ears or teeth) and so on. Painting of colors was usually done with a brush made of frayed yucca fibers attached to a stick.

Though the Hopi area on Black Mesa was not only rather barren of life but also of beautiful minerals, the Hopis obtained gem minerals, such as turquoise, from the Zuni and from the Pueblo tribes along the Rio Grande. They also obtained by trade beautiful sea shells from the distant Gulf of California, the Pacific Coast, and some even from the Gulf of Mexico. These they fashioned into fine ear pendants, necklaces and other attractive articles of jewelry, using hard and sharp obsidian or flint tools or by grinding and polishing with sandstone. Feathers of the eagle, gathered by special men who trapped the birds on the tops of the buttes, or imported feathers of the macaw, parrot and woodpeckers, were used in many of the ceremonies as decorations or parts of prayer sticks. The feather was said to "carry the breath of the spirit."

Social and religious culture

The circle of life. To prepare for a birth a layer of sand was placed over the earth floor of the room in the adobe apartment and near a fire. The mother, as the birth pangs increased knelt on hands and knees on this sand while a Hopi doctor and probably a midwife also began to help her. Their hands manipulated and rubbed her to help the baby come out straight. When the baby came the sand absorbed the blood, and the navel was cut, usually with a sharp arrowhead if the baby was a boy, to insure he would be a good hunter. The navel cord was turned back about two inches from the navel and tied with a string made of the mother's hair.

The mother was washed in warm yucca suds, dried and then wrapped in a blanket so she could lie warm by the fire and recover her strength. The father's mother was usually called at this time to wash the baby, also in warm yucca suds, coming with smiling face and happy heart to pass this spirit of goodness to the newborn. A part of the continued ceremony of new birth was to have the baby's ears pierced so they could later hold sacred earrings for the ceremonies. Wrapped in blankets and placed in a wicker cradle, whose bottom was padded with dry cedar bark as an absorbent, the baby was bound in place so later the mother could carry it this way on her back while she worked.

All boyhood and girlhood for the Hopis was a preparation for a life of work. Over and over they were taught that the "Way of the Hopi" meant hard work, no lies, obedience to elders, their actions to be peaceful and kind. The children were spanked more than in most tribes, as the Hopi believed in a fairly stern discipline.

Around 9 to 11 years of age the children were initiated into the Kiva societies, the girls into those for women, and the boys into those for men. Down in the dim and fire-lit Kiva an underground room they learned for the first time that the men in Kachina costumes and masks were really human beings and not gods or powerful spirits after all. The ceremonial fathers and mothers, one assigned to each child, sprinkled sacred corn meal on sand paintings on the floor of the kiva, each with symbolic spiritual meanings in the design that were explained. Afterward the children each stepped into a ring or wheel made of yucca leaves with a hawk's feather attached at each of four knots. Soon after this a large man masked and decorated in the form of the germination god Muyingwa descended the ladder and gave all the children a dramatic lecture on how to follow the "Hopi Way". By such ceremonial objects and figures the children were prepared to join the Kachina societies and their minds directed powerfully to follow the cooperative ways of Hopi society. Such training continued through other similar initiations and ceremonies producing Hopi juveniles who were more mature and self-controlled than white youth of the same age. The young men especially went through difficult ordeals, such as the two hundred mile round trip through the wilderness to gather salt at a special place in the Grand Canyon, that led them in time to take part in the complex ceremonial and work life of the tribe as trained and self-confident individuals.

Marriage usually involved the young man in asking his parents and the girl's parents for their consent as a first step. If granted, then many presents were exchanged. The clan of the girl next prepared the ceremony at which, among other things, the girl and boy would usually have their hair washed together in warm yucca suds in the same bowl and then the hair tied

HOPI CEREMONIAL BLANKET

together to sumbolize a long, happy and cooperative marriage. Then both girl and boy were bathed separately each by the women of the opposite clan. Afterward the young couple would likely go at sunrise to the edge of the mesa to pray together and so help make sacred the marriage.

Death, though supposedly leading those who were good Hopis to a very pleasant place in the underworld, was considered a disagreeable time by most Hopi. Death in the younger years particularly might arouse resentment and anger, especially from a spouse, as following the Hopi Way was supposed to lead to a graceful old age and a quiet death in one's sleep, while failing to do this would show lack of concern for one's family. Trying to prevent a disease or accident from bringing early death was usually done either by healing rites produced by a medicine man or a ceremonial association, or by the individual concentrating on "good thoughts", or by concentrating on driving away "bad thoughts." Medicine men often pulled objects out of the sick persons body, objects or an object they said had been put there by an evil person, such as a *Two Heart*. Two Hearts were men and women witches, people supposedly controlled by their evil passions and using black magic to gain their way with others or to kill them.

The dead person was usually formally bathed and then dressed for burial, being taken away on the back of one man, usually a clan kinsman, to an isolated place on the mesa. Here he was buried in a cave or deep hole, with the legs flexed as in birth, and many rocks piled over the entrance to keep out wild beasts.

Society and social relations. Hopi society was a theory, run by the priests who managed it by influencing the minds powerfully in ceremonies and in moral lectures rather than by force. The village chief had to do more with purely social observances, such as greeting and entertaining strangers, disciplining the youth with the help of other men, and planning feasts or hunts. The war chief, supposedly protected and guided by the famous war god twins, took charge when an enemy attack was imminent or a war party of revenge was organized and executed.

The Hopi concept of society involved not only human beings, but the whole web of life, and even lightning, rain, thunder, rocks and other supposedly non-living things were included and supposed to have special life. Thus to be in harmony meant to the Hopi to be in harmony with everything that might have influence on his life. In the continued struggle with the Navaho, a far more powerful tribe that has surrounded the Hopi for generations, the Hopi generally used magic, diplomacy and sheer peaceful determination rather than war to control and hold off these always potential enemies. However, if war came, as happened one time when Oraibi was attacked by two large Navajo war parties, the Hopi showed great bravery and used clever ambushes and enfilading tactics to overcome these enemies, demonstrating considerable discipline.

It is important to understand that the good Hopi placed his society and his religious first and himself decidedly second in his scheme of things. Almost every part of his life and thought was dedicated to his harmony with nature, with other Hopis and with his religion, meaning that even his work was done in a spirit of worship. Living as he did in a very stressful desert environment where a crisis of drouth or storm could come at any time, he felt that unless he and the bulk of his people faithfully followed the Hopi Way, they would upset the balance of nature and bring on themselves disaster. Since the legends of their past, and particularly the stories of their ancient migrations, are replete with accounts of times when some of their villages were destroyed because of the evil among them and the lack of harmony with their environment, the Hopi felt that he held in his hands and in his own conduct the fate of his people. Thus he created in himself a very strong force to obey his superiors and work cooperatively with all.

Religion was certainly a powerful influence on Hopi society and life. Spiritual dances and ceremonies were in operation almost throughout the year, but particularly in winter and spring when preparations for morally and spiritually producing the crops of summer and fall were underway. The intensity of Hopi concentration on religion and in bringing by its use their entire environment into harmony is shown by the fact that main ceremonies in the old days lasted from nine to

Gualetaga, the traditional Hopi Guardian Spirit.

seventeen days and nights, gathering in momentum and in spiritual power as eacy day and night passed. Though very complex in detail, the basic emphasis of these ceremonies is quite simple, they are to protect and give good life to the people.

Pivotal and a beginning for all of the other ceremonies is the Winter Solstice Ceremony or Soyal, which coincides with the turning back of the Sun god from his yearly retreat to the south, and also the coming of the Kachinas to Hopiland from their home in the San Francisco Mountains of what is now Arizona. The Kachinas are seen symbolically in the Hopi Kachina Dancers, but are supposed to be present also as invisible spirits.

It is a bit difficult to understand exactly what the Kachinas are, as sometimes they appear as the spirits of Good Hopis who have returned from the spirit land to help their people with the rain and crops, while other times some seem to be actual lesser gods, and still other times they appear like living human beings of some special sort, because there are legends of their being killed by Hopis who misunderstood who they were.

Tough identified with the Sun god, the Soyal or Winter Solstice Ceremony also relates to the Hopi harmony with all life and emphasizes the whole story of their travelling through three worlds and emergence into the Fourth World (the world we live in). Rites are

HOPI WEDDING SHAWL

performed to bring the sun back from the south, but prayer sticks are made also for almost every order of the universe, including animals, plants and rocks. Kachinas perform many dances in the town square and in the kivas and many prayers and rites are offered to insure rain and good crops in the year ahead.

The Powamu Ceremony or "Bean Dance" is conducted by the Powamu Society in February. The central design of the Powamu centers on the germination of beans. Corn is planted too at this time of year, but the beans are literally force-fed and warmed into the production of food even at this early season by keeping fires burning in the kivas where the beans are planted, making excellent greenhouses in cold weather. Speeches and dances at this time emphasize the growth of all cultivated plants and also the long journeys of the Hopi, including their emergence into the Fourth World through the *Sipapu* or earth hole. It is also in this ceremony that at least every four years the young boys and girls are initiated, as described earlier in this article.

In July the Niman Ceremony or "Home" Dance is contributed by the Kachina Society, as it is in July that the Kachinas returned to the San Francisco Mountains, the whole ceremony symbolizing and emphasizing the maturation or ripening of the corn, beans and other crops. Again the people give the children gifts, including sweet corn from the first crop.

The famous Hopi Snake Dances are included as part of the Snake-Antelope and Flute Society Ceremony in August, which emphasizes bringing the rain for the crops, since the snakes symbolize by their coming up out of their holes in the earth the water that is also found deep below the ground and rises as clouds. The Snake Dancers are not bitten because their hearts are pure, which means literally they are so relaxed that they do not upset the rattlesnakes they hold in their mouths. At the close of the dances the dancers send back the snakes to their holes to take messages to the under-earth people and to the Six-point Cloud People, who are supposed to be the spirits of holy people of long ago, asking them to help bring the rain.

The *Wuwuchim* or "Grown Man" Ceremony finally closes the ceremonial cycle in November. Symbolically and literally all the trails to the pueblo are closed, and the fires are put out, while the children and women hide in the houses. The chief priest impersonates Masau'u, who has grown in the last few centuries to be the chief Hopi god. The priest starts a "New Fire", which certain men distribute to all the kivas and houses. This ceremony includes the initiation of young men into the full adult rank where they can actively take part in the ceremonies. It also includes rites which symbolize the Hopi idea of death and rebirth of the Hopi in the underworld, where he lives much as he did in the upper world, but with rewards for his good conduct. There are also rites by the women's societies which give thanks if the harvests are good, emphasizing

also the role of the woman as the principle factor in the process of reproduction.

In all these ceremonies the deadly seriousness and intensity that characterizes so much of Hopi religious action and thought is tempered and countered by the clowns who go about making people laugh by burlesquing their actions and even appearing to act counter to all their beliefs of decorum and proper conduct. The clowns act with the freedom of untrained children, often doing things backward, such as coming down ladders head first. The people laugh and laugh, but the Kachinas, who are doing the serious dances, pay no attention to the clowns, for these grotesquely-masked figures symbolically represent the great powers of the universe, unchangeable and unshaken by the frailties of man. In the end the Kachinas whip the clowns and the women often pour water over the clowns to purify them.

The rhythm and organization of the whole complex ceremonial cycle can be compared to the work of a great symphony orchestra as all the many instruments combine harmoniously to complete the whole. The cycle includes gorgeously costumed dancers, with most beautiful rhythmic and coordinated movements, paintings, carvings, impersonations and many other elements of human art and acting. All this is not merely to bring rain, as some tourists watching it think, but, far more important, to orchestrate the harmony of Hopi life and ways with all in the universe, and especially with the spiritual powers.

Brief history and present condition

The complex history of the Hopi people is impossible to make clear in the limited space of this article. Basically their story is that of a tribe overwhelmingly tied up to their legends of emergence into the Fourth World and their wanderings and migrations in search of the home supposedly set aside for them by their principle god, Massau'u. It is doubtful if Massau'u was always so important, as originally he was simply the god of death, war and fire, a rather grim and not very pleasant figure, but the pressure of Christian missionaries since the first coming of Catholic Fathers to the Hopi in 1629 evidently caused the Hopi to gradually move Massau'u in the direction of being a Supreme God to counter that of the Christians.

The Spanish attempts to Christianize the Hopi from 1629 to 1680 were frustrated first by the general Pueblo revolt against Spain in 1680 when all whites were driven out of the southwest, and later by Hopi stubbornness, abetted by the Hopi isolated position in their far-off mesas. Awatowi on Antelope Mesa (see map), which had two Franciscan priests about 1700, was attacked and destroyed by other Hopi villages, presumably to protect the Hopi Way, a story of violent death the peaceful Hopi would like to forget.

The conquest of the southwest by the United States in 1848 brought a new and more forceful people, whose stronger armies frightened the Hopi into docility so they allowed other missionaries in their villages. Some even forced their way into the Kivas and tried to halt Hopi ceremonies.

Fortunately in the 1930s the Hopi, as well as other Indians, were granted religious freedom and protected in their right to have their own religion. At present no cameras or tape recorders are allowed where ceremonies are going on, nor are strangers allowed in the Kivas at ceremonial time. Education, at first forced on the Hopi in late nineteenth and early twentieth centuries, has changed in recent years to include helping them respect and revive their own culture and languages, as well as teaching them useful techniques and other wholesome knowledge that are preparing young Hopis for the modern world. There is still, however, a desperate fight against alcohol and drugs among the youth and against exploitation by industry of their ancient lands. But there is hope the beautiful Hopi Way will survive.

VINSON BROWN

HOPI RESERVATION, in Arizona, is the home of the Hopi Indians. It is more than 2,000,000 acres in size. All land is tribally-owned. An Executive order of 1882 granted the Hopi Tribe 2,600,000 acres in northeastern Arizona, entirely surrounded by the Navajo Reservation. The Hopi are presently living on only 650,000 acres, the remainder being occupied by the Navajo. Conflicting tribal claims to land have led to a series of ownership and boundary disputes. A 1963 court decision provided for an area of joint-use land and negotiation of disputes. The Navajo, however, have not cooperated.

The precise origin of the Hopi is unknown. Their own legends relate that their ancestors climbed upward through four underground chambers of kivas, living in many places before settling in their present location on the Black Mesa of the Colorado Plateau, where the Hopi have lived for nearly 1,000 years. Old Oraibi, built at least by 1150, is probably the oldest continuously occupied city in the United States today. The Spanish visited the Hopi area several times from 1540 until the Pueblo Revolt in 1680. During the revolt, the Hopi moved many of their villages to mesa tops for defense purposes, and sheltered other refugees from other pueblos such as Isleta. The Hopi destroyed the Spanish missions, and killed many of the priests. The Spanish made no effort to reestablish control of the Hopi. In the early 20th century, several new towns were founded. Many Hopi are moving from mesa tops to the new towns at the foot of the mesas.

The Hopi, westernmost of the pueblos, speak an Uto-Aztecan language rather than the Tanoan or Keresan spoken by most other pueblos. The old towns are constructed in typical adobe architecture. Each village is autonomous, an individual being a lifetime resident of his village even if he marries someone from another village. Both property inheritance and residence are matriarchal. Hopi as a whole is a closed community. The tribal members have a distinct pride in their nation or tribe which may be an important factor in maintaining the vibrancy and vitality of the culture. Considered by many to be outstanding intellectuals of Indian tribes, the Hopi are patient, peaceful, industrious people. They have developed a complex system of gods or Kachinas which are impersonated in many of the dances. These intricate dances, representative of their belief, are usually closed to the public. Kachina dolls, carved and decorated to resemble the gods, are used to teach the children. Hopi also produce excellent silverwork and silver overlay, polychrome pottery, baskets, and other art forms.

Each of the villages is organized independently, having either an elected governor or a hereditary village chief. The first tribal constitution was adopted in 1935; however, a tribal council was not elected until 1955. There is much resistance to change which might undermine their tradition and religion.

HOPOCAN (Delaware; ?–1794) was a hereditary sachem and a tribal war chief who fought with the British during the American Revolution, but later became a signer of the first peace agreement between the United States and the Indians on September 17, 1778. Whites called this Delaware chief Captain Pipe, but his own people knew him as Konieschguanokee.

Hopocan fought with the French during the French and Indian War and participated in Pontiac's Conspiracy (1763–64) to throw the English from their outposts west of the Appalachians. In the attempt to overtake Fort Pitt, however, Hopocan was captured and never took arms against the British again.

Following the failure of Pontiac's Conspiracy, Hopocan moved to the upper Muskingum River in Ohio. He had been a prominent member of councils held at Turtle Village and at Fort Pitt, and he enjoyed a reputation for possessing wisdom and superb oratory. When the colonists declared their independence from the British, the Delaware chief accepted a position on the side of the crown fighting against the Americans and their Indian allies. Hopocan foresaw, however, what might happen to him and his tribe when the conflicting whites patched up their differences. Therefore, he made a point of informing the British commander at Detroit that the Delaware would not act cruelly. His people had no interest in the struggle for independence and sought only to maintain their own well-being. Nevertheless, Hopocan did violate this pledge once during the Revolution. In retaliation for a party of whites massacring a group of Indians, Hopocan had U.S. Col. William Crawford put to torture after Crawford was captured during a rout of his regiment in May 1782.

Well before the war was over, though, Hopocan

signed a treaty with the United States. On September 17, 1778, at Fort Pitt, the Delaware chief endorsed the first treaty between the new government and an Indian nation. Later, he signed additional treaties, including those at Fort McIntosh, Ohio (January 21, 1785), and at Fort Harmar, Ohio (January 9, 1787). During the early 1780s Hopocan moved to what was called Captain Pipe's Village near the Upper Sandusky River in Ohio, where he died in 1794.

HOPSON, EBEN (Inuit; 1923?–   ), in the mid-1970s has been a member of the Alaska state legislature since Alaskan statehood in 1959. In 1974 he was also elected the first mayor of the North Slope Borough, Alaska, which includes the city of Barrow.

HORN CRAFT. *See* BONE AND HORN CRAFT.

HORNE, ESTHER BURNETT (Shoshoni; Nov. 9, 1909–   ), was a teacher for more than 30 years at the Wahpeton Boarding School, North Dakota, working to inspire her Indian students with pride in their culture. Descended from Sacajawea, the famous woman guide to the Lewis and Clark Expedition (1804–06), she was the guide for the Lewis and Clark Return Expedition (1956). She was named the first master teacher in the U.S. Bureau of Indian Affairs (1963), was North Dakota's Good Will Ambassador to Europe (1965), and was recipient of the U.S. Department of the Interior's Distinguished Service Award in Education (1966). Now retired, Horne teaches Indian folk dancing and singing and is a consultant to colleges on Indian culture.

HORNOTLIMED (Seminole; fl. early 19th century) was a chief who fought in the First Seminole War (1817–18). He lived in Fowl Town in northwest Florida at the beginning of the hostilities but was forced to flee to the village of Mikasuki. On November 30, 1817, Hornotlimed and his warriors attacked a contingent of 40 U.S. soldiers while they were unloading cargo from a ship at the mouth of the Apalachicola River. All but six of the soldiers were killed.

The Indians then attacked another group of 20 soldiers and about an equal number of women and sick. Hornotlimed and his men scalped the dead, returned to their village, and placed the scalps on red sticks for display. Shortly after this incident, U.S. troops attacked Mikasuki. Hornotlimed was captured and hanged.

Gen. Andrew Jackson called him Homattlemico, meaning "the old redstick," because he was chief of a band of Indians known for the red poles placed around their villages.

HORSE. The wild horse roamed over North America in late Pleistocene times; it became extinct less than 10,000 years ago. It was associated with the ancestors of the Indians as demonstrated in cave deposits in southern Chile; but Indians living in the New World have traditions of such an animal. The Spanish expeditions and settlements brought horses into the country during the 16th century.

The first horses seen by the Indians were those of the Spanish invaders of Mexico. A few years later De Soto brought the horse into Florida and westward to the Mississippi, while Coronado, on his march to Quivira

Indian children and travios.

The squaw pony.

in 1541, introduced it to the Indians of the Great Plains. When the Aztec saw the mounted men of Cortes they supposed horse and man to be one.

It was worshiped by the Aztec, and by most of the tribe was considered to have a mysterious or sacred character. Its origin was explained by myths representing horses to have come out of the earth through lakes and springs or from the sun. When Antonio de Espejo visited the Hopi of Arizona in 1583, the Indians spread cotton scarfs or kilts on the ground for the horses to walk on, believing it to be sacred. This sacred character is sometimes shown in the names given to the horse, as the Dakota *sunka wakan,* 'mysterious dog.' Its use in transportation accounts for the term 'dog' often applied to it, as the Siksika *ponokamita,* 'elk dog;' Cree *mistatim,* 'big dog;' Shawnee *mishawa* 'elk.'

The Indians of the forests learned to use them sparingly, but the Natives of Mexico and southwestern

United States took them readily, especially the Apache, Navajo and others. From here horses spread rapidly northward by trade and theft. Lewis and Clark found Indians using them in Washington and parts of Oregon. They were not adopted by the Indians of California and Nevada; but along the main range of the Rocky Mountains and eastward to the Mississippi all of the tribes soon became horse Indians, turning more nomadic. The Kiowa, for example, ranged more than 1000 miles in a summer. Some eastern forest tribes, formerly partially agricultural, moved out into the grassland, acquired horses and lived as hunting nomads, adopting the culture of the horse Indians.

Culture

The possession of the horse had an important influence on the culture of the Indians and changed the mode of life of many tribes. Before they had horses the Indians were footmen, making short journeys and

Apache horseman.

Brule war party.

Buffalo hunt.

transporting their possessions mostly on their backs. The hunting Indians possessed an insignificant amount of property, since the quantity that they could carry was small. All this was changed. An animal had been found which could carry burdens and drag loads. The Indians soon realized that the possession of such an animal would increase their freedom of movement and enable them to increase their property, since one horse could carry the load of several men. Besides this, it insured a food supply and made the moving of camps easy and swift and long journeys possible. In addition to the use of the horse as a burden bearer and as a means of moving rapidly from place to place, it was used as a medium of exchange.

The introduction of the horse led to new intertribal relations; systematic war parties were sent forth.

The horse was usually killed at the grave of its owner, just as his arms were buried with him, in order that he might be equipped for the journey that he was about to take. A number of Plains tribes practised a horse dance. There were songs about horses, and prayers were made in their behalf. On the whole,

however, the horse's place in ceremony was only incidental. On the occasion of great gatherings horses were led into the circle of the dancers and there given away, the donor counting a coup as he passed over the gift to the recipient.

Among some tribes a father gave away a horse when his son killed his first big game or on other important family occasions. In the dances of the soldier-band societies of most tribes 2,4, or 6 chosen men ride horses during the dance. Their horses were painted, the tails were tied up as for war, hawk or owl feathers were tied to the forelock or tail, and frequently a scalp, or something representing it, hung from the lower jaw. The painting represents wounds received by the rider's horse, or often there is painted the print of a hand on either side of the neck to show that an enemy on foot had been ridden down. In preparing to go into a formal battle the horse as well as his rider received protective treatment. It was ceremonially painted and adorned, as described above, and certain herbs and medicines were rubbed or blown over it to give it endurance and strength.

Moving camp.

Horse used to depict life of a Sioux.

Among some of the Plains tribes there was a guild of horse doctors who devoted themselves especially to protecting and healing horses. They doctored horses before going into battle or to the buffalo hunt, so that they should not fall, and doctored those wounded in battle or on the hunt, as well as the men hurt in the hunt. In intertribal horse races they "doctored" in behalf of the horses of their own tribe and against those of their rivals.

HORSESHOE BEND, BATTLE OF was an 1814 battle in Alabama in which anti-American Creeks were decisively defeated by white militia and pro-American Indian forces led by General Andrew Jackson.

As white settlers pushed forward into Creek territory in Georgia and Alabama after 1800, the Creek nation split into pro- and anti-U.S. factions. Civil war began in Creek towns in 1812. The anti-American factions led by chiefs Menawa and Red Eagle were called *Red Sticks* because they painted their war clubs red.

After Red Eagle's massacre of 350 men, women, and children at Fort Mims in August, 1813, an outraged United States demanded retaliation. Several surrounding states sent in militia under five volunteer generals to put down the warring Creeks. General Jackson of Tennessee, later 7th President of the U.S., engaged a large faction of Creek warriors at Tohopeka (Horseshoe Bend). The Tohopeka battle in east central Alabama on the Tallapoosa River proved to be the decisive engagement of the war.

Chief Menawa (Great Warrior), leader of the Creek Okfuskee towns on the Tallapoosa, had placed nearly 1,000 warriors on a peninsula connected to the river bank by a narrow, log-fortified neck. Jackson's 2,000-man force comprised Tennessee militia-men and Creek, Yuchi, and Cherokee warriors. The several hundred Creeks and Yuchis were led by William MacIntosh and Yuchi Chief Timpoochee Barnard. The Cherokees, under Chief Junaluska, numbered 600 warriors and scouts and with the Cherokees was young Sam Houston, who had been living among them in Tennessee.

The battle opened on May 27, 1814 with a 2-hour cannon barrage and the Red Sticks were then attacked from both river banks by Indian auxiliaries. Jackson's main militia force followed. Within a few hours, Creek opposition to white expansion was annihilated as only 70 Red Stick warriors, including Menawa, survived. More than 300 women and children were taken captive from a nearby village.

In the aftermath of the victory, Jackson became a national hero and a major-general in the U.S. Army. He built Fort Jackson at the confluence of the Coosa and Tallapoosa rivers where, in a treaty of August 9, 1814, the Creeks ceded their lands in Alabama.

HOUMA were a relatively small tribe which at the time of European contact lived a few miles east of the Mississippi River near the east-west Mississippi and Louisiana state boundary. They seem to have been one of several Muskogean tribes inhabiting the southern regions of Mississippi and Louisiana. The name *Houma* means "red" and it is believed that the tribe was once united with the Chakchiuma, whose name means "red crawfish". Scarcely any linguistic material has been collected in the Houma language. The few words that were recorded suggest the language was close to the Choctaw and Chickasaw languages.

La Salle was told about the Houma by other tribes during his voyage down the Mississippi in 1682, but he did not visit them. Their first known contact with Europeans was in 1686 when Tonti visited them and persuaded them to make an alliance with the French. The Houma were visited by Iberville in 1699 and again in 1700. Iberville left a missionary with them on the second visit. In 1706 the Tunica, fleeing the Chickasaw, sought and was given refuge among the Houma. The Tunica shortly afterwards abused this hospitality by massacring large numbers of the Houma. Those who escaped fled south and established themselves on a bayou near New Orleans. The Houma are believed to have soon moved north again and settled near the Mississippi River in Ascension Parish, where they remained for a considerable period. About 1805 some Houma went to live with the Atakapa near Lake Charles. Most eventually drifted southward to the coastal regions of Louisiana where their descendants live at the present time.

The Houma provided the French with agricultural produce, an indication that, like the other southeastern tribes, the Houma were agriculturalists. Corn was their major crop. The Houma also gathered the fruits and nuts of the forest. As for their religion and social organization, we know nothing, but it is safe to assume that in these and other cultural features the Houma resembled their Muskogean kindred.

The Houma population has been estimated at 1,000 in 1650. Their numbers were placed at about 700 in 1700. The massacre by the Tunica reduced the population to less than 500. By 1739 they numbered less than 300. In 1803 the total Houma population was placed at only 60. In 1907 an estimate of the mixed-blood population which called itself Houma was between 800 and 900. The 1930 census returned a total population of 947. In 1960 approximately 2,000 people, all of mixed blood, identified themselves as Houma.

Descendants of the Houma now live along the bayous in the southern parts of Terrebonne and La Fourche parishes and earn their living primarily as fishermen, hunters, and trappers. Tribal organization in modern times has been practically nonexistent, although they have succeeded recently in asserting their Indian identity for the purpose of acquiring federal aid for a few social projects.

HOUSE, LLOYD LYNN (Navajo-Oneida; Oct. 24, 1931–), was the first Indian to be elected to the

Arizona State House of Representatives (1966–68). He has worked extensively to provide educational programs for the Navajo tribe in Arizona. He was instrumental in getting social security benefits for self-employed Navajo, which included having Navajo medicine men recognized as self-employed doctors.

In 1973 he received his doctorate in education from Arizona State University. He was dean of instruction at the Navajo Community College (1973–74) and then became director of adult education and in-service training for the Navajo Division of Education in Window Rock, Arizona.

HOUSER, ALLAN (Apache; June 30, 1915–   ), the son of Apaches imprisoned at Fort Sill with the famous war leader Geronimo, overcame a childhood filled with hardships to win several honors for his painting and sculpture. Taking up drawing after an illness forced him to abandon plans of becoming a professional athlete, Houser first concentrated on painting and later became equally adept as a sculptor. He was commissioned to paint murals in Washington's Department of the Interior Building as well as a portrait of Geronimo in the State of Arizona's capital building. An artist in residence and instructor at the Inter-Mountain Indian School and later at the Institute of American Indian Arts, Houser received a Guggenheim Scholarship for Sculpture and Painting and the French Government's Palmes d'Academiques in recognition of his artistic achievements.

HOUSES. *See* DWELLINGS.

HOWE, OSCAR, (Yanktonai Sioux; May 13, 1915–   ), is artist-laureate of S. Dakota and one of the greatest Indian artists of the 20th century.

Howe was born at Joe Creek, on the Crow Creek Indian Reservation in South Dakota. His early schooling was at Pierre Indian School, and he completed his high school education in 1938 at the Santa Fe Indian School, where his art talents were first recognized.

In 1939 Howe returned to Pierre as an art instructor and the following year he painted the interior dome of the Carnegie Library at Mitchell, South Dakota, with symbolic designs. Study in the technique of mural painting brought a commission to execute 10 large oil murals on the walls of an auditorium in Mobridge, South Dakota. In 1948 Howe became artist-in-residence at Dakota Wesleyan University; while there he received the Harvey Dunn Medal in Art and in 1952 received his bachelor's degree. He continued to be both instructor and student, serving as director of art at the high school in Pierre from 1943 until 1957, and receiving his master's degree from the University of Oklahoma in 1954. In 1957 he was appointed assistant professor of fine arts at the State University of South Dakota and later became artist-in-residence as well.

Since 1936 Howe's masterful paintings have been shown in hundreds of group exhibitions and one-man shows throughtout the world. His works are in

Alan Houser.

Allan Houser, Apache, works with boarding school students from the Santo Domingo, Creek, Laguna and Eskimo tribes in sculpture processes.

major public and private collections, and his awards are numerous. In 1962 a citation presented to Howe by the U.S. government proclaimed that, through the media of brush and paint and with full knowledge of his people's way of life, Howe had become one of the foremost exponents of American Indian life in the world of art and that as an instructor he had endowed his students with a rich heritage that would endure.

HOWELL, JAMES PAYER (Cherokee; April 1, 1921–   ), is a career official in the U.S. Bureau of Indian Affairs (BIA) who in 1966 became superintendent of the Tuba City Agency in Arizona, the largest field unit in the BIA. Born in Fort Gibson, Oklahoma, he entered the BIA in 1940. He served as superintendent of the Fort Berthold Agency, New Town, North Dakota (1963–66), before accepting his present position.

HUACA PRIETA, a carbon dated mound in the Chicama River Valley on the north coast of what is now Peru has indicated that the cultivation of cotton *(Gossypium),* bottle gourd *(Lagenaria siceraria),* calabash, chili, beans, and the edible root achira was carried on about 2500 BC. Also found were pieces of cloth made by pounding thin layers of tree bark together. The inhabitants of the valley relied on fishing and harvesting of forest plants for the rest of their diet, as there was no hunting of land animals. They

made no pottery, but practiced weaving and the manufacture of rudimentary stone utensils.

HUACAS were some supernatural powers worshiped by the *Inca* as either places or objects, of importance. It is not entirely clear whether the Indians believed that the supernatural beings had a separate existence from the object in which they resided (animism), or whether the object was the supernatural being (animatism), although the latter appears to have been the case. The problem is complicated by the Spanish practice of speaking of the shrines as inhabited by devils, probably from their own rationalization of oracular responses.

The shrines called huacas were so numerous that very few inhabitants of any town could have known all the recognized ones in the neighborhood. Over 350 huacas in a radius of perhaps 20 miles around Cuzco are known, and they were proportionately numerous in most other Highland towns. Those for Cuzco include temples and cult objects, tombs of ancestors, places associated with mythological characters or dead *Inca* Emperors, battlefields, calendar markers, hills, caves, springs, palaces, prisons, houses, meeting places, bridges, forts, quarries, stones, and roots. The most numerous were springs and stones, which together formed nearly half of the total. Buildings and hills were also numerous.

A few of the most important huacas were worshiped as the residences of important natural powers. A flat

HUAREO (Arawak; fl. 16th century), was an important Arawak Indian chief of Jamaica when Columbus, on his fourth voyage, landed there in 1503. Columbus' subordinate Diego Méndez visited Huareo at his home on a site known to the Spanish as Melilla. Huareo and his eastern neighbor Ameyro were the two Jamaican chiefs known to the Spanish, and both supplied the Europeans with food and laborers.

HUARI was a pre-Inca empire which existed about 600 BC and originated in the Montana Basin, with its center at the town of Chakipampa, near the modern city of Ayacucho, Peru. By about AD 650, the sites of Ituari and Pacheco attained equal importance, but around 700 Huari became predominant. By the time of its decline around 800, the Huari empire had spread as far north as the Chicama Valley and south almost to the Titicaca Basin, thus covering almost all of what is now Peru.

HUARPE. A sedentary people who lived in present-day southern San Juan and northern Mendoza provinces, Argentina, the Huarpe were fishermen in the ancient swamp area of Guanacache. They constructed rafts with the stalks of rushes or reeds, knew the arts of pottery and basketmaking, and cultivated corn (maize) and quinoa.

HUASCAR (ca. 1495-1532) was the 12th Inca emperor, whose reign (1527-1532) was marked by a bitter struggle between himself and his half-brother, Atahuallpa, for the crown. At the same time that this civil war was in progress, the Spanish explorer Francisco Pizarro began his conquest of the Inca state.

Huascar was born near Cuzco, Peru in the 1490s, the son of the emperor Huayna Capac and his secondary wife Mama Rahua Ocllo. His given name was Topa Cusi Huallpa (Royal and Fortunate Turkey Cock), but he later took the name Huascar (Hummingbird). Little is known of Huascar's earliest years, but when he was about 11 years old, his father Huayna Capac, appointed him heir designate and co-ruler, just before leaving for Ecuador to put down native revolts in that area. In spite of this title the young prince was given little actual power, and during the 12 long years his father fought in the north, he spent his adolescence at ease and in splendor in Cuzco. To his father's disappointment, Huascar proved to be neither an able warrior nor was he highly endowed intellectually. History suggests that he was spoiled and pampered in the court.

While campaigning in the north, Huayna Capac had with him two of his other sons, Atahuallpa and Ninan Cuyochi, both of whom he held in high regard. Atahuallpa was proclaimed governor of Quito, and evidently Huascar was forced by his father to agree to this separation of a part of the empire. When an epidemic struck down Huayna Capac in 1526, he manifested his displeasure at Huascar's lack of potential by changing his mind on his deathbed and proclaiming his other son, Ninan Cuyochi, his heir. According to Inca law, Huascar had preference over Ninan Cuyochi since his mother was one of the Inca's sisters and Ninan Cuyochi's mother was a concubine, so Huayna Capac's decision was bound to cause problems. Huayna Capac had further instructed that, if the divine omens did not favor Ninan Cuyochi, then Huascar was to succeed him. The omens did prove unfavorable, and subsequently Ninan Cuyochi also died from the epidemic. Huascar then moved quickly to consolidate his position.

On taking power, Huascar eliminated those officials in Cuzco whom he felt were not loyal to him. He was particularly suspicious of his half-brother, Atahuallpa, who remained behind in Quito. A plot was uncovered to assassinate Huascar and his mother by member of the retinue who accompanied Huayna Capac's mummy to Cuzco. Huascar had the conspirators brutally murdered, including another innocent brother. Evidence suggests that at this time Atahuallpa had no designs on the crown, but Huascar's increasing paranoia and his ill treatment of emissaries sent to Cuzco by Atahuallpa led to the break. Huascar was crowned emperor on the return of his father's mummy to Cuzco, and he married his sister Chuqui Huipa.

In 1529 the Canar tribe in southern Ecuador acquired a new chief who soon allied himself with Huascar's faction. This tribe had been a buffer between the northern territory controlled by Atahuallpa and the remainder of the empire controlled by Huascar, and this alliance opened new tensions between the brothers. Atoc, a general of Huascar's, was sent to Quito Obstensibly to meet with Atahuallpa, but he had .secret orders from Huascar to gain Canar strength and to capture Atahuallpa. Atahuallpa was captured by this force but soon escaped, thus beginning the civil war that was to tear the empire apart.

Atahuallpa had two expert generals, Challcochima and Quizquiz, who led his army into battle. From the very first they were successful, routing Huascar's forces from Tumibamba and defeating them at Cajamarca, Jauca and Ayacucho. By 1531 Atahuallpa's forces were outside of Cuzco. The city was taken in bitter fighting, and Huascar captured. The emperor was forced to watch while his sisters Miro and Chimpu Cisa, the rest of his harem, and 80 of his children were executed in front of him. Their bodies were impaled on stakes along the highway leading out of Cuzco.

In the meantime the Spanish forces under Pizarro, taking advantage of the civil war, captured Atahuallpa in a surprise attack at Cajamarca, and held him prisoner. When Huascar's faction tried to contact the Spanish to enlist their support, Atahuallpa issued orders from his cell to have Huascar executed. In late 1532 Huascar, his queen, his two daughters, and his mother were executed by Challcochima at Andamarca.

Huascar's brief 5 year reign was marked by the violent civil war and countless court intrigues. The chroniclers characterize Huascar as emotionally unstable, envious, paranoid, and isolated. He broke with tradition and built his palace on the hills above Cuzco for protection and to avoid contact with the people. He alienated his family, especially his mother who despised him for disgracing her dead husband, his wife who was forced into marriage with him, and his daughter Cori Cuillor who is said to have provided information to Atahuallpa's faction to spite her father.

Huascar's achievements are minimal. He added no additional territory to the Inca empire, his entire reign being devoted to the civil war. He is said to have undertaken some religious reforms, including the elevation of the cult of Viracocha over Inti, the sun god, thus edging toward monotheism. He deified himself by identifying with the sun god, a step further than his father had taken. Yet he was a weak man in a time of crisis when internal and external forces were destroying all that his ancestors had achieved. We can only speculate about the fate of the Incas if Huascar had been as able as his predecessors.

DONALD A. PROULX

HUASTEC. An important group of Maya is the Huastec. This group, which extended the Maya culture to its northernmost limit, experienced a drastic reduction in the twentieth century. In 1950 there were only five towns in Veracruz and an equal number in San Luis Potosi that could claim a population of 18 percent or more Huastec inhabitants, and no town had over 72 percent Huastec residents. Their rapid dissolution can be measured in terms of the decrease in monolingual Huastec speakers and changing customs. Hunting, once important, is now a minor occupation. The white muslin shirts and pants once favored by the men are being replaced by factory-made clothes on the younger

Huastec clay figure.

generation. Even up to the late 1800s each village considered itself a republic, but the widespread attendance of Huastec children in the rural schools has encouraged the Huastec to become integrated into the national scene in Mexico.

HUAYNA CAPAC (ca. 1482-1527) was the 11th Inca emperor, reigning between the years 1493 and 1527. During the latter part of his reign the Spanish explorer Francisco Pizarro made first contact with the Inca empire, an event which marked the beginning of the end of Inca civilization. The sudden death of Huayna Capac, followed by a dispute over the succession between his sons Huascar and Atahuallpa, led to civil war and ultimate destruction at the hands of the Spanish.

Huayna Capac was born in Tumibamba, located near the present-day city of Cuenca, Ecuador, sometime in the 1480s. He was the son of the emperor Topa Inca Yupanqui (who reigned between 1471 and 1493) and Mama Ocllo, who named him Tito Cusi Hualpa; he later took the name Huayna Capac (Young Ruler). Topa Inca Yupanqui died in 1493, leaving the trone to his pre-adolescent son, Huayna Capac. Hualpaya, a cousin of Topa Inca Yupanqui, was chosen as regent until Huayna Capac reached maturity and could take over the affairs of state. During the 1490s there were at least two attempts to overthrow the young emperor, one by the regent Hualpaya who wished to place his own son on the throne. Huayna Capac barely escaped from the conspirators and was saved by his bodyguards who pushed him out a window of the palace, thus foiling his assassination. Because of these events Huayna Capac was elevated to the office of emperor even before he reached adolescence.

Soon afterward, as was the custom in the royal line, he married his sister, Mama Cusi Rimay, who became his Coya or queen. This union produced no offspring, so Huayna Capac later married a second sister, Mama Rahua Ocllo, who gave him a son, Huascar. He also had children by various concubines, including Atahuallpa, Ninan Cuyochi, Manco Inca, Paullu Topa, and Topa Huallpa.

About the year 1505, as he approached his twentieth year, Huayna Capac decided to make a complete survey of the empire. His father, Topa Inca, had expanded its territories from Ecuador in the north to central Chile and northern Argentina in the south. It had been nearly twelve years since the newly conquered provinces had been investigated. Huayna Capac sent his uncle, Huaman Achachi, to survey the north as far as Quito, while he himself inspected the Colla tribe in the Lake Titicaca Basin. As a result administrative reforms were made, and at the same time the emperor made changes in the state religion. He degraded the priesthood of the sun god, Inti, and proclaimed himself "Shepherd of the Sun," the first step toward the divination of the emperor. He further proclaimed his dead mother a goddess.

Huayna Capac next turned to the coast of Ecuador

which his father had not succeeded in capturing. He subdued the Huancavilcas near Quayaquil and took the Island of La Plata which later became the location of an Inca shrine. While campaigning he learned of a terrible disease ravaging his empire. He returned to Quito with his troops, but the disease had already reached the city. Huayna Capac contracted the disease and died in late 1526 or early 1527. This epidemic has not been definitely identified, but it most certainly was a pestilence introduced by the Spanish which spread from tribe to tribe, reaching the Inca empire before the Spanish themselves. It is believed to have been either smallpox or measles. In all Huayna Capac had spent over 12 years in the north without returning to Cuzco. His death caused a crisis in the succession and paved the way for the Spanish conquest.

Ordinarily the crown would pass to one of the Inca's sons by his principal wife, but as previously mentioned, Mama Cusi Rimay was sterile. Earlier Huayna Capac had chosen Huascar, his son by a second sister, as his co-ruler, but on his deathbed he changed his mind and selected another son, Ninan Cuyochi, to succeed him. Ninan Cuyochi, his son by a concubine, was to have the crown if the diviner's omens were favorable. If not then Huascar was to have the throne. The omens were unfavorable toward Ninan Cuyochi, and he soon died from the same disease that had killed his father. Huascar, the first son, was then proclaimed emperor.

Huayna Capac's mummified body was taken to Cuzco where traditionally it would be placed in the Temple of the Sun. When the Spanish attacked Cuzco in 1532, the body was hidden, only to be discovered in 1559 by the magistrate Polo de Ondegurda. The mummy was taken to Lima and is said to have been buried on the grounds of the Royal Hospital of Saint Andrew.

Huayna Capac was the last independent Inca emperor before the Spanish conquest. His reign witnessed the expansion of the empire to its greatest limits. His love for the northern provinces in Ecuador, where he had been born, led him to neglect the remainder of the empire and earned him the title "absentee emperor." The second capital that he founded at Tumibamba is indicative of the political split that was soon to follow his death.

DONALD A. PROULX

HUDSON BAY is a vast gulf or inland sea in northeastern Canada, which may be regarded as an arm either of the Atlantic Ocean or of the Arctic Ocean. With the Atlantic it communicates by way of Hudson Strait; it is connected with the Artic Ocean by several channels which run in a northerly direction. Hudson Strait is closed by ice during many months of the year; but the channels leading to the Arctic Ocean are practically unnavigable owing to the ice. Hudaon Bay is over 1,000 miles from north to south; and in maximum width about 600 miles. In latitude, it extends from 52°

to 62° 50′, and in longitude from 76° to 95°. Its watershed extends from the St. Lawrence Valley on the south, the Mississippi Valley in the southwest, and the Rocky Mountains in the west. Its shores are bleak and inhispitable.
inhospitable.

It was "discovered" by Henry Hudson in 1610, and was named after him. It was explored by Thomas Button in 1612, by William Baffin in 1615, by Jens Munck in 1619, and by Luke Foxe and Thomas James in 1631; and during these explorations the whole of the coast of Hudson Bay was charted. In 1662 Pierre Esprit Radisson and Medard Chouart des Groseilliers appear to have reached Hudson Bay overland from Lake Superior; and in 1668 Groseilliers, who had taken service with the English, sailed into the Bay and built the first trading-post on the shores. In 1760 the Hudson's Bay Company received the charter which gave it exclusive trading rights in the watershed of Hudson Bay; and in the same year Radisson founded, at the mouth of the Nelson River, what came to be known as York Factory. Trading-posts were later built at the mouths of the Moose and Albany Rivers. From 1682 to 1713 the French made an attempt to oust the English from Hudson Bay, and at times they were in almost complete control of the Bay; but by the treaty of Utrecht in 1713 the french posts on the Bay were handed over to the English, and for a century and a half the Bay was almost a private preserve of the Hudson's Bay Company.

Since to acquisition of the Hudson's Bay Company's territories by Canada in 1869, Hudson Bay has become an inland sea of the Dominion of Canada; and number of exploring expeditions have been sent to Hudson Bay by the Canadian government. In 1929 the Hudson Bay Railway was completed to Churchill, and in 1931 the first shipment of grain from western Canada to Europe was made from this port. In 1932 the Temiskaming and Northern Ontario Railway was completed to Moosonee on James Bay. Hudson Bay has thus been brought into railway communication with the rest of Canada.

HUDSON'S BAY COMPANY was an English corporation, established on May 2, 1670 to trade in the region of Hudson's Bay. For the next 200 years it controlled a profitable fur trade and had a major impact on the Indian and Eskimo cultures of the region.

The fur trade was the medium for the entry of Western civilization to those native peoples in the far north. The Hudson's Bay Company transformed their economies. Originally hunters of caribou and other animals for food, the Indians and Eskimos became fur trappers. They slaughtered herds of caribou to near extinction for the hide and thus became dependent on the European trading post for their food supplies. The Cree, for example, left their Canadian homeland with Hudson's Bay Company guns and moved south in the hunt for beaver. There they became the Plains Cree.

The English felt that Hudson's Bay would provide

Henry Hudson meeting with the Indians along the Hudson River.

easier access to the fur-rich area of the continent than the St. Lawrence River. From the beginning, they encountered strong opposition from French traders, a problem seeingly resolved by the Treaty of Utrecht in 1713. The French, however, continued to compete by sending men inland to the Red and Saskatcheqan rivers.

After the French ceded their territory in 1763, an English group financed the North-West Company of Montreal. Also engaged in the lucrative fur trade it began operation late in the 1770s. Antagonisms between the Hudson's Bay and North-West companies steadily increased, erupting into a bloody confrontation in 1816 on Canada's Red River. This "fur traders war" ended in 1821 when the two merged as the Hudson's Bay Company with exclusive rights as far as the Pacific slope.

Beginning late in the 1840s the company's monopoly was challenged by various Indian and American groups. The British government withdrew the exclusive license in 1859, and free fur traders entered the region. When the territory was transferred to the Dominion of Canada in 1869, the company became a commercial corporation involved in merchandising, land development, and oil exploration.

HUEMAC (Toltec; fl. 11th or 12th centuries), also Uemac or Vemac was the regal name of Texcatlipoca, a Toltec Indian king of Tula (Tollan), central Mexico, who usurped the throne of the famous Toltec king Topiltzin (Ce Acatl), in the 11th or 12th century. Huemac's reign saw disaster fall upon the Toltec empire, first with anarchy and famine, and finally with the destruction of Tula by the barbarians known as 'the Chichimecs. Though sources vary on dating Huemac's reign, the Toltec empire fell before the end of the 13th century.

The history of the struggle between Huemac and Topiltzin so closely parallels the myth concerning the gods Tezcatlipoca and Quetzalcóatl that there is doubt of the existence of the Toltec empire itself. Huemac, of noble birth, was appointed minister by Topiltzin. Huemac was the victor in a domestic struggle that drove Topiltzin to Cholula, in Mexico's Puebla area. Topiltzin's supporters followed him, and regrouped to attack Tula. When Huemac chose to counterattack, he completely vanquished Topiltzin and lay waste to much of Cholula.

However, Huemac had been neglecting domestic affairs. Late in his reign, famine befell Tula, and human sacrifice—outlawed under Topiltzin—

returned to the city. During Huemac's absence, the restless Toltecs chose as their leader one Nauhyotl, who attacked and easily defeated Huemac. The deposed king fled to the city of Chapultepec, where he allegedly committed suicide.

Like his patron god Tezcatlipoca, Huemac brought darkness and death upon his kingdom. Because of the weight of historical evidence, it is likely that, rather than history arising out of myth, the legend of Quetzalcóatl and Tezcatlipoca—later adapted by the Aztecs—had its roots in the accounts of the end of the Toltecs' golden age.

HUETZIN (Toltec; fl. 8th or 9th centuries), ruled the Toltec city of Tula (Tollan), Central Mexico, and was third of his line and apparently the first to inherit his title. The custom of this semi-legendary city was to turn political control over to a governor when a king had ruled for 52 years. Huetzin fulfilled his term and was succeeded on his death by his son Totepeuh. Under Huetzin the legitimacy of Toltec rule was firmly established.

HUICHOL Indians inhabit the rugged mountains and deep canyons of the Chapalagana River drainage in the states of Jalisco and Nayarit, Mexico. Many Huichol live interspersed among other traditional Indians (especially the Cora and Tequal), or in the regional cities and along the Nayarit coast.

Huichol is an Hispanicized form of *vishárika*, which means "us". *Xurúte* is the oldest ethnic name for the Huichol which the Spanish recorded. Other names used during the Colonial Period are: *Vitzúrita, Usilique, Uzare,* and *Guisol.* The term *Nayarita* was also used and applied not only to the Huichol but to the Cora and Tepecano, in addition.

The Huichol, after the Spanish conquest, were divided into three *comunidades* (titled and chartered land grants from the Spanish crown): San Sebastián Teponahuastlán. The former two are subdivided into *gobernancias, i.e.* districts with separate civil-religious hierarchies. The Huichol are not tribally organized,

Huichol dwelling near Santa Catarina, Jalisco.

but rather peasants. Culturally, the Huichol are quite diverse, a fact commonly ignored by anthropologists. Several thousand live outside the *comunidades.*

Before the Spanish arrived, the Huichol occupied a far larger territory. Their settlements extended toward the northeast and into the Bolaños River Valley. Huejuquilla and Tenzompa formerly were Huichol settlements. Settlements also extended to the south and southwest. Today, the core of Huichol territory is the inaccessible and rugged middle Chapalagana Canyon and nearby mountains.

Dialects among the Huichol exist, but all are mutually intelligible. The language, like Cora and Tequal, belongs to the Huicholan group—a subdivision of the Western Nahuatl language family of Uto-Aztecan. There is mutual intelligibility with the Tequal dialects in addition. Cora and Huichol, however, are only partially intelligible.

Most Huichol are ·subsistence farmers (maize, beans, squash gourds, chili, tobacco). Small quantities of cattle and sheep are raised, though some family herds are large. Most fields are prepared by cooperative labor groups using dig-stick, slash and burn techniques. Social organization is complex and rich. Most farmsteads are dispersed but loosely clustered into districts and organized as extended, bilateral lineages. Inheritance of farm site and cattle is often patrilineal, however. "Older Brother" and "Older Sister" are set off in kinship terminology from the rest of their siblings. Polygyny occurs, but it is not common. In the past, each district had a *kalihúe*, or religious compound. The central building of the compound is a communal structure called the *túki.* In many districts, these structures are no longer kept up. Large lineage oriented festivals used to be very common at the compounds. Agricultural rites stressing fertility, ancestor worship, and the health of the lineage are the most common themes of the traditional religious cycle. The consumption of peyote accompanies the chanting and dancing at the compounds. Peyote is gathered in the desrt of San Luis Potosi each year by specially formed groups organized as pilgrims. Their trek is heavily regulated by ritual and has to be on foot. Catholic ritual focuses on the small churches that the Franciscans built in the area during the mid-19th century. These rituals also are oriented toward the agricultural cycle and are heavily influenced by traditional symbolism. Carnival, Easter, Corpus Crhsti, and the birthday of the Virgin of Guadalupe are the most elaborate semi-Catholic rites. Peyote is consumed during these rituals as well, but, as with the traditional ceremonies, only within the context of religious supervision. The churches are controlled not by priests but by mayordomos, each in charge of a specific image and maintaining a confradia (endowment).

Singer-curers, called *mara'akáme*, are prominent among the Huichol. Their major function is to insure health, to cure, and to chant the long, individualized myths and legends that explain the Huichol cosmos. A

Groups of Huichol in native costume.

few men, never more than 5 in each *gobernancia*, are elevated to *kawitéro* (status). A *kawitéro* is a "man who knows everything". They serve as the repositories for each *gobernancia*'s history and legends. They aid the civil-religious hierarchy during the ceremonial cycle. That hierarchy is actually a council divided into two sections. As mentioned, the mayordomos are concerned with religious activities. The civil section of the council governs and presides at trials and ceremonies. Their authority is undisputed.

The Huichol are fine craft workers. Their bead work and weaving are well done and often still traditional. Recently, though, they have entered into the city-oriented tourist trade. The favorite product of the tourists (and museums) are the elegant, but totally nontraditional, yarn paintings.

Before the Spanish arrived, the Huichol had a long history as mountain and canyon agriculturalists. Archaeological survey and limited excavations show that village life with small circular ceremonial structures was well developed by the early Classic Period (*ca.* AD 200). During the Postclassic (AD 900-1,500), Huichol culture is very well documented archaeologically. Large, but dispersed villages are especially prominent near Tenzompa. Certainly, there is no evidence to suggest that the Huichol were recent arrivals in their area from a hunting and gathering background in the desert. This interpretation, while common, is a myth developed by uncritical anthropologists.

Like their neighbors, the Cora, the Huichol were not conquered by the Spanish until long after the conquest of the rest of western Mexico. A violent Spanish raid in the 1560s destroyed the northeastern Huichol settlements of Huejuquilla and Tenzompa. These Huichol were relocated and quickly acculturated. It was not until the end of the 17th century that the Huichol were pacified. Prior to this, they had been effective and violent raiders. Their deep mountain fastness in addition had become a refugee zone for other Indians. The Caxcan, Tepecano, and other groups took refuge among the Huichol after the revolutions of the 1540s. The Huichol had become a composite, response series of societies dedicated, like the Cora, to resisting the Spanish. The traditional date of their conquest is 1722, but that date marks actually the final Spanish campaign to control the western *Nayarita*, or Cora, and the beginning of Franciscan missionary activities. The Franciscans found the Huichol hard to control and it was not until the mid-19th century that the zone had permanent churches. During the middle and late 19th century, the Huichol joined the Lozada revolution. Lozada guaranteed the preservation of their *comunidad* status, something which the Republican government of Juarez had eliminated. The Huichol joined the 1910 Revolution in addition. Their participation in the 1926-9 Cristero Revolution (Christ-the-King) almost cost them their existence. The zone is still regarded as volatile and violent confrontations have again flared up in recent years. Inter-*comunidad* rela-

A Mexican medicine man. (Huichol of Sierra Madre).

tions are not always good, and oftentimes the Huichol are as distrustful of one another as toward outsiders. Contemporary missionary activity is only barely tolerated in the *comunidad* of San Andrés.

The wealth of the Huichol zone is its vast and rich natural pasturage, and the great, virgin stands of coniferous timber. The government is interested in developing these resources through development bank programs. New breeds of cattle have been introduced through a complex series of credit arrangements that the Huichol do not fully understand. Tick baths have been built in order to help upgrade the quality of stock now on the range. A timber survey is planned. The Huichol are suspicious of these programs and often do not cooperate. Corruption by bank officials is common. The city-oriented craft market for tourists is a major source of income for the Huichol. Almost all families gain some income through crafts. Slowly, the rugged mountain zone is being integrated into the national economy.

In the late 1700s, the Spanish estimated a total population of 1,000 for the entire Huichol zone. Archaeological surveys suggest a higher figure, at least several thousand, for the pre-Conquest period. Contemporary estimates range from 8,000 to 12,000, though the last figure is undoubtedly more accurate.

The Huichol are rapidly changing under the pressures for modernization. Many traditional ceremonies are no longer being held. Bilingualism and literacy are increasing. Social structure is no longer egalitarian, and class interests are important. In recent years, they have lost political and economic control over their own *comunidates*.

PHIL C. WEINGAND

HUIPIL. Indian clothing is elaborate in texture and embroiery, if not always in style, in Guatemala. It is not subject to rapid stylistic changes. Young women, however, do embellish traditional costumes with store-bought lace and ribbons and even, on occasion, wear Western-type blouses. Some Indian costumes appear to have survived from preconquest times, but most, particularly the men's, show marked Spanish influence, appearing to be rough copies of Spanish uniforms or other dress. For example, the short red coats worn by some Indian men are similar to those worn by Spanish colonial officials.

The Indian women wear *huipiles,* which are similar to blouses, though they may be very short or quite long, and one of two types of skirt. One type is the wraparound, requiring about 5 yards of cloth, which is close-fitting and is usually worn ankle-length. The other is the pleated skirt, requiring about 8 yards of cloth, which is also usually worn ankle-length. (Women also wear the *tzute,* a piece of decorated cloth, either as part of a headdress, as a shawl, or as a sling in which a baby is carried. Some pregnant women wear maternity belts for support. Occasionally the belts have talismans sewn into them because of the belief that, if one pregnant woman passes another, they will exchange babies. The talismans are believed to prevent this. Coin and coral necklaces are much prized by Indian women.)

Men wear trousers of varying lengths and shirts which are similar to the women's *huipiles.*

HUITZILÍHUITL (Aztec; fl. late 13th and early 14th centuries), also spelled Uitziliuitl, second *huey tlatoani* (chief speaker) of the Mexica (Aztecs) at Tenochtitlán ruled from *c.* 1391 to *c.* 1415 and gave his people previously lacking prestige and respect through politically important marriages, military successes, and new public buildings.

Huitzilíhuitl, which means "Humming Bird Feather," was elected by an electoral college of nobles to succeed his father, Acampichtli, and he began his reign as a vassal of the Tepanecs of Azcapotzalco, ruled by Tezozómoc. After marrying Tezozómoc's granddaughter, a marriage that produced the next Aztec ruler, Chimalpopoca, Tenochtitlán's tribute requirements were reduced to a token. After her death, Huitzilíhuitl married a princess from Cuernavaca, also important politi-

cally, resulting in the birth of the fifth ruler, Moctezuma Ilhuicamina.

Fighting for the Tepanecs, the Aztecs defeated Xaltocan in 1395 and were given that city-state's lands as a reward. They also, apparently independently, took Chalco in 1411 but had to give it back when their more powerful neighbors insisted, lest the Aztecs grow too powerful.

HUITZILÍHUITL (Aztec; fl. 14th century), was first single ruler of the Mexica (Aztecs) who was chosen to rule them during their second stay at Chapultepec (*c.* 1316–19).

Not counted in the list of Aztec rulers, Huitzilíhuitl was unable to prevent a coalition of neighbors, probably led by the Tepanecs of Azcapotzalco, from defeating his disliked people who were sent into slavery.

Huitzilíhuitl was either sacrificed or became a slave, depending on which account is followed.

HUMAHUACA (Omaguaca). This series of native groups inhabited the Quebradade Humahuaca River and its tributaries in Jujuy province, Argentina. They constituted an ethnic unity with their own culture, distinguished by a unified series of peculiar elements and their own characteristic ceramic style. Their economy and life-style were like those of the Diaguita.

HUMAN SACRIFICE. *See* CEREMONIAL SACRIFICE.

HUNAC CEEL (Maya; fl. 13th century), also called Cauich, was a Mexican mercenary who survived being sacrificed in the sacred Maya *cenote* (well) at Chichén Itzá, and rose to become the *halach uinic* (Real Man) or supreme ruler of the northern Yucatán around 1200 A.D.

Hunac Ceel was apparently imported from what is now the Mexican state of Tabasco to help an Itzá dynasty at Mayapan. With his military assistance, the dynasty seized control of the entire northern Yucatan, although Hunac Ceel ended up in the sacred well when the fighting ended.

Because the Maya believed survivors of the sacrificial ordeal had talked to the rain god and were returning with a message, such lucky individuals were pulled out of the well the next morning. Hunac Ceel came back and the feat made him a hero.

Rising rapidly, he soon became the most powerful in the League of Mayapán, a shaky alliance between Mayapán, Chichén Itzá, and Izamal that was increasingly dominated by Mayapán and Hunac Ceel.

Finally, so the traditional story goes, a war broke out after Chac Xib Chac, of Chichén Itzá, stole the bride of Ah Ulil, of Izamal, during the wedding celebrations. The "angry" Hunac Ceel, who may have arranged the abduction, joined with Ah Ulil to defeat Chac Xib Chac. Then he defeated Ah Ulil.

Hunac Ceel and his descendents, bearing the family name, Cocom, ruled the northern Yucatán for about 250 years, until their oppressive government caused a rebellion.

HUNT, WOLF ROBE (Acoma; Oct. 14, 1905–   ), is a painter, lecturer, author, and silversmith; he has been active in the promotion of authentic Pueblo dance groups. Also known as Wayne Henry Hunt, he was born at Acoma, New Mexico. As a young man, Hunt toured Europe with a dance group and since the 1930s has organized and led Pueblo dance groups, presenting educational programs throughout the United States and in foreign countries. For a time he served as an interpreter of Pueblo materials for the Smithsonian Institution.

Hunt wrote and illustrated a book entitled *The Dancing Houses of Acoma* which was published in 1963. In 1967 he won the Grand Award from the Philbrook Art Center for his painting "Dancing with Snakes."

HUNTING. Indians were keen naturalists. They knew the life-histories of the animals they hunted, the different stages of their growth, their seasonal movements and hibernation haunts, and the various foods they sought for sustenance. Difficulties of observation naturally prevented them from gaining as complete a knowledge of the habits of the fish, but they recognized every stage of the salmon from the egg to the adult, and the Nootka of Vancouver island artificially stocked their rivers by transporting salmon ova from one stream to another. Nor were the Indians less observant of the flora of their territories, noting not only the edible plants, and those that were useful for tools, weapons, and various household appliances, but many inconspicuous varieties that apparently served no useful purpose whatever. Their interest in their environment, and eagerness to experiment, led to their discovering the medical properties of many plants, and Indian simples gained a deservedly high repute among the early colonists. Several of them, indeed, have found a place in our culture, and others fail to appear there only because modern science has found better sources elsewhere for the same remedies.

Nowhere was the Indian's keenness of observation more displayed than in hunting. Few have equalled them in these pursuits, except when superior equipment has given them an initial advantage; for the aborigines employed practically every method that was known to the white man, and others that were

Ishi, the aboriginal hunter, calling game.

Ishi, shooting his favorite bow.

unknown. All tribes were not equally proficient in both pursuits; some excelled in hunting, others in fishing; and there were poor hunters, and poor fishermen, in every community. The Cree, who were among the most skilful hunters on the continent, regarded fishing as an occupation worthy only of women, and scorned their Chipewyan neighbours, who were keener fishermen but less proficient in hunting moose and caribou. Generally speaking, however, the average Indian, whatever his tribe, possessed more ability in both pursuits than the average white man, because from his earliest childhood he was trained to give the closest attention and study to every outdoor phenomenon.

Among all the methods of securing game, the still-hunt offers perhaps the greatest scope for individual skill. To the experienced Indian a turned leaf, a broken twig, a slight scraping of a tree, a faint track in the moss, each told a story. In the treeless Arctic the Eskimo who sighted a caribou tested the direction of the air-current by tossing up a shred of down or fur, or by moistening his finger to discover which side felt the cooler; then, if the topography of the ground prevented him from approaching his quarry under cover, he would wait in hiding for several hours, or he would imitate its actions and gait, and boldly advancing into the open, lure it within range of his arrows. Similarly, the Prairie Indian often masked himself under a buffalo hide and approached the buffalo herds unsuspected. Many of the natives could imitate the calls of various birds and animals; and the "moose-call" of the Algonquin tribes, usually performed with a roll of birch-bark, has been passed on to Europeans. The explorer Thompson, himself no mean hunter, pays tribute to the skill of one of his Cree. "An Indian came to hunt for us," he says, "and on looking about thought the ground good for moose, and told us to make no noise; he was told no noise would be made except the falling of the trees, this he said the moose did not mind; when he returned, he told us he had seen the place a doe moose had been feeding in the beginning of May; in two days more he had unravelled her feeding places to the beginning of September. One evening he remarked to us, that he had been so near to her that he could proceed no nearer, unless it blew a gale of wind, when this took place he set off early, and shot the moose deer. This took place in the very early part of October."

Most Indian tribes employed dogs for bringing to bay their game, especially moose, bear, and caribou; they then attacked the quarry with spears rather than with bows and arrows, which often failed to take effect. The Eskimo dog was strong and hardy, and, though not a match for the Arctic wolf, fierce enough to check the progress of a polar bear; but the dogs possessed by the Indians were in general small and ill-nourished.

Until the Indians obtained firearms, however, and even after they secured flintlock guns that required

Low Dog.

reloading after each shot, the still-hunt, whether with or without dogs, was less effective against animals that wandered in herds, such as the deer, caribou, musk-oxen, and buffalo, than the community hunt in which a large body of men participated, often aided by women and children. This community hunt corresponded in many ways to the "beating" of tigers and leopards in the Asiatic jungles, and the rounding up of ostriches by the Bushmen of South Africa. It was indeed an ancient method, successfully employed by men of the Old Stone Age in Europe, thousands of years before the Christian era, in hunting the wild reindeer, mammoths, and other animals that in those days migrated back and forth across the Carpathian mountains. The Salish Indians of the Columbia river practised it in a very simple form; they merely surrounded a herd of antelope in a plain and shot down a small proportion before the remainder broke through the circle and escaped. The Plains' Indians, the Iroquoians and other Eastern Woodland tribes, and the Indians of the Mackenzie River Basin adopted a more complex method; they drove or lured the buffalo, caribou, or deer into some kind of trap, usually an enclosed pound, and shot down entire herds. The old explorer Henry has left an excellent description of the buffalo hunts, which he witnessed among the Assiniboine.

"It is supposed that these people (the Assiniboine) are the most expert and dexterous nation of the plains in constructing pounds, and in driving buffalo into them. The pounds are of different dimensions, according to the number of tents in one camp. The common size is from 60 to 100 paces or yards in circumference, and about five feet in height. Trees are cut down, laid upon one another, and interwoven with branches and green twigs; small openings are left to admit the dogs to feed upon the carcasses of the bulls, which are generally left as useless. This enclosure is commonly made between two hummocks on the declivity or at the foot of rising ground. The entrance is about ten paces wide, and always fronts the plains. On each side of this entrance commences a thick range of fascines, the two ranges spreading asunder as they extend, to the distance of 100 yards, beyond which openings are left at intervals; but the fascines soon become more thinly planted and continue to spread apart to the right and left, until each range has been extended about 300 yards from the pound. The labor is then diminished by only placing at intervals three or four cross-sticks, in imitation of a dog or other animal (sometimes called"dead men"); these extend on the plain for about two miles, and double rows of them are planted in several other directions to a still greater distance. Young men are usually sent out to collect and bring in the buffalo — a tedious task which requires great patience, for the herd must be started by slow degrees. This is done by setting fire to dung or grass. Three young men will bring in a herd of several hundred from a great distance. When the wind is aft it is most favorable, as they can then direct the buffalo with great ease. Having come in sight of the ranges, they generally drive the herd faster, until it begins to enter the ranges, where a swift-footed person has been sta-

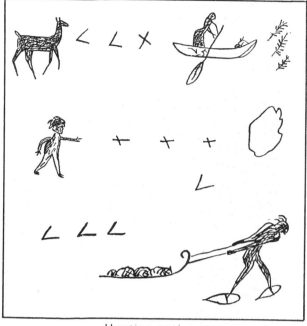

Hunting notices.

tioned with a buffalo robe over his head, to imitate that animal; but sometimes a horse performs this business. When he sees buffaloes approaching he moves slowly toward the pound until they appear to follow him; then he sets off at full speed, imitating a buffalo as well as he can, with the herd after him. The young men in the rear now discover themselves, and drive the herd on with all possible speed. There is always a sentinel on some elevated spot to notify the camp when the buffalo appear; and this intelligence is no sooner given than every man, woman, and child runs to the ranges that lead to the pound, to prevent the buffalo from taking a wrong direction. There they lie down between fascines and cross-sticks, and if the buffalo attempt to break through, the people wave their robes, which causes the herd to keep on, or turn to the opposite side, where other persons do the same. When the buffalo have been thus directed to the entrance of the pound, the Indian who leads them rushes into it and out at the other side, either by jumping over the inclosure or creeping through an opening left for that purpose. The buffalo tumble in pell-mell at his heels, almost exhausted, but keep moving around the inclosure from east to west, and never in a direction against the sun. What appeared extraordinary to me, on those occasions, was that when word was given to the camp of the near approach of the buffalo, the dogs would skulk away from the pound, and not approach until the herd entered. Many buffaloes break their legs, and some their necks, in jumping into the pound, as the descent is generally six or eight feet and stumps are left standing there. The buffalo being caught, the men assemble at the inclosure, armed with bows and arrows; every arrow has a particular mark of the owner, and they fly until the whole herd is killed."

Hunt bag.

Tropical forest hunters and fishers. Top, left: Spearing fish on the upper Xingú'. Bottom, left: Nambicuara hunter with carring basket. Right: Apalakiri man in bark canoe shooting fish.

Design on bow covers sides of birch bark hunting canoes.

Buffalo were occasionally driven over precipices instead of into a pound; and their bones may still be recovered in large numbers from certain ravines on the prairies. The northern Indians, who saw no buffalo, but who impounded caribou during the winter months, often set hedges and snares inside their enclosures, which were built only of saplings and brush. In summer they adopted the same methods as the Eskimo, forcing the caribou into lakes and rivers to spear them from canoes, or else driving them against a line of archers concealed in shallow pits. The Nootka Indians similarly drove the black-tailed deer into bays and fiords, and the Algonquian Indians speared the moose as it swam from one bank or headland to another.

Steel traps for the capture of fur-bearing game originated, of course, with whites, but Indians had long employed both dead-falls and snares, the former mainly for carnivorous animals, the latter for herbivorous. Dead-falls, operated by some kind of trigger, were especially common in British Columbia, where the Carrier Indians alone constructed at least four varieties. Most of the Athapaskan tribes in the north depended largely on snares for the capture of caribou and moose, and everywhere this was the accepted method for small animals like rabbits, hares, and marmots, and for birds like grouse and ptarmigan. Both snares and dead-falls required the exer-

cise of much ingenuity and woodcraft, and all the Indians were skilful trappers centuries before there were any trading posts where their furs could find a market.

Along with the more standard arrowheads the Indians designed several other point varieties primarily for hunting small game. Multiple-pointed arrows were used throughout the Arctic and Northwest Coast down to the Columbia River and by a few tribes in northern California, the Plateau, and the Southwest. Blunt or knobbed arrowheads were in widespread use. They had the advantages of greater durability and a smaller probability of sticking in trees if a shot was missed. A crossed-stick variety was made of from one to four small sticks, slightly larger than a match, glued or bound across the arrow shaft near its point. This type was used in the Southwest, Great Basin, and California, and in some parts of the Plateau and Northwest Coast. In the Arctic, multiple barbs or prongs were sometimes tied pointing forward near the middle of the arrow shaft. These afforded an additional chance of wounding small game if the arrow narrowly missed or glanced off.

The arrow shaft was usually of reed, cane, or stems or strips of wood. The Eskimo often used driftwood or pieces of bone lashed together. For durability, foreshafts of a harder material or grade of wood were often added.

The atlatl, also called spear thrower, throwing stick, throwing board, or dart sling, was a device for giving additional force and accuracy in throwing a dart, spear, or harpoon. It consisted of a shaft about one to two feet long with one end fashioned as a grip and the other notched to fit the trailing end of the spear. It was sometimes grooved lengthwise to accomodate the shaft of the spear. Some atlatls were apparently equipped with a stone weight or balance attached part way up the shaft for increased effectiveness.

The device was used in prehistoric times in the Great Basin, Southwest, Southeast, and southern Florida. It was used in both prehistoric and historic times by all Eskimo tribes, by the Tlingit on the Northwest Coast, in Baja California, and on the Mississippi Delta.

The atlatl appears to have lost much of its importance with the adoption of the bow and arrow.

HUNTING AND GATHERING SOCIETIES.

Human occupation of the Americas began more than 10,000 years ago. When bands of hunters drifted into the region on the track of Ice Age game — caribou and mastodon. They came into a landscape very different from that of today. They hunted in spruce forests and tundra, and across the exposed continental shelf far to the east of the modern shoreline. Since that time, climate, vegetation, and topography have changed greatly. The melting of the continental glaciers released vast amounts of water into the sea, so that the sea level rose, inundating the continental shelves. The warmer climate permitted the northward spread of deciduous trees, berry bushes, and other nutritious plants of the temperate zone. Moose, and then deer, replace caribou, and large numbers of smaller animals spread and settled into the region.

Successive human populations learned to adapt to new conditions, changing their lifeways in response to new opportunities and new restrictions. The story of human adaptation is of interest not only to the region's current residents, but to students of human behavior everywhere, who use such information in comparative studies, seeking to learn about regularities in human behavior through time and space.

Archaic (8000 BC-1000 BC) subsistence activities focused on gathering from localized areas a wide range of wild resources such as large and small mammals, birds, fish, nuts, and seeds. Through time Archaic populations developed from small, scattered groups "scavenging" resources over a wide area to larger groups forming greater regional populations which occupied more limited territories. Groups apparently moved from place to place to collect a variety of localized resources in a seasonal round. The Archaic period marks the beginning of the development of regional cultural traditions which persist into later times throughout the eastern Woodlands.

Woodland

The Woodland period is generally dated from about 1000 BC to between AD 1000 and AD 1600. The regional traditions which first developed during the Archaic continue through the Woodland period and are modified by new cultural developments. Subsistence activities continue to focus on intensive gathering and hunting, but domesticated plants become an important part of subsistence as well.

Middle Woodland subsistence activities relied on the intensive gathering and hunting of localized wild resources. A number of domesticated plants, including maize, also apparently became increasingly important. Middle Woodland subsistence activities have been characterized as "Mud Flat Horticulture" and "Intensive Harvest Collecting."

Late Woodland peoples were evidently primarily gatherers and hunters who focused their subsistence activities on hunting deer and small animals and collecting nuts and seeds along the many large and small streams. In some areas where a number of seasonally available resources occurred in close proximity, Late Woodland villages could be occupied throughout the year and had smaller settlements nearby which were probably occupied seasonally. In other areas settlements appear to have shifted with the seasons in order to allow for the collection of more dispersed resources.

The hunters and gatherers

Living sites of the early caribou hunters are rarely found and the few that are known have not been subjected to careful archaeological study. This rarity is a product of at least two different factors — the popula-

tions were probably never very large, and in the time which has passed since the sites were occupied geological forces as well as residential and industrial development have, no doubt, effaced many of them. The largest site of the early hunters known in New England was found within the survey area on a high terrace above Bull Brook in Ipswich. There, a great many of the characteristic stone tools of these early inhabitants have been found in clusters indicating family camp sites grouped together on the high terrace. The location may have been chosen for the overlook it provided onto the low plains to the east and north of the site, so that the hunters could remain comfortably around their campfires while keeping an eye out for the movement of the caribou herds below. Other sites are known in the area, but none has been explored in any detail. Stray finds of the characteristic early hunter artifacts have been made in Maine, New Hampshire, and Massachusetts.

The end of the caribou hunter period was defined by the climatic changes which drove the caribou slowly north. Ultimately, the caribou hunters had to move also, or learn new habits of hunting and new ways of life. We still do not know whether the descendants of the caribou hunters stayed and made adjustments or whether they left and reoccupation occurred again from the south.

After 7000 BC, there are indications that peoples whose culture was related to others farther south and west had come north where they were perhaps hunting moose and elk in the early deciduous forest of that time. Known sites of the next millennium are all very small, none has been carefully excavated in any detail, and very little is known about the adaptive patterns, group size, or ultimate fate of the people who lived there. Our only record of their passage is a few stone tools scattered over the landscape. We would like to learn more about them. These sites, like the older ones, will be small and fragile, because even as late as eight thousand years ago, the landscape differed from that of today.

We know a lot more about the people who lived here after about 6000 BC. By that time, the people who lived in southern New England had relatives all along the Atlantic seaboard south as far as Florida. Similar artifacts of similar ages are found throughout this area. The New England population was showing strong adaptation to the seasonal changes of available resources. Near Manchester, New Hamshire, they had a large spring fishing camp where they gathered during the spring runs of salmon, shad, and alewives. In the Shawsheen River Basin of Essex and Middlesex counties in Massachusetts, and the Cochato valley southwest of Boston, many small sites of the same age occur. These may have been winter sites located along the sheltered margins of inland ponds, where ice fishing would provide food through the winter. Some of the sites are situated along extensive marsh and swamp lands which may have been somewhat wetter, boggy meadows at the time. These would have been good places to intercept the spring and fall bird migrations and obtain an abundance of meat and feathers. The seasonal adaptations which we see established by this time produced a large variety of sites; no two duplicate one another, each has something new to tell us about the way these people were utilizing the ancient New England environment. We know nothing about the occupations of this age in southern Maine, but we know from scattered artifacts and sites as far north as Labrador that Maine was inhabited at this time.

By 3000 BC New England enjoyed a climate warmer than that of today, and the forest cover in the southern part was more like that of the Chesapeake Bay now. In these rich forests human populations expanded to a density similar to that existing when the English settled the area 4600 years later. By this time, New England inhabitants had become adept at exploiting the new resources of their habitat. Under the city of Boston, 20 feet below modern tide level, was found an ancient fish weir, constructed to intercept the spring runs of alewives, shad, and perhaps salmon. The construction of the weir required large amounts of labor expended over a short period of time each spring, when the weir had to be renewed from the ravages of winter storms. This indicates that the people, by this time, had very extensive knowledge of the seasonal resources and a large repertory of means for exploiting them. They were capable of cooperating in major tasks and probably lived together in fairly large numbers whenever the food supply was adequate in a particular place. They had, by this time, scattered over the entire landscape of southern New England. Sites may be found almost anywhere within that area, not only in the fertile floodplains of the rivers or along the seacoast, but upland into the hills near springs and ponds. Wherever food was available for any animal, human populations by this time had learned to expolit it. The diversity of lifestyles implied among the many sites is not understood, and needs to be examined in detail.

The relatively high population density of this period, between 3000 and 1000 BC produced conditions in which the social skills of the inhabitants became very important. From within the survey area, we have some interesting evidence of fairly elaborate burial rites. Sites showing such ritualism have been recognized in southern New Hampshire and widely in eastern Massachusetts. Along the Sudbury river in Wayland a very large cemetery, the limits of which cannot be known because it's destruction, produced evidence for repetitive ritualism involving fairly large numbers of people, perhaps seasonally, in ceremonies which were somehow related to notions of afterlife and provision for the soul's journey. The ceremonies also reinforced the sense of community among the surviving members of the social group. New England populations by this time had learned enough about the natural environment to have begun to express preference for certain kinds of raw materials and to establish means whereby they could maintain supplies of these goods, even from very long distances. We suspect, in other words, the existence at this time of long-distance trade on a fairly regular basis.

Around 1000 BC, a series of environmental and cultural changes transformed lifestyles in southern New England. The climate became a little cooler, and eventually, through the centuries, the forest composition changed toward that familiar to the early English settlers. Sea levels began to stabilize and estuaries began to form. Along the East Coast, the great clam beds of modern times developed. The Indians did not neglect this enlarged resource. The seashore had long been a dependable source of nutritious food for New England residents but about this time people began to rely more heavily upon coastal resources and to accumulate large shellheaps which were landmarks along the coast before modern destruction. The shellheaps which remain between Casco Bay and Boston Harbor are among our potentially most informative prehistoric remains, because the chemical conditions in shellheaps permit the preservation of objects of bone, antler, and shell which are usually lost in the region's acid soil. There have been few systematic explorations of these shellheaps of east-central New England. We do not know when they began to accumulate, whether there was a time lag between Boston Harbor and southern Maine, what the seasons were of maximum exploitation of the clamflats, and what the activities were in these middens other than shellfish gathering and consumption.

Within the last millennium BC the old adaptive patterns of southern New England changed. Fewer people lived in the hilly interiors; they gathered at the shore more often and perhaps for longer periods of time. The old trade routes broke down, and for a time people seemed to live in more parochial communities than they had before, with fewer outside contacts and more regional indivivuality than had been characteristic in the earlier mellennia. In these same centuries, the craft of pottery-making was introduced into New England, apparently from the west — across to Hudson River. The economic and social importance of this change in cooking vessels is not known.

South America

The scattered food-gathering tribes of the Orinoco Basin, South America, stand a striking contrast to the horticultural tribes of the Amazon-Orinoco area. The culture of these hunters and gatherers is not uniform. All of them hunt and gather vegetable food, but, to some of them, this is the principal subsistence activity, whereas others depend primarily on fishing and on gathering shellfish in rivers and lagoons. These differences in subsistence activities are correlated with other cultural differences, indicating that there was not one basic culture type but two, the Hunting

Culture and the Fishing Culture. Each in turn was divided into at least two subtypes.

Without further comparative research, it is impossible to say whether these subtypes were simply local variants of the two basic types or whether they too sprang from different origins. In any case it is highly significant that these food-gathering tribes formed an important link in the now-broken chain of food-gatherers that at one time must have stretched from Alaska to Tierra del Fuego, and that, like the tribes of the southern part of South America, they were divided into people who were mainly hunters and people who were principally fishermen and shellfish gatherers.

The territory occupied by these food-gatherers is very much larger than had been recognized previously. Whereas to the southeast, food-gathering tribes, like the *Shiriana* and *Waica,* appear as isolated remnants in an area character- ized by horticulture, food-gatherers predominated and farmers were the exception in an almost uninterrupted area north and west of the Orinoco River, stretching from the delta of that river, to the foothills of the Venezuelan Andes in the west and the Vichada River in the south

A considerable number of specific traits, such as the *Gayon* earth oven, linked these tribes with the food-gatherers of North America and with those farther to the east and south in South America. A few elements must have been borrowed from neighboring cultivating tribes, and portions of certain food-gathering tribes had even adopted farming. There was a small but significant number of traits — for example, *Guahibo* and *Chiricoa* rafts and *Guamo* vessels with two spouts — which seem to indicate that some of these tribes had been in contact with the Andean civilizations, though most of them are now separated from Andean tribes by peoples with a Tropical Forest culture of the Amazon-Orinoco type. The *Guamo* and *Taparita* tree-dwellings, on the other hand, may date from a time when these tribes were in contact with the *Choco* and the *Barbacoa* of dwellings that stretches from western Colombia and the pile-dwellers of Lake Maracaibo to the *Warrau* of the Orinoco Delta and to several horticultural tribes of the Guianas.

The immense savannas or llanos, covered with hard grass growing higher than a man, that stretch from the Meta River to the Vichada River, and the narrow strips of forest which separate the savanna from the river are inhabited by a number of nomadic tribes. The culture of these tribes differs as markedly from that of the sedentary tribes surrounding them on all sides as the country inhabited by them differs from the Tropical Forests. However, some traits in the culture of these nomads were undoubtedly taken from the nearby farmers. For the most part, the nomadic groups are confined to the savanna country, which is unsuited for Tropical Forest horticulture. There are also a few representatives of the nonfarmers just beyond the limit of the savanna, in the forests lying to the southwest. Interestingly enough, the latter, although considered to be related to the *Guahibo,* differ from them in some traits (such as permanent settlements and shields used in warfare). This marginal group of the forest is called by a name composed of *Guahibo* and the name of an *Achagua* subtribe from which they may have taken these elements.

Of other Indians still farther south, the first explorers say that they spoke a language similar to that of the *Guahibo* but that they differed from the *Guahibo* culturally, above all in being farmers. Thus it may be that the *Guahibo* and related tribes originally were forest dwellers, or inhabitants of both the forest and the savanna, being driven out from the former and into the latter by the advance of agricultural forest tribes. The invaders may have been the *Arawakan Achagua,* who seem to have had the closest relations with and influence upon these nomads.

The *Yaruro* appear to be the last representatives in this area of a type of culture different not only from that of their horticultural neighbors but also from the savanna-dwelling *Guahibo, Chiricoa,* and related tribes, which live largely by hunting land animals, the *Yaruro* live on sandy river banks and are mainly fishermen and hunters of river animals. While the former usually travel by land and have only wooden rafts for crossing of rivers and occasional downstream travel, the *Yaruro* are expert canoe men and spend much of their time on the river.

While there exist cultural differences as to both details and basic features between the *Yaruro* and the *Guahibo — Chiricoa* group, the nature of the sources and the kind of data they give probably exaggerate these differences.

As with the *Guahibo-Chiricoa,* the *Yaruro* have im-*portant cultural features, such as matrilineal moieties, which are isolated in the region of the Venezuelan-Colombian Llanos and are rare among or atypical of foodgatherers in general. The best explanation of their presence among the primitive Yaruro, Guahibo, or Chiricoa is that they are hold-overs from earlier contacts with western cultures, probably Chibchan* tribes. These relationships were later obscured when the hunting and fishing peoples were surrounded by tribes with an Amazonian type of culture.

The original habitat of the *Yaruro* or *Pumeh,* as they call themselves, is not well known. Today some of them are found on the banks of the Capanaparo River, and others are said to live on the Sinaruco River.

Subsistence Activities

They grew maize only on a very small scale and ate it green, as so many food-gathering tribes do when they first take to farming.

Animals hunted are, more or less in order of importance, crocodiles *(Crocodylus),* turtles (terracais, matamatas, galapagos, and tortoises), iguanas, manatees, chiguires (capybaras), stopped hunting land animals.

HUNTING RIGHTS. *See* FISHING AND HUNTING RIGHTS.

HUPA, Yurok and Karok were the three basic tribes of the rich Northwest Culture Area, which was itself a southern offshoot of the great Northwest Culture Region that stretched from Alaska to northern California. Since the Yurok were the largest of these three tribes and the most culturally diversified, it is under the Yurok that the main features of this culture are explained in more detail. In this description of the Hupa the factors that made them most distinctive are emphasized, as well as a brief outline of the qualities they held in common with the Yurok and Karok. Perhaps the main difference of the Hupa from the other two was their compact nature, as the great bulk of their people were confined in the single Hupa Valley just before the Trinity River enters the Klamath in what is now Humboldt County. They were close together there and knew each other well, unlike the other tribes whose villages were strung out over long distances of the Pacific Coast and the Klamath River.

The name Hupa was originally "Hupu", as given their valley by the Yurok. But the Hupa called themselves the *"Natinnoh-hoi"*, meaning "people of the Natinnoh," their name for the Trinity River, which pours northward here out of the high mountains.

Social and cultural boundaries and subdivisions

The bulk of the Hupa, who lived in Hupa Valley, had two major subdivisions, the South Valley, dominated by the large village of Takimitlding, and the North Valley, dominated by an even larger village, Medilding. South and higher up the Trinity, but not really identifiable as a division were a series of strung-out, very small settlements found wherever flat land along the winding and often cliff-lined river allowed them room. But it was the two first large villages that were the ceremonial centers of the Hupa. There are strong hints that Takimitlding even acted at one time or another as the political center of the tribe, with a head chief. If so, this was almost unique among California Indians, who were universally noted for their divisiveness into small bands each centered on one large village. It would be even more unique for the Northwest California Culture Area where conditions were generally quite chaotic, with political unity of any kind beyond the village very rare.

Language

The Hupa belonged to the very large Athapaskan Language Family that stretches from primitive hunting tribes of the Canadian northwest and the interior of Alaska south and east to the Navajo and the Apaches in Arizona and New Mexico. Athapaskans in California were all centered in the northwest corner of the state and included the Whilkut and Chilula, western and southern dialectically close neighbors of the Hupa, and the Tolowa and Nun-gah-hl branches.

Summary of tribal culture

Subsistence and economy. The principal food of the Hupa was the salmon, which came up the Trinity in

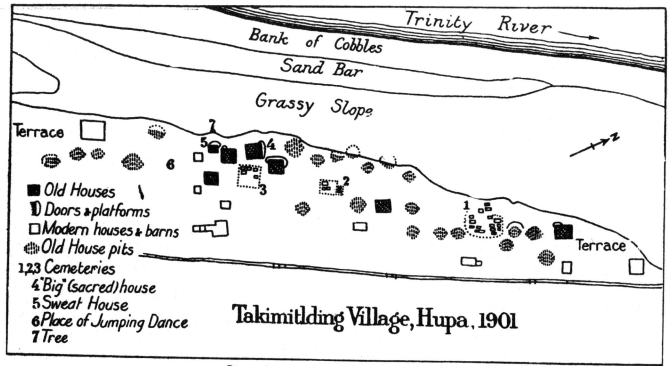

Plan of Hupa town of Takimitiding.

numbers almost any time of the year, but particularly in the spring and fall. The main method of catching them was by the aid of a platform stretched out over the river, to which was attached a large A-frame with the lower part of the A down in the water of an eddy, and on which was hung a large bag net, with the eddy flowing the net upstream. This was exactly where upstream swimming salmon liked to go, and the net was so fixed that the man above could tell when a fish had entered it, close the net entrance and haul the fish up to be clubbed and thrown into a large basket. Lambrey eels were also caught by this method, but using a small mesh net. Some harpooning of fish was done by fishermen not lucky enough to have a good place for a net, the harpoons as much as twenty feet long and usually with three prongs and a detachable head. Once every fall or so the two big villages, Takimitlding and Medilding, alternated in the construction of a huge permeable stick dam across the river, used to catch fish in traps placed in openings.

Acorns, particularly from the tanbark oak, were another major source of food supply, men and boys knocking the acorns down with sticks while the women gathered them and stored them in baskets. The usual California Indian method of leaching the acorn meal of its tannic acid with warm or cool water poured over it in a hollow in the sand was followed, but almost as important were two other methods. One was putting the acorns in the mud of swamps for about a year till freed of acid, then roasting them over coals, while the same thing happened by burying them in sand along the river, after first allowing them to mold in baskets. Bulbs and roots were gathered by the women with digging sticks in late spring and early summer, while seeds were obtained in the grassy meadows of some hill tops. They were much favored for flavoring. There was some hunting but it was not as important as acorns and salmon.

Trading was heavy with the Yurok down the Klamath River, with skins, bright-colored woodpecker scalps and acorns going downriver, while sea foods, dark bars of compressed seaweed, dentalium shell money, and canoes, burnt and chiseled out of redwood logs, were the chief items coming up river.

The Hupa, with their neighbors, had an economy far more based on money than other California tribes, and the only money that realy counted were the shells of dentalium, the dentalium shells being strung on strings that reached from a thumb to the point of the shoulder. A string with 11 2½-inch long shells (called *Kingket*) was worth about ten times as much as a string of 14 2-inch shells (*Hostanhit*) because of the far greater rarity of the longer shells. The high cost of the dentalium shells was due to their being traded down the Pacific Coast all the way from the Nootka of Vancouver Island, who had a virtual monopoly on their gathering.

Technology and arts. The Hupa and their neighbors had a similar technology to other California tribes, but only the Chumash of the Santa Barbara area, and possibly the Pomo of central California with their basketry, had the same interest in quality and artistic development of technical items. Hupa elkhorn and wood spoons were often handcarved in geometric designs of great beauty, for example. But it was in the quality of women's hats that the Hupa stood out, even above their near neighbors. As a woman might say: "they created the cutest little round basket hats you are likely ever to see!", some even decorated with abalone shell pendants that tinkled when a girl walked. What young hunter or warrior could resist that?! It was the designs of white and black, creatively pleasing and the white as sparkling as new snow, made out of *Xerophyllum* fibers, that helped make them stand out, with elaborate triangles and other geometric designs being used.

The houses and dance buildings, being made almost entirely of well-hewed boards, were far superior to the flimsier brush-covered houses built to the south, and the sweat houses were finely-made, with deep semi-underground pits. Even the ordinary houses had pits from 2 to 5 feet deep in the middle, with a kind of shelf all around. No beams or log framework were used in the construction, but the huge boards, lashed to squared poles, were strong enough to hold up a loosely-overlapping roof, with one roof board shifted when needed to provide a smoke hole and light. The women and children lived and cooked in the lower parts of

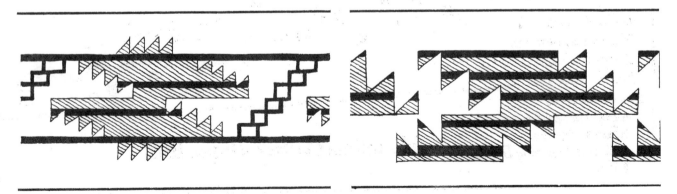

Hupa basket designs.

these houses, but the men only visited them for meals, spending much time in the sweat houses.

Social life. The men cohabited with the women mainly in the warm days, which meant most children were born in the spring. This was partly due to the men being avid seekers after riches and believing that dentalium, the symbol of wealth, and sex did not mix. Both men and women were very clean, taking baths every day, often two. The men spent the mornings working, but the afternoons and evenings were given over to talking and meditating, mainly in the sweat houses, which the men kept spotlessly clean. Gathering wood for the sweat houses from the tops of tall firs was a great social virtue for both men and women seeking power and wealth. The great amount of leisure of the men was due mainly to the ease with which food, particularly salmon, was gathered.

One social difference of the Hupa from the Karok and Yurok was the ceremony for the girl coming into adolescence. Certain men dancers, wearing feather-tipped caps, came often dancing arund the girl at night, shaking rattles made of flexible rods. Also seated women sang and tapped the girl with similar rattles.

Religion and tribal medicine. Religion and the great ceremonies of the Jumping dance and the White Deerskin Dance were so close to those of the Yurok.

Hupa Indians, White Deer Dance.

Family group of Hupa Indians.

Healing was done mainly by doctors, mostly women, who sucked out special "pains". But there were often among the Hupa separate dancing or singing doctors, who diagnosed illness by dreams or clairvoyance. Still another way was to cure through people who could say special magical formulas, and then use curing herbs, which were more in the order of placebos.

Summary of tribal history and contemporary condition

The Hupa were very fortunate to have a secluded valley where there was no gold to excite the miners, and having a reservation very early with soldier protection, though sometimes the soldiers were more harmful than otherwise. The result was their population only dropped from about 1000 in 1780 to 500 in 1910, and has come back strongly since that time. Today the tribe has a fine museum and library, a dictionary of their own language, which the children are learning, and there is a growing interest in and redevelopment of their past culture. A drawback is lack of work in the area.

VINSON BROWN

HURON. During the first half of the 17th century, French soldiers, explorers and missionaries observed and described a confederation of several tribes, living in a small region of southern Ontario between Lake Simcoe and Georgian Bay, which they referred to as the Hurons. These people were sedentary farmers, living in semi-permanent stockaded towns, and spoke a language belonging to the Iroquois language family. They were similar in culture and language to the Five Nations Iroquois of New York state, with whom they probably shared a biological ancestry. They had even closer affinities with other Iroquoian peoples in the Great Lakes area: the St. Lawrence Iroquois, the Neutrals of southwestern Ontario, and the Petun of the Blue Mountain region just west of the Huron.

Name

The name Huron is a French word which was applied to people in all the tribes of the Huron confederacy. The word itself means a "a wild boar", and may refer to the hairstyle of Huron men at the time; it was also used more generally as a name for rough or rustic people. The name used by the Hurons themselves to refer to the whole confederacy was *wendat*. This is often interpreted to mean "people living on an island", and could refer to the fact that the Huron territory in the 17th century was almost surrounded by water. It has also been translated as "people who speak a common language". This receives some support from the fact that the Hurons referred to neighboring Iroquoian

Hurons of Lorette. (1838).

groups, such as the Neutrals, as *attiwandaronk*, "people who speak a slightly different language", and this was the same name by which these neighbors referred to the Hurons themselves.

Social and cultural boundaries and subdivisions

By the early 17th century, when first contacted by Europeans, all the Hurons lived in a small region, referred to now as 'Historic Huronia', extending from the town of Orillia on Lake Simcoe to the Penetang Peninsula on Georgian Bay. This is a region of rolling sandy terrain which, at that time, would have been covered with areas of maple-beech forest and areas of more open country. There were uninhabited areas adjacent to Huronia, such as the valley of the Trent River system, which the Hurons controlled and used as hunting territories.

The Huron country was divided into five areas, each occupied by a tribe or 'nation'. The names of these tribes were *attignawantan* (Bear), *arendahrenon* (Rock), *attigneenongnahac* (Cord), *tohontaenrat* (Deer, or One-White-Lodge), and *ataronchronon* (People-of-the-Fens). These nations all shared a common language and essentially the same culture. The number of towns and villages comprising each nation varied considerably, ranging from one to fourteen.

Territory·

In the 17th century the Hurons were crowded into a territory measuring approximately 35 miles by 15 miles, in a band from Orillia to the Penetang Peninsula, It is clear from archaeological evidence that prior to AD 1600 the Hurons inhabited a much broader region than this. Pre-contact Huron village sites are known not only from historic Huronia, but all over an area bounded on the west by the Niagara escarpment, on the south by Lake Ontario, and on the east and north by the Canadian Shield. Villages appear to be concentrated in the region from Toronto northward to Huronia, along the shore of Lake Ontario, and in the valley of the Trent River system.

Language

The Huron nations spoke a common language belonging to the Iroquois language family. The Petun, just to the west, spoke the same language, while the Neutral to the southwest apparently spoke a language that was somewhat different. Huron is more distantly related to the languages of the League Iroquois, suggesting that the two groups have been linguistically separated for some time, perhaps more than 2000 years. The Iroquois language family also includes Cherokee, and the family as a whole is related to the Siouan family.

Culture

Subsistence and economy. Huron subsistence was based upon horticulture, hunting, fishing, and gathering of wild plants. Plants cultivated by the Huron included maize, beans, squash, pumpkins, sunflowers and tobacco. While men cleared the fields of trees and brush, planting, tending and harvesting the crops was the task of the women. After harvesting, corn was dried and pounded into a meal and stored for use during the winter, when it served as a staple food. During the fall and early winter, Huron men engaged in hunting. The animals most commonly hunted were white-tail-deer, beaver and bear. Other animals eaten included rabbits, ground hogs, squirrels, raccoons, skunks, turtles and birds. Hunting techniques made use of traps, snares, spears and bows and arrows. In at least some villages, substantial numbers of domestic dogs were raised for food.

Fish formed an important part of Huron diet, being used in soups, as well as eaten fresh, dried or smoked. Fishing was a communal activity, carried out primarily in the spring and fall. Fish were caught in lakes and streams, by nets, weirs and lines. In winter time, some ice-fishing was done with nets or lines.

Wild plant foods used by the Huron included several kinds of berries, nuts, plums, cherries, grapes, apples, beans and peas, and a few roots. Many of the fruits were dried for winter use.

An important aspect of Huron economy was trade, particularly in the historic period. During their involvement in the fur trade the Hurons traded corn and other items to the more northerly Algonkians in exchange for animal skins and fish. The animal skins, particularly beaver, were taken to Quebec, where they were traded to the French in exchange for European goods.

Settlement and yearly cycle. The focal point of Huron life was the semi-permanent village. Most villages were enclosed by a stockade of poles interlaced with bark or branches, and might occupy an area of from one acre to more than 20 acres. These villages were relocated every 10 to 30 years, when soil and firewood had been exhausted.

Huron houses were of the longhouse type, and accommodated several related families, being approximately 25 feet wide and anywhere from 30 to 200 feet long. Houses were constructed of poles bent over and tied together to form a roof, and covered with bark. Down the center of the house was a common passageway which contained cooking fires shared by individual families, who occupied compartments down each side of the house. On the average, a longhouse might accommodate about 10 families, or roughly 50 to 70 people. A small village might contain just a few such houses, while the larger ones might contain as many as 100. One large Huron village of the early 17th century was reported to have 200 longhouses.

The Huron population spent the winter in the villages, subsisting on the products of the hunt, and crops and other foods stored during the summer and fall. During this season, much time was spent at games, ceremonies and feasts. In spring, many people left the village for varying periods, the men spending the summer engaged in fishing and hunting, warfare, and trading. The women were involved in agricultural pursuits, and many of them built houses and lived in the cornfields during the growing season. During the fall, people gathered at favorite fishing places, after which men were busy hunting. The population finally reassembled in the village during December.

Technology. Prior to the introduction of European materials in the 16th century, Hurons had what could be termed a neolithic level of technology. Metallurgy was virtually unknown; most tools, weapons and utensils were made from wood, bone, antler, shell, stone or pottery. Native copper was sometimes used for implements such as awls, or for beads.

Household utensils included pottery vessels for cooking and storage, wooden bowls, spoons and forks, and other containers of wood and bark. Women's tools included flint knives, flint scrapers and bone fleshers for preparing animal hides, and bone awls and needles for piercing and sewing leather. Used in hunting were arrows tipped with flint, bone or antler, harpoons with barbed bone or antler points, and spears tipped with stone. Axes and adzes of ground and polished stone were used for felling trees, and dressing poles for houses and palisades. The principal weapons of war were bows and arrows, and wooden clubs. Also used were shields of leather or bark, and armor made of wooden slats laced together.

Following contact with the French, native technology was quickly replaced by articles of European manufacture, such as copper kettles, and iron axes, knives and awls.

Life cycle. For the first two or three years of its life, a Huron baby was breast fed and fed meat previously chewed by its mother. During this time, the infant spent the day in a cradleboard, wrapped in fur, or roaming the floor of the house. At night it slept between its parents. The period between infancy and adulthood was spent in games that anticipated adult activities. Boys spent their time shooting bows and arrows or playing games of physical skill, while girls engaged in play imitating the grinding of corn or other household activities.

Relations between the youth of different sexes seem to have been generally uninhibited, and girls apparently competed for the greatest number of lovers. When a girl became pregnant, her lovers would all claim that the child was theirs, and she would choose from among them the one she liked best for a husband. When a young man and woman had decided to marry, the man asked for the permission of the woman's parents. If he was an acceptable suitor to both the woman and her parents, a wedding feast was held for the couple's friends and relatives, at which their marriage was announced.

A man's own children were not his heirs, but rather the heirs of his wife's brother. Similarly, his own heirs were his sister's children; to them he would pass on his titles and possessions, and they, in turn, supported his in his old age. The elderly were respected, and their opinions sought on matters of importance.

Death was approached calmly by the Hurons. If a man was dying of natural causes, he might give a farewell feast for his friends and, as his death approached, he was shown the clothes and finery in which he would be buried. Immediately following death, the body was wrapped in a robe, and covered in furs and bark. The death was announced through the village, and feasts were held. Three days after death, the body was carried to the cemetery, just outside the village, where it was placed in a tomb made of bark. Sometimes bodies were buried in the ground, and a small hut of bark erected over the grave.

Every 10 years, several Huron villages cooperated in holding a Feast of the Dead, at which the bodies of those who had died since the last feast were removed from their graves and re-buried in a common pit, amid a great deal of feasting and exchanging of presents.

Social and political organization. The basic economic and social unit of Huron life was the family, which had the responsibility for providing for its members. A household accommodated a number of families related through the female line, thus approximating a matrilineage or a matrilineal extended family. The families sharing a house customarily cooperated in many ventures, and were expected to share and to help each other when necessary.

The village seems to have enjoyed a high degree of autonomy, but was tied to other villages by common concerns and activities. The affairs of the village were governed by a council of the older men. Among these councillors were chiefs of two kinds: those concerned with the government of the village, including such things as feasts, games and funerals; and those concerned with war. Chieftainships were largely hereditary, so that when a chief died, the successor was selected from among his sisters' sons. Certain of the chiefs were recognized as being pre-eminent by virtue of their personal qualities of wealth, and their influence was correspondingly greater than that of the other chiefs.

Above the village level, tribal affairs were governed by a council composed of the most respected chiefs from all the villages in that tribe. Of this council, one member was recognized as being the principal chief of the nation. This chief and his council had the responsibility for making treaties with other nations, declaring war, and giving permission for foreigners to cross the tribal territory. The entire confederacy of the Huron was likewise governed by a council, which probably consisted of a combination of the various tribal councils.

Religion. The Huron believed that every object, as well as people and animals, possessed souls or spirits. Some of these spirits had the ability to affect human affairs, and were propitiated by offerings. Among the most important spirits were those of the sky, and of certain geographical entities such as lakes, islands, large rocks, etc.

Some people, such as shamans, were believed to have a familiar spirit, acquired in a vision or dream, whose aid they could enlist. The most important function of shamans was curing the sick. This was accomplished by extracting an offending object from the patient's body, breaking a sorcerer's spell, or interpreting and fulfilling the patient's dreams. Other shamanistic functions included controlling weather, and bringing good luck in hunting, fishing or warfare.

The Hurons regarded dreams as the means whereby the soul made its thoughts and desires known, and to let such desires go unfulfilled could bring sickness and death. Thus, if a man dreamed that he would die if he were not presented with certain gifts, the required items would be found and given to him.

Charms were objects found or collected by Huron men which were believed to bring luck in hunting, war, and other activities. They were held in awe, and feasts might be given to maintain their power.

History

Huron culture can be traced archaeologically to approximately AD 1200, at which time the Hurons can be recognized as occupying several 'tribal' areas, each comprising a few villages, in a triangle bounded by Hamilton, Kingston, and Penetanguishene. These local groups appear to have been relatively independent.

At approximately AD 1500, European trade goods were introduced to the Hurons from the St. Lawrence Iroquois, who were in contact with Portuguese,

Basque and Breton people exploiting the Gulf of St. Lawrence. This led to competition among the Hurons for access to this trade, resulting in new patterns of inter-tribal alliances, warfare and migrations. At approximately 1550, probably because of a depletion of furs in the southern regions, as well as hostilities, there was a gradual movement away from Lake Ontario towards the upper Trent River valley and 'historic' Huronia. Following the intensification of hostilities between the Hurons and the New York Iroquois at the end of the 16th century, the Hurons all moved into Huronia, forming the Huron confederacy.

Hurons were first met by the French at Quebec in the opening years of the 17th century, after which an alliance was forged between the French and the Hurons, involving trade agreements, and commitments of military aid against their respective enemies. The most intensive contact between the Hurons and the French resulted from the establishment of Jesuit missions in Huronia in the 1630s and 1640s. During this time the Huron continued to trade with French commercial interests at Quebec.

As a result of competition for the fur trade, the Hurons were attacked and dispersed by the New York Iroquois in 1649, and many Hurons became captives of the Iroquois. Others fled to neighboring tribes such as the Neutrals, only to be attacked by the Iroquois again. One group fled westward with the Petun, and spent the next 150 years in a series of movements throughout the western Great Lakes. In 1815 they settled in Ohio and Michigan, only to move a few years later to Oklahoma, where they remain to the present day. A small group of Hurons made it to Quebec in 1656; this group is now known as the Hurons of Lorette.

An average estimate for the total population of Huronia in about 1630 is 25,000 to 30,000. Within the ensuing 20 years, warfare and disease had reduced the population to 10,000 or less. Considering the dispersal of the Hurons from their homeland, and the movements and probable mixing of populations in the intervening 320 years, present population estimates are virtually meaningless.

Conclusion

The available information on the Hurons depicts a relatively large aboriginal group being profoundly affected and disrupted by the complex events surrounding the arrival of Europeans in the eastern part of North America. Traditional Huron patterns of settlement, subsistence and politics were greatly modified by the effects of the European presence, probably as much as a century before the Hurons ever saw a white man. Huron involvement in European politics in North America helped to weld them into a confederacy, allied with the crown of France. It also led, a scant 50 years later, to their complete destruction as a social and cultural entity at the hands of the League of the Iroquois.

place in one of the squares at Cuzco was supposed to be the abode of the Earthquake, and a doorway in one of the palaces, the home of the Wind. Some objects associated with the cult were worshiped; for instance, the brazier from which fire for sacrifice was taken, a field dedicated to the cult of Huanacauri, and so forth. Places associated with an Emperor, especially with Pachacuti or Topa Inca, or Topa Inca's queen, Mama Ocllo, were huacas. The stones which had turned to men to help Pachacuti defeat the *Chanca* were very numerous. The city of Cuzco itself was sacred, as is clear form the fact that the places where a traveler caught his first and last glimpses of it were important shrines.

The most important huaca outside of the temples of the sky gods was Huanacauri (WANAKAWRI), a spindle-shaped unwrought stone on Huanacauri hill near Cuzco, which was believed to represent one of Manco Capac's brothers and was a special protector of the *Inca* royal family and a prominent feature in the maturity rites of the *Inca* youth. Certain other hills near Cuzco were also of exceptional importance (Anahuarque, Senca, etc.). In general, the supernatural power of a hill or mountain varied in direct proportion to its height, and all snow-capped peaks were very important deities. The powerful peaks of Ausangate (visible from Cuzco), Vilcanota, Coropuna, and Pariacaca were widely worshiped. This mountain worship is a very important element of modern *Quechua* religion. In modern times, mountain peaks are called APO ("Lord"), but this title does not appear to have been used in ancient religion.

Two kinds of huacas were associated with cultivated fields: the boundary markers (SAYWA) and the field guardians (WANKA). Field guardians were long stones set upright in the center of the field, and their importance is indicated by the fact that the principal WANKA of Cuzco was believed to have been a brother of Manca Capac.

Another special type of huaca was the APACITA, a pile of stones marking the top of a pass or other critical point on a road, where travelers stopped to make small offerings and pray for strength before continuing. The offering might consist of worn-out sandals, a coca quid, straw, another stone added to the pile, or anything else of little value. This custom is still general throughout the Andes on trails where the Indians travel on foot, and the ancient huacas are being constantly augmented.

Besides the localized huacas, the *Inca* used a variety of portable images and amulets for different purposes. Some were in human form, some represented animals, ears of maize, or potatoes, and others were natural stones of unusual shape or color, bezoar stones, or crystals. These were all called indiscriminately WAK'A, but were distinguished by function, as WASI-KAMAYOQ, "house guardian," SARA-MAMA, "maize mother," etc. Bezoar stones, favorite amulets, were called ILYA or AYAYLYA.

Bodies of the dead and all unusual things were also called huaca, regarded with awe, and worshiped. The following are examples: AYRIWA-SARA ("April maize"), two grains of maize growing together, or a stalk with a black and a white ear on it; twins (WAK'A-WACASQA or ISKAY-WACASQA); persons with six fingers like a puma (POMA-RONA); persons born feet first (chacpa). Similar terms exist for central Peru.

Each *Inca* emperor had a personal guardian, usually a portable huaca, which he called WAWQI, "brother," and which protected and advised him. It is not certain whether other men also claimed to have personal guardians, but it seems likely. These guardians were rarely animals. Pachacuti took an image of the Thunder God for his guardian.

HUALAPAI RESERVATION. Hualapai Reservation, Arizona, nearly one million acres in size, is home to more than 1,000 Hualapai (Yuma) Indians.

A January 1883 Executive order established a reservation of 500,000 acres. In June 1911, 60 acres in the Big Sandy area were added by Executive order. The Santa Fe Railroad deeded 6,440.68 acres in Clay Springs to the reservation in 1947. In May 1943, the Secretary of the Interior ordered odd sections which were released by the Santa Fe Railroad to be added to the reservation.

The Hualapai Indians formerly lived in northeastern Arizona occupying an area much larger than they do today. The mid-19th century was a period of friction with whites. Peace ended abruptly when the Indians felt the treaty had been violated. A stable peace was finally achieved in 1870. The Hualapai fulfilled their promise to preserve the peace. The Hualapai objected to their removal by the Bureau of Indian Affairs which placed them in the hot arid Colorado River Basin. Illness for many members resulted from living in the climate unlike that of their former cool mountain home. The principal Chief Schrum was instrumental in achieving the final settlements.

The Hualapai are of Yuman stock and closely related to the Havasupai. Ancient inhabitants of the Southwest, they lived mainly by hunting and gathering. They lived in mountainous areas and were described by whites as brave and enterprising. They are part of the Colorado River cultural group, less advanced in agriculture and architecture than the Pueblos. They also exhibit traits of the Great Basin area in their simplicity of social organization, ritual, and material culture. Religion is shamanistic. Clothing was made of bark or buckskin. They harvested seeds, grasses, pinon nuts, and game.

HUANCA occupy a broad basin of the Mantaro River (the basin a huge fossil Pleistocene lake bed) and the surrounding puna in the Andes of central Peru. This is about 3000-3400 meters, or 10,000-12,000 feet above sea level, in the present day provinces of Jauja,

Concepcion and Huancayo of the Department of Junin. The Mantaro River runs north-south, parallel to the Andes, making it a major route of communication—a branch of the Panamericana runs along it today, and the major Inca Royal highway ran through the same area 500 years ago.

The Huanca had three major political divisions at the time of the Inca and later Spanish conquests: Hatun Jauja, Hanansaya Huanca, and Lurinsaya Huanca. Alternative terms found are usually variants in spelling, such as *Wanka, Guanca, Sausa, Xauxa, Atunjauja, Ananguanca, Uringuanca,* or *Guanca Guamani*. The meaning of both "wanka" and "xauxa" appear to reflect the agricultural importance of the area. "Wanka" refers to the name of one of the important agricultural field gods in Inca times, and the term is still used today in some communities to refer to small stone field gods. "Xauxa" is believed to derive from a local dialectical name for the llama.

The Huanca language belongs to one of the two major subdivisions of Quechua, that of Quechua I or B. Recent research has shown that Quechua I/B is older than the second subdivision, Quechua II/A. Quechua II/A is the language spread by the Inca in their imperial expansion just prior to the Spanish arrival. Quechua I/B is therefore an earlier, pre-Inca language, which is identified as the language of the Second Great Andean Empire (the Inca being the Third) known as the Huari or Wari, whose height of power was about AD 500-800.

The Huanca at the time of the Inca and Spanish conquests were an agricultural folk. They grew a large number of plants, including such important contemporary domesticates as potatoes, *ocas, ullucu, mashua, maca, quinoa, tarwi,* beans and corn. They also herded large numbers of alpacas and llamas. Today this agricultural emphasis continues, although such plants as wheat, barley, and onions, and such animals as sheep, cattle and donkeys, introduced from the Old World, have largely supplanted many of the indigenous species. The Huanca area is currently a "breadbasket" zone for Peru. It was also such a major agricultural zone for the Inca, and appears to have been so for much of the last 1500 years.

The Huanca may have been some of the very first herders of llamas and alpacas in the Andes. Archaeozoological evidence indicates that the Junin area was one of the first zones where the wild guanaco underwent the process of domestication into these modern varieties. Llamas and alpacas have played an important part in Huanca history until the present century. One of the most important methods of transporting goods in the Andes, until the advent of the modern fossil-fuel powered conveyances, has been the llama caravan.

The Huanca maintained a large number of caravan animals. Control of numerous transport animals gave the Huanca significant political and economic power. An extremely important development in the Huanca

area was the development of a mercantile economy. This contrasts sharply with other tribes such as the Incas. The Inca and many of the other typical Andean groups did not rely on markets for supply but rather relied upon mutual reciprocal obligations through kinsfolk living in slightly different ecological zones on the steep Andean slopes to provide them with necessities. The Huanca, in contrast, became skilled entrepreneurs, trading goods in long distance caravan networks, resulting in a market-oriented economy. A measure of the kind of market orientation among the Huanca is that when the Spaniards first reached the largest of the three Huanca capitals, Juaja, they found a market of an estimated 100,000 people, with regular governmental specialists overseeing the flow of market goods and other marketing procedures. Such skills and emphasis continue in the Huanca area until the present. The weekly trade fair in Huancayo is the largest in Peru, and has become one of the mandatory tourist attractions.

Huanca housing patterns have changed much in the last 500 years. Before the Inca conquest, the Huanca lived in villages and towns, reaching sizes of 2,500 to 3,500. These settlements were on the top of low hills, affording them view over the surrounding area, and providing a more readily defensible location, for there were frequent small raids from surrounding outside peoples. There were irregular streets running through the towns, but since there wre no wheeled vehicles, only llama caravans and foot traffic, the streets took sharp corners, and ascended narrow stairways. The houses were clustered around narrow courtyards. In the poorer sections of town, there might be a dozen or more small circular houses clustered around such a courtyard. In the more affluent parts of town, the houses were larger, and more equally spaced, sometimes no more than one house to each side of a courtyard. On the downhill or exposed flanks of the town, there were one or more rows of storage buildings (colca), usually numbering 20-50 buildings, but sometimes as many as 100 or more. Early Spanish explorers tell us of the wealth stored in these buildings—hundreds of cloaks and ponchos; pairs of sandals; freeze-dried tubers such as potatoes, oca and ullucu; parched corn; quinoa; sun-dried llama meat; dried fish; fruits from the jungle; corn beer; pottery vessels; gold, silver, copper, lead, and various bronze metal goods; dried peppers and salt; and sometimes firewood and straw (for bedding and animal fodder). The towns and villages were well provisioned, and could withstand occasional years of loss of crops through frosts or loss of animals through similar natural causes, as well as the occasional seige. The location of the storage buildings on the lower, exposed flanks served an important and obvious function in providing additional fortification and a rampart surrounding the town.

The individual house was built of unmodified stone from the fields, cemented together with clay, and housed a single family of an average of 5-6 persons.

Walls were built to 6-8 feet high, and the house was covered with a domed roof, thatched with native ichu grass. The houses were small, usually no more than 3-5 meters or 10-15 feet in diameter, with a single small door about 2 feet wide and 3 feet high through which one entered the house. Some of the better built houses also had one small window, and clay plastered walls decorated with red and white designs. Furniture was sparse. The bed was nothing more than woven textiles placed on masses of ichu grass bundles on the dirt floor. There were occasional stools of rock or wood. Decorated ceramics for cooking, eating and food storage; wooden and stone agricultural tools; some weapons; and equipment for simple crafts such as weaving formed the bulk of other goods in the houses, stored in wall niches or hung from poles protruding from the wall.

The Huancas dressed much like their neighbors throughout the Peruvian Andes at this time. They had shirts, ponchos, and dress-length shifts for clothing. These were homespuns, woven in each household for its own use. As a tax obligation for the local chief, the homeowners spun finer grades of textiles from alpaca wool. On ceremonial occasions, metal pins (tupu) made of copper and silver, were worn to fasten the clothing together, and to serve as decorations. Within the Huanca area prior to the Spanish conquest, the people wore four-cornered woven hats: black hats for the men of Hanan and Lurin Huanca, and multi-colored ones for the Jauja-Huanca. These four-cornered hats were three inches high, and are identical to those worn a thousand years earlier by the ranking officials of the Second Andean Empire of Wari. Later, during the Inca empire, they continued to wear similar four-cornered caps, but the Inca ordered the Lurin-Huanca and Hanan-Huanca to change their hat colors, so that one could easily distinguish a Lurin-Huanca from a Hanan-Huanca from a Hatun-Jauja simply by glancing at the cap color. Sandals were made from the tough leather of the neck of llamas, and from woven plant strips and fronds. More important members of the group wore jewelry such as earspools, necklaces, and headpieces as insignia or badges of office on appropriate occasions. The Huanca took pride in wearing their hair longer than that of their neighbors.

Political power resided with the more important families in the village, but the most important offices did not necessarily pass down from father to son. If the current chief (curaca) did not have sons judged suitable for leadership, then the village council of elders elevated to power that individual felt to have these characteristics. There was a great deal of local village autonomy, so within a larger region power rested more on persuasion than coercion. Our picture is seen only imperfectly through the eyes of Spaniards interviewing the last few surviving elders. What appears is a view of changing political fortunes. Individual towns rose and fell from power as individual families or strong rulers appeared. The provincial capital thus was not a set locale, but changed with the fortunes of the success of local politicians.

Huanca religion had both a broader theological thrust and a particularistic pragmatic quality. On the one hand, there was an important branch of the Oracle of Pachacamac, that of the temple of Huariwilka in Hanan-Huanca territory (just south of present Huancayo). The oracular tradition, though focussed in part on agricultural processes, with Pachamama or Earth-Mother the moving force, was also a more ideological or theologically oriented system. Religious philosophers and priests were attached to this complex. On the other hand there were a number of localized or even individualized spirits. Each house had household gods (kamac) looking after its residents. There were gods of the fields (wankas), and a series of other spirits, associated with mythological places of origin such as springs and lakes, and mountains. For the Inca, the Sun was the paramount diety; one early Spanish source suggests that for the Huanca it was the Moon.

The important dead of a village were buried in the skin of a llama or alpaca. The individual was sewn up in this hide, and was brought forth on a litter for various religious occasions in order that the spirit of the dead might add force to the ceremony. Sacrifices of llamas and alpacas frequently took place during religious celebrations. Other frequently mentioned offerings were cocoa leaf, food items, sea shells, and a special totem of the Huanca, the dog. Little is known about the early medical practices and beliefs. Bleeding an individual to let the bad spirits escape was one frequent method of curing. Intestinal problems were handled by using the purgative vilca and other native herbal remedies. Tobacco powder, and a whole range of pharmaceuticals from the Amazonian lowlands were inhaled through the nostrils by curers in various ceremonies, and also taken by the patients in many of these sessions.

The Huanca became very involved in the Inca civil war in the decade just prior to the Spanish arrival, and later in the Spanish civil wars of the first three decades after the Spanish conquest. For a short while they were able to parley their political intrigues into a unique stance of power and importance, but in the end they succumbed to the Spanish manipulations as did all other Andean peoples. At the time of the Spanish conquest of Peru, the Inca were just finishing a bitter eight-year long civil war over the question of which of two sons of the previous Inca emperor was to be the legitimate heir to power. For a time there were two Inca capitals—one in the north in Quito, and one in the south at Cuzco. The Huanca aided both sides of the Inca power struggle, but in the end were most closely allied with Huascar, an unfortunate choice in that he ended up losing. Before the winning side could consolidate power, the Spanish appeared on the scene. The importance of the Huanca might best be seen in the fact that the Spanish did not choose either of the Inca capitals, Quito or Cuzco, to be their own capital city, but rather chose as the first capital city of Spanish Peru the Huanca town of Jauja (the largest of the three Huanca political centers). Because of the difficulty of supplying Jauja from the coast, the Spanish later moved the capital to the present location, Lima.

The Huanca area was to be a pivotal supply area for the conquest of Peru. At the time of the first Spanish invasion, more than 500,000 llamas and alpacas were given to Pizarro and his men at the city of Jauja, and thousands of additional animals were supplied by the Lurin and Hanan Huanca. During the nearly successful seige of Lima by Manco Inca only a few years after the Spanish arrived, the Huanca arrived from the hills at the eleventh hour and helped break the seige, and defeat Manco Inca. In the time of the subsequent civil wars, the Huanca area became a frequent winter camp and supply depot. Even after several decades of looting, the Huanca store houses had enough food surpluses and supplemental war material to maintain Spanish forces of thousands for several months. In reward for these services, Don Felipe Guacra Paucar, the ruler (curaca) of the Lurin Huanca, became the only Indian in Peruvian history to be granted the right to have a Royal Coat of Arms, to pass this right down to his descendants in perpetuity, and to act in the same manner as other Spanish *encomenderos* (Royal Decree, King of Spain, March 18, 1564).

The Huanca were initially allies of the Spanish and fared well. Later, as need for labor supply in the mercury mines of Huancavelica grew (mercury being crucial in the silver mines in Potosi), and more workers were needed at the tambos, in Lima, at surrounding haciendas, and to replace other Indian favored status. At the time of the Spanish conquest, there were more than 175,000 Huanças. But by less than 100 years later, they had been as badly decimated by disease, deaths in silver mines and mercury poisoning, and mistreatment by Spanish officials, as other Andean groups. In the year 1608, there were only 30,000 Huanca left. Nearly 85% of the population had been destroyed, basically destroying the integrity of the Huanca as a separate culture group. In the intervening years, some additional groups have been moved into the valley, and the Huanca have become westernized and hispanicized. Although there are still rural Huanca villages, where the people speak the original pre-Inca dialects, little of the original culture still exists. The Huanca have become integrated into the general Peruvian culture.

DAVID L. BROWMAN

HUANCAVELICA inhabited most of the presentday Province of Guayas in Ecuador. Some of their settlements were: Yagual, Colonche, Chinduy, Chongon, Daule, Chonoma, Colonchillo, Guayaquil, Yaguachi, Racual, Guaya, Cachao, Veindal, Uchicacao, Chadai, Chandui, Tantomo, Mopeñitos, Payo, Belin, and Guare. Both culturally and linguistically, this group was closely related to the *Manta* of the western Coast. Their language is extinct.
Subsistence. The *Huancavelica* cultivated maize, yuca (sweet manioc), and other crops characteristic of this area. Fish were an important item in the diet.
Dress and ornaments. Men wore short cotton shirts and a loincloth. In their hair they wore crowns of very small gold and silver beads, and sometimes of juguar skin. Women wore a cloth hanging from the waist and another over their shoulders. As elsewhere along the Coast, the teeth were ornamented with gold, and removal of three upper and three lower teeth is consistently mentioned.
Burial. The dead were placed in a round vaulted grave, opening to the east. Living women and weapons were included in the burials of chiefs.
Religion. To insure fertility, it is said that human blood was sacrificed in the fields. Cures were also effected through sacrifice. Cieza mentions that human hearts extracted from sacrificial victims were revered as gods. Old men were reported to have communicated with "devils."

HUAVE, a tribe belonging to the Mizocuavean stock, formerly considered independent, living in the coastal parts of the districts of Juchitlan and Tehuantepec, State of Oaxaca, Mexico.

Snow covered pass near Huancavelica.

HYDABURG, on Prince of Wales Island, Alaska is the largest Haida village with a population of 400. Hydaburg is incorporated as a town in Alaska. The term "Indian Reservation" has been applied generally to any lands in Alaska set aside for the benefit of Indians. The lands in established native townsites are held in trust by an employee of the federal government for disposal as provided by the 1926 Alaska Native Townsite Act which authorizes the townsite trustee to issue a restricted deed to an Alaskan native for a tract of land occupied by and set apart for him in a townsite established under the 1891 Townsite Act.

The Haida Indians were emigrees from Canada in the early 18th century. Hydaburg was established in 1911 by Indians from the villages of Klinkwan and Howkan with the common interest of bettering their conditions. Many live today in Hydaburg and derive their income from fishing. They take an active interest in Alaska's political affairs.

According to tradition, totem carving originated among the Haida. Their carvers were sometimes hired or enslaved by the Tlingit to provide totems or carved embellishments for Tlingit homes and villages. They also produced fine slate carvings and delicately worked articles of wood, bone, and shell.

Incorporated as a city in 1915, Hydaburg is governed by a mayor and council form of government.

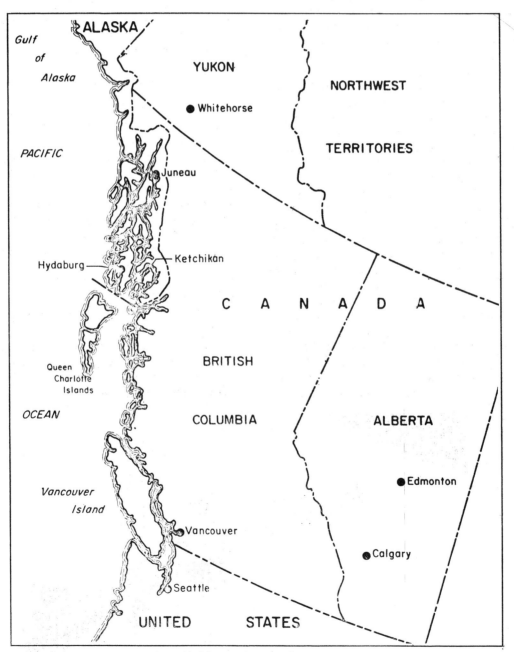

Hydaburg and surrounding area.